The Diversity
of Discipleship

THE PRESBYTERIAN PRESENCE:
THE TWENTIETH-CENTURY EXPERIENCE

Series Editors

Milton J Coalter

John M. Mulder

Louis B. Weeks

The Diversity of Discipleship: Presbyterians and Twentieth-Century Christian Witness

Edited by
Milton J Coalter
John M. Mulder
Louis B. Weeks

Essays by
Milton J Coalter, Robert H. Bullock, Jr.,
James A. Overbeck, John R. Fitzmier,
Randall Balmer, Theodore A. Gill, Jr.,
Erskine Clarke, J. W. Gregg Meister,
Joel L. Alvis, Jr., Gayraud S. Wilmore,
Henry Warner Bowden, Francisco O.
García-Treto, R. Douglas Brackenridge,
Michael J. Kimura Angevine,
Ryô Yoshida, and Sang Hyun Lee

Westminster/John Knox Press
Louisville, Kentucky

© 1991 Westminster/John Knox Press

First edition

Published by Westminster/John Knox Press
Louisville, Kentucky

PRINTED IN THE UNITED STATES OF AMERICA
9 8 7 6 5 4 3 2 1

Library of Congress Cataloging-in-Publication Data

The Diversity of discipleship : Presbyterians and twentieth-century
Christian witness / edited by Milton J. Coalter, John M. Mulder,
Louis B. Weeks ; essays by Milton J. Coalter . . . [et al.]. — 1st
ed.
          p.   cm. — (The Presbyterian presence : the twentieth-century
experience)
    Includes bibliographical references and index.
    ISBN 0-664-25196-X

    1. Presbyterian Church—United States—History—20th century.
2. Presbyterian Church (U.S.A.)—History—20th century.   3. Church
and social problems—Presbyterian Church.   4. Church and social
problems—Presbyterian Church (U.S.A.)   5. Christian union—
Presbyterian Church.   6. Christian union—Presbyterian Church
(U.S.A.)   7. Race relations—Religious aspects—Presbyterian Church.
8. Race relations—Religious aspects—Presbyterian Church (U.S.A.)
9. Ethnic relations—United States.   I. Coalter, Milton J.
II. Mulder, John M., 1946–   .   III. Weeks, Louis, 1941–   .
IV. Series: Presbyterian presence.
BX8937.D58   1991
285′.1—dc20   91-4517

Contents

Series Foreword

This series, "The Presbyterian Presence: The Twentieth-Century Experience," is the product of a significant research project analyzing American Presbyterianism in this century. Funded by the Lilly Endowment and based at Louisville Presbyterian Theological Seminary, the project is part of a broader research effort that analyzes the history of mainstream Protestantism. By analyzing American Presbyterianism as a case study, we hope not only to chronicle its fate in the twentieth century but also to illumine larger patterns of religious change in mainstream Protestantism and in American religious and cultural life.

This case study of American Presbyterianism and the broader research on mainstream Protestantism arise out of an epochal change in American religion that has occurred during the twentieth century. Mainstream American Protestantism refers to those churches that emerged from the American Revolution as the dominant Protestant bodies and were highly influential in shaping American religion and culture during the nineteenth century. It includes the Presbyterians, Episcopalians, Methodists, Congregationalists (now the United Church of Christ), Disciples, and American or northern Baptists.

In this century, these churches have been displaced—religiously and culturally—to a significant degree. All have suffered severe membership losses since the 1960s. All have experienced significant theological tensions and shifts in emphasis. All are characterized by problems in their organization as institutions. And yet they remain influential voices in the spectrum of American religion and retain an enduring vitality in the face of a massive reconfiguration of American religious life.

The result is a complex phenomenon that is not easily described. Some would say the term "mainstream" or "mainline" is itself suspect and embodies ethnocentric and elitist assumptions. What characterized American religious history, they argue, was its diversity and its pluralism. Some groups may have believed they were religiously or culturally dominant, but the historical reality is much more pluralistic. Others would maintain that if there was a "mainstream," it no longer exists. Still others would propose that the mainstream itself has changed. The denominations of the evangelical awakening of the nineteenth century have been replaced by the evangelical churches of the late twentieth century—Southern Baptist, charismatic, Pentecostal.

Some propose that the term "mainline" or "mainstream" should be dropped in favor of talking about "liberal" Protestantism, but such a change presents additional problems. Like "evangelical," the term "liberal" is an extremely vague word to describe a set of Christian beliefs, values, and behavior. Furthermore, virtually all the "mainstream" churches contain large numbers of people who would describe themselves as either evangelical or liberal, thus making it very difficult to generalize about them as a denomination.

Despite the debates about terminology and the categories for analyzing American Protestantism, there is general agreement that American culture and American Protestantism of the late twentieth century are very different from what they were in the late nineteenth century. What has changed is the religious and cultural impact of American Protestantism. A study of American Presbyterianism is a good lens for examining that change, for in spite of their relatively small numbers, Presbyterians are, or were, quintessential mainstreamers, exerting a great deal of influence because of their economic, social, educational, and cultural advantages.

When did the change occur? In a pioneering article written more than fifty years ago, Arthur M. Schlesinger, Sr., pointed to the period from 1875 to 1900 as "a critical period" in American religion. In particular, American Protestants confronted the external challenges of immigration, industrialization, and urbanization and the internal challenges posed by Darwinism, biblical criticism, history of religions, and the new social sciences.[1] Robert T. Handy has maintained that the 1920s witnessed a "religious depression." The result was a "second disestablishment" of American Protestantism. When the churches lost legal establishment in the U.S. Constitution, they attempted to "Christianize" American culture.[2] But by the 1920s, it was clear that both legal and cultural establishment had been rejected. Sydney Ahlstrom points to the 1960s as the time when American religion and culture took a "radical turn" and the "Puritan culture" of the United States was shattered.[3] Wade Clark Roof and William McKinney build on Ahlstrom's argument, proposing that the 1960s and 1970s represent a "third disestablishment," in which mainstream churches lost their religious dominance.[4]

These diverse interpretations underscore the fact that the crises of mainstream Protestantism did not appear suddenly and that the developments within one tradition—American Presbyterianism—are mirrored in other denominations as well. While some of our studies reach back into the late nineteenth century, most of our studies focus on the period after the fundamentalist controversy within Presbyterianism during the 1920s and 1930s. For a variety of reasons, that became a watershed for Presbyterians and ushered in the twentieth century.

The value of this substantial Presbyterian case study can be seen from at least two perspectives. First, this research is designed to write a chapter in the history of American religion and culture. It is the story of the attempt of one tradition—its people and its institutions—to respond to the crosscurrents of the twentieth century. Second, it is an attempt to illumine the problems and predicaments of American Presbyterianism so that its members and leaders might better understand the past as a resource for its future direction.

The series title was carefully chosen. Presence is more than passive existence, and it connotes the landmark that we hope these groups of studies provide for comparing the equally important pilgrimages of other mainline Protestant denominations through the past century. Missiologists have characterized the Christian responsibility as one of "profound presence" in the world, patterned on the presence of God in providence, in the incarnation, and in the work of the Holy Spirit. In the words of missionary and theologian John V. Taylor, Christians "stand" in the world in the name of Christ to be "really and totally present in the present."[5]

Has the Presbyterian presence declined into mere existence? Have the commitments of Presbyterians degenerated into lifeless obligations? What forces have informed, transformed, or deformed our distinctive presence within the Christian community and the society? And can changes in Presbyterianism invigorate their continued yearnings to represent Christ in the world today? These are the questions posed in the series and the queries addressed by the Caldwell Lectures at Louisville Seminary from quite different perspectives.

More than sixty researchers, plus students at Louisville Seminary and generous colleagues in seminaries, colleges, and universities throughout the United States, have cooperated in the research on American Presbyterianism. Many are historians, but others are sociologists, economists, musicians, theologians, pastors, and lay people. What has excited us as a research team was the opportunity of working on a fascinating historical problem with critical implications for the Presbyterian Church and mainstream Protestantism. Animating our work and conversations was the hope that this research might make a difference, that it might help one church and a broader Christian tradition understand the problems more clearly so that their witness might be more faithful. It is with this hope that we issue this series, "The Presbyterian Presence: The Twentieth-Century Experience."

Milton J Coalter
John M. Mulder
Louis B. Weeks

Acknowledgments

The management of the Louisville research project on American Presbyterianism would have been impossible without the assistance of our secretaries: Elna Amaral, Beverly Hourigan, Kem Longino, Dana Rohde, and Ingrid Tanghe. They took care of a mountain of correspondence and frequent phone calls, and kept everything orderly amidst many other responsibilities.

We are also grateful to our colleagues at Louisville Seminary for their encouragement and support, and to the Board of Directors for generously allowing each of us time to carry out the research and planning for this series.

We are equally thankful to the scores of people who have listened to the results of our research and offered helpful suggestions and criticisms that have influenced the final result. The researchers themselves have been a wonderful group of people with whom to work. They have been unfailingly patient with our suggestions for revision and extremely cooperative in meeting deadlines. Others have been generous with their time in reading drafts and offering new insights. The Louisville research project created new friendships, and in so doing the researchers became not only a community of scholars but also a community of faith.

We are also appreciative of the staff at Westminster/ John Knox Press, especially our editor, Alexa Smith, Editorial Director Davis Perkins, Publisher Robert McIntyre, Director of Publicity Sally Telford, and Director of Copyediting Danielle Alexander. Their personal interest in this series has encouraged and sustained us.

This project would not have been possible without the financial support of the Lilly Endowment and the creative stimulation provided by Dr. Robert Wood Lynn, Senior Vice President for Religion. He retired in mid-1989, but it was his vision that prompted the research on American mainstream Protestantism. For his wise advice, patience, and encouragement we give thanks. He has been and continues to be a perceptive mentor and a discerning critic.

The Louisville research project on American Presbyterianism assumed new dimensions in the fall of 1990 with the establishment of the Louisville Institute for the Study of Protestantism and American Culture. Funded by the Lilly Endowment, the Louisville Institute will plan and stimulate research and leadership education programs in mainstream Protestantism. We are delighted to be working with Dr. Craig Dykstra, Vice President for Religion at the Lilly Endowment, in creating the Louisville Institute. We hope this series, "The Presbyterian Presence: The Twentieth-Century Experience," and the Louisville Institite will offer new insights into American religion and provide new perspectives on the renewal of mainstream Protestantism.

Contributors

Joel L. Alvis, Jr., is the pastor of the St. Pauls Presbyterian Church in St. Pauls, North Carolina. He attended the University of Mississippi before receiving a Ph.D. in history from Auburn University. He served on the reference staff at the archives now known as the Presbyterian Study Center of the Presbyterian Church (U.S.A.) in Montreat, North Carolina, and later acquired an M.Div. from Louisville Presbyterian Theological Seminary.

Michael J. Kimura Angevine is the senior pastor of Makiki Christian Church in Honolulu, Hawaii. He completed his graduate work at San Francisco Theological Seminary and the sociology department at the University of California, Berkeley. He taught in the Asian American Studies program at U.C., Berkeley, before becoming the Assistant Dean for Interracial Cross-Cultural Education at the Graduate Theological Union in San Francisco. He has also served on the faculty of San Francisco Theological Seminary.

Randall Balmer is Tremaine Associate Professor of Religion at Columbia University. He holds degrees from Trinity College, Trinity Evangelical Divinity School, and Princeton University, where he received a Ph.D. in religion. He is the author of *A Perfect Babel of Confusion: Dutch Religion and English Culture in the Middle Colonies* (New York and Oxford: Oxford University Press, 1989) and *Mine Eyes Have Seen the Glory: A Journey Into the Evangelical Subculture of America* (New York and Oxford: Oxford University Press, 1989).

Henry Warner Bowden is Professor of Religion at Rutgers University in New Brunswick, New Jersey. He received degrees from Baylor and Princeton universities and has held various posts at Rutgers since 1964. In addition to numerous studies on American church history and historiography, his most notable monograph on Native Americans is *American Indians and Christian Missions* (Chicago: University of Chicago Press, 1981).

R. Douglas Brackenridge is Professor of Church History at Trinity University and serves as associate editor of *American Presbyterians.* He was trained at Muskingum College, Pittsburgh Theological Seminary, New College in the University of Edinburgh, and the University of Glasgow, Scotland, from which he received his doctorate. Among his numerous publications are works coauthored with Lois Boyd: *Presbyterian Women in America* (Westport, Conn.: Greenwood Press, 1983) and *Presbyterians and Pensions* (Louisville, Ky.: Westminster/John Knox Press, 1989).

Robert H. Bullock, Jr., is the editor of the journal *Presbyterian Outlook.* He is a graduate of Austin College, Austin Theological Seminary, the University of Michigan, and Princeton University. He holds a doctorate from the latter institution. He has also worked as both a campus chaplain and a parish minister.

Erskine Clarke is Professor of American Religious History at Columbia Theological Seminary in Decatur, Georgia. He attended the University of South Carolina and Columbia Theological Seminary prior to completing a Th.D. at Union Theological Seminary in Virginia. He is the author of *Westlin' Jacob: A Portrait of the Old South* (Atlanta: John Knox Press, 1979).

Milton J Coalter is the library director and Professor of

Bibliography and Research at the Louisville Presbyterian Theological Seminary. He was educated at Davidson College, Princeton Theological Seminary, and has a Ph.D. in religion from Princeton University. In addition to coediting the present series, his publications include the study *Gilbert Tennent, Son of Thunder* (Westport, Conn.: Greenwood Press, 1987).

John R. Fitzmier is Associate Dean and Associate Professor of American Church History at the Vanderbilt Divinity School. Educated at the University of Pittsburgh, he has an M.Div. from Gordon-Conwell Theological Seminary and a Ph.D. from Princeton University.

Francisco O. García-Treto is Professor of Old Testament at Trinity University. He has degrees from Maryville College, Princeton Theological Seminary, and a Ph.D. in Old Testament biblical studies from Princeton Seminary. Among his publications is *Iglesia Presbiteriana: A History of Presbyterians and Mexican Americans in the Southwest* (San Antonio: Trinity University Press, 1974, 1987), which he coauthored with R. Douglas Brackenridge.

Theodore A. Gill, Jr., is the editor of *Monday Morning.* He attended the University of Wisconsin, Princeton Theological Seminary, and currently is in Princeton's doctoral program for ecumenics, missions, and the history of religion. He also holds an M.Lit. in New Testament from Oxford University.

Sang Hyun Lee is Kyung-Chik Han Associate Professor of Systematic Theology and Director of the Asian American Program at Princeton Theological Seminary. He is a graduate of the College of Wooster, Harvard Divinity School, and Harvard University, where he received his doctorate. Before joining the faculty at Princeton Seminary, he taught at Hope College in Michigan.

J. W. Gregg Meister was a Presbyterian pastor in San Francisco for several years before becoming a television producer with his own media company, Interlink Video Productions. He attended Williams College and Princeton Theological Seminary before receiving a master's degree in television production at San Francisco State University and a master's degree in communications research from the Annenberg School of Communications at the University of Pennsylvania.

James A. Overbeck is the librarian and Associate Professor of Church History at Columbia Theological Seminary. He is a graduate of Carthage College, the University of Chicago Graduate Library School, and the University of Chicago Divinity School. He previously served for several years as the librarian of the School of Theology at Claremont, California.

Gayraud S. Wilmore, Distinguished Visiting Professor at the Interdenominational Theological Center in Atlanta, was before his retirement the Professor of Afro-American Religious Studies and Dean at New York Theological Seminary. His works on the Black Presbyterian experience have been both numerous and authoritative.

Ryô Yoshida is on the faculty at Dôshihsha University School of Theology in Kyôto, Japan. He is also a researcher with the university's Institute for the Study of Humanities and Social Sciences, the foremost research institute and archives on Meiji period Japanese Christianity. He did his graduate work at Dôshihsha University and the Graduate Theological Union. He is a member of the Presbyterian Church in Japan (Nihon Kirisuto Kyôkai).

Introduction

This volume is about discipleship, the common pursuit of Christians. Each volume in The Presbyterian Presence series examines some facet of Presbyterian discipleship in the twentieth century. But this volume is unique because it considers three issues that have proved particularly perplexing to the Presbyterian witness in the last one hundred years. Those issues are outreach, ecumenism, and pluralism.

Although all three concerns have deep roots in the Christian gospel, their interaction in the last century has created a complicated tangle of sometimes enriching, sometimes conflicting, but always interlocking emphases. As a result, a clear and distinctive definition of a coherent, commonly accepted Presbyterian discipleship has become increasingly elusive.

The question of outreach has been bounded by two scriptural texts often cited today in Presbyterian circles. These are the Great Commission of verbal witness in Matthew 28:16–20 and the equally well-known and momentous commission of service encapsulated in Matthew 25:31–40.

These two texts have served Presbyterian mission like magnetic poles, providing gravity and grounding to Presbyterian discipleship. But the press of twentieth-century events has disrupted their balanced pull. Conflict over which polar star should serve as "true north" in the contemporary Christian pilgrimage has resulted, sapping Presbyterian energies for outreach of both types.

As Jesus departed from his disciples, he instructed them to go and make disciples of all nations, baptizing them in the name of the Father and of the Son and of the Holy Spirit, and teaching them to obey everything that he had commanded. This mission nurtured the hope for centuries that the earth's inhabitants would be made followers of the Christ through the proclamation of the good news of salvation. This trans-mission in word was to be matched by the complementary co-mission of merciful acts of servanthood, emblematic of Christ's own self-identification with the oppressed and repressed in Matthew 25:31–40.

Verbal outreach and physical outreach were then parallel missions in Christ's ministry and, as such, became parallel allegiances for his Presbyterian disciples. But the story of the first four essays in this volume illustrates that in this century troubling questions about the church's witness divided Presbyterian opinion in the midst of critical American social problems. Verbal outreach and physical outreach became competing priorities. Outreach efforts of both varieties continued, but internal dissension crippled full-bodied support of either.

The article on Presbyterian evangelism by Milton J Coalter chronicles the increasing difficulties of balancing these parallel allegiances. The essay discusses the long evangelistic tradition of Presbyterianism but focuses on the path of Presbyterian evangelism in the twentieth century. During this century, the Presbyterian churches were among the first denominations to create separate "evangelism" agencies; and in the late 1940s, they spearheaded major programs of evangelistic outreach, later pursued throughout the ecumenical community. This situated Presbyterian and mainstream Protestant congregations so they could take full advantage of the revival of religious involvement that swept through American society in the

1950s. However, as the decade of the 1950s waned, questions about the faithfulness of these evangelistic efforts arose. Critical in this reevaluation of Presbyterian outreach were several factors: new doubts about the numerical successes of former evangelistic programs, growing concern about the church's possible complicity in contemporary social problems, a rising belief that the church's past actions did not measure up to its verbal witness, and an emerging anti-institutionalism that envisioned the church's mission as fundamentally one of self-sacrifice.

All of these developments contributed to a laudable surge in Presbyterian social action during the 1960s and 1970s. Yet this move was accomplished at the expense of a vibrant verbal declaration of the faith that undergirded Christian service. Ironically, at the same moment that Christian action assumed ascendency, the social institutions by which Presbyterians continued to express their physical witness began to distance themselves from their traditional church affiliations. This was particularly debilitating. Presbyterians' verbal outreach was already being muted in order to avoid conflict in the ecumenical community and within the mixed coalitions of Christians and non-Christians addressing the crisis of contemporary social problems. Now, though, the motivation behind Presbyterian social service was equally obscured by the "neutral" identity assumed by the public agencies through which Presbyterians acted out their faith. Like the Cheshire cat in Alice's wonderland, Presbyterian social outreach disappeared from the public eye.[1] Although Presbyterian discipleship continued unabated, this combination of a silent and largely invisible witness eclipsed Presbyterian evangelism.

Robert Bullock's article, which follows, indicates the serious consequences of these shifts for new church development. As social mission overshadowed verbal outreach, the number of new church starts slumped dramatically. During a critical period in the 1960s and 1970s, new church starts in the PCUSA/UPCUSA churches dropped from a peak of 70.8 in the 1950s to 44.6 in the 1960s and

21.7 in the 1970s. The PCUS followed suit with a peak in
new church development also in the 1950s, but the 60.2
new congregations of the 1950s were followed by only 30.4
in the 1960s and 13.5 in the 1970s.

As the numbers of new congregations shifted, so too did
their location. Bullock documents that Presbyterian denominations in the 1950s situated new churches in growing suburban areas to take advantage of their phenomenal
growth. But in the 1960s and 1970s, concern for social
witness led the church to focus on new experimental ministries and inner-city congregations. Many of these church
development projects never became self-supporting, and
spiraling costs for land and construction during the same
decades significantly weakened the denomination's ability
to create new churches.

A study by James Overbeck provides a slightly different
angle on the conflict generated by Presbyterians' mixed
mind during the latter half of the twentieth century. In this
case, the focus is on official Presbyterian journals. These
periodicals proved particularly vulnerable targets for grass-
roots discontent with the denomination's social policy.
Most of these publications began as house organs, or journalistic bulletin boards for announcements of denominational plans and activities. But in the 1950s and 1960s,
experienced representatives of professional journalism assumed editorial positions within these organizations. More
forthright coverage of the volatile church and societal issues of the day ensued. In most cases, this resulted in Presbyterian periodicals' losing subscriptions, and either being
terminated or being consigned to a house organ status and
content. The history of Presbyterian journals, then, becomes a testimony to the severe divisions inflicted by
post–World War II debate over proper Presbyterian discipleship.

The domestic patterns of Presbyterian outreach are even
more graphically exhibited in the history of international
missions. John Fitzmier and Randall Balmer employ a
1932 benchmark report on Protestant missions to measure
changing Presbyterian emphases in this area. Known as

the Hocking Report, it soundly condemned Protestant missionaries' Western imperialism, urged toleration of other world religions as well as ecumenical cooperation, and deemphasized verbal evangelism in the interest of a greater "ministry to the secular needs of men [and women] in the spirit of Christ."

Although Presbyterians protested vehemently against the report immediately following its publication, Fitzmier and Balmer find recent Presbyterian mission policy virtually indistinguishable from that suggested by the Hocking Report in 1932.

International mission was a natural locale for early ecumenical ferment among traditionally competitive Christian denominations. The formidable task of Christianizing the American frontier had already led Presbyterians to cooperate individually in interdenominational benevolent societies during the early nineteenth century. In a similar fashion, the daunting mission of discipling the world led missionaries to cooperate locally on the mission field and later prompted their denominations to support worldwide missionary conferences and the World Council of Churches (WCC).

Theodore Gill's essay on global ecumenism illustrates that this move was not free from conflict. Controversy erupted over the methods and theology of outreach as well as the value of ethnic and theological pluralism.

Gill chronicles the development of a more pluralistic vision in member denominations of the ecumenical community, as well as the resulting ironies. For instance, over a century of mission work in Third World countries had elapsed before a more egalitarian terminology for missionary personnel was developed; and even then, the term "fraternal worker" arose because mainstream American Protestants found themselves engaged in mission services to their historic parent churches in devastated post–World War II Europe. Similarly, as indigenous churches in the mission fields matured and their unique spiritual insights were acknowledged, the notion of foreign "missions" surrendered its place to one of a shared "mission" in the worldwide, pluralistic, though common body of Christ. This provided a solid theological base for once "foreign" churches to finance and speak out openly on social Christian witness in their "mother" churches in the United States during the civil rights movement.

The Faith and Order conferences of this world ecumenical movement fostered reevaluations of the boundaries separating Christian theological traditions and later encouraged dialogue with other faith communities. Ecumenical Life and Work conferences, on the other hand, propelled a social action agenda with their notion that "doctrine divides; service unites." The Faith and Order talks clearly affected the urgency felt in participating churches for making denominational disciples. Their critics have also claimed that these conversations diminished the perceived need to make Christians of all the earth's peoples. The Life and Work discussions, in contrast, fueled the already mounting priority of social witness in American churches during the 1960s and 1970s.

International ecumenism parallels the domestic ecumenical movement in the twentieth century. Erskine Clarke aptly quotes Robert McAfee Brown when he wrote, "To be ecumenical is as Presbyterian as predestination." He might have added that to be ecumenical may be even more Presbyterian than predestination today, considering the abandonment of that traditionally Reformed doctrine by many in the contemporary church.[2]

The most prominent embodiment of U.S. ecumenism during the early twentieth century was the Federal Council of Churches (FCC). According to Clarke, this agency served as the religious counterpart to the Progressive Movement through its proclamation of the social gospel. As such, it provided an avenue for exhibiting Christian unity and a force for sustaining the old Protestant establishment's dominance over the social, political, and economic values of the nation.

The National Council of Churches (NCC) superseded the FCC in 1950, but the paradigm for domestic ecumenism did not change significantly until the birth of the

Consultation on Church Union (COCU) in 1960. Initially, COCU transformed the American ecumenical ideal from one of coordination among denominations to that of con- solidation into a single, organically reunited church. Clarke contends that this new engine for ecumenical union was again motivated by the declining influence of old-line Protestant denominations in American life. But he also suggests with John Leith that the Presbyterian emphases on "the action of God in word and sacrament" rather than "structures or even correct doctrine," plus a Calvinistic concern for transforming society, propelled Presbyterian involvement in the movement.

Clarke sees the recent disintegration of organized ecu- menism as a visible sign of a cultural turn inward, a move from social activism to the "therapeutic and narcissistic." Nevertheless, one element of past ecumenical enthusiasm endures and even thrives today with no foreseeable end in sight. That element is evident at the grass roots. Because of the mixed denominational backgrounds of the Presbyte- rian membership and internal reformist impulses that have spawned social services and community ministries, Presbyterians have led local interdenominational efforts.

In an interesting study of the potentially contradictory ideals of ecumenism and evangelistic outreach, Gregg Meister considers next the use Presbyterians have made of modern mass media. Churches, he claims, are "in essence, message production centers" because of their mission to proclaim the good news. During the twentieth century, the possible avenues for this mission have mushroomed, but two media in particular have had stupendous effect upon American culture. They are radio and television.

Meister notes that at their inception both radio and tele- vision were given considerable attention by Presbyterian denominations. But in the late 1960s and the 1970s, church use and even church capabilities for employing television declined precipitously in reverse proportion to television's meteoric rise in influence.

Along with other mainstream Protestant denominations, the Presbyterian churches pursued a policy that doomed their effective use of television. They decided that Christian programming and evangelism through this mass medium should remain free of denominational labels, and on-air time for religious programming should be requested rather than purchased. The latter decision worked only so long as the NCC held a privileged position with the national media networks. When networks were permitted to charge for programming, evangelical organizations alone thrived because they were accustomed to paying.[3]

The decision to avoid denominational labels was equally momentous. Though it was certainly ecumenically correct, the policy was technologically naive, because the media of radio and television require a clear, readily identifiable message for "brand recognition." Here Presbyterians were doubly handicapped. First, their commitments to ecumenical cooperation led them to spurn denominational promotion. Second, they were unable to determine exactly what elements of the Christian faith, much less which parts of the Presbyterian interpretation of that faith, should be highlighted. This was particularly debilitating in a medium that requires selective emphasis in the broadcast message. Frustrated and unwilling to pay the cost of television production, the Presbyterian churches concluded that television was an inappropriate environment for transmitting sophisticated theological content.

Meister also notes an equally interesting problem with the churches' use of television. The world created by this medium has values that are often antithetical to those of the churches. Meister contends that the dismantling of television capabilities that most mainstream Protestant churches had completed by the 1970s was the wrong answer to this conflict of value systems. The number of hours that Americans, particularly youth, spend before a television set translates such an answer into an act of unconditional surrender.

From the articles on ecumenism and international missions' outreach, it is clear that one of the "great awakenings" of the latter part of the twentieth century has been a rising sensitivity to the diversity of voices proclaiming

Christ domestically and around the world. The final six essays of this volume examine racial ethnic Presbyterians' search for their own place within this diversity. Like previous articles, these essays offer further examples of the interlocking and sometimes interfering interplay of outreach, ecumenism, and pluralism in the quest for a distinctive Presbyterian discipleship.

In each of these essays one hears three common themes. First, there is a struggle—the struggle of several unique cultures seeking a voice of witness appropriate to their own community's insights into Christ and Christian discipleship. The struggle is complicated by the desire for a voice that is at once harmonious with the larger chorus of American Presbyterian discipleship and yet not drowned out by the predominantly Anglo lyrics and chords of traditional Presbyterian proclamation.

Second, each essay testifies to a cornucopia of feelings in these communities. One perceives their anger toward the cultural chauvinism that infected the all-too-fallible Christians who introduced their forebears to Christianity. One feels the profound comfort they have found in Christ. And one senses their steadfast allegiance to the church despite the perplexing difficulties of a hoped-for pluralism where particular communities retain their singular identity even as they are integrated into the larger community of the Presbyterian Church (U.S.A.).

There is also the message in all of these essays that the church's ability to deal with racial ethnic pluralism within its own boundaries may decide how well the church will handle the increasingly pluralistic situation in American culture. Indeed, some essays claim that marginalized Presbyterian groups provide a much-needed lesson to the larger denomination's discipleship. The church must remain in conversation with its surrounding culture, but it must avoid its cultural captivity of former times.

In a sense, the story of Presbyterians' struggles with racial ethnic pluralism is a tale in microcosm of the Gordian knot of issues that torments American mainstream Protestant ecumenism as well. How shall these churches main-

tain a single body of Christ, while encouraging the
interaction of many different, independent, though mutually supportive communities?

Joel Alvis and Gayraud Wilmore begin the discussion
of racial ethnic Presbyterians with complementary treat-
ments of Blacks and whites in the Presbyterian Church.
Joel Alvis first provides a survey of Black-white Presbyterian interaction reaching back to the Civil War. He shows
how this relationship significantly affected allegiances
between and within the "northern" and "southern" Presbyterian churches. It also galvanized Presbyterians' latter-
day "recognition of ethnic pluralism as an organizing
principle."

Over the last century and a half, Presbyterians have
moved from a policy of segregation to one of integration
and, later still, self-development of the Black Presbyterian
constituency. Through it all, Alvis credits the racism of
white Presbyterians for past segregation practices. The ecumenical movement's theology of "brotherhood" and the
civil rights movement's spur to concrete action were instrumental in the integration phase, and the development
of a Black Presbyterian caucus founded on contemporary
Black Theology gave rise to self-development programs.

Gayraud Wilmore takes a slightly different angle by examining the deep ambiguities in Black Presbyterians' association with their predominantly white church and their
white Presbyterian allies during the civil rights effort. The
Black Presbyterians' relationship to the church has been
clouded with ambiguity since Blacks first encountered
Christ on the slave ships of their white oppressors. More
recently, their ambivalence has continued because of the
inevitable tensions between "racial and cultural identity
and racial integration," two common goals of Black Presbyterians. Yet Wilmore sees the Black experience as a
potentially redemptive example for the entire church because it epitomizes the dilemma of Christianity within
America's pluralistic society.

A second racial ethnic group that has endured white
oppression even longer than Blacks is Native Americans.

Henry Bowden briefly chronicles Presbyterian missionary work among Native American tribes, and, like Alvis, notes the importance of women in funding missions to racial ethnic constituencies. Bowden notes that the dominant expectation of missions until the 1960s was that Native Americans would assimilate. Thus, missionaries preached a "gospel of soap" alongside a "gospel of grace." This began to change with the civil rights movement and an emerging sensitivity to the pluralistic implications of the Christian gospel, manifested in the Confession of 1967.

Bowden sees several significant barriers to Presbyterian growth in Native American communities. Primary among these are the dire poverty of these communities, wide cultural differences over leadership qualifications and administrative style, and the questions of control and land ownership.

Francisco García-Treto and Douglas Brackenridge follow with a discussion of Hispanic Presbyterians. Much like the label "Native Americans," the term "Hispanic Americans" is misleading by suggesting an undifferentiated group with shared values and cultural backgrounds. In actual fact, Hispanic Presbyterians in the Southwest draw from quite different cultural experiences than do those with Cuban or Puerto Rican roots. Moreover, their first contacts with the Presbyterian Church varied. García-Treto and Brackenridge examine these variants before discussing critical issues that the Presbyterian Church must address if Hispanic Americans are ever to be incorporated into its community.

Two fundamental issues for Hispanic Presbyterians are leadership and language. Their community suffers from a lack of officially approved leadership for present and future congregations. Hispanic Americans are also fast becoming the largest racial ethnic group in the United States, and they reside in areas where their numbers are often significant, if not dominant. The Spanish language will likely remain their preferred tongue, but Presbyterian efforts to respond to this fact have been quite limited.

The language problem, in one sense, only points to an

even deeper question—the Presbyterian Church's own cultural self-perception as a " 'Scottish' or a Scots-Irish/English church." If this cultural myopia could be overcome, García-Treto and Brackenridge believe that the Hispanic Presbyterian community could become more than just a "special interest group." Indeed, it could provide a source of much-needed revitalization in this mainstream Protestant establishment communion.

Two final essays in this volume raise similar questions and prospects for the Presbyterian Church, this time from the Asian American perspective. Michael Angevine and Ryô Yoshida offer a history of the Presbyterian Church and Japanese Americans in northern California between the late 1860s and the mid-1920s. Their tale is one of Presbyterian ministries' paternalism toward the Japanese.

Japanese Americans found it difficult to distance themselves from this mixture of cultural chauvinism and Christianity for two reasons. First, they deeply appreciated the white missionaries and leaders who had brought Christianity to them. Second, contemporary policy in Meiji-Taishô Japan taught them to equate westernization with civilization before their immigration to the United States.

Angevine and Yoshida explain the development of a new theology and self-identity among Japanese American Presbyterians that followed. These creations allowed Japanese American Presbyterians to resist paternalism and to articulate a vision of their equality in the church of Jesus Christ.

The essay of Sang Lee, which concludes this volume, considers the reaction of Korean Americans to American Presbyterianism. This group is the fastest-growing racial ethnic constituency in the Presbyterian Church (U.S.A.) today.

Sang Lee discusses Korean American Presbyterians' struggles with an alien culture and church. Their difficulties with the church are particularly ironic. American Presbyterian missionaries were in large part responsible for the introduction of Christianity into Korea during the nineteenth century. Nevertheless, recent Korean Presbyterian immigrants have discovered that Presbyterianism in Korea and Presbyterianism in America have traveled quite different paths in the intervening years. Korean Presbyterianism, for instance, has maintained a more conservative interpretation of the Bible than has its American counterpart, and American Presbyterianism has come to accept the ordination of women leaders and the rotation of church elders, both of which many Korean Presbyterians find objectionable. Consequently, Korean Americans have endured the double shock of finding themselves at odds with their "mother church" in addition to encountering the cultural and racial prejudice that other racial ethnic minorities face.

As with other groups discussed in this volume, the American church's requirements for leadership certification has created a crisis for Korean American Presbyterians. Language is also a problem, particularly for early generations of Korean immigrants. But two even more fundamental issues are Korean Americans' conservative theology and their unique resistance to cultural assimilation.

The Presbyterian Church's response to the last two factors has created a dilemma. On the one hand, the church has acknowledged Korean Americans' right to be "ethnically particular"; this has been accomplished by such acts as the creation of a Korean language presbytery, Hanmi Presbytery. At the same time, the church expects Korean American Presbyterians to participate fully in the larger church and to follow what are for them theologically and culturally alien polity requirements, such as the ordination of women.

Lee counsels both Korean Americans and their Presbyterian Church (U.S.A.) to recover the sense of being a pilgrim people. This will inevitably involve a "leave-taking," as he puts it, where lesser loyalties to self, denomination, or nation are surrendered to the inclusive demands of divine love. In this way, all parts of the American Presbyterian community will be reformed as they travel together in a common pilgrimage.

The discussions provided in this volume point to a single need, namely, that the marginalized and the mainstream learn to travel light and together. Few Presbyterians today would deny the need to travel together as a denominational body as well as with the wider world Christian community. But how lightly can Presbyterians travel together, and how shall they weight their load? Which pieces of their denominational baggage are non-essential cultural trappings, impeding their companionship on the journey of faith? Which are vital necessities for survival on the road of Christian discipleship? What measures of Christian proclamation in word and service or ecumenical communion and denominational identity are appropriate gear for the varied and treacherous cultural terrain of this age? These questions have thus far defied a Presbyterian or mainstream Protestant consensus.

1

Presbyterian Evangelism: A Case of Parallel Allegiances Diverging

Milton J Coalter

American historians have often framed Calvinist controversies as a running battle over the question of "order" versus "ardor" in Christian piety. However, another problem has troubled the Reformed community equally as much since the seventeenth century. It centers around the church's responsibility for the unconverted.

Calvin himself believed that most of those who would be brought into the communion of the faithful had already been converted by his time. He designated the "evangelist," which Paul listed among the divine gifts, as a temporary office, largely unnecessary after the Apostolic Age. The English Puritans perceived the Church of England to be more Roman than gospel "pure," and their New England cousins encountered a continent of unconverted Native Americans. Thus, they saw the situation quite differently from their theological mentor. Evangelism for the Puritans became a pressing need, a divinely ordained opportunity, and a Christian responsibility punishable by damnation if ignored.[1]

As battles over the relative value of "order" over "ardor" resurfaced during the eighteenth-century First Great Awakening and its nineteenth-century revival sequel in

America, a secondary debate was engaged. Its combatants wrestled over whether one should "await" or "awaken" the divine election of sinners. Cultural and revival winds propelled the Arminian "sales" of American Protestantism during the nineteenth century. By the turn of the century, awakening the elect by human means had become the preferred option for most Presbyterians. For this reason, all of the denominational antecedents of the current Presbyterian Church (U.S.A.) entered the twentieth century with one or more boards responsible for the church's evangelistic outreach.

Debate over evangelism continued into the twentieth century. Yet the conflict over the unconverted changed keys, so to speak, as Presbyterians contested not the value but the methods of human evangelism. The new battle lines formed around the relative priority of word and action in outreach.

The denominational agencies engaged in evangelism during the last decades of the nineteenth century supported ministries to Blacks, Native Americans, immigrants, Jews, and communities on the frontier. But they were also responsible for a range of church programs beyond evangelism. In the twentieth century, American Protestantism developed the unique notion that its structures needed separate "evangelism" agencies. Unlike their predecessors, these units were responsible exclusively for two efforts. First, they were to reinvigorate the evangelical spirit of the current membership. Second, because other agencies in these denominations were assigned ministry responsibilities for minority racial ethnic groups, immigrants, and communities on the frontier, the evangelism units were to reach the masses of American citizens residing within the official state borders of the nation.

The concern to bring these Americans into the Presbyterian Church was not new to the denomination, but the creation of formal, ongoing, programmatic structures to promote and oversee evangelism to this group was largely unprecedented.

One can also chronicle a shift of emphasis in the methods of evangelism that such agencies pursued over the century. From an initial program focused largely on "mass evangelism," Presbyterians moved to more interpersonal approaches at midcentury. Later still, they subordinated these methods to what might be called a social transformation or action evangelism. This last shift in particular was not smooth. In fact, the story of its development illuminates a serious and debilitating division of Presbyterian evangelical impulses by the late 1980s.

The Presbyterian tradition had long-standing parallel allegiances to the salvation of individuals while simultaneously promoting a redemptive transformation of American culture. Events within and without the church have led Presbyterians in the last three decades, however, to view these parallel thrusts as, at best, sequential rather than concurrent means, and frequently even conflicting options, for spreading the evangel.

Although other mainline Protestant denominations did not always share the dual allegiances of Presbyterians, they too came to regard evangelism as a program designed primarily for membership recruitment rather than the sustenance of a forthright Christian witness. The resulting ambivalence toward the purpose and methods of evangelism confused, divided, and debilitated efforts at galvanizing the evangelistic energies of the Presbyterian Church and its mainstream Protestant allies after the mid-1960s.

Evangelism by Mass Revivals
with a Simultaneous Twist

In 1901, John H. Converse and a group of fellow elders expressed their concern over what they considered a low annual increase in membership. They offered to fund a special promotion of the evangelism issue if the General Assembly of the Presbyterian Church in the United States of America (PCUSA) would appoint a committee for that purpose. The General Assembly created a Special Committee on Evangelistic Work the same year with Converse as its chair. The new committee appointed J. Wilbur

Chapman its corresponding secretary in 1902 and was soon providing varying levels of support to over fifty evangelists, singers, and related personnel in the new evangelism program.[2]

The United Presbyterian Church of North America (UPCNA) followed this lead soon after by establishing its own committee. This group did not employ permanent staff to promote its programs until the year before the UPCNA's merger with the PCUSA in 1958.[3]

The PCUSA special committee initially served as a direct stimulus to local church evangelism efforts. It acted as a clearinghouse for the names of effective evangelists within the denomination. It oversaw the production of literature, and it promoted conferences and the establishment of evangelism committees at the presbytery level.[4]

Chapman's earlier close association with the evangelist Dwight L. Moody led him to develop a new urban revival form known as the Simultaneous Movement. The movement consisted of a series of evangelistic campaigns in major cities where Chapman and a cadre of associates conducted a range of revival events. Unlike city revivals of the late nineteenth century, these campaigns were not restricted to a large central, but normally secular, meeting place or "tabernacle." Instead, the program maintained close ties with local congregations by also holding evangelistic services in major local churches simultaneously.[5]

In organizing his evangelistic team, Chapman borrowed from the emerging American corporation the notion of specialization. Evangelists within his group honed their skills at leading services directed specifically to men, women, youth, the laboring class, or what one writer has called the "less than reputable." After his General Assembly appointment to a special mission with the working class, Charles Stelzle cooperated in simultaneous campaigns with Chapman. His involvement indicates apparent support for the evangelism program by social gospel elements in the church at this early stage of the program's development.[6]

The Simultaneous Movement was a uniquely ecumenical event. Other denominations were welcomed to participate in the citywide revivals. Their congregations' activities were listed in the promotional literature, and Chapman himself insisted that there were two things that he would not do in his campaigns. "I won't allow anyone to tell me the days of revival are over, for they have just begun, and I will not preach a denominational sermon. I am first, last and all the time a Christian."[7]

Throughout their history, the evangelism programs of the Presbyterian churches would exhibit the same emphasis on ecumenical cooperation. Nowhere in the official records is a single question raised about such interdenominational evangelism cooperation, even though individuals might join other denominations with different theology or practice.

This early allegiance to ecumenism within evangelism swiftly spread to more formal ties in the early twentieth century. Converse and Chapman were appointed to participate in a worldwide soul-saving movement sponsored by the Alliance of Reformed Churches in 1910. One year later, the PCUSA initiated an overture to the Federal Council of Churches that occasioned the creation of a formal Evangelistic Commission within that body. Through that body and its successors in the National Council of Churches, the Presbyterian churches would share their literature, ideas, and even programs with other mainstream denominations.[8]

In 1908, the Presbyterian Church in the United States (PCUS) developed a separate committee with staff for evangelistic work. The following year, this Permanent Committee on Evangelistic Work hired its first general secretary, Rev. J. Ernest Thacker.[9] The organization of the evangelism program in the PCUS did not approach the sophistication of that in the PCUSA until the late 1940s for one reason—money. In 1910, Thacker's title was downgraded to "general evangelist." This indicated that he was now an official evangelist-for-hire to local judicatories rather than the director of a denominational program.[10]

By 1911, the Permanent Committee disappeared, and

its work was subsumed under the executive committee of
the Board of Home Missions. A superintendent of evangelism appointed in 1914 had his title changed to "assembly
evangelist" four years later. Not coincidentally, a "new"
funding plan, again based largely on local judicatory pay-
ment, was also set in place.[11]

A second "permanent" committee arose during a flurry
of enthusiasm for the evangelism cause in 1938. Promises
of voluntary funding from presbyteries and churches ig-
nited new hope after a rousing speech at General Assembly. Within a few years, though, complaints of unfulfilled
pledges surfaced, and the committee began to insist that a
reliable financial base must be found for staffing and program development. Simultaneous campaigns were employed in the South and in the UPCNA long after they fell
out of regular use in the PCUSA.[12]

J. Wilbur Chapman resigned in 1911, and George Gordon Mahy was named secretary for evangelism in the
PCUSA.[13] Mahy oversaw several major shifts in the evangelism program between 1912 and 1932. First, the Special
Committee on Evangelistic Work acquired permanent status in 1913. The founders of the special committee had
opposed the notion of making their committee a fixed
landmark on the bureaucratic landscape. Two factors influenced the General Assembly to alter its status. Like other
mainstream Protestant denominations, the PCUSA had
begun to adopt throughout its boards and agencies the corporate structure that it found so successfully employed in
contemporary business. A permanent office to handle the
regular "marketing" of the faith made eminent sense
within this paradigm, both for efficiency and corporate order. But equally important were the 229 of 295 presbyteries who by 1913 established evangelism committees as
requested by the special committee. These local agents depended on the national committee for literature and assistance. Their call for a reliable national agency ultimately
persuaded the General Assembly.[14]

Ten years later, during the reorganization of the General
Assembly, the denomination declared formally why a sep-

arate evangelism arm was needed. The 1923 restructuring of the PCUSA transformed the Permanent Committee on Evangelism into a "division" of a new Board of National Missions. The board's first report explained the link between what it called the "four motives" that had "controlled our church through all its history." They were evangelism, service, Christian education, and Christian fellowship. The heart of the statement stated: "Our church has time and again expressed its conviction that our purpose must be a saved soul in a saved body in a saved community."[15]

The General Assembly of the same year reaffirmed what its prior Board of Home Missions had insisted since its conception: "Evangelism, in its broad sense of bringing men [and women] to Jesus Christ for personal salvation, being the primary business of the Church, should be carried through each Division and Department of the Board . . . , and should not be regarded as the exclusive function of any one Division or Department."[16] However, the General Assembly then proceeded to take away much that it had generously given by explaining the formation of a new Division of Evangelism in this way: "The promotion of the evangelistic spirit, instruction in evangelistic methods, and training in the practice of evangelism, is a sufficiently specialized and technical branch of Christian work to call for the erection, as a constituent part of the National Board's organization, of a Division of Evangelism."[17]

This new rationale redefined evangelism's place in the church's ecology, and in a curious way, it limited its role. Evangelism had previously been assumed to be the motive force and purpose behind all programs of the church's many boards and agencies. Now it became one of several ecclesiastical offices of technical expertise competing for the attention and funding of the larger church. In this new and constricted definition of the evangelism division lay the seed for later friction and questioning from social action advocates. Increasingly, proponents of social involvement would view evangelism efforts as manipulative, number-oriented programs that were largely unconcerned about the commitment and holistic discipleship of those who were added to membership rolls.[18]

Ironically, at the very moment when evangelism found a permanent base and rationale within the church's national structure, it decentralized its operations and assumed a more passive administrative style. The simultaneous campaign program continued under Mahy but with far more emphasis on presbyteries assuming primary responsibility. Chapman had largely orchestrated his campaigns with some local assistance. Mahy and his division fostered "presbyterial simultaneous campaigns." The division provided evangelists and training, but presbyteries planned and executed campaigns that now involved an entire presbytery rather than just an urban area.[19]

After 1923, Mahy followed the lead of the denomination's reorganization plan by further decentralizing the program. The reorganization gave special emphasis to synods as intermediaries between presbyteries and the General Assembly. The evangelism division likewise made the synods the primary consultative body for formulating evangelistic programs for a region.[20]

Mahy and his successor after 1932, William F. Klein, also took a nondirective approach to program development. They no longer created and charted new activities for the larger church. They preferred to base programs "upon the known experiences of the pastors of the Church and their expressed desire rather than upon any theory of its [the division's] own."[21]

The ten-year period from 1913 to the 1923 denominational reorganization proved slightly more fruitful than the initial years of the Special Committee on Evangelistic Work. Net member gains rose, and the number of Presbyterian members required to bring in one new member dropped. But after reorganization and decentralization, complaints were raised. A lack of program and direction from the division and a significant slippage in the denomination's rate of growth were noted.[22]

Blame for the latter development is hard to place squarely on the evangelism division alone. This time span included a puzzling demographic glitch across the American religious scene and a formal schism within the PCUSA. During the early 1930s in particular, losses for reasons other than members' deaths or moves to other communities increased dramatically. Yet every mainline Protestant denomination experienced a similar slump in membership during this period of what Robert T. Handy, the noted historian of American religion, has called a "religious depression." Also, division over fundamentalism climaxed in 1936 when J. Gresham Machen led a number of Presbyterians to form a new denomination.[23]

A hostile overture in 1940 called for the creation of a special commission on evangelism, free from the current bureaucracy, to formulate a five-year plan for evangelism. The General Assembly responded by forming a special commission to suggest better ways of unifying the current evangelism effort.[24]

The Special Commission recommended in 1942 that a national commission be established with representation from the major boards and the church-at-large. This body would formulate program, using the Unit of Evangelism as its administrative agent, but would report directly to the General Assembly.[25]

New Life Through Increased Person-to-Person Evangelism

The National Commission on Evangelism signaled a shift in evangelism's profile within the PCUSA, since its composition and relative autonomy prefigured the exclusive focus evangelism would enjoy during the late 1940s. George Sweazey signed on as the new general secretary of the Unit of Evangelism in 1945. One year later, the unit announced a major evangelistic push called the New Life Movement.[26]

The New Life Movement was impressive in both its scope and its organization. Its motto was "If any man [or woman] be in Christ, he [or she] is a new creature." Its dates set January 1, 1950, as the finale to the effort so that the church could enter the last half-century revived and re-equipped for the future. But the influence of the program was to continue long past its formal climax because, as its literature suggested, "This is a 'movement' and not a 'campaign.'" Where "a campaign is something that is promoted for a period and finished forever," the New Life Movement's intent was "by three years of concentrated attention" to start something that would "remain for the permanent endowment of the Church."[27] *Concentrated* was the operative word here. The evangelism unit insisted that the church make evangelism its primary focus for the projected three-year plan.

The effort's tools were varied but largely centered around the notion of person-to-person contacts.[28] Moreover, each of the three years in the New Life Movement had a special orientation and audience for those contacts. The first year, 1947, was to be one of preparation in which the church strengthened itself spiritually. The second year aimed to reach those with whom the church already had some contact, and 1949 would emphasize work among those never before touched by the church community.[29]

The movement's goals captured the imagination. By 1950 there would be 1,000,000 new Presbyterians on the rolls, 300 new churches or Sunday schools, and 100,000 lay people trained in personal evangelism. The ultimate accomplishments of New Life approached but never reached those targets. The program did train 100,000 lay people. It did attract almost 700,000 new people by either profession or reaffirmation of faith. But perhaps most important of all, its timing and organizational scope coincided with actions by the UPCNA and PCUS that poised the three denominations for riding the crest of a significant cultural wave.[30]

The multi-year pattern, with special emphases for each year and specific numerical goals, was not unique to the New Life Movement. The UPCNA employed a similar strategy as early as 1940 and continued in a series of such multi-year programs until the merger of the UPCNA and PCUSA in 1958. One of the more statistically successful of these efforts by the UPCNA was the United Evangelistic Crusade of 1948–1952. Evangelism enjoyed the singular focus of all UPCNA boards and agencies. And, like the PCUSA New Life Movement, the Crusade coincided with the 1949–1950 United Evangelistic Advance, an event involving approximately twenty-five major Protestant denominations.[31]

The PCUS did not attempt a program of New Life dimensions in the 1940s, but evangelism enjoyed a higher profile starting in the mid-1940s. Until 1944, a reliable financial base eluded the evangelism program of the PCUS, and a permanent director for evangelism was not in place for two more years.[32] The new secretary, H. H. Thompson, formulated a five-year evangelism plan to complement the denomination's "Presbyterian Program of Progress." Its goal was to take advantage of southern population growth and rising economic prosperity. It required an increase in both office and field staff and ambitious annual goals for membership increases.[33]

The "Presbyterian Program of Progress" provided a checklist of congregational evangelism activities. It expected regular monitoring by presbyteries of these efforts. Person-to-person evangelism through visitation, Sunday service invitations to membership, evangelistic preaching at least ten days a year, and church school growth goals were emphasized in order to make evangelism an integral and consistent part of local church life.[34] The net result was that the church "received more on profession of faith and had more net gains [during Thompson's tenure (1947–1952)] than in the previous 20 years combined."[35]

Religious historians and sociologists all recognize the 1950s as a decade of "faith in faith" in which church and synagogue membership became the norm for most Americans. It is often assumed that outside forces largely caused this cultural surge. But the experience of the PCUSA, UPCNA, and PCUS indicates that mainstream Protestant denominations mounted major evangelistic campaigns just as the wave began to build momentum. How much this work propelled the wave is still uncertain, but it certainly set these churches firmly at the wave's crest just as it reached its apex.

The New Life Movement acquired a mythical stature in later decades when membership figures declined. For those intimately involved in the national church's program, however, its successes were soon tarnished by questions. The first question was, Where do we go from here? After receiving the denomination's exclusive attention, what does one do for an encore? The initial answer was to continue the momentum by maintaining the basic program under a new name but with less denominationwide attention. In 1951, the New Life Movement became the New Life Advance. Its projected life span was for at least three more years. A new membership goal was later set of three million Presbyterians in the PCUSA by 1958. This target was achieved, but by merger with the UPCNA in 1958 rather than by new-member recruitment.[36]

As the decade of the 1950s wore on, a growing sense of exhaustion and the need for a new beginning permeated the evangelism division's rhetoric. Sweazey resigned his post in 1953. The same year, the division acknowledged that its role now was less a bugler to arms than a nagging spouse reminding the church of its unfinished chores.[37]

The division sustained its litany of reminders during the late 1950s as it confronted a new round of questions concerning the New Life Movement's statistical success. Troubling signs of problems with the assimilation of new members surfaced as early as the middle year of the program, but a study reported in 1962 raised further doubts. The church had commissioned research to answer why people joined the church in general and the United Presbyterian Church in the United States of America (UPCUSA) in particular. The researcher unexpectedly discovered a significant number of members brought onto the PCUSA rolls around 1958 who were now inactive.[38]

Compounding questions about the long-term efficacy of the New Life triumph was the concurrent production of an in-house history of PCUSA evangelism programs. This history offers insight into important tactical rethinking within the national office. A staff member and one-time acting director of the division, Richard R. Gilbert, challenged the New Life Movement where it had supposedly been most potent—its generation of spectacular statistical growth. Gilbert charged that the yield of the New Life Movement, with all its hoopla, horsepower, and hierarchy of organization, was not significantly superior to that of the Division of Evangelism's first six years under the decentralized, passive, and comparatively silent administration of George Mahy. Gilbert then proposed that "the statistics race toward a harsh conclusion: No matter what the top does and says programmatically, the bottom comes up with similar patterns of growth."[39]

The UPCUSA evangelism unit had already decided to move to a regionalization scheme, because "action in [the] Executive Suite makes little difference on Main Street numerically." Under this new plan, the congregation could discover "on its own, through a 'blood, sweat and tears' struggle" an "authentic and effective" evangelism program for its particular situation.[40]

The national staff had been moving to a specialized consultant model for some years under its secretary, Donald Lester. Each staff member had become an expert for a specific church situation. Under regionalization, this pattern continued. But the staff's role became one of "participant-observer." The staff would use their expertise to facilitate and challenge local formulators of evangelism. However, they would remain one step removed from actually formulating programs.[41]

Although the PCUSA/UPCUSA experienced a gradual loss of faith in the New Life success, the "test of faith" for the PCUS arose rather abruptly. The PCUS celebrated its centennial in 1961. At the request of the Centennial Celebration Committee, the evangelism division under its secretary, Albert E. Dimmock, prepared a campaign as the anniversary's centerpiece.[42]

This "Presbyterian Mission to the Nation" was pursued to a rather bitter end. It began with a series of preaching cavalcades to over eighty selected metropolitan centers in

October 1960. Teams of three outstanding church leaders and speakers moved about the South to inspire and inform local Presbyterians about the mission. A period of self-study in each congregation followed. It culminated in a tripartite program of evangelism known as the "mission of friendship" (person-to-person evangelism), the "mission of Christian action" (a program addressing a local human need chosen by the local church), and the "mission of proclamation" (evangelistic preaching on Sunday mornings).[43]

Carefully planned and organized in consultation with seminary and church leaders, the mission offered a range of printed materials to educate and inspire. It employed radio and television to spread its word. It provided training schools to instruct selected individuals how to evangelize so that they could later teach others the same. But the PCUS experienced a decline in professions of faith and net growth during the year of its climax. Astonishment and disappointment pervaded all postmortems, despite the mission's early warnings that numbers would not be its ultimate criterion of success or failure.[44]

The PCUS and UPCUSA reacted quite differently at first to the troubling events at the turn of the decade. Where the latter moved swiftly to a new structure in "regionalization," the PCUS served up a mighty jeremiad. Nevertheless, both churches entered a new stage of rethinking, retooling, and restructuring evangelism. This process the church continues today.

Rethinking, Retooling, Restructuring

By 1963, the evangelism leadership of both denominations was convinced of two things. First, the key to evangelism lay in grass-roots commitment rather than bigger and better "New Life"-style programs generated from the national office.[45] Both churches sensed that fundamental shifts were occurring in American culture that undercut members' commitment to Christ, to evangelism, and to discipleship. Both were also concerned that the church itself might be deeply implicated in the problem.

Where the late 1950s and early 1960s raised questions about Presbyterian evangelism's statistical health, the middle and late 1960s challenged the very character of evangelical outreach. The civil rights movement quickly taught Protestant denominations that the church was not the sole purveyor of divine revelation. Evangelism rhetoric through the latter part of the 1960s overflowed with claims that the world's social ferment was as much, if not more, a source of revelation for God's will as was the church. This insight led naturally to the notion that the church should listen more to the world and its social movements of divine justice.[46]

Race captured the UPCUSA's attention shortly after regionalization took effect. Under the title "Evangelism and Race," the evangelism office produced in 1964 its first and only policy statement dealing with a specific social problem. The statement insisted that all aspects of the evangelism program must be geared to the promotion of equal rights within the church.[47] The same year, the Commission on Evangelism went so far as to request that the Division of Evangelism be fused with the Office of Church and Society. This would witness to their close interrelationship in the Christian life. The action was never taken. But within a few short years, the evangelical act of verbally claiming allegiance to Christ was subordinated theoretically to the social action mission.[48]

After a period of flux in the division's leadership, George T. Peters was named its new chair. In keeping with the division's shifting interest, Peters had been much more active at the denominational level in church and society issues than in the church's formal evangelism programs.[49]

The division drastically redefined evangelism one year later. Entitled "Mission and Evangelism," this policy statement of the division insisted:

> All evangelism is mission but all mission is not necessarily evangelism. Christians often are engaged in the mission of the Church without any explicit or self-conscious verbal reference to their being Christian or to the teachings of Christ. They simply allow their Christ-formed consciences and con-

cerns to cooperate with, and to take part with, other men [and women], whether Christians, Jews, humanists, or atheists, in working for the welfare of other men [and women].[50]

The expressed concern for cooperation with those who did not share the faith grew out of the church's experience in social justice movements of the 1960s. But this statement made two departures from past rhetoric that indicated a signal shift in perspective. First, the distinction that all mission might not be evangelism was entirely new. Repeatedly, the mission boards of the PCUSA and UPCUSA had insisted that the central purpose of all their divisions or departments was evangelism.[51] This 1967 statement denied evangelism such a place in part because it assumed a much narrower definition of evangelism tied largely to the verbal witness of the church. Second, this statement subordinated the verbal witness of evangelism to the physical witness of social action and, as such, promoted a "muting" of the Presbyterian witness.

There were several reasons why a "muted" witness seemed preferable at the time. For one, the new emphasis on listening to the world militated against too swift a resort to speech on all occasions.

There was also the commitment to transform the culture through coalitions of churched and nonchurch activists. Resorting too quickly to verbal witness could have disrupted such cooperative efforts.

Related to this concern, the 1960s witnessed a new surge of ecumenical enthusiasm. The Stated Clerk of the UPCUSA, Eugene Carson Blake, and Episcopal Bishop James A. Pike issued the call in 1960 for a new and final stage in American ecumenism. Not content with mere cooperation, the church participated in the proposed Consultation on Church Union (COCU). Its ultimate goal was the actual reunion of the major Protestant denominational families. A muted witness now proved attractive to ecumenical advocates for the same reasons that it did to promoters of social action coalitions. That is, it neutralized a potential source of friction in the delicate negotiations required for church union.

Finally, the church's past emphasis on verbal witness became identified in some Presbyterians' minds during the 1960s with the church's instincts for institutional self-preservation at the expense of courageous Christian witness in society. The 1960s exposed a host of moral contradictions in American society, not the least of which was the church's acquiescence to and complicity with bigotry, sexism, and poverty. To many Presbyterians, past words had been an empty smoke screen for the complacency of the church in the face of major social evils and in service to its own self-preservation. Now actions to redeem the substance of those words were needed. The actions must emulate Christ's own works of self-sacrifice. Therefore, the rhetoric of the division, and indeed that of the larger board, acquired a strong anti-institutional bent.[52]

The evangelism literature of the division in this period repeatedly alluded to Christ's admonition that those who would lose their lives for his sake would preserve it.[53] The adoption of this pericope as the paradigm for the church's witness had one unintended destructive effect. The UPCUSA began to hemorrhage in 1966 with an average net loss of 54,294 members per year over the next decade. As the magnitude of the losses became evident, cries for a reexamination of the evangelism program multiplied.[54]

The logic of self-sacrifice proved impenetrable to questioning from these statistical losses. The Board of National Missions parried one thrust by the Stated Clerk's statistical report in 1968 by charging that "the Church has no warrant for substituting a statistical graph for a cross." Moreover, "if it [the church] takes seriously the gospel of its Lord; if it is willing to lose its life that it may find it, the apparent winnowing of its membership may yet prove to be its restoring."[55]

The Council on Evangelism overseeing the work of the division made a Solomonic attempt at calming the furor following the division's 1967 statement by formulating one of its own. Entitled "Evangelism Through Mission: Promise and Danger," it summarized five approaches to evangelism and listed the potential benefits and dangers of each. "Evangelism Through Mission" resolved nothing. In keeping with the denomination's growing affection for diversity over a single lockstep approach, no one style of evangelism or combination of the five was suggested as preferable.[56]

The PCUS was no more successful in resolving the growing split between verbal and social action evangelism. Following the failed "Mission to the Nation," the church produced a jeremiad to chasten its collective soul and its members' flagging evangelical impulses. "A Call to Repentance and Expectancy" blamed not the program but the people for evangelism's failure. There was selfishness among an affluent membership. There was narrow denominationalism. There was pride of class and education. There was prejudice, backbiting, and crass materialism. There was a lack of faith, shallow theological understanding, and no fervent expectancy for God's reviving touch. All of these lay at the heart of the failure.[57]

To begin the redemption of these many sins and to revive its sagging evangelism, the PCUS began a two-pronged reevaluation. One task force traveled the hinterlands to hear what the people said about past and future evangelism; another worked on a new theological definition of evangelism appropriate for the times. "Appropriate for the times" was the key phrase here, for the new executive secretary of the Board of National Ministries, John F. Anderson, Jr., was convinced, along with his UPCUSA counterparts, that everything was new and in movement in the mid-1960s. The church should illustrate its awareness "of the peril of stopping places" by keeping pace.[58]

The effort at theological redefinition was not easy and almost ended in a deadlock. At one point, those overseeing the process despaired that any common statement could be reached. They considered presenting two separate papers to the church. "A Theological Basis for the Evangelistic Work of Our Church" was completed in 1967, however. It represented an admirable attempt not to succumb to any of the polarities current in discussions of evangelism. Yet the official implications drawn from the document differed little from those found in contemporary statements of the UPCUSA. They insisted that "faithfulness to mission is more important than serving the demands of ecclesiastical structures; . . . witness by the church is more important than recruitment into the church; and the total style of the church's life is more important witness than the verbalization of its creed."[59]

Throughout the remainder of the 1960s and all of the 1970s, the evangelism divisions of both churches funded experimental ministries. The intent was twofold. First, they searched for innovative ways of conducting evangelism that would fit what they viewed as a rapidly changing social situation. Second, they hoped to produce concrete, albeit limited, pilot projects that local churches or lower judicatories could then modify for their own locale with some degree of confidence.[60]

By 1971, both the UPCUSA and the PCUS were experiencing net losses of members. Restructuring at the national level disrupted programmatic efforts to address this problem in the next decade. The evangelism programs lost both continuity and visibility under the two churches' reorganizations. Before 1971, the leadership and program thrusts of national evangelism efforts had been well publicized and supported by the denominational structure. This changed dramatically as responsible General Assembly staff and their plans were accorded a low profile in the new organizational patterns.

During the 1970s and 1980s, several special studies relating to evangelism proved largely ineffective at redeeming enthusiasm for evangelistic outreach. The PCUS Board of National Ministries completed a "Study of the Specific Role of Preaching Evangelists" in 1971. It upheld evangelistic preaching but discouraged the use of itinerant preaching evangelists despite cries in some church quarters to return to the practice.[61]

Two years later, the PCUS participated with other denominations in the national movement known as Key '73.

The effort fostered some enthusiasm, but the effects were short-lived. The UPCUSA refused an invitation to join Key '73.

In 1976, the UPCUSA General Assembly received a major study on church membership trends. The report dispelled a number of popular myths about membership loss. It indicated, however, that members were ambivalent about sharing their faith. They exhibited low motivation for such activities and felt little competence at doing so. Moreover, they lacked clarity in their Christian convictions due to the social climate of uncertainty, individualism, and relativism.[62]

The report provided a battery of statistics indicating Presbyterian ambivalence toward evangelism. When asked, the laity and clergy placed high value on sharing their faith and on new-member recruitment. But low participation in and organization for such efforts belied their declared interest. Presbyterian seminaries had had little or no instruction in evangelism for the last ten years. In fact, they exhibited a suspicion toward emphasizing the subject in their curricula. And lower judicatories under the regionalization plan had, for the most part, saved their "blood, sweat and tears" by not struggling to develop such programs.[63]

A report by the Strategy Development Committee for Reaching People Who Are Without the Gospel deflected this troubling challenge to the state of evangelistic concern in the UPCUSA a year later. The committee offered strategies that required and got little change in the division's plans. They essentially confirmed programs that the division had already begun, most notably the RISK evangelism program. This child of the regionalization process had been officially parented by the Synod of the Trinity.[64]

More recently, a Special Committee on Evangelism and Church Growth proposed a new program called New Day Dawning.[65] It is premature even to guess at the ultimate fate of this dawning initiative in Presbyterian evangelism. But this effort, plus the creation of a General Assembly Council Task Force on Church Membership Growth and a call for redirecting significant funds to the denomination's

Evangelism Unit, indicate the national church's desire to revitalize an evangelistic outreach.[66]

One observation about Presbyterian and mainstream Protestant evangelical impulses can be ventured. The tensions between advocates of social action evangelism and those who favor a verbal evangelism have yet to be resolved. In part, this is because neither can be dissolved adequately into the other. The two options are, in fact, not options in the Reformed tradition or, more broadly, in Christianity. They are, instead, the twin outgrowths of the *euangelion* proclaimed by Christ, who came to save sinners and to teach them a redemptive transformation of relationships that unavoidably involves Christians in reforming cultures.

In the 1960s in particular, mainline Protestantism awoke to the full magnitude and urgency of contemporary social problems. At the same time, it expressed a renewed will to restore the fractured body of Christ to real unity through COCU. This prompted the Presbyterian churches, with their denominational colleagues in ecumenical talks, to question the efficacy, propriety, and motivation of past evangelism efforts. They believed that evangelistic outreach had ignored serious social evils and the demands of full Christian fellowship for too long in an effort to bolster the size and financial strength of their particular institutions. As a result, actions took priority over words in evangelism. Actions, not words, would embody what had become the empty mouthing of concern for fellow humans' spiritual and temporal welfare. Actions, not words, would also allow cooperation across theological and ideological boundaries.

If this move meant a muted verbal witness in the interest of cooperation with non-Christians for social justice, many recalled Jesus' contact with publicans and prostitutes in service to the kingdom. If it also meant that church rolls would dwindle, many exclaimed, "So be it!" for the church's mission was witness, not self-preservation.[67]

For others in Presbyterian and mainstream Protestant circles, words of invitation and witness to Christ continued to be seen as the necessary preliminaries to action. The words interpreted the motives and meaning behind acts of love and solidarity. Claiming that the denominational leadership remained inattentive to their position, several special interest groups, such as Presbyterians United for Biblical Concerns and the Presbyterian Lay Committee, Inc., were organized to sustain a prominent voice for this position.

The significant decline in membership of the last two decades has accentuated the division between the two sides of this debate. It has exacerbated the underlying suspicions held by each group that their counterpart is prepared to sacrifice willingly a critical element of the Reformed tradition's parallel allegiance and Christianity's dual thrusts. Fervor for these two brands of evangelical outreach remains strong among their proponents today. Yet the debate continues inconclusive, because neither party has captured the imagination of the Presbyterian or mainstream Protestant masses who exhibit in varying degrees significant ambivalence, apathy, and/or discomfort with the topic of evangelism.

2

Twentieth-Century Presbyterian New Church Development: A Critical Period, 1940–1980

Robert H. Bullock, Jr.

Introduction

Home missions, church extension, new church development—all these terms have been used by American Presbyterians to describe the process of extending the gospel and planting new congregations of the church of Jesus Christ.

The purpose of this study is to examine a critical period (1940–1980) in the life of three members of the American Presbyterian family of churches: the Presbyterian Church in the United States of America (PCUSA), the United Presbyterian Church of North America (UPCNA), and the Presbyterian Church in the United States (PCUS). In 1958, the PCUSA and the UPCNA united to form the United Presbyterian Church in the United States of America (UPCUSA). In 1983, the UPCUSA and the PCUS reunited after a 121-year separation to become the Presbyterian Church (U.S.A.).

The forty-year period 1940–1980 is particularly fruitful for study because the first twenty-year period exhibits a high degree of success in the single-minded work of new church development accompanied by tremendous membership growth. By contrast, the second twenty-year period exhibits a broadening of emphases in national mission, a de-emphasis on new church development, and a precipitous decline in membership.

Some have argued that the reason for today's membership decline was the diversion of denominational funding away from evangelism and new church development into experimental ministries in the 1960s. The unintended consequences of neglecting the task of building up the base is at least in part responsible for the membership decline that continues at the present time.

The findings of this study lend general support to this hypothesis, although the slowdown in new church development between 1960 and 1980 can hardly be the only cause for the UPCUSA/PCUS combined membership losses of 885,609, or 21.3 percent of the 1960 combined membership total of 4,158,127 (see Table 2.2).

This study is about "conventional" new church development—church development aimed at the white middle- and upper middle-class constituency, which even today comprises about 95 percent of the membership of the Presbyterian Church (U.S.A.).[1]

The PCUSA/UPCUSA, UPCNA, PCUS: 1880–1980

The PCUSA/UPCUSA

1880–1940: From the cities to the suburbs. With the closing of the frontier and increasing industrialization, urbanization, and immigration, the mission focus in the PCUSA turned to the cities and their attendant problems and opportunities. The PCUSA developed both evangelistic and service strategies. Within this complex of activity, new church development was steadily becoming a particular, identifiable function within denominational structures.[2]

An Immigration Department, coordinated with an existing Department of Church and Labor, was established in 1908 to meet immigrant needs through education, literature, visitation, and Bible reading. A Social Service Department was created in 1910.[3]

The general urban strategy in this period was to meet the pressing physical needs of the immigrants in the large cities through institutions such as neighborhood houses, with evangelism and church development expected to follow.[4]

There were significant developments in funding and organization for new church development after 1890. For example, in 1910 the Board of Church Erection was authorized to establish a Church Extension Fund for site purchase and construction, and the following year, presbyteries were requested to assist in fund-raising. In 1912, a Special Fund for site purchases was established and a Land Purchase Department approved two years later. By 1924, however, Board of Church Erection funds had nearly been exhausted.

In a major denominational organizational overhaul, the Board of National Missions was created in 1923 and relationships among synods and presbyteries in new church development established, allowing for more centralized planning and direction than in the past.

There was a great deal of building in the 1920s in the PCUSA. In 1924, a Bureau of Architecture was established, and in 1927 a full-time church architect, who also reviewed congregational grant and loan proposals, was employed.

Funding for new work came from a three-year Advance Fund, begun in 1928, which solicited individual contributions throughout the denomination for the purpose of supporting new church development in suburban areas. By the late 1930s, however, with giving down and churches hurting financially because of the Great Depression, many had difficulty in repaying their capital debts. With 46 percent of total denominational loans delinquent in 1938, a Church Debt Service was created at the national level.[5]

1940–1960: The suburban boom years. The World War II period was a time of preparation for the surge in new church development and membership growth that was to follow.

In 1943, the Synod of New Jersey gave $75,000 to the denomination for new church development on condition that an equal amount would be raised churchwide for purchase of sites in promising areas.[6] The following year, the Assembly set up a Restoration Fund for postwar new church development and requested advance giving of 12 percent of the annual benevolence budget for "church extension in industrial and suburban areas."[7] The board approved participation in the new interdenominational Cooperative Field Research Program.[8]

Following World War II, suburban new church development was the major focus of the PCUSA, and new patterns of organization, staffing, and funding were required for the effort. Urban immigrant work decreased correspondingly.[9]

Beginning in 1945, in addition to other available funds, the Board of National Missions appropriated $240,000 for new church development. Debt repayment of existing loans in growth areas was urged, authority was given to executive officers of the board to approve limited new site and construction grants immediately, and liberalization of denominational building loan policies was considered. The Assembly approved additional annual funding in the general benevolence budget in 1946.[10]

In 1947, the Office of New Church Development and Building Aid was created and directed to develop an overall plan in consultation with synods and presbyteries. In 1950, the renamed Department of New Church Development and Church Extension would be subdivided into an Office of New Church Development Organization and Promotion and an office of New Church Development Building Aid.[11]

In 1948, the board declared new church development to be a high priority for the church as a whole and "a major emphasis" for the next five years. It followed that expanded organization and funding ($1 million in the general benevolence budget) at the national level would be necessary, and such was requested in the same year.[12]

During the 1950s, increasing sums of money were committed at the national level to finance new church development. In 1951, the Assembly approved a capital needs campaign, including $7.5 million for new church development. Two years later, it directed that 66 percent of the $7.5 million building fund be allocated for loans, to be administered through a revolving fund. It recommended an additional $1 million for personnel grants.[13]

But in 1955, the board estimated the total need to be an additional $5.5 million. With a general mandate from the Assembly, the board voted to secure $3 million commercially, another $1.5 million from the reserves of the four denominational boards (including $600,000 from the Board of National Missions), with the remaining $1 million to be secured from the denominational benevolence budget. That year the Assembly authorized the General Council to provide not less than $300,000 per year in the benevolence budgets from 1957 through 1964 to support the loan program for "*carefully selected* new church projects," with the expressed hope for $200,000 more each year, for a total of $500,000 annually. By 1956, all boards had provided funds from their reserves for new church development.[14]

But still more money was needed. In 1957 the board proposed selling bonds, a plan that was not implemented. Instead, the 1958 Assembly created a Guaranteed Loan Fund for new church development by authorizing the board to borrow up to $10 million with the following guidelines: (a) funds were to be used only as needed annually; (b) interest charged was not to be less than interest paid; (c) there should be presbytery and synod guarantees of all loans; (d) there should be an annual reserve of $250,000 to be established for four years, beginning in 1960, to guarantee loans; (e) any additional deficiencies were to be guaranteed by the annual benevolence budget; and (f) there should be annual reports to the Assembly on the loan program.[15]

During 1958, the board held seven fund-raisers for new church development. These brought in $7.6 million in building funds and an additional $1,687,000 for the current operating budgets of the congregations involved.[16]

In 1960, *A Guide for the Development of a New Church* was published, reflecting the church's experience in the postwar era.[17] In the same year, the Assembly requested all judicatories to create strategy committees and to take advantage of board support services in new church development planning, toward the goal of establishing new churches that could be self-sufficient in three years.[18]

1960–1980: New directions in mission. As previously noted, in the period 1880–1940 the denominational focus on the immigrants and their needs gradually gave way to urban/suburban residential congregational development. In the period 1940–1960, the focus was clearly on suburban residential congregational development. From the early to mid-1960s on, however, the denomination moved steadily away from the earlier thrust until the mid- to late-1970s, when concern about downward membership trends prompted renewed emphasis on conventional new church development and church redevelopment.

In retrospect, the early 1960s was a time of gradual shifts in priorities. The trends between 1960 and 1966 included (a) interest in less promising fields (such as inner city, town and country); (b) concern expressed about the number of delinquent loans; (c) a recognized need to recruit and provide specialized training for new church development pastors, reflecting the increasing complexity of starting new churches; (d) ever-increasing funding (an additional $10 million in borrowing authorized by the Assembly in 1962), reflecting the realities of rising costs; (e) better planning for new church development (now coordinated by the Division of Church Strategy and Development); (f) a significant shift in emphasis within the board toward social ministries and perceived inadequacies in "traditional" new church development approaches; (g) and promotion of various types of ministries in urban settings.[19]

These trends were reflected in the new guidelines for new church development approved by the Assembly in

1966: more judicatory involvement in planning and funding, an ecumenical emphasis, new directions envisioned for congregational ministry generally, and the importance of social ministries.[20]

A major strategic turning point came in 1967 when the board approved the paper "Strategy for the Development of New Congregations," itself based on the core theme of the newly adopted Confession of 1967—reconciliation. New church development would now be aimed at a considerably broader field, including commercial areas (shopping centers), "vocational and special purpose communities, age group communities, communities of special concern or interest such as urban issues, public affairs, the arts, etc., and communities of leisure and recreation."[21]

As long-time Board of National Missions staff members Everett and Margaret Perry point out in their excellent outline of PCUSA/UPCUSA policy developments, the new model "was in sharp contrast to the earlier themes of evangelizing the frontier, of serving immigrant peoples and incidentally developing congregations, and churching burgeoning suburban communities with a strong survival goal [successive strategies of the PCUSA/UPCUSA]. It saw the new congregation as *an instrument of mission in its inception, rather than an instrument for meeting personal needs out of which it had been anticipated mission would develop*" (emphasis added). Ecumenical mission was stressed.[22]

A variety of "experimental" congregations were established as a result of the new strategy and policies. The 1971 Assembly affirmed this new direction, commended it to the presbyteries for study, and reminded presbyteries that they had chief responsibility for organizing new churches.[23]

A 1972 UPCUSA report showed that since 1959, $20 million had been loaned to 503 churches, with 222,354 members whose total receipts were $168,180,090, of which $20,643,619 had been given to general mission.[24] The board expressed its opinion that "strong, high potential, self-supporting churches of this type must be developed

. . . in order to support the general mission of the Church" and recommended a new $10 million Guaranteed Loan Fund.[25] It noted that $6,124,506 had been granted to minority and ethnic churches. By this time, however, the board was beginning to incur operating deficits—$2 million reported for 1971.[26]

A major denominational restructure took place in 1973. The Program Agency was established, replacing the long-standing board system. Emphasis on new church development decreased, because "conduct of mission, support of mission, and personnel matters in mission were placed in three different agencies, all of which were considered to be mission agencies." New church development was not specifically mentioned in the plan for the Program Agency.[27]

During the 1970s, there was growing concern, however, about membership decline and, consequently, later in the decade a rekindled interest in new church development, along with what was now called redevelopment of existing churches with potential.

In 1973, a Mission Development Grants Committee was established whose purpose was to provide seed money for new projects, including new church development. Two years later, comprehensive new guidelines were approved for site and building loans. The 1977 Program Agency guidelines relating to new church development limited aid to residential church development, but the listing of possible settings continued to be very broad—from rapidly growing communities to shopping centers. Joint new church development with other denominations, especially the PCUS, was strongly encouraged.[28]

The 1976 Assembly emphasized the critical importance of new church development to the future of the denomination, urged presbyteries over the next five years (1977–1981) to take the initiative and to give it the highest priority, and commended to them the massive 1976 Assembly "Membership Trends" study as a basis for new program development. That study strongly recommended the new church development and redevelopment thrusts, including ethnic work.[29]

It also revealed the following summaries about new church development in the period 1953–1974: Between 1953 and 1962, the denomination averaged 77 new congregations per year (with a high of 106 in 1956). In 1963, the number of new churches organized was 49. It declined annually to 33 in 1966.[30]

The study noted that in the five-year period beginning in 1967, when the new national strategy was approved (with emphasis on "experimental" and "noninstitutional"), only 116 churches were started, no more than 25 in any one year, only 19 in 1971. Few, if any, of these achieved membership of over 40 adults.

From 1972 to 1975, primary responsibility for new church development was shifted down to the middle judicatories as a result of the restructure, thus requiring time and energy spent developing appropriate strategy and plans at the lower levels. In these four years, only 75 new congregations were started.

The summary for the period 1964–1974 was as follows: Of the 293 new congregations begun, 93 percent were still functioning in 1976. The report noted: "While the denomination averaged a 1.9% loss for each of those years, these congregations grew by 9.8%. They now have over 50,000 members and have in the ten-year period contributed $3,252,151 to General Mission. However, during this same period the U.S. population grew, despite declining birth rates, by over 16 million persons, or 8%." The report made it clear that adequate funding for the existing new church development program was in place; all requests had been met. The problem was the lack of interest in starting new churches.[31]

The 1977 Assembly set five-year new church development goals to begin the following year—at least one new church in each presbytery during the five-year period. It expressed hope that people of a broad range of backgrounds would be attracted to the denomination. Consideration of the handicapped and conservation of energy were new concerns related to building.[32]

The following Assembly affirmed the Program Agency

commitment to growth and the need for funding for "loans, grants, increased staff, and staff services, including racial minority staff."[33] The Program Agency was directed to expand consultation with synods and presbyteries so as to establish advance goals and plans for new church development projects in the period 1983–1988, with an interim report to the 1981 Assembly.[34]

In 1981, however, the Assembly voted not to make a commitment to a 1985 national capital funds campaign for church development and redevelopment (for sites and buildings), opting instead for support of campaigns in the synods and presbyteries. It also urged congregations with a total of $58 million in outstanding denominational loans to accelerate payment so as to make funds available for new loans.[35]

In the period 1975–1982, the UPCUSA started 244 congregations (an indeterminate number of these jointly with the PCUS in union presbyteries), an eight-year average of 30.5 per year. The low was in 1977 (15); the high in 1980 (46).[36]

The UPCNA

The United Presbyterian Church of North America was a small denomination created by several bodies from the Scottish Associate and Reformed Presbyterian traditions in 1858. At the time of its founding, it had a membership of 55,524. Over the years, its membership was largely concentrated in three states: Pennsylvania, Ohio, and Illinois, although home mission activity, including new church development, involved it in work in the upper and lower South as well as the Far West.[37]

In the latter part of the nineteenth century, the Board of Home Missions (responsible for planting new churches) and the Board of Church Extension (loans for buildings and manses) coordinated new church development operations in the Mid and Far West.[38]

Shortly after the turn of the century, the UPCNA turned its attention to the immigrants and their needs, but after

World War I and the enactment of restrictive immigration legislation, the church focused on church extension in non-immigrant fields.[39]

In a 1928 denominational reorganization, three boards—Home Missions, Freedmen's Missions, and Church Extension—were merged into the Board of American Missions with three departments: Negro Work, Home Missions (starting new churches and locating potential sites), and Church Erection (financing and erecting buildings).[40]

In its first year, the new board set a goal of 150 congregations in the next five years. The following year, speakers representing the board were sent out to publicize the need for "organizing, developing and maintaining of English-speaking congregations."[41]

By 1931, the board realized that its goals had been overly ambitious, but it encouraged continued development, especially, as the Assembly noted in 1933, in view of depression-era price levels.[42] However, from 1930 to 1939 only 29 new churches were started.[43]

In 1938, the board shifted the work for initiating new work to the presbyteries and individual congregations, requiring careful planning to qualify for board assistance.[44]

Wartime preparation for new church development at the conclusion of hostilities took the form of amassing some $300,000 for postwar building and purchasing of sites for new churches in 1943 in these cities: Buffalo, N.Y.; Detroit and Dearborn, Mich.; Long Beach, Calif.; and a relocation site in Philadelphia.[45]

In 1945, as part of a larger denominational $2 million campaign, the board proposed $350,000 for organizing 20–25 new congregations and $35,000 for new Negro work in northern cities.[46]

Two of the more innovative ideas from this small denomination were prefabricated chapels in the late 1940s and so-called package churches in the early 1950s. The latter involved the erection of a small first unit, paid for by the board. The first $15,000 was a donation, the balance a loan. Four had been built by 1951. The package church was seen as one of several available options.[47]

Denominational funding was always inadequate. In 1949, the board declared a two-year moratorium on any new church developments involving a building and set the limit at four new congregations for that year. The next year, the board reported to the Assembly that the wartime accumulation of funds had been exhausted, and unless new funding were secured, only four or five new congregations per year could be begun. In 1951, the Assembly requested that the presbyteries take the initiative in locating new fields.[48]

However, the board reaffirmed the priority of new church development in 1952, guaranteeing funds for three new churches before any would be released to existing churches in that year. Furthermore, although the board pledged to make grants and loans available, it encouraged large churches to offer their buildings as collateral, with the board guaranteeing the loans up to a total for the denomination of $100,000.[49]

In 1956, the Assembly instructed the board to appoint an experienced "missionary" in new church development situations who could bring the new church to self-support in 3–5 years, all debt being liquidated or refinanced by the end of the first year after organization.[50]

Finally, in 1958, with union with the PCUSA coming soon, the board approved a slowdown in site acquisitions, applying the funds to building expansions.[51]

The PCUS

1880–1940: Establishing the foundations. Following the Civil War and Reconstruction, the PCUS, which had begun its existence as the Presbyterian Church in the Confederate States of America in December 1861, was in a position and had the desire to begin growing as a new denomination. This desire was reflected in the changing of the name of the Executive Committee of Sustentation to Home Missions in 1879, with two departments: Sustentation (including church erection) and Evangelism.[52]

Although there were periods of evangelistic fervor, the most effective means of growth in this era, as Ernest Trice

Thompson has pointed out, was the planting of new churches, especially in the rapidly growing areas of the Southwest (Texas) and the Southeast (Florida), whose strength today was established in those years. Neglected areas such as Oklahoma continue to be weak numerically.[53]

Denominational strategy and funding patterns varied, the two basic issues always being (a) Assembly versus synod/presbytery responsibility for new church development, including funding, and (b) the allocation of funds between new church development and sustentation.[54]

By 1930, fully half of all PCUS congregations were receiving aid, resulting in a scarcity of funds at all levels for new church development. This situation continued for a number of years.[55]

During 1930–1939, the PCUS started only 173 churches, the high being 28 (1930), and the low, 6 (1937).[56]

1940–1960: Expanding the base. Between 1940 and 1960, the PCUS registered a net gain in membership of 69 percent (see Table 2.2). This result was a predictable consequence of the combination of a tremendous postwar denominational growth potential coupled with strategic planning, organization, and funding.

After the stagnation of the depression years and the constraints imposed by the war years, there was a tremendous pent-up desire for church growth.

Both evangelism and new church development were given the highest priority, the plans beginning to be laid in 1938 with the appointment of a Permanent Committee on Evangelism and the authorization for an Assembly's Home Mission Council. In the years ahead, the former would sponsor a succession of well-planned denominationwide evangelism programs, whereas the latter would be the instrument for achieving maximum coordination of efforts by the Assembly, synods, and presbyteries.[57] The priority of the new church development strategy was symbolized by the change in name from the Executive Committee of Home Missions to the Board of Church Extension, following reorganization in 1949.

The developing denominational new church development strategy was designed to plant as many PCUS congregations in the growing suburbs of the South as rapidly as possible. Sustentation of weaker churches in declining areas continued throughout the period, but the major emphasis was on new church development in the so-called investment areas; that is, those in which new churches could be started relatively easily and inexpensively and which would presumably soon be economically self-sufficient, producing dividends in the form of benevolences to the denomination at large.[58]

The so-called weaker churches—most frequently either racial, ethnic, or rural in this period—continued to be supported: the former racial and ethnic churches because the PCUS had always sponsored ministries directed toward the less fortunate within its bounds, but the latter rural congregations more especially because they were seen to be a "seedbed" for the urban congregations. The dividend from the rural investment was a steady supply of new members in the growing city churches.[59]

A series of consecutive capital fund-raising and denominational growth programs gave the new church development program high visibility and provided the financial undergirding for the great leap forward from 1940 to 1960.

The five-year Home Mission Emergency Fund (1942–1947), with a goal of $1.25 million, was undertaken to retire the debt of congregations in growth areas and to raise money for new ones in the expanding suburbs as soon as the war was over.[60] It produced a total of $1,083,766, with 4.1 percent allocated for expenses, 50.5 percent distributed by the Executive Committee, and 45.3 percent by the synods.[61] By the end of 1947, 196 new churches were organized. They had a charter membership of 9,663, which had increased 73 percent by the end of 1947.[62]

A five-year Home Mission Program of Advance (1947–1952), with emphasis on suburban new church development, immediately followed and was part of an overall "Presbyterian Program of Progress," with a goal of $1.5 million for home missions, including $250,000 for continuing Emergency Fund projects and $500,000 to create a Revolving Extension (loan) Fund to supplement an existing Church and Manse Loan Fund. At the end of six years (1953), $1,044,965 had been collected (69.7 percent of the goal) and 316 new churches organized.[63] In the same period, a strong visitation evangelism program produced more additions on profession of faith and more net gain in membership than the combined totals of the twenty years preceding.[64]

In the latter part of the decade, however, signs of slowdown in advance begin to appear. The evangelism–new church development "Forward with Christ" program (1955–1957), for example, set ambitious goals—two new churches organized per week and a net gain in membership of 50,000 per year—which were not met.[65] Second, a "Presbyterian Mission to the Nation" evangelistic emphasis in 1960, in preparation for the observance of the PCUS centennial in 1961, was a notable failure. The results were termed "shocking" by the Assembly standing committee: "the lowest number of additions on profession of faith in five years, the greatest number of losses, the smallest net gain."[66]

During the 1950s, there was a gradual shift of funding responsibility to the presbytery level. In 1953, following the "Program of Progress," a supplemental Capital Gifts Plan had been approved, involving the presbytery Men of the Church organizations and encouraging planning and fund-raising for new church development at the presbytery level. And in 1957, a supplementary $1 million Challenge Fund plan was begun, which continued through 1963. It allowed presbyteries to keep 80 percent of the funds collected for new church development.[67]

In 1955, the Revolving Extension Fund ceiling had been increased to $1 million. By 1959, the board's loan program was so completely inadequate that $300,000 was placed in escrow so that the board could begin guaranteeing loans validated by presbyteries.[68]

Between 1940 and 1960, some $5 million had been granted for the purchase of church and manse sites and the erection of buildings. In the same period, 508 low-interest building loans totaling $4,535,000 were approved.[69]

Between 1940 and 1960, the Executive Committee/board worked closely with synods and presbyteries, most of which had church extension committees. Organizational structure at the denominational level became increasingly specialized to provide essential support services along with the funding. Following the 1949 reorganization, the new Board of Church Extension had divisions of home missions, evangelism, Negro work, chaplains, media, and Christian relations. Later, survey and church location, church architecture, and urban church, among others, were added.[70]

· The massive investment in new church development in the postwar years produced impressive results. Between April 1, 1946, and December 31, 1960, 785 new churches were organized in all 16 synods and in 81 of the 83 presbyteries, slightly more than one a week. The synod leaders, in order, were Texas (110), North Carolina (105), Florida (81), Virginia (80), and Appalachia (60). Nine presbyteries organized 20 or more new churches.[71] For the period 1946–1959, the greatest increases in membership were in Texas, North Carolina, Florida, Virginia, and Georgia. The largest percentage increases in membership were in Florida, Texas, Georgia, Alabama, and Louisiana. The membership in the postwar new churches at the end of 1959 represented 15.69 percent of total PCUS membership, according to Board of Church Extension calculations.[72]

For the 747 churches organized 1946 through 1959, membership was 138,946; total Sunday school enrollment was 144,472; total contributions were $14,400,072; total benevolences were $1,984,414; and total per capita giving was $103.64 (compared with the denominational average of $99.83).[73]

The largest number of churches organized in a single year in this period was 70 (1955); the smallest was 34 (1946). In 1960, 35 new congregations were organized.[74] The slowdown was attributed at the time to greater selectivity in starting new churches, rising costs of land and building, and increasing scarcity of funds. These concerns had been noted for several years.[75]

1960–1980: Expanding the scope of mission.

In the period 1940–1960, the PCUS was able to focus considerable energies and resources on both evangelism and new church development in the rapidly growing suburban areas. By the end of the 1950s, however, resources were wearing thin, and resolve seemed to be weakening. The failure of the previously mentioned "Presbyterian Mission to the Nation" in 1960 was a turning point.

Meeting with the Board of Church Extension in October 1961, the Assembly Moderator spoke these prophetic words: "Our great concern, therefore, should not be the rising or falling of statistics but whether or not we are an *instrument of God's purpose for these times.*"[76]

Concern, however, continued to be expressed by the board and the Assembly about the slowdown in the church extension effort and signs of loss of vitality in the PCUS. The board cited a number of factors in the decline of new church starts: rising land and building costs, borrowing limits reached by presbyteries and congregations, building programs in larger churches diminishing their ability to support denominational campaigns, the proliferation of such campaigns, and the lack of priorities.[77] In 1964, it decried "the apparent lack of evangelistic concern which has fallen like a miasmic fog" on the church and declared "the era of rapid church extension" to be over.[78] A year later, the Assembly adopted "A Call to Repentance and Expectancy," which called on the church to "wait on the Lord" for further guidance.[79] In the Annual Report for 1966, the executive secretary said that the denomination should be starting 50–75 churches per year. The actual number was 37 in 1962 and 33 in 1966.[80] The last major capital funds drive that benefited new church development was the Presbyterian Development Fund begun in 1963; the church extension share was set at $2,308,500.[81]

New directions in mission began in the early 1960s as urban problems began to grow. A critical turning point was the creation of a new Department of Urban Church in 1962, the department with that name since 1950 becoming the Department of Survey and Church Location. Beginning in 1963, the board made a major commitment to saving urban churches in changing neighborhoods, admitting that the work could not be undertaken without cutting into existing programs.[82]

In the same year, the board approved guidelines for inner-city "creative ministries." The following year it urged presbyteries to create subcommittees on the urban church and to commit major funding to inner-city churches. In 1965, it included $100,000 for "inner city evangelism" in its Advance Program supplementary budget. In 1966, the Advance Budget included $50,000 for continuation of "special ministries such as high-rise apartments, trailer camps, inner-city settlement houses, etc.," together with a $150,000 challenge fund for new church development and $40,000 for seminary evangelism courses.[83]

In the same year, $253,618 was set aside for the new "experimental ministries, . . . instead of for the purchase of property and the erection of church buildings which would have been the usual procedure."[84]

The new focus was confirmed in the board's name change from Church Extension to National Ministries in 1967. In the accompanying restructure, new church development was located in the "area of parish development."[85]

The urban crisis came to a head in 1967–1968 at the same time the financial woes of the board were beginning. Substantial funds were being committed to new ministry projects over and above the support given for new church development and maintenance of the home mission churches—at a time when living donor receipts were generally decreasing each year (after peaking in 1966).[86] Transfers from reserves were frequently made in the years ahead in order to meet operating expenses.[87] An added pressure was rising inflation. In 1968, the board received authority from the Assembly to guarantee up to $3 million in new local loans.[88]

An important paper on evangelism was adopted by the

board in 1968, which expanded its definition and provided the theological rationale for the board's new directions.[89]

In the 1973 PCUS reorganization, the board structure was completely dismantled and in its place a General Executive Board (renamed the General Assembly Mission Board in 1976) was created to end perceived interboard rivalry. New church development was placed in the Division of National Mission, in the area of mission strategy with middle judicatories. In the new organization, distinctive "programs" were replaced by "strategies."[90]

In the early 1970s, evangelism and new church development were given priority, and a Council on Evangelism and Lay Renewal was appointed in the hopes of stimulating growth again; but new church development in the PCUS continued to be anemic and membership decline continued.[91] (See Tables 2.2 and 2.3.)

In line with previously described UPCUSA trends, the PCUS denominational new church development policies in the 1970s encouraged formation of house churches and other experimental congregations without walls as well as ecumenical new church development, including shared facilities, if facilities were to be built.[92]

In 1979, the Office of Review and Evaluation took note of the PCUS failure to revive a strong national new church development program at a time when membership was declining. The report, however, expressed some encouragement that at least ten presbyteries had initiated or were planning capital fund drives wholly or in part for the support of new church development.[93]

Comparative Analysis and Conclusions

The preceding section demonstrates many similarities among the three denominations, in the period being given primary consideration: 1940–1980. Each had great desire to grow after the Depression and World War II era. Goals were set, plans laid, organization developed, and major financial campaigns for new church development undertaken. Then, the UPCUSA and the PCUS followed a downward trajectory, beginning in the mid-1960s.

New church development was the primary domestic mission emphasis for all three denominations in the first twenty-year period. The fruits of their efforts are summarized in Table 2.1, which displays peak new church development for all three denominations (1954–1957) and peak membership for the UPCUSA (1965) and the PCUS (1968). Peak membership for the UPCNA was in 1956, the last year for which separate statistics are available.[94]

TABLE 2.1

Years of Peak Membership and Peak Numbers of New Churches Organized, 1940–1980: PCUSA/UPCUSA/PCUS/UPCNA

Church	Peak Membership	Year	Peak New Churches Organized	Year
PCUSA/UPCUSA	3,308,622	1965	84	1957
PCUS	957,430	1968	70	1955
UPCNA	330,904	1956	7[a]	1945
				1954
				1955

[a] Seven new churches were organized in 1945, 1954, and 1955.

The decline in both churches following peak strength was steady, along with new church development. The low point for the UPCUSA was fifteen new churches organized in 1974 and 1977; in the PCUS it was eight in 1972.

Conventional new church development in the modern period has been considered an investment enterprise. In investing to build up the base, a future return can be expected in terms of net denominational growth and giving for denominational mission.

Tables 2.2–2.6 represent an effort to measure the effectiveness of the respective new church development efforts of the denominations in producing net membership growth.

Table 2.2 indicates that PCUS percentage growth, by period, exceeded that of the PCUSA and the UPCNA in every period except 1950–1960, when it was equal (33.1 percent). PCUSA percentage growth by period, in turn, exceeded that of the UPCNA.

TABLE 2.2
PCUSA/UPCUSA/PCUS/UPCNA
Membership Growth/Decline, 1880 – 1980

Year	PCUSA UPCUSA	Net Increase/ Decrease	Percentage Increase/ Decrease
1880	578,671	—	—
1940	2,021,901	1,443,230	249.4
1950	2,447,975	426,074	21.1
1960	3,259,011	811,036	33.1
1970	3,095,791	−163,220	−5.0
1980	2,434,033	−661,758	−21.4

Year	PCUS	Net Increase/ Decrease	Percentage Increase/ Decrease
1880	120,028	—	—
1940	532,177	412,149	343.4
1950	675,489	143,312	26.9
1960	899,116	223,627	33.1
1970	953,600	54,484	6.1
1980	838,485	−115,115	−12.1

Year	UPCNA[a]	Net Increase/ Decrease	Percentage Increase/ Decrease
1880	82,119	—	—
1940	255,898	173,779	211.6
1950	297,266	41,368	16.2
1960	330,904	33,638	11.3
1970	—	—	—
1980	—	—	—

[a] Figure given on Line 4 is for 1956.

Table 2.3 indicates that the average number of churches organized, by period, was in order of the size of the three denominations: PCUSA/UPCUSA, PCUS, and UPCNA. The highest annual rate of new churches organized for the PCUSA and the UPCNA was in the period preceding 1940, and for the PCUS, in the period 1950–1959. In terms of the average number of churches organized per year, by denomination, the 1960s resembled the 1940s; the 1970s resembled the 1930s, when the PCUSA, PCUS, and UPCNA averaged 31.5, 17.3 and 2.9, respectively.

Tables 2.4 and 2.5 reveal that the percentage increase in membership of all three denominations exceeded the percentage increase in population in their respective areas served up until 1960 (except for the UPCNA, whose final statistics reported were for 1956). But the PCUS figures were higher: 2.2 times the percentage of population growth in the states served by the denomination between 1880 and 1940, 2.4 times between 1940 and 1960 compared with the PCUSA, whose figures were 1.5 and 1.7 for the same periods. The figures for the UPCNA were 1.3 and 0.8 (the latter for the 17-year period ending in 1956).

Table 2.6 represents an effort to measure the "bottom line" effectiveness of the new church development of the three denominations: the ratio of the net increase in membership to the number of new churches organized, by period.

Whereas the PCUS did better in terms of percentage growth (Tables 2.4 and 2.5), the UPCUSA and the UPCNA did better in every period in terms of net membership growth when compared with the number of new churches, except for 1960–1969 when the UPCUSA suffered a net loss, whereas the PCUS registered a net gain. In that decade, although the UPCUSA was organizing 446 new churches, it still lost 5.0 percent of its membership. And although the PCUS organized 304 new churches, it managed a net gain of only 6.1 percent.

Finally, in the period 1970–1980 (Tables 2.2 and 2.3), even with 217 new churches, the UPCUSA lost another 21.4 percent of its membership at the same time the

TABLE 2.3

PCUSA/UPCUSA/PCUS/UPCNA New Churches Organized, 1880 – 1979

Period	PCUSA UPCUSA[a]	Average Per Year	PCUS[a]	Average Per Year	UPCNA[b]	Average Per Year
1880 – 1939	7,344	122.4	3,133	52.2	635	10.6
1940 – 1949	351	35.1	329	32.9	38	3.8
1950 – 1959	708	70.8	602	60.2	35	3.5
1960 – 1969	446	44.6	304	30.4	—	—
1970 – 1979	217	21.7	135	13.5	—	—

[a] Figures for PCUSA and PCUS for years 1880 – 1926 taken from tables in Herman C. Weber's *Presbyterian Statistics Through One Hundred Years, 1826 – 1926* (The General Council, Presbyterian Church in the U.S.A., 1927), pp. 24, 31, 99.

[b] Figure given on Line 3 is for 1950 – 1956.

TABLE 2.4

**PCUSA/UPCUSA/UPCNA Membership Growth/Decline
Compared with United States Population Growth, 1880, 1940, 1960, 1980**

Year	United States Population (1)	Net Increase (2)	Percent Increase (3)	Percent Increase/Decrease PCUSA/UPCUSA (4)	Ratio of Col. 4 to Col. 3 (5)	Percent Increase/Decrease UPCNA (6)	Ratio of Col. 6 to Col. 3 (7)
1880	50,155,283	—	—	—	—	—	—
1940	131,669,275	81,513,492	162.5	249.4	1.5	211.6	1.3
1960	179,323,175	47,653,900	36.2	61.2	1.7	29.3	0.8
1980	226,545,805	47,222,630	26.3	−25.3	—	—	—

SOURCES: U.S. Bureau of the Census, *Historical Statistics of the United States, Colonial Times to 1970, Bicentennial Edition, Part 1* (Washington, D.C.: U.S. Government Printing Office, 1975), p. 9.; U.S. Bureau of the Census, *Statistical Abstract of the United States, 1988, 108th Edition* (Washington, D.C.: U.S. Government Printing Office, 1987), p. 8.

TABLE 2.5

PCUS Membership Growth/Decline Compared with United States Population Growth (PCUS Area), 1880, 1940, 1960, 1980

Year	PCUS Area Population	Net Increase	Percent Increase	Percent Increase/Decrease PCUS	Ratio of Col. 4 to Col. 3
1880	18,335,000	—	—	—	—
1940	47,087,000	28,752,000	156.8	343.4	2.2
1960	60,707,000	13,620,000	28.9	69.0	2.4
1980	81,646,000	20,939,000	34.5	-6.7	—

SOURCES: U.S. Bureau of the Census, *Historical Statistics of the United States, Colonial Times to 1970,* Bicentennial Edition, Part 1 (Washington, D.C.: U.S. Government Printing Office, 1975), pp. 24 – 36; and U.S. Bureau of the Census, *Statistical Abstract of the United States, 1988,* 108th Edition (Washington, D.C.: U.S. Government Printing Office, 1987), p. 18.

NOTE: PCUS area includes Alabama, Arkansas, District of Columbia, Florida, Georgia, Kentucky, Louisiana, Maryland, Mississippi, Missouri, North Carolina, Oklahoma, South Carolina, Tennessee, Texas, Virginia, and West Virginia.

TABLE 2.6

Number of New Churches
Compared with Net Membership Growth, 1880 – 1980:
PCUSA / UPCUSA / PCUS / UPCNA

Period	PCUSA UPCUSA New Churches[b] (1)	Net Growth (2)	Ratio of Col. 2 to Col. 1 (3)
1880 – 1939 (40)[a]	7,344	1,443,230	196.5
1940 – 1949 (50)	351	426,074	1,213.9
1950 – 1959 (60)	708	811,036	1,145.5
1960 – 1969 (70)	446	—	—
1970 – 1979 (80)	217	—	—

Period	PCUS New Churches[b] (4)	Net Growth (5)	Ratio of Col. 5 to Col. 4 (6)
1880 – 1939 (40)[a]	3,133	412,149	131.6
1940 – 1949 (50)	329	143,312	435.6
1950 – 1959 (60)	602	223,627	371.5
1960 – 1969 (70)	304	54,484	179.2
1970 – 1979 (80)	135	—	—

Period	UPCNA New Churches[c] (7)	Net Growth (8)	Ratio of Col. 8 to Col. 7 (9)
1880 – 1939 (40)[a]	635	173,779	273.7
1940 – 1949 (50)	38	41,368	1,088.6
1950 – 1959 (60)	35	33,638	961.1
1960 – 1969 (70)	—	—	—
1970 – 1979 (80)	—	—	—

[a] New churches organized 1880 – 1939, percentage increase in membership 1880 – 1940.

[b] See note a, Table 2.3

[c] Figure given on Line 3 is for 1950 – 1956.

PCUS, with 135 new churches, lost 12.1 percent of its membership. The PCUS Stated Clerk calculated in 1978 that 50,180 members had been lost to the Presbyterian Church in America following the schism that began in 1973.[95]

Clearly, something more was going on than simply a slowdown in new church development.

A critical factor has surely been the spiraling costs associated with new church development. The PCUS Board of Church Extension reported that between 1940 and 1960 a total of slightly more than $9.5 million had been granted or loaned for new church development. In that period 1940–1959, 931 new churches had been organized, an average of approximately $10,204 from board sources per church. Between 1940 and 1960, the consumer price index increased from 47.3 to 88.8, which is to say that costs were approximately twice as high as they had been at the beginning of the twenty-year period. And then, by 1980 the consumer price index had risen to an astounding 246.8 (x2.8).[96]

Even by the end of the 1950s, the denominations were experiencing the pressures of rising costs. A new Presbyterian congregation today will require an investment of from $500,000 to $1 million in grants and loans from outside sources if it is strategically located in a high-potential suburban area. Assuming self-sufficiency after five years (and, therefore, an average annual subsidy of $100,000, including the purchase of land), 52 new churches per year would cost the church approximately $5.2 million in grants and loans *annually!* Although precise figures are not available, a large portion of that total today must come from local and regional sources.[97]

Along with increasing costs, this study has documented an ever-expanding mission scope, with a focus on urban problems, in both the UPCUSA and the PCUS beginning in the early 1960s. This included new funding for urban and experimental ministries, which meant that new church development would get less attention throughout the church. Furthermore, the new church development/evangelism programs were perceived, at least in the PCUS, to be yielding fewer dividends by the end of the 1950s. At the time, some interpreted the decline in evangelism and new church development as a loss of vitality. The study has also documented the rapid decline in new churches organized in both denominations beginning in the early 1960s and membership losses beginning in the mid-1960s.

The conclusion of the study is that there seems to be a relationship between new church development and church growth. The exact nature of that relationship, however, is complex. In sum, new church development is a necessary but not a sufficient condition for overall membership growth. New church development cannot by itself compensate for existing churches that are no longer growing.

3

The Rise and Fall
of Presbyterian Official Journals,
1925–1985

James A. Overbeck

It is surprising that official Presbyterian church journals in the twentieth century have not been a topic of extensive research, because their story during the social changes between 1925 and 1985 is a fascinating and instructive chapter of American church history.

Martin E. Marty observed in 1963 that denominational periodicals were imprisoned in a triangle of competing roles. On one side, their staffs wanted to address the major issues of the day with the same freedom and breadth of focus as did the secular press. From a second angle, this desire was frustrated by the compulsion to build denominational loyalty by interpreting all events from the compartmentalized perspective of their sponsoring church. But journals were also squeezed by a third concern, namely, the need to provide an ecclesiastical bulletin board for the sundry organizational activities of their churches.[1]

Marty's observations highlight the unique yet ambiguous place that church-sponsored magazines occupy in the history of their denominations and American journalism. As publications of the church, they are house organs designed to support and foster the mission of their denomination. As part of the American press, however, their leadership often yearns for the independence and journalistic respect enjoyed by secular and independent publications. When their ecclesiastical allegiances conflict with their journalistic aspirations, church-sponsored journals can become the source of intense denominational conflict. When the denomination is itself of mixed minds on volatile contemporary issues, its journals are easy targets for anger and criticism from all parties.

The history of Presbyterian journals in the twentieth century illustrates both types of difficulties. The Presbyterian journals existing in the late 1920s were largely house organs under the management of board agencies. They chronicled without comment those agencies' activities. Only one of the publications, the *United Presbyterian,* managed to escape this pattern. It considered contentious social issues and still survived.

Around 1950, a signal shift occurred in Presbyterian periodicals. The denominations began to struggle more seriously with professional religious news analysis. The journals gained some independence from close church supervision. Separate boards of directors were established and professional journalists hired as editors. Thus, the magazines were freed to address several significant but controversial social problems for the church. Candor about volatile issues—such as war and peace, church and state, school prayer, the ordination of women, civil rights, labor disputes, and the reunion of Presbyterian churches—proved too much for the church's membership. These issues divided the Presbyterian community much as happened elsewhere in mainstream Protestantism during the period.[2]

Presbyterian periodicals proved particularly vulnerable in this situation. They were dependent on support from the denomination, yet the denomination was itself divided over the proper perspective with which to approach the newsworthy issues of the day. By the 1970s, only two journals had survived. One of these publications, *Presbyterian Life,* eventually went out of existence. The other, *Presbyterian Survey,* the church quietly brought back under direct control and reduced the reporting of potentially explosive topics.

Within this broader framework, this essay traces the development of officially sponsored Presbyterian journals. Only those periodicals published for the General Assembly or its agencies and directed to the entire church membership are considered. These include the *Presbyterian Magazine, Presbyterian Life,* and *A.D.* of the Presbyterian Church in the United States of America (PCUSA) and the United Presbyterian Church in the U.S.A. (UPCUSA) traditions; the *United Presbyterian* of the United Presbyterian Church of North America (UPCNA); and *Presbyterian Survey,* originally from the Presbyterian Church in the United States (PCUS) denomination.

The *Presbyterian Magazine* began in 1898 as the *Assembly Herald* and changed names in 1921. It ceased publication in 1933 and was not replaced until 1948, when *Presbyterian Life* appeared. The union of the PCUSA and the UPCNA in 1958 resulted in the merger of the UPCNA's *United Presbyterian* into *Presbyterian Life. Presbyterian Life* continued publication as the UPCUSA journal until 1972, when the UPCUSA and the United Church of Christ jointly began to produce *A.D.* In 1983, *A.D.* was in turn superseded by *Presbyterian Survey.* The PCUS's journal since 1924, *Survey* now serves as the official magazine of the present PC(USA).[3]

The PCUSA Journals

An article in the *Presbyterian Magazine* for October 1926 stated that a religious paper is an "educating medium" giving the church correct information that helps ministers, a "stimulating medium" bringing the church fresh points of view and ideas, and a "broadening medium" combating parochialism and provincialism. The *Presbyterian Magazine* intended to be all three.[4]

In order to bring the *Presbyterian Magazine* into every Presbyterian home, the editors asked their readership to subscribe to a "Magazine Creed." The creed affirmed that every minister, church official, and Presbyterian family should have *Presbyterian Magazine,* because the publication would "strengthen the local church" and provide support for the "work of the church, both at home and abroad." Church members were also asked to recruit subscribers to the magazine.[5]

Presbyterian Magazine had over 33,000 subscriptions by 1929. Rev. J. G. Bailey, the editor for several years, died in 1929, and the following year, Rev. William Thomson Hanzsche was hired as part-time editor. It was he who saw the magazine through the difficult economic crisis of the early 1930s. It was Hanzsche as well who fought valiantly against the denomination's decision to shut the magazine down.

The *Presbyterian Magazine* underwent serious stresses and tensions in the early 1930s. In 1931, the PCUSA General Assembly addressed "the problems of publicity for church causes through periodicals." It reported "publicity through periodicals is far from ideal because it introduces competitive elements with our program."[6]

Pastors were designated as the key persons in any program of promotion. Thus, the publication would graphically describe the work of the denomination and offer sermon illustrations. The membership of the church also needed to be informed. But in contrast to its practice since 1926, the Assembly maintained that the church should ideally support a publication for pastors only. A single unofficial church magazine should, it claimed, supply the general membership's needs. At the time, there were several independent church papers, none of which had enough subscribers to be self-sustaining.[7]

The same report recommended the termination of *Presbyterian Magazine.* Although the recommendation was not accepted, it significantly complicated editor Hanzsche's task. The magazine was finally terminated in 1933. The public reason given was finances, but the more likely cause was animosity toward the magazine's past discussions of controversial issues like prohibition, church and state, and politics.[8]

One small example of prior conflict over the publication concerned its cover. The magazine began to appear with a red cover in 1929. The color red's association with the Communist movement angered the readership. Disgruntled readers demanded that the color be changed to Presbyterian blue, but the editor ignored their annoyed pleas.[9]

After the demise of the *Presbyterian Magazine* in 1933, a special committee was almost immediately appointed to draw up plans for a new church periodical. A pastors' magazine, *Monday Morning,* resulted in 1935. Plans for a new periodical for the laity seemed forgotten until the Board of Christian Education established a journal in 1938. Called the *Pageant,* it appeared in tabloid format. Hopes that the *Pageant* would evolve into a general magazine for the denomination never materialized. After one year of publication, it ended.

The General Council then appointed a Special Committee on a Church Paper, which reported plans for still another journal in 1941. The committee proposed an official church magazine similar to the *Presbyterian* (see n. 3). The *Presbyterian* had never been officially sanctioned by the denomination. It had also lost a large segment of its readership by becoming embroiled in the fundamentalist-modernist controversy.

The proposed magazine was to be a house organ in *Reader's Digest* format. It was to be written in an unemotional editorial style with no pictures, no editorials, no arguments or theological controversies, and no local or personal news. Each of the church's six boards or agencies would provide one article per issue.[10]

Of course, such an uninspiring plan aroused opposition. A letter from a pastor to the head of the Board of Christian Education pointed out that similar plans had been hashed over before and discarded. The church as a defender of freedom and democracy should not support a house organ magazine. Instead, the church should face the world and its issues head-on. The proposed journal never materialized. Instead, adoption of an existing periodical or merger with the official magazine of the PCUS was considered.[11]

In 1945, the PCUSA General Assembly appointed a committee to put "into production at the earliest possible moment an adequate Presbyterian journal." The committee's chair and the former editor of *Presbyterian Magazine,* William Hanzsche, announced a new journal, *Presbyterian Life,* in 1947.[12]

Presbyterian Life began publishing with over 69,000 advance subscriptions. Soon it would also have a board of directors who alone would direct editorial policy. They would, however, be responsible through the General Council to the General Assembly. At least two-thirds of the board's members were to be from the church-at-large. William Hanzsche had not rested until a new magazine rose from the ashes of *Presbyterian Magazine* some fifteen years after its demise. He was chosen the new board's chair.[13]

The board quickly elected Robert J. Cadigan, then associate editor of *Holiday* magazine, as the general manager of *Presbyterian Life.* Hanzsche explained to Cadigan the problems of publishing an official church magazine. On February 14, 1948, the first issue appeared.[14]

According to its Articles of Incorporation, *Presbyterian Life* was to be "a journal of religious news and information, in the interest of the PCUSA." It was to bring the church and its membership "into intimate contact with the whole task of the Church and with all that transpires in the field and world of religion."[15] Every Presbyterian home would receive *Presbyterian Life* each week. *Presbyterian Life* would bear all the marks of modern journalism, and it would be well illustrated. It would cover Presbyterian churches worldwide and offer information on all of Christianity. But unlike past church journals, it would not engage in theological subject matter "except as is needed to stimulate the thinking of the people of the Church."[16]

Presbyterian Life's editor stated in 1949 that an official church magazine's value lay in keeping members informed. He reminded church members that a desire to serve Christ certainly must unite all Presbyterians despite the divisiveness of various issues. He also insisted that from a journalistic point of view, crime does not necessarily make better reading than Christianty.[17]

William Hanzsche was enthusiastic about *Presbyterian Life.* In his words, "each of the issues [of *Presbyterian Life*] is a milestone in religious journalism. It is now an established fact that a Christian magazine can be attractive, fascinating and readable."[18]

Hanzsche insisted that *Presbyterian Life* was not just another magazine, however. It had no intention of competing with gaudy secular magazines. It was designed to bring all Presbyterians together into one fellowship. As the circulation of *Presbyterian Life* increased, so too Presbyterians would increase their interest in the church. When *Presbyterian Life* was sent into Presbyterian homes, those homes would certainly have been reached by the church. In fact, in Hanzsche's view, the magazine was the best way to reach inactive church members. For that reason, all those persons who worked for the promotion of *Presbyterian Life* did so as if it were a sacred task.[19]

Although subscriptions in 1950 went beyond the 80,000 mark, circulation did not dramatically increase until the introduction of the Every Home Plan in 1950. The magazine was financed through subscriptions, paid advertising, and church subsidies. By 1951, there were nearly 448,000 subscriptions.[20]

The Every Home Plan employed representatives on the presbytery and synod level to enlist churches. Congregations wrote into their budgets a set amount for subscriptions to each of their family units. This allowed the very low subscription fee of about one dollar per family to congregations enrolled in the plan. The editor argued that advertising revenues would increase as the circulation of the magazine rose. Thus, the plan anticipated that advertising income would eventually offset the extra denominational subsidy that the Every Home Plan required. To some degree the editor was correct. In the 1950s and early 1960s, advertising accounted for more than 15 percent of *Presbyterian Life*'s income and brought in increasingly larger sums of money.[21]

The UPCNA Journal

The merger of the PCUSA with the UPCNA brought *Presbyterian Life* a new subscription base as the UPCNA's *United Presbyterian* was merged with *Presbyterian Life.* The UPCNA'S association with the *United Presbyterian* had begun in 1925, when a group of interested persons purchased the magazine, developed a nonprofit organization for its control, and offered its services to the denomination. The journal was not officially sponsored by the church until 1941, when it began to print on its masthead: "The Assembly Authorized Adult Weekly." The same year, editor William J. Reid and manager John C. Downs retired. The corporation chose Rev. Raymond L. Edie for its new editor and manager. Edie attempted closer collaboration between the magazine and the UPCNA.

The slogan for the *United Presbyterian* was: "The truth of God with forebearance in love." When Edie took over in 1941, he described the editorial policy of the magazine as never vitriolic nor denunciatory. Controversial issues would always be dealt with fairly. Differing points of view would be given equal opportunity for expression. Such a policy, he claimed, required grace and gumption. The magazine was not a promotional weekly but an informational one.[22]

The *United Presbyterian* seemed to enjoy a certain freedom from controversy because it was primarily a newsmagazine and because its editorial policy was not closely controlled by the church until 1956.[23] In 1956, when the magazine became an official church publication similar to *Presbyterian Survey* or *Presbyterian Life,* editor Edie elaborated further on the purpose of the paper. It was to inform church members about all denominational matters. It should be inspirational and devotional and build up the spiritual life of the church. Yet it should be filled with news.[24]

The *United Presbyterian*'s message included a strong emphasis on education, solid support for civil rights, concern for labor issues, and a balanced assessment of the arguments for the ordination of women to the ministry. Hardly an issue of the magazine went by without some article on Christian education, a church college, or the denomination's seminary. Every year the seminary graduating class was pictured, sometimes on its cover. No other Presbyterian magazine under consideration here gave such strong support to education.[25] Articles on Presbyterian seminaries are rare in the pages of *Presbyterian Life* and *Presbyterian Survey.* The *United Presbyterian* supported efforts for civil rights from the 1920s on. However, it was astute enough to recognize that segregation should not only be eliminated from society; it should also be eliminated from the church.[26] The issue of women's ordination was thoroughly debated in the pages of the *United Presbyterian.* Because nothing in the Bible forbids such ordination, the journal concluded, why not do it?[27]

The issue of union with the PCUSA received much coverage in the magazine. For some readers, it was too much coverage.[28] Many people in the UPCNA were afraid that their small denomination would be swallowed up by the larger church. Nevertheless, the merger of the PCUSA and the UPCNA was consummated in 1958, and with it came the merger of the *United Presbyterian* and *Presbyterian Life* as well.

The UPCUSA Journals

Presbyterian Life had been able to build up a large readership during the 1950s because *Presbyterian Life* gave the impression of supporting conservative issues. It seemed to be anti–Roman Catholic because it opposed a United States ambassador to the Vatican, and stood for the teaching of religion as an academic subject in the schools, and was also foursquare against the use of alcoholic beverages.[29]

By 1960 things had changed. The magazine did not speak out against the candidacy of Roman Catholic John

F. Kennedy for President. It favored the Supreme Court
ruling in 1964 against school prayer, and it supported the
UPCUSA General Assembly's stand on the importance of
church and state separation. *Presbyterian Life* took a severe beating on the last issue, when readers complained
that *Presbyterian Life* had departed from true Presbyterianism. The editors explained that they were merely reporting what the church had done. But readers asked why the
magazine had to follow the lead of the church![30]

Circulation of *Presbyterian Life* peaked at about 1.2 million subscriptions in 1963. This made it the most widely
circulated religious newsmagazine in the United States.
But after a leveling-off period, circulation began to decline
in 1966. By 1968, it had fallen below the one million mark
to 993,000. The Board of Directors' report to the 1968
General Assembly stated that the previous year had been
one of controversy and debate in which the witness of the
church "to a world in change, turmoil, and revolution"
had been criticized as being unfair and one-sided.[31]

The editors attempted at least two promotional efforts to
keep the magazine alive. A brochure entitled *A Magazine
for a Church with a Conscience* was distributed in 1968.
The brochure explained that *Presbyterian Life* was the
magazine for the pastor who struggled with doubts about
the Vietnam War and concerns over civil unrest in the
streets. *Presbyterian Life* regarded such matters concerns
of the church.

It was a time of controversy for the magazine and the
church. The editors attributed the conflict to four factors.
First, some members felt that the ecumenical movement
diluted Presbyterian resolve and sold the church out to
Rome. Second, the civil rights movement illustrated that
those who get involved in it find trouble. Third, many
church people regarded the Confession of 1967 as little
more than an attack on scripture. And finally, the doubts
expressed in the magazine about the Vietnam War seemed
unpatriotic. Nevertheless, *Presbyterian Life* claimed to be
the best prophetic voice that the church had.[32]

Cesar Chavez, head of a California farm workers union,

was pictured on the front cover of the October 1, 1968, issue, and subscriptions continued to decline. In the issue for July 1, 1971, the journal reported on the church's support for the Angela Davis defense fund. An overwhelming outcry in letters and calls to the magazine followed. It appeared that the end of the magazine was near.

A "Report on Readers' Attitudes Toward *Presbyterian Life*" provided an eleventh-hour defense in November 1971. This public opinion poll found that church people had their first contact with socially controversial topics through the magazine, because such subjects were seldom addressed in the pulpit. Hence, church members vented their frustration and discomfort with social changes by rejecting the messenger, the magazine. The editors had an impossible task. The expression of any point of view resulted in infuriating someone.[33]

Readers also expressed the belief that *Presbyterian Life* lacked articles on Christian spirituality but provided an abundance of articles on social issues. In fact, *Presbyterian Life* had numerous offerings on spiritual development.[34]

When asked if churches that took strong stands on social issues experienced a decline in membership, between 40 and 50 percent of those polled responded positively.[35] When asked if churches that held a neutral position on social issues increased in membership, 30 to 40 percent responded positively. Sixty-seven percent of the respondents felt *Presbyterian Life* did not represent conservative interests; 80 percent believed it represented liberal interests.[36] The authors of the report concluded that church members did not want their church magazine to report on social issues. Moreover, when it reported on any social issue, it would likely be criticized as being a liberal magazine. The defensiveness of the report was very evident.

By 1972, circulation had slipped to 567,000. Editor Cadigan had decided to retire. The General Assembly was asked to disband the first Board of Directors of *Presbyterian Life* in favor of the establishment of a second board. The latter was commissioned to establish a new religious

periodical called *A.D.* in a joint venture with the United
Church of Christ.[37]

The *A.D.* Publishing Committee included an equal number of representatives from the UPCUSA and the United
Church of Christ. It carried the responsibility for publishing the magazine and making reports to the General Assembly. The committee elected as editor Rev. J. Martin
Bailey, the former editor of the *United Church Herald.*
Rev. Robert H. Heinze was the publisher of *A.D.* He was a
UPCUSA minister who had come on the staff of *Presbyterian Life* as a circulation manager shortly after it began in
1947. He considered himself the chief administrative offi-
cer of the magazine, but there were many indications of
unrest in the staff because of differences of opinion between the editor and the publisher on personnel and
finances.[38]

At first, an attempt was made to preserve the *Presbyterian Life* name by publishing a Presbyterian and a United
Church of Christ version of *A.D.* This gave the impression
that *Presbyterian Life* was not dead. But it was dead, and
an editorial by Robert Cadigan in the February 1973 issue
stated that *Presbyterian Life* had been taken over by *A.D.*[39]
By May 1974, the Presbyterian version of *A.D.* was called
the UPCUSA edition.

The subtle reference to time in *A.D.*'s title was not acci-
dental. The journal was to become the religious counterpart to *Time* magazine, much as Robert Cadigan had
previously expected *Presbyterian Life* to be the Presbyterian *Life* magazine of its day.[40] To that end, it was hoped
that *A.D.* would find its way into newsstands and become a
very popular religious magazine.

A.D. faced a financial crisis from the start. Church subsidies were available to it, but never in the amounts it
needed. There was hope that other church magazines
would join this bold, new ecumenical venture and swell
the subscription list. That did not happen. Funds left from
the defunct *Presbyterian Life,* the so-called Emergency Reserve Fund, were transferred to *A.D.* The periodical was
forced to dip into these funds year after year just to keep

going. By 1976 there was hardly any reserve left. In that year, Robert Heinze decided to retire, now thoroughly disheartened over the lack of progress of the magazine.[41]

The editor, J. Martin Bailey, had become equally discouraged. Bailey lamented the financial crisis that the magazine faced. He noted that other church magazines were facing similar situations. The church magazine was less and less needed by the church, according to Bailey, and there was a massive communications problem between the church hierarchy and its membership. If this problem remained unsettled, it would make American Christians increasingly parochial. He further predicted that as church magazines experienced the loss of subscriptions, they would eventually be disbanded. Churches too would lose members and eventually be forced to close their doors. Because of their constant outcries, the critics of the church magazines were blamed for the destruction of the church's channels of communication.[42] Valiant efforts were made to keep *A.D.* going. New staff appointments were made right up to the end, but suddenly in 1983 the magazine was shut down.

A commissioned evaluation of Presbyterian publications in 1983 polled opinion on *A.D.,* even though it was a moot point, in order to evaluate a magazine no longer in existence. *A.D.* did not receive high marks. Only 10 percent of the laity found the magazine very interesting, although 27 percent of the clergy gave it that rating.[43] The magazine was regarded as a liberal journal, often biased in its treatment of social issues. It was often criticized for not including enough human interest stories, even though it was praised for forthright reporting and good layout.[44]

PCUS Journals

Although the official journal of the PCUSA/UPCUSA went through several incarnations, the PCUS sustained a single journal after 1924. In April of 1924, *The Missionary Survey* magazine became the official periodical of the PCUS and changed its name to the *Presbyterian Survey.*

PCUS General Assembly Minutes indicate that the *Presbyterian Survey* remained substantially a house organ for decades after 1925. During the 1920s, subscriptions ran at about 33,000, but they had declined to about 30,000 by 1940.[45]

During the 1930s, *Presbyterian Survey* claimed that "a reading church is a wide-awake church and a generous church."[46] All of the official Presbyterian magazines suggested that members who read the denominational magazine were more likely to contribute generously than those who did not read it. In 1933, the editorial staff also noted that the church magazine's purpose was to make the work of the church possible.[47]

Editor Gilbert Glass died in March 1934, and the head of the Board of Christian Education, John Fairly, took over the editorship of *Presbyterian Survey* during 1934. He held that position until 1949.

There were many articles in *Presbyterian Survey* during the 1930s depicting the horrible rise of Nazism in Germany. They described all of the fanaticism and racism involved. Reprinted from other religious journals and written by church historians, these articles articulated the fate of the Jews as well as predicted terrible suffering for them. But in the early 1940s, such articles could not be found in *Presbyterian Survey*. Almost no pictures of wartime destruction were printed during the war. Instead, one found pictures of the beautiful beaches of Brazil!

Holmes Rolston became editor in 1949. Under his leadership, the magazine remained largely a house organ publication. News coverage on the General Assembly was improved, and seminary education was given some attention. *Presbyterian Survey* discussed race relations in terms of the growing number of Blacks voting and holding political positions. It noted that Negroes were making much progress and that there was a trend against bigotry.[48] The problem of racism did not seem to be recognized.

The 1951 General Assembly established a Special Committee on Publications in order to deal with unrest over competition between boards and agencies. Such rivalry had reduced the effectiveness of church promotional materials, including *Presbyterian Survey.* The "general membership," the committee stated, "is not being informed through any single publication. . . . An informed church is a working church" and "the effectiveness of the promotional work of the Church will be enhanced when a majority of the families in the Church have access to a publication which promotes the total program of the Church."[49]

The committee recommended that an ad interim committee from the church-at-large be appointed. The proposed committee would confer with *Presbyterian Survey*'s editors and others. Together they would develop a plan for the production and promotion of a publication suited to the informational needs of the church.[50]

The Special Committee on Publications brought several recommendations to the General Assembly during 1953. It affirmed the role of *Presbyterian Survey* as the official PCUS magazine bringing news, information, and inspiration to the entire church. It insisted that the five agencies and the General Council should contribute on a percentage basis if the magazine needed subsidies. It also suggested that the magazine find a new name.

The special committee recommended that a Board of Directors be given sole direction and control of *Presbyterian Survey,* including its editorial policy. Responsible directly to the General Assembly, the board was to have fifteen members. Each of the denomination's agencies would provide one representative. The remainder of the board would have no connection with any of the six agencies; five of the nine would be lay people.

As a house organ, *Presbyterian Survey* could publish materials from the boards and agencies without editorial modifications. Little editorial control was exercised over the contents. The special committee recommended no change in the editorial direction of the magazine, even though it intended to free *Presbyterian Survey* from house organ status through a thoroughgoing reorganization.[51]

After the plans for reorganization were completed in

1953, the magazine showed some spunk as it attacked McCarthyism.[52] But overall, *Presbyterian Survey* gave the lion's share of its pages to foreign and domestic missions until the end of Rev. Holmes Rolston's editorship in 1954.

William Thompson, a professional journalist, a lay person, and a non-Presbyterian, began his term as editor and general manager in November 1954. Frances Furlow was hired as associate editor in 1956. Under these two editors, *Presbyterian Survey* began to address controversial issues in earnest. The failure of plans for reunion was much lamented in 1955. An October issue claimed that the church was too self-centered to know what needs to be done in society.[53] The magazine added a "letter to the editor" column because of increased correspondence from readers, and because it wanted to recognize the importance of their opinions. In June, the issue of the role of women in the church was raised again. This time, the *Survey* asked what roles women play in the church and whether they could be ordained as elders and as ministers.[54]

The magazine was no longer simply a house organ journal. The August 1954 issue pondered presbyterial support for the General Assembly's action on civil rights.[55]

One goal of *Presbyterian Survey*'s reorganization was to extend its reach into the homes of church members by increasing subscriptions to 200,000. To that end, editor Thompson introduced the Every Family Plan in November 1954. This allowed each church a special subscription rate if the congregation would underwrite the cost of a subscription to every family. Ted Pratt became the promotional director at *Presbyterian Survey* in 1955, and circulation statistics show that he made the plan work. Although there had been little growth in the magazine's distribution since the 1930s, *Presbyterian Survey* had about 30,000 subscriptions by 1954. Four years later, circulation reached 191,000 and was still growing.[56]

Presbyterian Survey had adopted a *Manual of Operation* by 1956. The General Assembly gave continuing support to the manual by reprinting it in its minutes for years on end. This reaffirmed again and again the General Assembly's approval of the magazine's mission.

The *Manual* expected *Presbyterian Survey* to stimulate an interest in and an understanding of the PCUS. It was to clarify problems that confronted churches and lead individuals into deeper personal commitment to Christ. It was to provide information, inspiration, and guidance for the individual. It was also "to show the relationships of the PCUS to the total impact of Christian forces in the world."[57]

During the 1950s, *Presbyterian Survey* was not considered the equal of its sister denomination's *Presbyterian Life.* Consequently, its Board of Directors reorganized the editorial staff and created the position of executive director for Ted Pratt in February 1958. It appears that this encouraged William Thompson's resignation, because his former staff assistant now became his boss. Thompson left early in 1959 and took a staff position with the Disciples of Christ. He died suddenly about a year later.[58]

Ben Hartley took the editor's position vacated by Thompson. The Board of Directors, which included some prominent journalists, apparently agreed with Hartley. They felt that the magazine should continue to be edited by a professional journalist rather than an ordained minister. Hartley had such experience from his work with the *Pet Milk Magazine.* He took to heart the purposes set out for *Presbyterian Survey* in 1956 and made the journal his personal ministry as a lay person.

During April 1959, the church finished a study of subsidies to *Presbyterian Survey.* It rejected a recommendation to cut support for the magazine.[59]

In 1959, the *Survey* became embroiled in controversy. Ben Lacy Rose had begun what was to be a long association with the journal through a new column that first appeared in July 1959. Rose was called *Presbyterian Survey*'s Dear Abby, but he generated conflict when he claimed that a Presbyterian could also be a Communist.[60] The new editor soon after let it be known that the magazine was going to support the civil rights movement. A reader's letter the following July criticized the civil rights movement and compared it to communism. Over the years, the magazine was repeatedly accused of being communistic.[61]

Another July letter to the editor demanded that an article be written explaining why a Roman Catholic must not be elected to the White House. No such article appeared in *Presbyterian Survey.* The editor claimed that the magazine should support no particular candidate for office. Yet when the election was over, the editor let it be known that "the man we preferred lost."[62] This was no way to win friends and influence readers.

Circulation figures in the early part of the 1960s show that the magazine was reaching more and more families in the PCUS. By 1963, there were 262,000 subscriptions. The Board of Directors noted the next year that the official church magazine provided a forum in which the opinions of individual members could be expressed for the enlightenment of church officials. They suggested that this airing of members' opinions allowed the magazine to deal with their concerns and help them over their difficulties.[63]

Hartley steered *Presbyterian Survey* through the most difficult period in its history. The 1960s proved to be some of the most tempestuous and stormy years of recent history. Editor Hartley decided in 1965 that he should make a visit to the war zone, just as Cadigan had done in 1951 during the Korean War. When he returned, Hartley declared his confidence in the way the armed forces were conducting the war. During an Atlanta talk show interview, Hartley also stated that the war in Vietnam was politically necessary even under threat of nuclear war.[64]

Although the magazine reported the war in terms of its difficult contradictions, the general feeling was that *Presbyterian Survey* supported governmental policies. This left the magazine in a no-win situation. Liberals were angry with the journal's position on the war, and conservatives were irritated by its position on civil rights.[65]

Civil rights proved ultimately the decisive difference. At the beginning of 1968, the magazine's staff planned to make civil rights the major topic of the year. *Presbyterian*

Survey had pointed out as early as 1964 that civil rights programs were failing in the PCUS because church members would not invite Black persons to worship with them or visit them in their homes.[66] A printed letter in May of the same year doubted that *Presbyterian Survey* represented the PCUS.[67] A letter the next month asked why *Presbyterian Survey* could not support religion in the public schools and a campaign against pornography rather than support civil rights, the National Council of Churches, and ecumenism.[68]

The editorial staff projected the June 1968 issue to be one on civil rights, with articles written in large part by members of the Presbyterian Black Caucus. With that issue still in the development stage, Martin Luther King, Jr., was assassinated in April. A *Presbyterian Survey* photographer happened to be on hand as the funeral procession made its way through the streets of Atlanta. The journal used a photograph of the funeral bier for the June issue's cover.[69]

During July, controversy broke loose. Readers concluded that *Presbyterian Survey* was certainly a Communist magazine, and the church was doomed if it supported civil rights. Subscriptions were canceled immediately. A financial crisis forced a reduced format on cheap paper for the last few issues of 1969. The editor tendered his resignation, but it was not accepted. Hartley weathered the storm and tried to show that the magazine was not superliberal but dedicated to integration.[70]

The Board of Directors reported to the 1966 General Assembly that *Presbyterian Survey* had attempted "to bring into focus the tensions between those who want a silent Church and those who want an involved Church." But the loss of subscriptions was beginning to be felt.[71] Circulation was down to about 252,000 in 1966, but dropped even further to 234,000 after the turmoil of 1968. Thereafter, *Presbyterian Survey* lost so many subscriptions that it was in constant financial difficulty. By the end of 1970, subscriptions had tumbled to 149,083!

The slump in subscriptions brought with it a loss of confidence in the magazine's editorial direction. It was alleged that the editor not only supported integration; he also approved of interracial marriage. Hence, the controversy surrounding race relations engulfed the magazine. At a rump meeting of the Board of Directors in February 1971, Ben Hartley was asked for his resignation. By July he had left the magazine.[72]

In September, John Templeton, a Methodist and a journalist, took over editorship. A letter printed three months later asked directly if the magazine and its editors supported miscegenation. Templeton responded with a long explanation on marriage and then suddenly stated that neither he nor the magazine supported miscegenation![73] The church disbanded *Presbyterian Survey*'s Board of Directors in 1972, and the magazine was put under the control of the General Council. The end of an era had come.[74]

The controversy surrounding *Presbyterian Survey* would not go away just because *Presbyterian Survey* had a new master, however. In May, a reader recognized that *Presbyterian Survey* had been through some rough times. The reader suggested that the changes in the magazine over the years had been for the worse.[75] Another reader thought that *Presbyterian Survey* was some kind of Baptist magazine. Still another reader was convinced that *Presbyterian Survey* was a Communist magazine.[76] In August, a letter opposed the ordination of women. It claimed that the PCUS and *Presbyterian Survey* cared more for the majority opinion in the church than the Word of God, and asserted that the Bible forbade women to speak in the church.[77] An article published in the March 1973 issue dealt with freedom of the press. The author explained that *Presbyterian Survey* did not print simply what people wanted to read but what was actually out in the world. It reported not the way we want things to be, but the way things are.[78]

The PCUS elected its first Black Moderator in 1973. Some of the disaffected left the church, and confidence about the discussion of social issues seemed to gain a certain comfortable status among the leadership of the PCUS.

Issues of reunion, a new confession of faith, marriage and divorce, and organizational restructuring all seemed to demand larger and larger portions of the magazine's copy. The magazine also came out against capital punishment and for discussion of homosexual rights. The issue of world hunger appeared almost every month after 1972.

Finally, a new editor for *Presbyterian Survey,* Bill Lampkin, wrote that readers who found the church paper wrong would most likely have followed the medieval practice of killing the messenger who brought bad news.[79] Nevertheless, letters critical of *Presbyterian Survey* kept coming, so much so that a letter in the June/July 1980 issue lamented the number of persons in the PCUS who wrote to the magazine but did not conduct themselves as members of a "Christian Brotherhood."[80]

Quietly, *Presbyterian Survey* was once more brought under the direct control of the General Assembly. The PCUS underwent reorganization in 1973, and the General Council was disbanded. *Presbyterian Survey* was put under the General Executive Board Division V, Central Support Services. Later in 1980, when the reorganization of the Presbyterian Publishing House was proposed, *Presbyterian Survey* was assigned to it.[81]

Presbyterian Survey's future was by no means secure, for the General Assembly Minutes of 1982 discussed the need to reduce costs if the magazine was to survive. It then added the rather plaintive statement: "Assuming that the denomination wants to continue publication of its only magazine, additional funds must be found."[82]

After reunion in 1983, the PC(USA) General Assembly established a Publications Policy Task Force to evaluate existing Presbyterian publications. The task force commissioned the Simmons Market Research Bureau to determine the usefulness of church publications, including *Presbyterian Survey.* A questionnaire sent out in April 1984 went to church members, elders, and clergy. Of 4,262 questionnaires sent, 2,270 were returned. The survey found about one-fourth of the lay people polled and about one-half of the clergy were subscribing to *Presbyterian Sur-*

vey. When respondents were asked what sources they had for church news, only 8 percent of the laity and 22 percent of the clergy answered *Presbyterian Survey.* Nevertheless, most respondents felt that *Presbyterian Survey* was a very useful magazine.[83]

Presbyterian Survey survived this test and yet another attempt to change its name. By special arrangement, *A.D.* subscribers received *Presbyterian Survey* for a limited time, so that circulation had improved to about 170,000 by mid-1984.[84] Late in 1983, Vic Jameson, who for many years directed the United Presbyterian Office of Information, became the editor of *Presbyterian Survey.* He listed the following goals for the reunion church's magazine:

> Honor the heritages we all bring, while pointing not to the past but to the future. Work in all our settings to become truly one church. Be Presbyterians who are attentive to voices and needs and gifts of all of us. And get a vision—for all of us, shared by all of us—of what kind of church this ought to be.[85]

Today, religious journalism in the secular press enjoys a renaissance. Yet the denominationally sponsored journal is struggling. Four of the five journals reviewed here no longer exist, and whereas three Presbyterian magazines had almost 2,000,000 subscriptions in the 1960s, current subscriptions for *Presbyterian Survey* are about 130,000.

The failure of the denominational effort to bring news and Christian commentary into the home via professionally produced Presbyterian religious magazines is cause for serious reflection. Can it be that the dual demands of journalistic integrity and denominational promotion are so contrary that such journals are doomed to debilitating conflict? Have denominationally sponsored journals been the unwitting, and perhaps the most obvious, victims of the general decline in denominational allegiances found by Robert Wuthnow throughout mainstream Protestantism in the twentieth century?[86] The story here told suggests the answer to both queries is a troubling "yes."

4

A Poultice for the Bite of the Cobra: The Hocking Report and Presbyterian Missions in the Middle Decades of the Twentieth Century

John R. Fitzmier and Randall Balmer

In January 1930, a group of Baptist laymen, meeting in New York at the behest of John D. Rockefeller, Jr., concluded that the time was right for an assessment of the Protestant mission enterprise. With Rockefeller's financial backing, seven denominations—Methodist, Baptist (Northern), Reformed Church in America, Congregational, Episcopal, Presbyterian Church in the U.S.A., and United Presbyterian of North America—each delegated five representatives to constitute the thirty-five directors of the Laymen's Foreign Missions Inquiry. Under the aegis of the Inquiry, the Institute for Social and Religious Research was organized for the purpose of collecting data and conducting interviews in India, Burma, China, and Japan. Those findings were then entrusted to a Commission of Appraisal, chaired by William Ernest Hocking, Alford Professor of Philosophy at Harvard University. The Commission issued a seven-volume assessment of Protestant missions, together with detailed recommendations.

Coming on the heels of the fundamentalist-modernist controversies of the previous decade, the Commission's report, especially its one-volume summary entitled *Re-Thinking Missions,* attracted enormous attention in Prot-

estant circles. "There is a growing conviction that the mission enterprise is at a fork in the road," the report began,
"and that momentous decisions are called for."[1] Reflecting
the generally liberal theological sentiments of Hocking and
the rest of the Commission, and building upon earlier calls
for ecumenicity, *Re-Thinking Missions* urged a threefold
recasting of missions in light of "the many changes in the
world during the past century."[2]

First, the Commission called attention to an "altered
theological outlook" within the Western churches. Western
Christianity had shifted "its stress from the negative to the
affirmative side of its message"; it was now "less a religion
of fear and more a religion of beneficence." These changes
were largely theological; modern Christians, the report
claimed, were not apt to mouth traditional claims about
the everlasting torments of hell, God's punitive justice, or
similar "otherworldly" realities—all of which had given
"the original motive of Protestant missions much of its
urgency." In a backhanded stab at the fundamentalists, the
report declared triumphantly that Western Christianity
had "passed through and beyond the stage of bitter conflict
with the scientific consciousness of the race over details of
the mode of creation, the age of the earth, the descent of
man, miracle and law, to the stage of maturity in which a
free religion and a free science become inseparable and
complementary elements in a complete world-view." Despite these progressive trends, in many places—and here
one wonders if the report was pointing an accusing finger
directly at the missionaries—Christianity still suffered
"from the poverty, the rigidity, the inertness of the conceptions which Christians have of its significance."[3]

Given the new theological outlook, missionaries (and,
by inference, Christians generally) should back away from
their exclusive claims to truth, seek a fuller understanding
of those with different convictions, and promote "a steady
growth of mutual understanding and respect among these
seekers of various faiths." "The mission of today," the report concluded, "should make a positive effort, first of all,
to know and understand the religions around it, then rec-

ognize and associate itself with whatever kindred elements there are." The Commission betrayed its universalist leanings when it declared that "there is little disposition to believe that sincere and aspiring seekers after God in other religions are to be damned."[4]

Second, the report asserted that the emergence of a new "world-culture" demanded a reorientation of Protestant missions. The Commission heralded "a simpler, more universal, less contentious and less expressive religion coming into human consciousness which might be called the religion of modern man, the religious aspect of the coming world-culture." The increased education and sophistication of those in the East, moreover, required a more intelligent missionary, and the Commission called into question "the mediocre work which is now proceeding upon momentum without regard to the changes in the mental and spiritual environment." Although acknowledging that the "task of the missionary is an extremely difficult one," the Commission's researchers found that far too many of the missionaries were "devoted, patient and unimaginative people, content with the dull round of a conventional service and so encumbered with administrative routine as to be incapable of thinking freshly and planning wisely." To redress this problem, the Commission argued that "a much more critical selection of candidates should be made, even at the risk of curtailing the number of missionaries sent out."[5]

Third, the Commission cited the rise of nationalism in the East, which it called a "deliberate reaction against western domination and cultural control," as a mandate for rethinking Protestant missions. Here, the Commission's report advanced a thinly veiled criticism of capitalism as it noted "a disconcerting consciousness of the defects of western culture" and "a much more critical attitude toward our institutions, our democracy, our education." Moreover, the report continued, the "failure of Christianity to dominate our economic and political life has brought about widespread skepticism regarding the value of our religious professions, if not of our religion itself." The identification of

Christianity with Western culture, therefore, should be called into question: "For the sake of securing Christianity a fair hearing it is necessary to separate it, as far as possible, from *our* history and our promoting agencies and to present it in its universal capacity."[6]

The Commission's progressive appraisal of the missions effort immediately placed it in a tenuous position; many of the professionals to whom *Re-Thinking Missions* was directed were theologically conservative. Well aware of the political fragility of the denominational alliance on which it was founded, the Commission sought an ecumenical—albeit elusive—*via media*. To appease nervous conservatives, the Commission intoned traditional affirmations of the central importance of verbal proclamation of the gospel: "Nothing can displace, or minimize the importance of, a true and well-qualified evangelism." In the next paragraph, however, the Commission offered a grand concession to theological liberals: "But the Christian way of life is capable of transmitting itself by quiet personal contact and contagion, and there are circumstances in which this is a perfect mode of speech. Ministry to the secular needs of men in the spirit of Christ, moreover, *is* evangelism, in the right sense of the word."[7] Having thus appealed to the polar extremes of theological opinion by attempting to stretch the definition of evangelism to include both verbal proclamation and social action, the Commission offered its considered opinion about how these two aspects of evangelism were most efficiently promoted:

> We believe that the time has come to set the educational and other philanthropic aspects of mission work free from organized responsibility to the work of conscious and direct evangelism. . . . We must work with greater faith in invisible successes, be willing to give largely without any preaching, to cooperate whole-heartedly with non-Christian agencies for social improvement, and to foster the initiative of the Orient in defining the ways in which we shall be invited to help.[8]

The message was clear to anyone: soul saving, the traditional shibboleth of the nineteenth-century Protestant missionary, was now but one item on the crowded missions agenda.

Reaction to Re-Thinking Missions

Predictably, *Re-Thinking Missions* caused a stir among foreign missionaries and the congregations and boards that supported them. Perhaps one of the most controversial responses to the Hocking Report came from Pearl S. Buck. Novelist, university educator, daughter of missionaries, and wife of a Presbyterian missionary to China, Buck had returned to the United States on furlough about the time the Hocking Report was released. Asked by the *Christian Century* to review the volume, Buck wrote a lengthy, and quite laudatory, essay. She remembered well the visit of the Commission's researchers and, although they had struck her at the time as people "of very small caliber," she was impressed indeed with the report itself, hailing it as "a masterpiece of constructive religious thought" imbued with a "spirit which to me is nothing less than inspired."[9]

"I think this is the only book I have ever read that seems to me literally true in its every observation and right in its every conclusion," Buck wrote, a wry salvo doubtless aimed at the biblical literalism of the fundamentalists. Although she vigorously defended the character and quality of missionaries in the field, Buck said that their limitations were reflections of the limitations of those in America who sent them. "Where the missionary is mediocre," she wrote, "it is because the group who sends him is mediocre." The root of the problem, she argued, was a fixation with money:

> We missionaries have been made to feel that we are judged by numbers of converts and by the accuracy and economy with which we spend the board's money. It has made us of necessity men and women of limited outlook. We are money-minded. Instead of doing our real work we spend hours of our precious time discussing infinitesimal items on budgets.

These concerns, she said, included the missionaries' concern over "the wretched little salary on which we and our

children must depend." Together all these financial worries
had eclipsed the purpose of missions.[10] Like *Re-Thinking
Missions,* Buck lamented the poor training that mission
boards provided missionary candidates, and she echoed
the Commission's call for fewer, better qualified missionaries.

Buck's opinions gained a wide hearing, not least because
of her emerging fame as a novelist; *The Good Earth* was
published in 1931 and won the Pulitzer Prize in 1932. She
elaborated her views on missions in an address before
Presbyterian women and missions officials at the Astor
Hotel in New York City, a speech reprinted as "Is There a
Case for Foreign Missions?" in the January 1933 issue of
Harper's. Buck's response to her own rhetorical question
was a qualified "yes."[11] She allowed that most Protestants
no longer believed that "a soul can in a moment choose its
eternity or that God can let such a weight of responsibility
hang on the uncomprehending limited human will." But if
conversion, as traditionally understood, no longer lay at
the center of mission efforts, then what possible justification remained for missions? Buck believed that Christianity's virtue lay in its influence on individuals, making
many of them kinder and more compassionate people:

> In nations where the figure of Christ has been perceived,
> however dimly, I find something I do not find elsewhere. To
> some degree the sick are cared for, the weak and defective
> are housed and cared for with tenderness, women are more
> honored, people do struggle somewhat for goodness; some-
> how the poor are helped a little. It is all too little, too badly
> done, and there are many failures and much suffering, but—
> here is the point—it is better than where the figure of Christ
> has never been known.

This alone, Buck concluded, justified the perpetuation of
foreign missions.[12]

Buck's strident criticisms of mission policy both echoed
and built upon the findings of the Hocking Commission.
Not all Presbyterians found *Re-Thinking Missions* so laudable, however. Robert E. Speer, the most prominent Pres-

byterian missionary spokesperson of the day, issued a generally balanced assessment, although he remained quite suspicious of the Commission's more liberal sentiments.[13] The fundamentalist J. Gresham Machen, having just formed the conservative Westminster Seminary (1929), and soon to withdraw from the PCUSA to form what would become the Orthodox Presbyterian Church (1936), considered the Commission's report beneath contempt; it represented, he claimed, an attack "against the very heart of the Christian religion."[14]

Nor did the Presbyterian Boards of Foreign Missions suffer the criticisms of *Re-Thinking Missions* in silence.[15] In the PCUSA, the Standing Committee on Foreign Missions (the General Assembly body that oversaw the work of the Board of Foreign Missions) met almost continually during the twelve months after the Hocking Report was published. In response to the "prevalent criticism of the Board," and hoping to assure the church that all was well, the Standing Committee forwarded several recommendations to the 1933 Assembly. The Assembly should reaffirm, the board urged, "its loyal and complete adherence to the doctrinal Standards of the Presbyterian Church." Indeed, it should repudiate "any and all theological statements and implications in that volume [*Re-Thinking Missions*] which are not in essential agreement with the doctrinal position of the Church." More important, the Assembly should announce that Presbyterian orthodoxy was neither theologically wooden nor politically naive. Presbyterian missionaries *did* respect other religions, although "complete and final truth is to be found in Jesus Christ alone through the religion of which he is the center." Affirmations of the importance of the social character of the gospel appear throughout the report; Presbyterian missions touch the "whole life of the people," the report insisted, "their physical ills, their mental slumber, their social evils, and their spiritual darkness."[16]

Despite the solace these defensive rhetorical bulwarks may have provided, however, the PCUSA board and its Standing Committee continued to feel the sting of the

Hocking critique. In one of its final recommendations to the 1933 Assembly, aptly entitled "Method of Expressing Criticism," the Standing Committee urged the Assembly to encourage healthy, constructive criticism but "deplore the dissemination of propaganda calculated to break down faith in the sincerity" of representatives of the church. In common law and in Christian charity, "a man must be held innocent until he is proven guilty of any charge," they said; "suspicion of motives is not adequate evidence against any man."[17] In 1934, nevertheless, the year after Machen formed his own Independent Board for Presbyterian Foreign Missions, the PCUSA formally declared its disavowal of "those parts of the volume *Re-Thinking Missions* which are not in harmony with New Testament teachings and not in agreement with the doctrinal position of the Presbyterian Church."[18] The following year, in what appears to be part of its larger defensive strategy, the board published its statement of purpose:

> The supreme and controlling aim of Foreign Missions is to make the Lord Jesus Christ known to all men as their divine Savior and to persuade them to become his disciples; to gather these disciples into Christian churches which shall be self-propagating, self-supporting and self-governing; to cooperate, so long as necessary, with these churches in the evangelizing of their countrymen, and in bringing to bear on all human life the spirit and principles of Christ.[19]

Although missionaries would inevitably err—"All who are involved in this work are human and none is infallible," they conceded—the Standing Committee pled for a fair hearing in the face of the "propaganda troubling the Church," for "some of it is small, some of it is misleading, some of it is false."[20]

Although the PCUS had not been a constituent member of the Laymen's Inquiry, their Standing Committee on Foreign Missions did not hesitate to offer the following venomous response to presbyters gathered at their 1935 Assembly: "With utmost emphasis we repudiate that monumental folly miscalled 'Rethinking Missions.' Its true title should the rather be: 'Rejecting Missions and Crucifying Our Lord Afresh.' It offers a bread and milk poultice for the bite of the deadly cobra."[21]

Despite this storm of controversy in the 1930s, the story of Presbyterian missions over the next four decades can be understood as a gradual process in which American Presbyterians adopted the proposals set forth in *Re-Thinking Missions*. A close examination of the annual reports of the mission boards in the PCUSA, the UPCUSA, and the PCUS—with special attention given, first, to statements concerning the exclusive truth claims of Christianity, and, second, to Western and American cultural imperialism abroad—will make this evident. In this respect, *Re-Thinking Missions* was doubly prophetic: It both called for and accurately predicted enormous changes in missions policy.

Evangelism, Ecumenicity, and Interfaith Dialogue

Even a cursory reading of the annual missions reports in the 1930s verifies at least one observation contained in the Hocking Report: The boards' primary focus fell on individual soul winning and otherworldly concerns. Very often, moreover, this evangelistic zeal was cloaked in aggressive martial rhetoric. Churches were urged to raise funds to enable young men and women "to be sent as recruits for the great battle line at the front," from which they would go "forth in heroic faith to obey His marching orders," never sounding "retreat."[22] The call to duty was clear: "Fall into line; touch elbows, forward; and take the world for your glorious Savior—the only hope of sin-wrecked humanity in all its tragic helplessness and need."[23] Ironically, even while expressing concern over the ghastly prospect of a second world war, Presbyterians in both the PCUSA and the PCUS employed the language of military conquest: The church's "supreme mission" was "taking the world for Christ"; it must "move steadily forward to occupy for Christ the lands that are still in darkness."[24] If spirits should flag in the heat of spiritual battle,

the history of the American Presbyterian missions movement itself could inspire hope: "Surely the great head of
the Church has given us an honored place in the saving of
the nations and is calling loud to our people to go forward
with the foreign mission endeavor."[25] Indeed, delegates to
the PCUSA Assembly were urged to take up a model song
of triumph, one ostensibly chanted by those victorious
agents of U.S. foreign policy, the Panama Canal engineers:

> Got any rivers that are uncrossable?
> Got any mountains that you can't tunnel through?
> We specialize on the wholly impossible,
> Doing things that no one can do.[26]

This triumphalism, however, was gradually tempered. At
home, the sending agencies struggled throughout the Great
Depression to raise funds to protect established work in
the field.[27] Inevitably, financial setbacks slowed growth on
the field. This pruning forced missionaries to cooperate
with the other denominations on the field as well as with
"nationals" whose churches, planted by missionaries decades before, were now mature.

In 1935, the PCUSA board reiterated its commitment
to gather converted nationals "into Christian churches
which shall be self-propagating, self-supporting and self-
governing."[28] This promise of cooperation was carefully
circumscribed, however. Should allied bodies promulgate
"teachings unsound or injurious to the Evangelical Faith,"
or should they "compromise our evangelical witness or the
true advance of Christ's Kingdom," the board must either
insist upon correction or withdraw from further participation.[29]

By the mid-1950s, in response to ecumenicity, this concern for doctrinal purity abated somewhat. The PCUSA
board stressed a new commitment in 1956 to meeting
"this-worldly" concerns of people in concert with other
Christians:

> Our sensitivity to the need of peoples is not keeping pace
> with their rising demand for justice, equality, and brother-
> hood. . . . Ecumenical mission is the whole Church in the

whole world releasing its whole life in dynamic mission, with
the purpose of entering directly and vitally into an encounter
with the world in the name of Jesus Christ. Too long the
Church has ignored His command to be one in Him, that the
world may believe. In the urgency of our time it dare do so
no longer.[30]

Nor was the PCUS immune to the new spirit of cooperation. In a remarkably self-critical evaluation presented to
the 1954 Assembly, the Standing Committee noted: "The
Ecumenical Idea is Implicit in Missions," "Missions is Implicit in the Gospel," and "The Gospel is Implicit in
Christ." Indeed, the board made the consequences of these
"implicit" claims explicit, insisting that "more rapid progress must be made toward an indigenous church in every
mission field."[31]

This ecumenical spirit was not limited to other Protestant mission efforts or to the nationals with whom Presbyterians had worked in the field. Increasingly, there was a
new openness to the value, if not the validity, of other
religions. Working from the 1933 declaration that, whereas
"certain truths may be found in other religions, complete
and final truth is to be found in Jesus Christ alone through
the religion of which he is the center," the boards took
steps in the direction of interfaith dialogue.[32] In 1943, the
PCUSA changed the language of its bylaws to be more
sensitive to people of other faiths. It dropped references to
"unevangelized or pagan nations" and described the pur-
view of its efforts simply as those regions "outside the con-
tinental area of the United States of America, and the
general diffusion of Christianity."[33] In 1961, a hint of uni-
versalism crept into their description of the ministry of the
church—to "prophetically proclaim the uniqueness of
Christ and the encompassing love of God for the whole
world."[34]

With the convening of the Second Vatican Council in
1962, Presbyterians were suddenly faced with the possibility of new dialogue with Protestantism's oldest nemesis—
Rome. In an effort to make a positive response to the overtures of Vatican II, the board recommended that the As-

sembly approve a large statement, part of which read: "Fidelity to the truth as each understands it is a condition of responsible and fruitful ecumenical discussion. Neither side should seek concessions requiring compromise of belief." Presbyterians should reflect their Protestant and Reformed heritage, but they should also seek insights from Roman Catholics, "who have been giving careful and competent study to the issues of the Reformation period." Encounters between Presbyterians and Catholics "should be approached as opportunities for mutual understanding and for joining together in seeking more complete comprehension of the obedience to God's truth and its meaning for his Church and his world."[35]

The churches' increasing stress on humanitarian aid, their move from "talking" the gospel to "doing" it, was due in large measure to the massive destruction of the Second World War. In the immediate postwar years, many missionaries became transfixed with the human dimensions of the destruction: homelessness, disease, food shortages, death. Whereas in the late 1930s the PCUSA board had to fend off the criticism that its medical and educational work was merely "bait" for evangelism, by 1941 the minutes resound with pathos about human suffering.[36] Presbyterian missionaries were doing more relief work than ever. More important, perhaps, was the claim that "never before has the love of Christ been preached more effectively than through this ministry."[37] In 1949—the year in which the PCUSA board changed its letterhead to read "Foreign Missions and Overseas Interchurch Service"—the notion that relief work was part and parcel of the missionaries' task was duly noted. The board lamented to the Assembly that in Palestine—where both Christians and Muslims had been displaced by Israelis—Roman Catholic and Jewish groups have done better at relief than have the Presbyterians.[38]

By the 1960s, on the heels of the 1958 merger of the PCUSA and the UPCNA to form the UPCUSA, the Presbyterian missions enterprise was wholly transformed.[39] No longer was the gospel restricted to the verbal proclamation of a body of doctrinal data. UPCUSA missionaries eschewed the 1930s notion that the "supreme and controlling aim of Foreign Missions" was "to make the Lord Jesus Christ known to all men as their divine Savior and to persuade them to become his disciples."[40] In the 1960s, the purpose of missions was far different: "To make Jesus Christ known, to enter into the common life of men, healing the enmities which separate them from God and from each other, and to encourage all men to become Christ's disciples and responsible members of the Church."[41] Though the term "evangelistic outreach" was still used, its meaning had been broadened to include ministry to a spectrum of human needs—spiritual, physical, educational. The board noted the need for new programs designed to address new social circumstances; they wondered whether the careful use of drama and fine arts might be useful for evangelism in industrial areas, for instance.[42]

As the United States struggled with its own history of racism, the board noted that racial unrest in Birmingham, Nashville, Evanston, or Detroit reverberated "in the four corners of the world where men and women listen to the echoes of violence and injustice in our land." It called for programs of education on race relations.[43] Anticipating the theme of reconciliation that would figure so prominently in the UPCUSA Confession of 1967, the Assemblies of 1966 and 1967 stressed "Christian responsibility in international affairs . . . response to situations of human need . . . the mission opportunities within the developing technological world civilization."[44] Indeed, mere verbal proclamation of the gospel, the 1967 Assembly noted, "falls on deaf ears if the Church in its total life has not continued to stand for social justice, to minister to people in physical need, to express concern for those in the darkness of illiteracy, to provide educational opportunities for children." Service and social action, they continued, "are inseparably related to the evangelistic task, and without such activities the Church's witness in the world is incomplete."[45] The next year the UPCUSA would herald the importance of reconciliation as "the crying need" of the hour: "Reconciliation is built upon justice, sensitivity developed through open channels of communication, and human dignity is an inseparable part of the new humanity in Christ."[46]

Western Imperialism in a Changing World

As the otherworldly triumphalism that characterized many of the boards' early statements abated over the years, so did the confident sense that the West, or, more specifically, the United States, could provide the answers to the world's problems. In the early 1930s, the churches displayed a remarkable naïveté about the ways in which international politics and foreign missions became entangled. In 1931, for instance, the PCUSA board rejoiced in the conversion and baptism of the president of the Chinese Republic. This conversion, the board felt, "has made it less logical to consider the Christian faith a foreign religion and has opened new doors for the introduction of the faith of Christ unconfused by political or international complication."[47]

When confronted with the suggestion that their gospel might be too Western, that they may have sullied the purity of the "good news" with American values, the board became defensive, claiming that it was neither naive nor uninformed. In 1933, for example, with reference to the emerging political power of Mohandas Gandhi, the PCUSA board boasted that it had a "grasp of the political and social tensions" in India and had "anticipated current recommendations by twenty years." Indeed, the church in India was growing less dependent on American missionary efforts, they believed, and Indian nationals would soon "take over complete control of an ever increasing share of the work." Despite the goal of self-sufficiency, the West was still needed in India, however. Many in the "Depressed Classes" were moving toward Christianity; and because they were a politically strategic group, poised between the Hindus and the Muslims, the West had to respond: "The door of religious opportunity is wide ajar; the call to the Western churches is clear and commanding." The situation in Latin America was similar; governments in the region were interested in leading their "people out of ignorance and sin into cleanliness and righteousness, health and the wealth of Godliness," and hence the missionaries had a strategic opening.[48]

The message of the American Presbyterian missionaries promised spiritual salvation together with cultural and political benefits. This was made disturbingly clear in 1937 when the PCUSA board claimed that the influence of Christianity goes "beyond the pale of the Church, for in addition to winning the individual the preaching of the Gospel has acted like leaven in cultures and civilizations of Asia, hoary with age." And in India, Christianity had become revolutionary in both religious and political terms; the models of democracy, the board claimed, had been the churches.[49]

Although the chief complaint of the boards during World War II centered on foreign nationalism, their patriotism masked—even to themselves—their own cultural chauvinism. In 1939, one of the pamphlets published by the PCUSA board noted that "nations are seeking substitutes for God, and nationalisms are replacing old religious loyalties." Nonetheless, the board confidently stated that in "Siam there is a great and inviting openness to the American Christian approach."[50] That missions were tied to the outcome or the purposes of the war seems quite evident. In 1942, the PCUSA board celebrated the start of a $200,000 financial campaign with a rhetorical question: "Will the church enter these open doors [into West China, India, and Brazil] through a gift of $200,000 to dominate situations affecting the future world order?"[51] The next year, the board acknowledged that although "the world is far from fully accepting the spiritual implication of all that we mean by Foreign Missions," there has never "been a greater opportunity to show the reasonableness, the urgency, the indispensability of the spiritual dynamics of the Christian Gospel. The things people want to accomplish by this war, if they are disposed at all, are the very things that are being accomplished by our Board of Foreign

Missions."[52] Very often in these patriotic war years Presbyterians juxtaposed American democracy with eternal commitments: "We herewith proclaim again our love of religious freedom, and our belief in it as a fundamental principle of Christianity, of American democracy and of any satisfactory ordering of human relationships."[53] In 1943, the PCUS even took credit, on behalf of all Protestant missionaries, for China's allegiance to the Allies during the war.[54] Indeed, by the close of the war, the churches saw themselves as an instrument, not only of the establishment of Christianity abroad but also of American political philosophy: "We give hearty approval to the Board's plans to work with these churches [in Europe and Asia] as the major hope of achieving true democracy and of developing the moral and spiritual life of these nations."[55]

After the war, however, the churches began to recognize the leadership potential of nationals in the field, thereby appropriating, perhaps inadvertently, one of the recommendations of the Hocking Report.[56] The ultimate goal of our work, said the PCUS board, always was, and now continues to be "to establish in all lands where our Church is at work a native, self-supporting church which will be able to evangelize its own people and send the Gospel to the people in regions beyond."[57]

The task to conduct missions in the spirit of sacrificial service, and to do so with little expectation of establishing outposts of American democracy abroad, became the central challenge of the postwar years. This difficult agenda—differentiating between spiritual ministry and cultural domination—was made far more challenging by a cultural and political force that took the churches by surprise—communism. In both the PCUSA and the PCUS, communism wrought fear in the hearts of believers. "Communism threatens with atheism and lawlessness," the PCUS board declared in 1948.[58] The PCUSA echoed that sentiment several years later: "We are deeply alarmed by the terrible and devastating forces of Communism and Materialism which seek to divide and conquer the world and to destroy the cherished values and institutions which Christianity has brought about."[59] As the churches armed themselves for their "battle against the mounting forces of evil which would wipe Christianity from the world," they came to believe that communism was even more sinister than the older world religions.[60] The only answer seemed to lay in fighting fire with fire; the churches' "daring venture" would be to start a true "World Revolution—Christian style."[61]

Ironically, in the very years that the Cold War began chilling American self-confidence, the churches expressed optimism in the face of the Communist challenge: "Whether tomorrow's world will be ruled by the Spirit of Christ, or by fear and ignorance and materialistic totalitarianism, may well be determined by the response we make to the needs which our mission enterprise seeks to meet. The Christian Church will determine the outcome of the world revolution."[62] Nor was this confidence broadcast in wholly ideological terms; it was the result, in part, of serious theological reflection. The preamble to the PCUSA board's 1955 report was grounded in truly self-critical theological reflection on the problem of missions and imperialism. It is essential, the preamble stated, that the church work for the healing of the nations. Because the present world situation is complex and unstable, our work must take place in the knowledge of our former imperialism and with a sense of expectancy of new revolutionary governments and cultures. The church must stress partnership and not paternalism. All this means greater and not lesser mission.[63]

This sort of self-criticism produced concrete results. In 1958, the UPCUSA board noted its gratefulness to God that several national missions are now "no longer ecclesiastically dependent upon the General Assembly of our Church." The new stress fell on partnership in "ecumenical mission, whereby Churches everywhere share as partners in a total mission effort."[64]

By the early 1960s, the boards had acknowledged that the times were revolutionary—both abroad and at home. Although they continued to reaffirm their eschatological hope—"The Church is entrusted with another force, the Gospel, which God intends for the redemption of all men"—there were serious changes afoot. Instead of insisting upon vigorous, almost militant evangelism, as in the past, American Presbyterians began to employ the language of cooperation and conciliation; the UPCUSA board, for instance, spoke of "the uniqueness of Christ" but also emphasized "the encompassing love of God for the whole world."[65]

By 1964, Presbyterian missions felt caught in the inexorable currents of change. With the "cultural revolution" forcing enormous changes in American society, the UPCUSA board waxed hyperbolic: In the face of "the most radical revolution that has taken place since the dawn of civilization," the call of God on Presbyterians is to engage in change, for "this revolution, like all revolutions, is God's opportunity. . . . God does not call us simply to sit around and wring our hands and bewail the good old days when we could impose on any people our aspirations and goals." Rather, we are called to "share in this movement to secure more and more freedom for more and more people."[66]

Conclusions

The liberal theological platform of *Re-Thinking Missions* had offended many conservative Presbyterians in the 1930s. But *Re-Thinking Missions* did more than exacerbate tensions between fundamentalists and modernists; it also formulated the outlines of a substantive criticism of an ethos dear to many Presbyterians in the middle decades of the twentieth century—middle-class, capitalistic, Protestant, American.

By the late 1960s, however, the self-confident assertions about evangelism, American righteousness, and the superiority of Christianity were consigned to the "good old days." Like other mainline Protestant denominations, Presbyterians came gradually to discard both the militant rhetoric and the exclusive truth claims that had character-

ized their earlier statements of mission.[67] But the abandonment of former verities engendered confusion for not a few
mainline Protestants, Presbyterians included. In 1973, for
instance, the General Assembly of the UPCUSA heard an
urgent call "to take large steps toward the affirmation of
mission," an entreaty followed on the next page by the
concession that "tension exists in the church as to precisely what the church's mission is."[68] Even if the new approaches were still ill-defined, however, the Presbyterian
missions enterprise had become remarkably like that pre-
scribed by the Hocking Commission four decades earlier.
Despite initial resistance, even reaction, to *Re-Thinking
Missions* for its inadequate response to the "bite of the
deadly cobra," American Presbyterians had come to embrace the attitudes and strategies of the report, especially
its ecumenicity, its toleration of other traditions, and its
directive to fashion a missions strategy that took into account the nuances of an increasingly complex world.[69]

Appendix

Presbyterian Missionaries, 1930–1970

The information listed in Table 4.1 is taken from the annual
reports of the boards. It represents the number of foreign missionaries sent out by the PCUSA/UPCUSA and the PCUS in the
years 1930 through 1970. Because the reports were submitted
after the *close* of the calendar year, the figures listed actually represent the "missionary force" in place during the year *preceding*
the date of the reports. (For example, the PCUSA deployed 1,491
missionaries during the year 1929.) The use of these figures is
subject to several caveats. In general, the figures represent only
full-time "career" missionaries. The data do not include those
designated as "interns," "short-term missionaries," "educators,"
or "medical staff." It should also be noted that the methods of
computation of the two bodies differed slightly, and that the
methods of computation within each of the bodies varied over
the period in question.

TABLE 4.1

Missionaries of the PCUSA/UPCUSA and PCUS, 1930 - 1970

Year	PCUSA/UPCUSA	PCUS
1930	1491	427
1931	1491	420
1932	1474	420
1933	1474	409
1934	1425	403
1935	1344	395
1936	1305	402
1937	1262	393
1938	1260	379
1939	1242	376
1940	1222	377
1941	1203	369
1942	1173	340
1943	1135	329
1944	1160	398
1945	1136	321
1946	1173	337
1947	1184	333
1948	1185	359
1949	1170	369
1950	1140	369
1951	1118	388
1952	1045	373
1953	1070	391
1954	1042	443
1955	1001	464
1956	1004	481
1957	1003	483
1958	967	504
1959	1284	483
1960	1261	493

Year	PCUSA/UPCUSA	PCUS
1961	1215	485
1962	1217	496
1963	1198	487
1964	1185	519
1965	1042	553
1966	1092	567
1967	1082	543
1968	1035	531
1969	1032	527
1970	904	504

5

American Presbyterians
in the Global Ecumenical Movement

Theodore A. Gill, Jr.

In May of 1958, the General Assembly of the newly formed United Presbyterian Church in the U.S.A. (UPCUSA) created the Commission on Ecumenical Mission and Relations (COEMAR). This commission continued the functions of the Permanent Commission on Interchurch Relations of the Presbyterian Church in the U.S.A. (PCUSA), the Committee on Ecumenical Affairs and the Permanent Committee on Inter-Church Relations of the United Presbyterian Church of North America (UPCNA), as well as the foreign mission boards of both predecessor denominations.[1] The ideal it sought to achieve was a merger of "mission" and "unity" in the thought and practice of church life.[2]

Halford Luccock, writing in the persona of Simeon Stylites for his popular column at the back of the *Christian Century,* heralded the nativity of COEMAR with conflicted feelings. He admitted that "there has been an attitude of condescension associated with the term 'foreign missions,' a sort of playing the Victorian role of Lady Bountiful to the poor heathen," but he worried over the psychological impact of replacing a Board of Foreign Missions with a Commission on Ecumenical Mission and Relations.

"Ecumenical" is a great word and it represents a great idea, called truly "the greatest fact of our time." But it is not quite the gift of God to meet this need and to meet the danger of throwing out the emotional power of "foreign missions" when we throw out the term. For "ecumenical" is one of the most colorless words in the English language. . . . One reason, of course, is that at present it does not convey any concrete pictures. It does not come "out of the everywhere into the here." It conveys only the picture of a company of church leaders with well filled brief cases hurrying to catch a plane for a conference at Timbuktu. A noble company of saints. But thought of them does not arouse unrestrained enthusiasm.[3]

Throughout the twentieth century, the history of the global dimension of American Presbyterianism has been the story of involvement in and reaction to the worldwide ecumenical movement.[4] Even so, many church members have consistently restrained their enthusiasm for the ecumenical enterprise. Few organizations within the local church have embraced the "noble company of saints" and their ecumenical partners with the sense of adventure or ownership that local churches had attached to "our missionaries" and "our missions overseas."

In action and discussion on ecumenical mission, church unity, and social action, American Presbyterians have encountered (a) the ancient churches of the East, (b) the churches that have grown up from what once we saw as "our mission fields," (c) the Roman Catholic Church as renewed by the Second Vatican Council, and (d) representatives of other Christian traditions, world faiths, and ideologies. At times, this exposure to heretofore unfamiliar cultures and traditions has left U.S. Presbyterians with a greater sense of foreignness, of alienation, than the subject of foreign missions ever did. For some dedicated church members, denominational commitment to ecumenism has come as a threat to a distinctively Presbyterian identity.

The ecclesial internationalism of ecumenism grew up in tandem with the League of Nations, the United Nations, and a host of secular international organizations. Just as the spirit of the League was dampened by a rising tide of U.S. isolationism, and as the United Nations has been viewed in the West with varying degrees of suspicion, segments of mainline Protestantism in the United States, including American Presbyterianism, have responded to ecumenism's challenges with a concern that cooperation with other traditions might lead to a blurring of specifically Presbyterian identity and to theological syncretism. The tension between maintaining one vision of the Reformed interpretation of the gospel and a commitment to patterns of partnership with other churches in global mission stretches back in U.S. history at least as far as the creation of the Presbyterian Board of Foreign Missions and the split between the Old and New Schools in 1837;[5] on other shores, its antecedents can be found in the Acts of the Apostles.[6]

Early Sources of International Cooperation

American Presbyterians of the nineteenth century defined themselves theologically in relation to one another largely in terms of adherence to the Westminster Confession of Faith. By the beginning of the twentieth century, the tenets of fundamentalism were also proposed by some, including some Presbyterians trained in the Princeton Theology, as related standards of orthodoxy.

In 1861, when Presbyterians in the South declared their independence from the Presbyterian Church in the U.S.A., the first General Assembly of what would become the Presbyterian Church in the U.S. (PCUS) claimed for itself the title of "church" based on its commitment to evangelical orthodoxy as expressed in the Westminster Standards: "Truth," insisted the Assembly, "is more precious than union."[7] Against PCUSA claims that the southern Presbyterians were politically motivated schismatics, the Assembly argued that it had been necessary to separate from the PCUSA Assembly in order to avoid open hostility between church representatives from the two warring sections of the country; indeed, the PCUS Assembly presented its withdrawal as an act of Christian unity in that secession aimed at making less likely a "breach of charity" among Presbyterians.[8]

After the end of the Civil War, with the reunion of the Old and New Schools in the PCUSA, the PCUS came to question the doctrinal purity of their separated brethren and sisters.[9] Presbyterian orthodoxy became a crucial issue for the PCUS in regard to the organization of the World Alliance of Reformed Churches Holding the Presbyterian Order (or the World Presbyterian Alliance, one predecessor body to today's World Alliance of Reformed Churches). Dr. James McCosh of Princeton University was among the founders of the Alliance, and the PCUSA General Assembly of 1873 passed his resolution calling for steps toward the establishment of an "Ecumenical Council" of "sister Churches holding to the Westminster Standards."[10] The United Presbyterian Church of North America, formed through a union in 1858, readily agreed to membership. The PCUS Assembly of 1875 cautiously debated the wisdom of joining the proposed Alliance. Opponents of a motion to join the Alliance feared that it "might not be orthodox," but they were defeated following an appeal by Assembly Moderator Moses D. Hoge, who challenged commissioners to consider their own fallibility.

> If the only pure church is the Presbyterian Church of the Southern States; if the problem of the development of Christianity as symbolized in the Presbyterian faith and form of government has been solved only by us; if, after all the great sacrifices of confessions and martyrs of past ages, we alone constitute the one true church; if this alone is the result of the stupendous sacrifices on Calvary and the struggles of apostles and missionaries and reformers of all generations; then may God have mercy on the world, and on his church.[11]

The PCUS, too, became a founding member of the Alliance in 1877; even so, early southern Presbyterian participation in the Alliance was noteworthy for a continuing PCUS crusade to force the expulsion of the Cumberland Presbyterian Church on the grounds of Cumberland Pres-

byterians' refusal to require strict allegiance to the Westminster Confession and Catechisms.[12]

Following the turn of the century, plans were laid for
cooperation in the field of education between the responsible boards of various Protestant communions. On the international level, this would lead in time to the World
Sunday School Association (later the World Council of
Christian Education, which then became a division of the
World Council of Churches). American Presbyterians provided leadership in this movement; in 1912, both the
PCUSA and the PCUS were among the six founding U.S.
denominations of the Council of Church Boards of Education.[13] Prior to the Edinburgh Missionary Conference of
1910, however, participation in nondenominational, international movements of students, social activists, and missionary enthusiasts tended to occur through the
commitments and memberships of individuals rather than
of church bodies.[14] It would not be until 1910 that the
Edinburgh International Missionary Conference would
consist of official representatives of missionary societies,
including denominational boards of foreign missions.

The International Missionary Conference,
Edinburgh, 1910

It has become commonplace in the literature of ecumenism to ascribe the birth of the modern ecumenical movement to June 1910—the International Missionary
Conference in Edinburgh, Scotland. American Presbyterians, with their remarkable record of missionary accomplishments, were an important force in the international,
interdenominational activity that made Edinburgh possible. The ecumenical approach to mission, in turn, has
shaped subsequent American Presbyterian attitudes to
global mission.

By the beginning of the twentieth century, the European
and North American journey in "foreign missions" had
led missionaries and Protestant officials to a series of regional and international conferences. Beginning with gath-

erings in both London and New York in 1854, interested individuals had assembled to discuss the common problems of missionaries and their sending bodies.[15] Each such gathering was an isolated event, with only the most incidental continuity from one event to the next.

In 1893, North American denominations seeking cooperation in their work overseas organized the Conference of Foreign Missionary Boards of the United States and Canada. In 1895, Arthur Judson Brown was elected secretary of the PCUSA Board of Foreign Missions and immediately dedicated himself to interdenominational cooperation in mission. He was a prime organizer of the Ecumenical Missionary Conference, which met in New York in 1900, and became conference secretary.

Arthur Tappan Pierson, editor of *Missionary Review of the World,* originator of the phrase "the evangelization of the world in this generation" and chair of Philadelphia Presbytery's committee on foreign missions, was one of the self-selected participants in the conference of 1900. Noting the lack of continuity in coordination of missionary efforts between conferences, Pierson moved that a continuing committee be established. In 1900, the motion failed, but it was the adoption of a nearly identical motion at Edinburgh in 1910 that is said to mark the beginning of a sustained "movement" in ecumenics.[16] Arthur Judson Brown, who had chaired the executive committee of the Edinburgh conference, served on the Continuation Committee for the next eighteen years.

Edinburgh 1910 led directly to the creation of the International Missionary Council. Participants in Edinburgh would also found two other great movements: Faith and Order and Life and Work. By 1937–38, the latter two entities would move to join in a World Council of Churches (WCC), the first Assembly of which would be delayed by World War II until 1948; the International Missionary Council (IMC) would merge into that World Council in 1961. The PCUSA, PCUS, and UPCNA were, from 1910 onward, active supporters of each of these elements of the ecumenical movement.

Sources of Controversy, Delays, and Mission
Policy Reformulation

Origins of dissatisfaction with the movement that grew out of Edinburgh may be traced to the conference planning that succeeded in attracting wide participation, in part, by limiting the scope of missions and types of missionaries to be included. Anglo-Catholics, who thought little of Protestant missions aimed at members of ancient Christian traditions such as Orthodoxy and Roman Catholicism, and German Evangelical leaders, who resented Baptist and Methodist missionaries to Germany, gave their support to Edinburgh once it had been agreed that the conference would be representative only of missions operating among "non-Christian peoples."[17]

North American Presbyterians had strong ties to missions and churches in Latin America, an area in which many Protestant missions were aimed at the proselytization of Roman Catholics. The decision not to represent these missions at Edinburgh caused widespread resentment among Latin Americans and among champions of their cause in the United States. This hostility would later be directed at the International Missionary Council, which in its early years continued Edinburgh's policy on membership.

At Edinburgh itself, a number of dissatisfied delegates convened an unofficial discussion section on Latin American needs. This section was chaired by Robert E. Speer, a representative of the PCUSA. Out of the discussion arose plans for an ecumenical conference specifically on Latin America, which was held in New York in 1913 and which led in turn to the foundation of the Congress on Christian Work in Latin America.[18] Members of the PCUS, UPCNA, and PCUSA and their missions were active in this organization. Robert Speer and John Alexander Mackay, in particular, used their position of respect within the IMC to persuade other leaders of the ecumenical movement that evangelical missions in Latin America deserved a place in the councils of world Christianity.

During the decades following the Edinburgh conference,

the churches of the United States were caught up in controversies over fundamentalism and modernism. Controversialists who tried to base their arguments on Westminster, or the five fundamentals, came to question the value of missionary and ecumenical circles in which other traditions of orthodoxy were to be given equal weight. Many American Presbyterian leaders, including those most profoundly committed to the IMC, were troubled by tendencies they considered "liberal" in the report from the 1928 IMC conference in Jerusalem. The subsequent ecumenical dialogue with nascent neo-orthodoxy was, for some, equally troubling. Conservatives and fundamentalists in the PCUSA attempted to organize a board of missions independent of ecumenists like Speer; their defeat and censure resulted in the founding by J. Gresham Machen of the Orthodox Presbyterian Church in 1936, and of the Bible Presbyterian Church by Carl McIntire in 1937. It has been said of the PCUSA in this period that "only among Northern Baptists were the battles waged by the fundamentalists as intense."[19]

The internal troubles of U.S. denominations were only one impediment to the ecumenical movement between 1910 and the First Assembly of the World Council of Churches in 1948. Two world wars within one generation, originating among the traditionally "Christian nations" of Europe, were a humbling experience for the peoples on either side of the North Atlantic. In the rebuilding of Europe, North Americans found themselves involved in mission to societies racially and culturally like their own; in some cases, American Presbyterians found themselves as "sending churches" providing service and supplies to their own historic "parent churches" in Europe. It was in this context that the PCUSA began referring to its missionary personnel as "fraternal workers."[20] This term would replace "missionary" in the vocabulary of COEMAR once UPCNA and PCUSA united to form the United Presbyterian Church in the U.S.A. (UPCUSA).

A new approach to mission was being pioneered in the IMC as the European colonial empires crumbled. Changes in attitudes of Western churches provided a new dynamic in mission. One of the essential elements of this dynamic was the recognition of a maturation in relationships between the traditional "sending churches" of the West and the churches that had grown up from the "mission fields" of Africa, Asia, Oceania, and Latin America. The mature relationship of a postcolonial age moved from missionary paternalism to a global partnership based on the equality and interdependence of all churches.[21] A postwar belief in the capacity of newly independent states to develop economically and spiritually, and a recognition of the increasing secularism of the West gave birth to an ecumenical missiology promoting a multilateral, multidirectional "mission on six continents."[22]

This new style and strategy of mission was exemplified in the UPCUSA by COEMAR and particularly by its 1961 paper *An Advisory Study,* which challenged the UPCUSA to embrace the ecumenical approach to mission. Perhaps the most remarkable feature of the study was its authorship: a committee of fifteen made up of ten members from partner churches outside the United States, three members of COEMAR, and two fraternal workers under appointment by COEMAR but working outside the United States.[23] *An Advisory Study* was to make quite a splash among partner churches, but even the general secretary of COEMAR was to conclude that the "one place where we failed" to make an impact on people's thinking about mission "was in the United States."[24]

While the uniting Presbyterians of the PCUSA and UPCNA were designing COEMAR, ecumenical missions were a bone of contention in the mission strategy of the PCUS. C. Darby Fulton, longtime executive secretary of the Board of World Missions, held to the old system of a PCUS-supported "Mission" in a given country, often ruled by extremely conservative missionaries who were reluctant to engage in partnership with national churches or in interdenominational movements or unity movements. Fulton's position was also championed by the independently published, conservative evangelical *Presbyterian Journal.* Opposition to Fulton was led by a professor of church history and missions from Austin Theological Seminary, T. Watson Street.

By 1960, Street had been named to succeed Fulton as executive secretary and directed the PCUS Board of World Missions toward an in-house consultation on mission that culminated at Montreat, North Carolina, in 1962. The Montreat consultation produced a paper calling for mutuality in an international mission that would recognize the equality of all Christians, the unity of the church universal, the need to evangelize through deeds as well as words, and the courage to experiment, to be flexible, and to be responsive to changing times.[25]

In 1972 and 1973, both the UPCUSA and the PCUS underwent a flurry of organizational restructuring. In the UPCUSA, the principal work of COEMAR became the province of one unit within the new Program Agency that combined national mission, global mission and ecumenics, and Christian education. In the PCUS, the new General Assembly Mission Board acted globally through its Division of International Mission. The PCUS, like COEMAR in 1958, had learned from ecumenical missiology to use the singular term "mission" as opposed to the plural usage of the far-flung "missions" over which previous generations of Presbyterians had felt such pride of ownership. Presbyterians were no longer said to engage in the promotion of a variety of "missions" in "foreign" lands, but claimed to be engaged in the mutuality of the one "mission" of God. In its theology of *Missio Dei,* American Presbyterianism joined the rest of the ecumenical movement in linking the missionary calling of the church with the quest for Christian unity.[26]

Faith and Order

American Presbyterians were no strangers to discussion of unity. They had met with their greatest successes in the 1758 reunion of New Side and Old Side Presbyterians, the union that created the UPCNA in 1858, and the reunion of the Old and New Schools in the PCUSA in 1869. The early nineteenth-century Plan of Union with the Congregationalists had borne witness to good intentions on each side, even if it had not borne fruit in visible unity of the churches.

As preparations were laid for New York's Ecumenical Missionary Conference of 1900, the PCUSA Board of Foreign Missions adopted a new declaration of policy for the denomination's work abroad.

> Believing that the time has come for a yet larger measure of union and cooperation in missionary work, the Board would ask the General Assembly to approve its course recommending to its missions in various lands that they encourage as far as practicable the formation of union churches, in which the results of the mission work of all allied evangelical churches should be gathered, and that they observe everywhere the most generous principles of missionary comity. In the view of the Board, the object of the Foreign Missionary enterprise is not to perpetuate on the mission field the denominational distinctions of Christendom, but to build upon Scriptural lines, and according to Scriptural methods, the Kingdom of our Lord Jesus Christ.[27]

At the time that this declaration was drafted, and the Assembly of 1900 was approving it, the PCUSA was engaged in a union process with the Cumberland Presbyterian Church that would come to fruition in 1906. In 1907, the PCUSA approached the UPCNA. UPCNA leaders found little support for union, however. A process of exploring the possibility of union between the PCUS and UPCNA, begun in 1912, failed because of lack of enthusiasm by the two denominations' General Assemblies in 1915.[28] In 1920, the PCUSA would successfully effect a merger with the Welsh Calvinistic Methodist Church.[29]

One of Edinburgh's Protestant Episcopal delegates from the United States, Bishop Charles Brent, spent the months and years following the International Missionary Conference promoting a vision of church unity. He persuaded the highest councils of his denomination to enter into dialogue with other communions, from the Disciples of Christ to the Vatican. Although charmingly rebuffed by Pope Benedict XV at an audience in 1919, Brent pushed for a world conference on faith and order.[30]

In 1920, the Ecumenical Patriarchate of Constantinople addressed an encyclical "unto the churches of Christ everywhere," calling for the creation of a *koinōnia tōn ekklēsiōn,* a council of churches devoted to dispelling mistrust and strengthening bonds of love among the Christians of the world. The encyclical appealed to Christian leaders not "to fall piteously behind the political authorities, who, truly applying the spirit of the Gospel and the teaching of Christ, have under happy auspices already set up the so-called League of Nations in order to defend justice and cultivate charity and agreement between the nations."[31]

These actions by a U.S. Episcopal bishop and the Greek Orthodox synod of Constantinople were initial steps in the Faith and Order movement. Though the avowed purposes were said to be a lessening of hostility among Christians and a building up of charity, some evangelical Protestants were doctrinally uncomfortable with a movement that even in its infancy was making approaches to Rome. By the spring of 1920, the PCUS Assembly would look askance at both Faith and Order and the recent union of the Welsh Calvinistic Methodists with the PCUSA, refusing in the quest for church union to deviate from the traditional doctrinal, ecclesiastical, and cultural orthodoxies.

> The Assembly and the Church would view with uneasiness any structure of Union which failed to take into account and safeguard in the United Church the historical convictions and position of this Church with respect to sound doctrine, just and effective discipline, the plenary inspiration and inerrancy of the Scriptures, and vicarious atonement, the spiritual mission of the Church and its obligation to abstain from interference in matters purely of civil or political concern, its position as to its Negro constituency in the South and other matters of like interest and importance.[32]

Faith and Order began in cautious conversation, but out of conversation would grow future bilateral dialogues between the great Christian communions. The World Alliance of Reformed Churches would find itself in conversation with similar bodies of Lutherans, Baptists, Anglicans, Orthodox, Methodists, and Catholics. On national levels, these encounters would lead to church unions and union conversations such as the Consultation on Church Union (COCU).

The trend in Faith and Order discussions toward the possibility of mutual recognition of ministries and organic church unity raised fears in diverse quarters. In evangelical circles, there was talk of an emerging "superchurch" more concerned with union than with purity of doctrine. The clearest rejection of such a goal came not from Protestants, but from the Russian Orthodox Church in its decision not to join the World Council of Churches at the time of its First Assembly at Amsterdam in 1948.

> The direction of the efforts of the ecumenical movement into the channels of social and political life, and towards the creation of an "Ecumenical Church" as an influential international force, appears to us to be a falling into the temptation rejected by Christ in the wilderness. For the Church to accept it would involve departure from its own true path through attempting to catch souls for Christ by using non-Christian means.[33]

Similar sentiments emerged from Presbyterian circles (though conservative politics often made them distrustful of one potential ally, the Russian Orthodox Church, once it joined the WCC in 1961). In time, the 1975 WCC Assembly in Nairobi described the goal of the World Council as "unity in conciliar fellowship" rather than organic unity.[34] A survey of presbyteries in the PCUS following Nairobi suggested that the conciliar approach was reassuring to many who continued to feel that "truth comes before unity."[35]

In 1982, a conference at Lima sponsored by the WCC Commission on Faith and Order adopted the text *Baptism, Eucharist, and Ministry,* which explored common Christian understanding of the dominical sacraments and ordination. In the United States, study and response to the document engaged church members from all levels, and had particular impact on member denominations of COCU. The official response of the recently reunited Presbyterian Church (U.S.A.), when it was approved by the 1986 General Assembly, stressed the classically Reformed themes of God's prevenient grace, justification by faith, the eschatological dimensions of the Lord's Supper, the ministry of the laity, and the priesthood of all believers.[36]

Another theme, not so clearly sounded in the sixteenth century, is made plain in the Presbyterian Church (U.S.A.)'s response to *Baptism, Eucharist, and Ministry.* The theologically and culturally diverse participants at Lima are reminded of the mid-twentieth-century commitment of American Presbyterians to the equality of women in all offices of the church.[37] In this, the Presbyterian Church (U.S.A.) challenges the WCC to take new, potentially divisive positions. Blame for differences of opinion and divisions arising out of ecumenical debate is sometimes laid at the doorstep of the World Council of Churches, but that Council is reflective of the communions of which it is constituted; church members frequently project onto the WCC their objections to stands taken by their own denominations. Within a conciliar fellowship, the member churches each have their chance to take the leadership in causes of mission, unity, and social action.

Life and Work

As the Faith and Order movement was coming into being, a parallel movement concerning Life and Work evolved under steady pressure from Swedish Lutheran archbishop Nathan Söderblum. Although the watchword of this social action oriented campaign was "doctrine divides; service unites," early gatherings, like those of Faith and Order, spent more time recognizing disagreements than celebrating common commitments. The report of the first world conference, held at Stockholm in 1925, was punctuated by the recurring phrase "Some of us believe . . . , while others affirm . . . ." There were wide differences between theories of natural law, the social gospel, orthodox Lutheranism, and a spirituality requiring political neutrality.

The second Life and Work conference, at Oxford in 1937, came in the midst of a worldwide depression and in the face of totalitarian oppression of national churches and missions at the hands of both Fascists and Communists. It was the genius of the planners of that conference to plead for the elaboration of "middle axioms" with which all participants could agree. John Bennett, one organizer of the meeting, defined middle axioms as "those goals for society which are more specific than universal Christian principles and less specific than concrete institutions or programs of action."[38] No one policy was *the* Christian position; ecumenical ethics presented a range of options for the social strategist.

This is not to say that Oxford could not speak forcefully against the evils of racial hatred and unbridled militarism that lay outside the bounds of Christian axioms. In economics, both communism and undiluted capitalism were assaulted; in surveying the empires of the world, racism and class distinctions were deplored; most of all, in the contemporary European situation, the Nazi persecution of Jews and of the churches was condemned. Presbyterian discussion leaders included John A. Mackay, Henry Van Dusen, John Foster Dulles, and Charles Taft.

Despite Oxford's importance within the ecumenical movement itself, especially as the World Council of Churches was in process of formation during World War II, the conclusions drawn at Oxford were not always well communicated to church members in the United States. The historian Peter H. Hobbie has shown that religious press coverage of Oxford in PCUS-related journals focused the racial question exclusively on Nazi treatment of the Jews. This seems to have been a public relations ploy in favor of ecumenism on the part of well-intentioned church journalists who "realized that Oxford could be discredited if its racial statements were understood to apply to the South."[39]

In 1937, the Oxford conference and the Faith and Order

conference that followed it at Edinburgh voted to enter a dialogue aimed at the creation of a world council of churches. The final decision to form this council was taken on the eve of war in Europe. Among the American Presbyterians instrumental in this decision were James Alexander of the UPCNA, J. R. Cunningham of the PCUS, and Ross Stevenson, Samuel McCrea Cavert, John MacCracken, Charles Leber, and William Adams Brown of the PCUSA.

Suspicions of the tendency toward a superchurch, coupled with perceptions that the World Council of Churches was too "political," were voiced in certain sectors of American Presbyterianism. The PCUS, PCUSA, and UPCNA were founding members of the WCC; this marked a continuation of the PCUS's return to ecumenical circles following its reconciliation with the Federal Council of Churches during World War II. In the same period, the Cumberland Presbyterian Church rejoined the World Presbyterian Alliance for the first time since the merger of the majority of Cumberland Presbyterians with the PCUSA in 1906; agreement on the WCC was not so easily achieved. Although the Cumberland General Assembly of 1943 had approved membership in the World Council, reaction against conciliar policies caused the 1944 General Assembly to overturn the action of the previous year.[40] Ever since 1948, Carl McIntire of the ultraconservative Bible Presbyterian Church, founded in 1937 to oppose "liberal" PCUSA practices, has picketed major ecumenical gatherings in the name of his own association of anti-Communist, anti–Roman Catholic purists.

The war period was one in which social action centered largely on the coordination of relief, an undertaking that continued years after the cessation of hostilities. With the breakup of the Western colonial empires, thoughts turned to economic development of newly independent nations. For the first decade after the WCC's organization at Amsterdam, ecumenical social ethics were dominated by the concepts of middle axioms and the First Assembly's goal of "the responsible society."

The social policy of the ecumenical movement was ap-

plied in the United States as the civil rights struggle grew
in magnitude. With the adoption of the goal of mission on
six continents, the World Council began to direct resources
to the churches in the United States that were engaged in
improving race relations. Funds were channeled through
the National Council of Churches (NCC) to such projects
as the Mississippi Delta Ministry, administered by Kenneth Neigh and the UPCUSA's Board of National Missions.[41] Such activities were not a strong selling point for
ecumenism in the South; in 1965, T. Watson Street wrote a
popular Christian education text on ecumenism in which
social action was barely mentioned.[42]

Within the WCC, the functions of Life and Work were
being carried out in the Department on Church and Society. This office organized the 1966 WCC conference in Geneva on "Christian Response to the Technical and Social
Revolutions of Our Time." The Central Committee of the
WCC gave latitude to the conference participants, as-
signing them the responsibility of "speaking to" rather
than "speaking for" the churches of the conciliar movement. Geneva was to be the first conference following the
election of Eugene Carson Blake, up to that time Stated
Clerk of the UPCUSA, as general secretary of the World
Council; Blake would be noted for his leadership in a time
of intense social action, as well as for administrative skills
that for the first time in its existence put the WCC on
sound financial footing.

Paul Abrecht has commented that "ecumenical social
thought is a theological and sociological reflection of its
constituency."[43] This helps explain the divergence of Geneva 1966 from Oxford 1937. In the postcolonial era, and
with the addition of the Russian Orthodox and other Eastern Orthodox churches to the WCC at New Delhi in 1961,
ecumenism was becoming increasingly representative of
Christians outside the West. The membership of the Geneva conference broke down thus: North America and
Western Europe, 40 percent; Eastern Europe, 20 percent;
the developing nations, 40 percent.

At Geneva, the "middle axioms" approach to social policy fell by the ecumenical wayside as clear-cut positions were taken on issue after issue, from patterns of economic growth to U.S. involvement in Vietnam. Objection to this war cannot be attributed entirely to the enlarged constituency of the WCC. The UPCUSA, for example, was by now critical of the Vietnam War, and it was Richard Shaull of Princeton Theological Seminary who issued a call for the churches to throw in with "guerilla units with a clear sense of self-identity, a vision of a new social order and a commitment to constant struggle for change, inside or outside the social structures."[44]

One of the most outspoken public critics of the 1966 conference on church and society was Paul Ramsey, a professor of social ethics from Princeton University who served in Geneva as one of the United Methodist Church's conference consultants. In his book *Who Speaks for the Church?*[45] Ramsey deplored the abandonment of the "middle axioms" approach to ecumenical ethics. The role of a conference like Geneva, Ramsey argued, is to provide an opportunity for dialogue among persons from many cultures holding conflicting viewpoints. He thought it presumptuous for so large and diverse a group to meet under such severe pressure of time to prescribe specific cures for society's ills, which, in any case, is not the place of the church. Ramsey contrasted the haste of the section meetings at Geneva with the painstaking series of consultations that led to such contemporary documents of the Second Vatican Council as *Gaudium et Spes;* he asserted that policy statements of sections, which never came before the plenary, were presented as the thought of the whole body; he objected that conclusions were often pronounced without any written explanation of theological and ethical bases that might support them. He condemned U.S. participants in the conference who promulgated their own denunciation of their government's actions in Vietnam.

Although some U.S. Presbyterians supported Ramsey in his complaints about the Geneva conference, Donald W. Shriver gave a particularly Presbyterian answer to the question posed in Ramsey's title.

Paul Ramsey's implied doctrine of "representation" must be charged with over-simplicity: At the highest level, only God "speaks for the church"; at the lowest, every individual Christian speaks for it. But in between, representatives of various church bodies speak for it, and these representatives are "sometimes more, sometimes less pure." The Bible, church tradition, and "sound reason" are doubtless the tests of the purity; but no church body speaks with simple authority according to these tests. In ways that only centuries can unravel, majorities, minorities, and elected leaders can on occasion all embody some of this churchly authority. (In this connection, I wish that Ramsey were more tolerant of the Geneva Conference: deficient as it may have been, it too was one voice in the chorus of the contemporary church. His own voice is another.)[46]

Eugene Carson Blake commented:

Who *does* speak for the church? Certainly not the World Council, much less an ad hoc conference called by it. At most, either speaks to the church and to the world on the basis of the intrinsic truth of its utterance.[47]

With the 1968 Uppsala Assembly of the WCC, social action took on a high profile in the Council's work. Critics of the Council felt that the missionary mandate for global evangelism had been replaced in ecumenical thinking by an accommodation with secular structures and political agendas. The creation of the Program to Combat Racism in 1970 and the program's humanitarian aid to armed antiapartheid groups in southern Africa led to charges in the United States that the Council was actively pro-Marxist.

As the WCC continued its emphasis on social justice during the 1970s and 1980s, evangelicals sought an alternative means of cooperating in a depoliticized style of world evangelization. Many evangelicals objected to the WCC's openness to emerging forms of liberation theology, with economic presuppositions rooted in Marxist analysis, espoused by some ecumenical theologians from the developing world. It should be noted, however, that other theologians connected with the World Council of Churches have been highly critical of liberation thought.[48]

In 1974, with key sponsorship from the Billy Graham organization, the Lausanne International Congress on World Evangelization marked the adoption of the "Lausanne Covenant" proclaiming the urgency of offering salvation in the name of Jesus Christ alone. The Lausanne movement opposed the WCC's method of dialogue with peoples of other living faiths and secular ideologies, and questioned the WCC's acceptance of liberation theology.

Membership in the Lausanne movement is on an individual basis; participants include members of the Presbyterian Church (U.S.A.) and a number of its partner churches, as well as members of more conservative branches of the Reformed family. At the second Lausanne Congress, at Manila in 1989, Patricia M. Roach, of the PC(USA)'s Evangelism and Church Development Ministry Unit, found that most congress participants felt the WCC's mission thinking was irrelevant to the task at hand.[49] On the other hand, one prominent Latin American leader of the Lausanne movement has suggested a need for future cooperation, contrasting the WCC's 1989 World Conference on Mission and Evangelism with the 1989 Manila meeting.

> Behind the two gatherings are two different approaches to mission, one stressing the social dimension of the gospel and the other the need for conversion to Jesus Christ. Would two conferences need to be held if the two emphases were fully recognized for what they are—complementary aspects of the Christian mission?[50]

Recent Notoriety and Perceptions
of International Ecumenism

From the mid-1960s, ecumenical commitment to social action has come under attack from American Presbyterians active in such organizations as the Presbyterian Lay Committee, the Executive Commission on Overseas Evangelism, and the Institute on Religion and Democracy (IRD). The media-conscious IRD drew public attention to the social policies of the NCC and the WCC in January

1983 through testimony to authors of an article in the *Reader's Digest* magazine and a telecast of the CBS news program "60 Minutes." Both presentations alleged that the churches involved in the NCC and the WCC were sponsoring inflammatory anti-U.S. publications, supporting Marxist-Leninist governments and terrorist movements, and funding policies administered by dishonest and arrogant ecumenical leaders who felt no sense of accountability. The cover of *Reader's Digest* asked, "Do You Know Where Your Church Offerings Go?" The visual images on "60 Minutes" contrasted white, middle-class U.S. Protestants dropping money into offering plates, with conferences and projects populated by Africans, Asians, and Latin Americans. Although CBS's argument was based on the *Reader's Digest* and uncritical repetition of IRD claims, it improved on the print medium by its ability to stress visual differences of race and culture.[51]

At its reuniting General Assembly of 1983, the Presbyterian Church (U.S.A.) appointed a special committee to investigate charges against the NCC and WCC. The committee's extensive report to the 1986 Assembly on the history and practice of ecumenism presents a mid-1980s snapshot of American Presbyterian attitudes toward the global ecumenical movement.[52]

In the course of its investigations, the special committee commissioned a scientific survey by the Presbyterian Panel of PC(USA) members. A summary of the June 1984 panel data appears in the report to the General Assembly.[53] Clergy were shown to be best informed about the WCC; among elders and members, the top two sources of information about the ecumenical movement were *Reader's Digest* and "60 Minutes." Clergy were three times more likely to have a positive rather than a negative view of the WCC, whereas among elders, 41 percent were negative and only 32 percent expressed positive opinions. Self-identification according to theological categories had no discernible bearing on negative or positive bias, but regional differences were acute, with the most negative feelings in the South and the most positive in the Northeast.[54]

Among PC(USA) clergy questioned in the Presbyterian Panel, 85–98 percent saw the objectives of the WCC as being "to foster ecumenism, to help churches give visible expression to their unity in Christ, and to provide a means of carrying out projects that would be impossible for individual denominations because of limited resources." Among members and elders, 70–80 percent agreed. Only 45 percent of respondents said one goal of the WCC was "to provide funding for groups fighting racial injustice, even though some of the groups promote or are engaged in violent revolution."

Women were almost twice as likely as men to have a positive attitude toward the WCC. This may reflect the high quality of information made available through women's conferences at Purdue and Montreat, and the educational programs of organizations such as Presbyterian Women and Church Women United.

As one commentator has observed, "In many Southern communities," Church Women United was "the only organized ecumenical expression that had the staying power to stand the racial stress of the 50's and 60's."[55] In the 1980s, Presbyterian Women continued strong, as contrasted with the near total eclipse of the national organization for Presbyterian men. It may be that the personal involvement of local women in such churchwide networks explains why mission and ecumenics are better supported by local church women's organizations, just as local councils of churches win widespread support because trusted members of neighborhood congregations are prominently involved and able to communicate actions directly to the local church. Networks of women reaching into nearly every church are able to provide trusted local spokespersons for national and international councils and agencies. Women's organizations around the world have been one of the finest channels for ecumenical communication.[56] And, although the ecumenical movement was no quicker than many other church organizations to benefit from women's leadership, women insiders at or near the pinnacle of the traditionally male hierarchy had from at least midcentury lobbied the ecumenical councils for a more equitable distribution of power and authority.[57]

The 1986 PC(USA) General Assembly again stressed the importance of its role in the ecumenical movement, while calling for improved communications on the part of the denomination's ecumenical representatives, the NCC, and the WCC. As the special committee reported to the Assembly:

> Participation by the PC(USA) in both councils, and especially the WCC, emphasizes the reality that the PC(USA) is only one communion among many. The process of involvement in council activities leads to a discovery of insights, perspectives, and opinions not previously understood or appreciated. Presbyterian participation demands humble openness to these other viewpoints and a readiness, in many instances, to submit to Christian sisters and brothers and their insights into Christian truths.[58]

In these words, and in spite of continuing concern among some church members and autonomous organizations of Presbyterians that interdenominational and interfaith encounters may lead to doctrinal impurity and blurring of group identity, the PC(USA) General Assembly renewed its commitment to global ecumenism.

6

Presbyterian Ecumenical Activity in the United States

Erskine Clarke

"I Am a Presbyterian—Therefore I Am Ecumenical" was the message spread across the front cover of the September 1987 *Presbyterian Survey,* the official magazine of the Presbyterian Church (U.S.A.). The headline was the title of an article by Robert McAfee Brown, Professor Emeritus of Theology and Ethics, Pacific School of Religion, and distinguished commentator on religion and ethics in the twentieth century. "To be ecumenical is as Presbyterian as predestination," declared Professor Brown. To back up such an assertion, he pointed out that "it never was the intention of John Calvin, John Knox or other Presbyterian forebears to 'divide' the church." On the contrary, they "conceived of themselves as doing just the opposite—recovering the heritage of the early *un*divided church." A public reminder of this ecumenical stance, says Professor Brown, is the Presbyterian practice of "open communion"; that is, welcoming to the Lord's Table not just Presbyterians but all who confess Jesus Christ as Lord and Savior. [1]

This essay's review of the history of Presbyterians in the United States in the twentieth century provides substantial evidence that confirms Professor Brown's assertions.

There is also, however, ample evidence of Presbyterian behavior that contradicts his claims. Many Presbyterians, and not a few Presbyterian courts and organizations, have exhibited decidedly antiecumenical stances. Not infrequently there have been calls for limitations on ecumenical activity by Presbyterian churches and for reaffirmations of the "distinctive doctrines of the Reformed Tradition." Yet even those who have wanted to limit certain types of ecumenical activity—particularly in councils of churches—have themselves often been involved in important ecumenical ventures. As will be seen, many conservative Presbyterians who have spoken vigorously against Presbyterian participation in such organizations as the National Council of Churches have themselves been leaders in conservative ecumenical ventures.

This essay seeks to explore the varying and often contradictory ways in which an ecumenical spirit has expressed itself among twentieth-century Presbyterians. Of particular concern is the influence of social forces in shaping their ecumenical perspectives and activities.[2]

Background

The ecumenical activities and perspectives of twentieth-century U.S. Presbyterians did not, of course, fall suddenly from the sky in 1900. A brief introductory look at developments in the nineteenth century can provide a historical framework for understanding developments in the present century.

Among the most important ecumenical efforts by Presbyterians in the last century was the Plan of Union of 1801. The plan united Presbyterians and Congregationalists in an effort to "win the West." Large-scale comity arrangements allowed Presbyterian and Congregationalist settlers to combine and form either a Presbyterian or a Congregational church. Through these arrangements, many Congregationalists came into the Presbyterian Church and brought with them a strong ecumenical spirit, a fervent evangelicalism, and a commitment to the great interdenominational benevolent societies that were being organized in the early decades of the nineteenth century.[3] Most important of these societies were the American Bible Society, the American Education Society, the American Home Missionary Society, the American Sunday School Union, the American Tract Society, and the American Board of Commissioners for Foreign Missions. Presbyterians and Congregationalists were the primary supporters of these societies, which were often connected through "interlocking directorates."[4]

Presbyterians were also vigorous participants in the formation of the Evangelical Alliance.[5] The Alliance, founded in London in 1846, brought together evangelical Christians from eight countries and eight major denominational families. An American branch was organized in 1867 and held six conferences before the end of the century. Although the participants were interested individuals and not official representatives of any denomination, the Alliance was a forerunner of the modern ecumenical movement.

Nineteenth-century Presbyterians not only participated in ecumenical activities, they also exhibited a remarkable ability to continue old European divisions within the Presbyterian family and an inclination both to divide among themselves and to resist moves toward broader ecumenical involvements. Covenanters and Seceders from the Church of Scotland remained separated from the larger Presbyterian bodies in the United States.[6] The Cumberland Presbyterian Church was organized in 1810 as a result of the revivals of the Second Great Awakening. In 1837, the Presbyterian Church in the U.S.A. was divided between the Old School and the New. The Old School, the larger and the most rapidly growing of the two, rejected participation in the Plan of Union and in several of the important interdenominational benevolent societies. The New School divided along North and South lines in 1858 and the Old School in 1861. New School and Old School were united, both North and South, by 1869, but the division remained between the Presbyterian Church in the U.S.A. (largely northern) and the Presbyterian Church in the U.S. (south-

ern). This meant that at the beginning of the twentieth
century there were four major Presbyterian denominations
in the United States: the Presbyterian Church in the
U.S.A. (PCUSA), the Presbyterian Church in the U.S.
(PCUS), the United Presbyterian Church of North
America (UPCNA), and the Cumberland Presbyterian
Church.[7]

Major social factors that helped to shape the ecumenical
activities of Presbyterians in the nineteenth century included the frontier and the need to win the West; slavery
and the Civil War; and immigration, the rise of cities, and
the consequent challenges to Protestant values and hegemony. Major theological and ecclesiastical factors included revivalism and the common experience of being
"touched" by revival fires; a romanticism that encouraged
both a return to earlier denominational roots and an emphasis on the organic nature of the church; and a scholastic
theology that largely rejected ecumenical cooperation or
activities.

Participation in National Ecumenical Bodies

The early years of the twentieth century saw the major
Presbyterian churches as important participants in new ecumenical bodies.

The Federal Council of Churches.   The Evangelical Alliance had, in a series of important meetings in the 1880s
and 1890s, called attention to the need for united Protestant action to meet the challenges of a rising urban and
industrial society. A series of important, if short-lived, interdenominational organizations followed and helped to
prepare the way for the formation in 1908 of the Federal
Council of Churches.[8] Among the thirty-three denominations that joined in calling for the Federal Council were the
Presbyterian Church in the U.S.A., the Cumberland Presbyterian Church, and the United Presbyterian Church of
North America.

From the first, the Council was a forceful advocate for

the theological perspectives and social concerns of the social gospel. Among its purposes was to "secure a larger combined influence for the churches of Christ in all matters affecting the moral and social condition of the people, so as to promote the application of the law of Christ in every relation of human life." At its organizing meeting, the Council adopted a social policy presented in the report of its Committee on the Church and Modern Industry. Section 9 of the report, later known as "the Social Creeds of the Churches," called upon the churches to stand for "equal rights and complete justice" for all people in all stations of life and for various reforms in the emerging industrial society.[9] In this social agenda of the Council, Presbyterians gave vigorous leadership, especially through the work of Charles Stelzle (1869–1941). After serving a number of city congregations, Stelzle was made superintendent of the PCUSA's Department of Church and Labor. Under his vigorous leadership, the department became an outstanding success. When the Federal Council was organized, Stelzle became the "voluntary secretary" of the Council's Commission on the Church and Social Service. He played a major part in the commission's investigation and report on the Bethlehem steel strike of 1910. In the report, the "twelve hour day" and the "seven day week" were condemned as a "disgrace to civilization," and the churches were called on to address the problems of working people.[10]

This social agenda of the Council, which provided its distinct accent and gave "vitality to the Council in the years of its infancy,"[11] linked the Federal Council to the Progressive Movement in American political life and to the political agendas of Theodore Roosevelt's Square Deal, Wilson's New Freedom, and later, in modified form, Franklin D. Roosevelt's New Deal. Progressivism saw in the rise of an urban, industrial society and in the "immigrant invasion" of the period serious threats to the nation's moral and social life.

Presbyterian participation in the Council can consequently be seen not only as the result of an important impulse toward Christian unity and a genuine concern for the weak and oppressed, but also as a part of a widespread attempt by the old Protestant establishment to maintain the values of its Puritan heritage in the nation's social, political, and economic life. Not incidentally, it was also an attempt by Presbyterians and other mainline Protestants to maintain their own status and influence in the nation's life.[12] Perhaps even more, the Federal Council and the ecumenical impulse it represented reflected a changing social context. A rising new middle class was seeking in the ecumenical movement concerted action that would bring stability and equilibrium to American life. The churches of the Council, including the Presbyterian, had deep roots in a largely rural and small-town Protestant America. Their members, however, were being transformed into a new, bureaucratic-minded urban middle class who were concerned for order and efficiency amid the disorders and turbulence of an emerging urban, industrial society.[13]

The Presbyterian Church in the U.S., still largely rural and small-town in 1900, still preoccupied with issues surrounding the Civil War and defeat, was conspicuous in its absence in both the calling for and the initial shaping of the Federal Council. The PCUS did join in the first meeting of the Council in 1908, only to withdraw in 1911 and then reenter in 1912.[14] Conservatives in the church were alarmed over the Council's social and political agenda and its violation of the doctrine of the "spirituality of the church," which southern Presbyterians had long held sacred. This doctrine, articulated in the nineteenth century most forcefully by James Henley Thornwell in regard to the question of slavery, insisted that the spheres of church and state were separated. The state, it was said, is "designed to realize the idea of justice. It is the society of rights." The church, on the other hand, is "designed to realize the idea of grace. It is the society of the redeemed." Church and state "are as planets moving in different orbits, and unless each is confined to its own track, the consequences may be as disastrous in the moral world, as the collision of different spheres in the world of matter."[15]

Southern Presbyterians' concerns over the "social pronouncements" of the Federal Council indicate, as will be seen, a primary focus of the opposition to ecumenical activity by Presbyterians from all parts of the country throughout the twentieth century. For southern Presbyterians, the Federal Council's Commission on the Church and Social Service became a target for heavy fire. Year after year, overtures were sent to the General Assembly demanding that the church withdraw. These were defeated, with reminders that the Council did not speak for the church and with warnings about the dangers of isolation from other evangelical churches. The increasing identification of the Council with not only social activism but also theological liberalism led finally in 1931 to the church's withdrawal from the Council. Ten years later, the PCUS again entered the Council and was a vigorous participant in the Council's reorganization and consolidation in 1950 as the National Council of Churches.

The National Council of the Churches of Christ in the U.S.A. The Federal Council of Churches represented denominations as total entities. There were, however, other important ecumenical bodies throughout the first half of the twentieth century that represented denominational boards. These included the Home Missions Council, the Foreign Missions Conference of North America, the United Stewardship Council, the National Protestant Council on Higher Education, the International Council of Religious Education, Church World Service, the Protestant Radio Commission, the Protestant Film Commission, and the Inter-Seminary Movement. Presbyterians participated in all of these and were among the leaders who began in the late 1940's—as the movement intensified to form a world council of churches—to push for a more efficient organization of interdenominational activities in the United States. In 1950, this was achieved with the formation of the National Council of Churches (NCC), which brought together the nine interdenominational agencies mentioned above so that their work could be more efficiently coordinated in one body. The Presbyterian Church in the U.S.A., the United Presbyterian Church of North America, and the Presbyterian Church in the U.S. were all part of the National Council from the first. They have played a conspicuous role in the financial resources they have provided to the National Council, always being among the most generous contributors and frequently the largest contributors on a per capita basis.[16] As will be seen, Presbyterians have also filled important leadership positions in the National Council.

Other Ecumenical Agencies and Organizations. Even after the creation of the National Council with its consolidation of ecumenical bodies, there remained a number of important independent ecumenical agencies. In 1989, those related to the General Assembly of the Presbyterian Church (U.S.A.) included the American Bible Society, Church Women United, Church World Service, Coalition for Appalachian Ministry, Commission on Religion in Appalachia, Japan–North American Commission of Cooperative Mission, Joint Educational Development, Joint Strategy and Action Committee, Inc., The Lord's Day Alliance of the United States, Presbyterian Council for Chaplains and Military Personnel, Religion in American Life, United Ministries in Education, World Alliance of Reformed Churches, and the World Council of Churches.[17] Of special note is the work of Joint Educational Development (JED) in providing ecumenically oriented church school materials. The *Christian Education: Shared Approaches* curriculum materials were prepared for twelve denominations and were widely used in Presbyterian churches.

Presbyterian theological seminaries have not only attracted students from a wide variety of backgrounds, they have also participated in significant ecumenical ventures through consortia. These generally allow for a sharing of library resources, cross registration of students, and faculty exchanges. More extensive is Johnson C. Smith Seminary's participation as a member institution of the Interdenominational Theological Center. This consortium of six predominantly Black theological institutions has one faculty and administration and a shared campus. All of the theological schools have had their ecumenical perspectives broadened by the presence of international students on their campuses.

Consultation on Church Union.   If the National Council represented a movement beyond the Federal Council in the degree of coordination of activities among American denominations, the Consultation on Church Union (COCU) represented a move beyond cooperation toward organic union. On December 4, 1960, Eugene Carson Blake, Stated Clerk of the General Assembly of the United Presbyterian Church in the U.S.A., preaching in Grace Episcopal Cathedral, San Francisco, issued a call for a union of churches that would be both "truly catholic" and "truly reformed." By "truly catholic," Blake meant the confession of the historic Trinitarian faith expressed in the Apostles' and Nicene Creeds; the observance of the two dominical sacraments, Baptism and the Lord's Supper; and a continuation of the historic episcopate. By "truly reformed," Blake meant a tradition of continuing reformation under the Word of God and the leading of the Holy Spirit, a democratic understanding of the church as the people of God, and the acceptance of diversity in worship and in the theological formulations of the faith.[18] When the General Assembly of the UPCUSA met the following May, it issued an overture to the Episcopal Church to join in inviting the United Methodists and the United Church of Christ to consider the proposal. The result was the formation of the Consultation on Church Union. The PCUS also joined the Consultation.

The historical context for the calling of the Consultation was of no little significance. Blake's proposal in San Francisco came one month after the election of the first Roman Catholic President of the United States and at the beginning of an era of precipitous and continuing decline in the membership of all the participating denominations. The

Consultation itself would take place in "Post-Puritan America,"[19] a time when the old Protestant hegemony had clearly come to an end in American life. The Consultation can thus be interpreted as not only an indication of a growing ecumenical spirit, but also as an attempt by the participating denominations to regain through union their declining influence in American life.

Presbyterian Leadership in National Ecumenical Bodies

One way to measure the level of Presbyterian activity in the ecumenical movement in the United States is by the leadership Presbyterians have provided in national ecumenical bodies. Even a cursory review indicates an impressive list of outstanding Presbyterian leaders in the ecumenical movement.

During the first thirty years of this century, Presbyterians helped to lead the way on a variety of ecumenical fronts. William H. Roberts, longtime Stated Clerk of the General Assembly, PCUSA, joined in calling for the formation of the Federal Council and was in charge of the arrangements for the first preliminary meeting. Charles L. Thompson, general secretary of the PCUSA Board of Home Missions, also joined in issuing the call for the formation of the Federal Council and served from 1908 to 1924 as president of the Home Missions Council. Charles Stelzle was the "voluntary secretary" of the Federal Council's Commission on the Church and Social Service, the Council's field secretary for special service, and during the First World War was the publicity director of the World Alliance for International Friendship Through the Churches. William P. Merrill, pastor of the Brick Presbyterian Church, New York City, was president of Church Peace Union, 1918–1947. William Adams Brown, Roosevelt Professor of Systematic Theology at Union Theological Seminary, New York, was chair of the General Wartime Commission of the Churches, 1917–1919, chair of the Federal Council's Department of Research and Education,

1920–1936, and co-president of the Oxford 1937 Conference on Church, Community, and State. From the PCUS, Walter Lingle gave outstanding leadership, serving in the 1920s as chair of the Federal Council's Executive Committee. Perhaps most influential were Robert E. Speer and Samuel McCrea Cavert. Speer, a lay person and "Champion of the Cause of Missions," was president of the Federal Council of Churches from 1920 to 1924. Cavert was general secretary of the Federal Council from 1921 until 1950, and of the National Council from 1950 to 1954.[20]

During the next thirty years, southern Presbyterians began to play a more active role in leadership positions. J. McDowell Richards, president of Columbia Theological Seminary, served as vice-president of the Federal Council and was a staunch supporter of the Council in the Deep South. Of the merging agencies that united to form the National Council of Churches, three had southern Presbyterians serve as chair during the immediately preceding years: C. Darby Fulton, the Foreign Missions Conference of North America; James Patton, the United Stewardship Council; and Ed Grant, the National Protestant Council on Higher Education. The founder and first president of the Protestant Radio and Television Center, John M. Alexander, was a southern Presbyterian, as was his successor, Ernest Arnold.[21] The PCUSA provided two seminary presidents who were highly respected leaders in the ecumenical organizations during this period: Henry P. Van Dusen of Union Theological Seminary, New York, and John A. Mackay of Princeton. Two lay people active in the early years of the National Council were John Foster Dulles, Secretary of State under President Eisenhower, and J. Howard Pew, head of the Sun Oil Company.

During the last thirty years, probably the single most influential Presbyterian leader in ecumenical affairs was Eugene Carson Blake. During the 1950s, he served as president of the National Council of Churches; in 1960, he issued the challenge that led to the formation of the Consultation on Church Union; and from 1966 to 1972 he served as general secretary of the World Council of

Churches (WCC).[22] Other leaders during this period include William P. Thompson (president of the World Alliance of Reformed Churches and of the National Council of Churches), William A. Benefield (chair of the committee that drafted the "Plan of Union" for the Consultation on Church Union), David W. A. Taylor (general secretary for COCU), and J. Oscar McCloud, who has served on numerous ecumenical committees including the Executive Committee of the World Council of Churches. James Costen presently serves as president of the Interdenominational Theological Center, the consortium of seven theological seminaries.

Presbyterian women, although long active in ecumenical affairs, have come to play an increasingly important role. Early ecumenical leaders included Dorothy Shaw MacLeod, who for years was executive director of United Church Women. More recently, Claire Randall served as the first woman executive secretary of the National Council, and Rachel Henderlite served as vice-president and then president of the Consultation on Church Union. Patricia McClurg was recently elected president of the National Council.

Although this list could be substantially extended, it does point to the significant involvement of Presbyterians in the ecumenical movement. The major Presbyterian denominations have encouraged and honored such involvement through an insistence that their churches are but part of one holy catholic and apostolic church, and by frequent reminders that divisions within the body of Christ are a cause of scandal.[23] Because Presbyterians have defined the church "primarily in terms of the action of God in word and sacrament, not in terms of structures or even correct doctrine," they have been able to "recognize the ministries, sacraments, and memberships of other churches."[24] Moreover, the concern of Calvinistic churches for the transformation of society has encouraged Presbyterians to seek cooperation in meeting the social challenges of the twentieth century.

Unions and Divisions

Although Presbyterians have been active supporters in a variety of ecumenical endeavors, they have also been seeking in the twentieth century to heal some of their own deep divisions. In 1906, the Cumberland Presbyterian Church and the Presbyterian Church in the U.S.A. were reunited after a separation of almost a hundred years. After seventeen years of debate, a Plan of Union was brought in 1954 before the General Assemblies of the PCUSA, the PCUS, and the UPCNA. The General Assembly of the PCUS voted for the plan 283 to 169, but the presbyteries voted 42 in favor and 43 against. It appeared to many who had worked long and hard for the union that they had been dealt an ironic blow by the United States Supreme Court. Only a few months before the vote by the presbyteries, the Court had outlawed segregation in the public schools. The reaction in the South was massive resistance to what was regarded by many as northern interference and renewed aggression against southern ways. In the midst of such a climate, hopes for union between the PCUS and the two other major Presbyterian churches all but disappeared for the foreseeable future.[25]

Undeterred by the defeat of 1954, the UPCNA and the PCUSA united in 1958 to form the United Presbyterian Church in the U.S.A. (UPCUSA). By this union, a division that had its roots in eighteenth-century Scotland was healed.

However dismal the chances for reunion between the PCUS, the PCUSA, and the UPCNA appeared in 1955, powerful social and economic forces were at work undermining the resistance of white southern Presbyterians to union. Most important in this regard was their increasing loss of identity as white southerners with their own history as a distinct part of the American experience. The mobility of the American people (including white southerners), the rise of the Sun Belt, and the increasing realization in the 1960s and 1970s that racism was not only a "southern problem" but a national scandal, all helped to prepare the way for reunion in 1983.[26]

There have also been, however, during the twentieth century, divisive forces at work among Presbyterians. The modernist-fundamentalist debate in the 1920s led to the formation in the 1930s of the Orthodox Presbyterian Church, a small but outspoken fundamentalist church. In 1972, a number of conservative southern Presbyterians, protesting the great traumatic changes of the 1960s, withdrew from the PCUS and formed the Presbyterian Church in America. Others withdrew and joined the Associate Reformed Presbyterian Church, a church with its roots in an eighteenth-century Scottish controversy. In 1980, a few congregations in the UPCUSA withdrew to form the Evangelical Presbyterian Church.

Conservative Ecumenical Groups

Among conservative Presbyterians, those with fundamentalist perspectives have been highly critical of the ecumenical movement. Indeed, they have generally regarded it as signs of the approach of the Antichrist.[27] Other conservative Presbyterians, however, although distancing themselves from such mainline ecumenical organizations as the National Council of Churches, have played a remarkable ecumenical role among evangelicals. Presbyterians Harold Ockenga and Dan Fuller, along with a host of Presbyterian faculty and trustees, turned Fuller Theological Seminary into the largest independent regularly accredited theological seminary in the world. This "Princeton of Evangelicalism" was drawing by the 1970s and 1980s the bulk of its students from an evangelical constituency within mainline denominations.[28] Gordon-Conwell Theological Seminary, also strongly influenced by Presbyterian leadership, has played a similar ecumenical role among evangelicals. Leighton Ford, a member of the Billy Graham organization, has been a leader in the international ecumenical endeavors among evangelicals. L. Nelson Bell, retired southern Presbyterian medical missionary, was instrumental, with Presbyterian J. Howard Pew, in founding and setting the direction for the magazine *Christianity Today* with its massive circulation among evangelicals of many different denominations. Bill Bright was founder of Campus Crusade for Christ, an evangelical para-church organization that has received substantial financial support from Presbyterians. Presbyterian lay person Ralph Winters founded and heads the U.S. Center of World Missions.[29]

Conservative Presbyterians, in other words, have played an ecumenical role among evangelicals comparable to that pursued by more liberal Presbyterians among the official ecumenical agencies and organizations like the National Council of Churches.

"Grass Roots" Ecumenism

The ecumenical activity of Presbyterians, although highly visible on an international and national level, has perhaps been even more extensive on a presbytery or congregational level. One factor that has encouraged such activity is the amount of "religious switching" from other denominations into Presbyterian churches. Statistical studies in the 1960s confirmed what had long been observed: An "upward" social mobility has brought conservative Protestants into more liberal and "higher status" churches such as the Presbyterian, with their greater accommodations to modern life and thought.[30] Presbyterian congregations with significant numbers of people from other denominational backgrounds consequently have been open to cooperate in a wide variety of ecumenical activities. At the same time, the traditional reformist concern of Presbyterians has led them into a wide range of ecumenical activities that address specific local community issues: prison ministries, Meals on Wheels, soup kitchens and night shelters for the homeless, campus ministries, day care, youth services, elderly services, and other community organizations. Some of these activities are organized through ministerial alliances or local councils of churches. Increasingly, they are part of "community ministries"—ecumenical activities by members of different denominations to meet social needs in a particular geographical area.[31] Once again, Presbyterians have taken a lead in providing substantial leadership and financial resources to such movements.[32] David Bos, Presbyterian minister in Louisville, Kentucky, is the chair of the newly organized National Steering Committee for Community Ministries.

In some regions of the country, particularly in the Midwest, there have been long-established patterns of union congregations and more recently "yoked parishes." These arrangements have often reflected the need for cooperative action in areas where rural or small-town conditions made ecumenical cooperation necessary for the survival of local congregations.[33] One presbytery executive in the South, after noting a number of local congregations that were involved in union Sunday schools, youth fellowships, and interdenominational service projects, commented that "people who are adamantly opposed to conciliar or formal ecumenical activities by the denomination are most willing to be involved in ecumenical endeavors with friends and neighbors who are members of other denominations."[34]

Opposition

Not all Presbyterians have been strong supporters of ecumenical activity or of the union of separate Presbyterian denominations. Some have opposed ecumenism or union because it appeared to them to involve compromises with important theological beliefs or polity commitments. Most have objected to what they have regarded as the political and social agendas of ecumenical bodies or the denominations involved in union discussions. Several Presbyterian magazines, newsletters, and journals have been particularly outspoken in their opposition.[35]

In the early years of the century, the *Southwestern Presbyterian* opposed southern Presbyterians entering the Federal Council because the Council was sure to reject the doctrine of the spirituality of the church and address social questions. Although such questions were important and needed serious attention by thoughtful people, declared the paper, they were beyond the sphere of the church, for "Her mission is spiritual. . . . [H]er governing principles should be to preach Christ and His Gospel." A half-century later this was a primary argument by southern whites against union with the PCUSA and the UPCNA. The titles of articles in the *Southern Presbyterian Journal* point to the old arguments against union: L. Nelson Bell, "It Is *Historic Presbyterianism* Which Is at Stake"; G. Aiken Taylor, "Can Two Walk Together Except They Be Agreed?"; William Childs Robinson, "The Kingship of Christ and the Plan of Union" and " 'The Radical Principles' Exalted in the Plan of Union."[36]

For the last twenty years, the *Presbyterian Layman* has consistently opposed the participation of first the UPCUSA and then the Presbyterian Church (U.S.A.) in COCU, the National Council of Churches, and the World Council of Churches. A brief review of its opposition illumines important aspects of Presbyterian ecumenical activity during these years.

The *Presbyterian Layman* began publication in January 1968 in the midst of one of the most turbulent periods in American history. A publication of the Presbyterian Lay Committee, Inc., the monthly newspaper had the backing of a number of affluent Presbyterian businessmen.[37] It was, said the masthead of the *Layman,* "an organization of Presbyterian laymen dedicated to the adherence of our Church to its primary mission—the teaching and preaching of the Gospel of Jesus Christ." From the first, it has taken a position on the side of the "Spirituality of the Church," although it has itself championed particular social and economic perspectives.[38] At the same time, it has expressed a concern for the role of the laity in the church's life and has emphasized what it regards as the laity's growing distrust of denominational leaders.[39]

During its first year, the *Presbyterian Layman* began a sustained attack on COCU and Presbyterian participation in it. The primary focus of the attack was on the proposed Plan of Union's abolition of the office of ruling elder, the perceived diminution in the role of the laity, and the dangers of "a super-church." "A Hierarchy of Bishops to Replace Presbyterian Governmental Structure" was a typical heading.[40] In November 1970, the *Layman* published the resolution of the Board of Directors of the Presbyterian Lay Committee opposing COCU. The heart of the opposition was that, with the COCU Plan, many provisions "discard our present form of democratic government and substitute therefor the episcopal form headed by bishops and councils," and that the board "finds no substantial benefits but many grave dangers inherent in the 'super-church' concept set forth in the Plan."[41] In explaining the COCU system of structure and authority, the *Layman* declared that the line of authority was "really a line of *disenfranchisement,*" the "disenfranchisement of laymen in local congregations."[42] This opposition was so intense that it succeeded, much to the distress of General Assembly Stated Clerk William P. Thompson, in having the United Presbyterian Church in the U.S.A. withdraw from COCU in 1972.[43] The vote, said an editorial of the *Layman,* was a message from the "little people, the grassroots, both lay and clergy . . . a trend in our Church—a swing of the pendulum back toward greater participation by the people in the Church." It represented, declared an article heading, "Mistrust Between Members and Leaders."[44] Although the Assembly voted the next year to rejoin COCU, much of the original enthusiasm for it had left, and membership in COCU apparently no longer appeared to the *Layman* as a pressing danger.[45]

From its first issue, the *Layman* has consistently criticized the National Council of Churches and the World Council of Churches and opposed Presbyterian support of these ecumenical agencies. Most of the criticism has focused on the political, social, and economic pronouncements and activities of the Councils. One line of criticism has emphasized that the Councils are not competent to judge complex issues. In April 1968, after reporting the

NCC's call for changes in U.S. foreign policy, the article ended with an editorial note: "It is inconceivable that NCC has competence to deal with military, diplomatic, and economic problems, yet it has no hesitancy in offering solutions just as though it had the competence." Following this was a quotation from Archbishop William Temple: "It is of crucial importance that the Church, acting corporately, should not commit itself to any particular policy. . . . [I]t must never commit itself to an ephemeral program of detailed action."[46] Another line of attack has emphasized what the *Layman* regards as the Councils' support of policies and groups that are not in the best interest of the United States.[47]

Behind many of these attacks are opposing views of the American experience and the role of the United States in the world. The *Layman* expresses the older view, long held by the Protestant establishment, that the United States has been a great source of hope for the world and a defender of justice and democracy. An alternative view, often found in the pronouncements of the NCC and WCC, is that the United States is the source of many of the world's most serious problems because of its racism, consumerism, militarism, and imperialism.[48] Such an alternative view of the American experience and the United States' place in the contemporary world has contributed ironically to the decline of the ecumenical movement in the United States. Much of the impulse for the ecumenical movement in the United States has flowed from a vision of a Christian America united in great crusades to right ancient wrongs. Without that vision, an important motivation for ecumenical activity—for "a united Christian front"—has been significantly drained of its power. It is perhaps not by chance that the quotation that introduced this essay—"I Am a Presbyterian—Therefore I Am Ecumenical"—was written by a retired professor and not a rising young theologian or prominent pastor.

The opposition to formal ecumenical activities has been particularly effective because it has accompanied significant cultural shifts taking place in American society. The great inward turn of the 1970s and 1980s away from social activism toward a therapeutic and narcissistic culture undercut much of the dynamic that had fueled the ecumenical movement. The need for united action to address "the great social issues of the day" no longer had as much appeal among a people increasingly preoccupied with "getting in touch with their feelings" and discovering "my true self."[49] At the same time, many who remained concerned about social issues and the common good were increasingly skeptical of bureaucracies and their need for efficiency and standardization.[50] In such a context, ecumenical agencies such as COCU, the National Council, and the World Council no longer evoked the passionate commitments they once had. The result has been a general waning of the ecumenical movement in the United States.

Conclusions

The ecumenical activity of Presbyterians, no less than other areas of their lives, reflects a complex interaction between religious beliefs and social forces within a particular historical context. Religious beliefs have encouraged Presbyterians, both liberal and conservative, to be active participants in ecumenical endeavors. Presbyterians have clearly played an outstanding role in an exceedingly wide range of ecumenical activities, from the National Council of Churches to evangelical organizations and institutions through local cooperative efforts. They have provided much leadership and a disproportionate share of the financial support of ecumenical agencies and activities.

The nature of much of this ecumenical activity reflects powerful social and economic forces at work in the twentieth century. Perhaps most obvious is the rise of the technological society, with its emphasis on efficiency and centralization. In order to organize more efficiently so that the yield of its bureaucracy might be increased, Presbyterian churches, like modern corporations, have standardized and centralized much of their work with other denominations through ecumenical agencies.[51] At the same time the declining role of the old mainline denominations in American life has encouraged a closer cooperation and ecumenical activity in order to advance the values and perspectives of those denominations most active in the ecumenical movement.[52] An increasingly pluralistic and secular America, the rapid growth of Third World churches and their calls for changes in dominant social and economic orders, and the varied reactions of Presbyterians to these changes have all helped to shape the perspectives and activities of Presbyterians as they have sought to express their beliefs about the nature of the church and its mission in the world.

7

Presbyterians and Mass Media:
A Case of Blurred Vision
and Missed Mission

J. W. Gregg Meister

Messages emerge out of a complex relationship between the author of the message and its content, medium, audience, and effect. When institutions produce messages, the relationship becomes even more intricate. Invariably, groups within the organization vie for control of the message content, generally within the context of competing organizational goals. The production of institutional messages requires the allocation of precious institutional resources. Competition for these resources influences the selection of the medium used for message distribution. Moreover, institutional messages do not occur in a cultural vacuum. Frequently societal factors beyond the control of the institution shape the messages, or at least the interpretation of the messages, that the organization produces.

Christian churches are among those American institutions engaged in the production of messages. In fact, it could be argued that institutional Christianity has as its primary purpose the production of messages. Certainly, churches have no products to sell, like hamburgers or gasoline. They are not service institutions like dry cleaners. Their mandate to exist comes from their call to proclaim the gospel message to both church members and those outside the fold. Churches are, in essence, message production centers. Their task is to produce the good news of the gospel through various media and to diverse audiences.

In the biblical past, the media that the church used consisted of the oral tradition, Luke's "orderly" written account, Paul's letters, and, of course, the preacher's platform speech. Today, local congregations use a greater variety of media in their efforts to produce messages. These range from bulletins to newsletters, radio, audiocassette, and cable television. Church leaders compete for the resources and set the policies for defining, producing, and distributing the institution's messages through selected media to specific audiences within any given historical context. All of these factors operate together, in various combinations and subject to numerous forces, in order for any church or denomination to carry out its mandate to produce and distribute messages.

Given Christendom's historic interest with messages, it is not surprising that Presbyterians in America have, over the past four decades, given considerable attention to the use of radio and television to reach mass audiences. Presbyterians have issued theological pronouncements on the importance of using the mass media for spreading the gospel to the unchurched. They have sponsored radio and television programs, designed production studios, created communications boards and agencies, encouraged seminary courses, and trained church leaders in the use of mass media. What is surprising, however, is that Presbyterian commitment to using mass media markedly decreased as the twentieth century progressed, even while the influence of television as a message-producing system exponentially increased and church membership rolls declined.

The rise of television's cultural impact and the fall of mainline religion's impact may not be causally connected. But because both television and organized religion are message-producing systems, and because the messages each produce are often in conflict with each other, there may be underlying tensions that deserve exploration. Although a detailed examination goes beyond the scope of this essay, we can hope to lay bare some of those key policies that Presbyterians developed regarding the use of mass media. This in turn may help illumine the stance of mainline Protestantism toward the mass media—television, in particular—as well as advance the discussion regarding the relationship between two message-producing systems, television and religion.

The Early Enthusiasm

In 1949, the General Assembly of the Presbyterian Church in the United States of America (PCUSA) entered the second half of the twentieth century with great expectations for church involvement in the mass media. To lead the church into that future, the Assembly, which was itself broadcast on coast-to-coast network radio programs, formed the Department of Radio and Television. The department, in turn, established policies that strongly influenced the Presbyterian relationship to the mass media—especially television—into the 1990s. Those policies include the department's early commitment to produce programming ecumenically, its intention to train church leaders in the use of radio and television, and its assumption that the church's message could forge a harmonious partnership with the broadcast industry.

The efforts of the Presbyterian Church in the United States (PCUS) Radio and Television Division largely paralleled the work of its PCUSA counterparts. Under the leadership of John M. Alexander, the division participated in the "Protestant Hour" and the "National Radio Pulpit." In the early 1950s, the division joined with three other denominations (including its PCUSA counterparts) in constructing the Protestant Radio and Television Center. From this location, the PCUS participated ecumenically in mass media ministries, but it also from the beginning produced strictly Presbyterian programming.

With mass media ministries firmly in place in both the PCUSA and PCUS hierarchies, the 1950s were characterized by exuberance for the mass media by Presbyterians on both sides of the Mason-Dixon line. The PCUSA's seventeen-page report in the 1950 Minutes of the General Assembly seeks to capture that enthusiasm with accounts of coast-to-coast radio broadcasts, mass media evangelism efforts, radio and television production facilities, and workshops and seminary courses for church leaders throughout the country.[1] The PCUS was equally enthusiastic. Its Radio and Television Division provided programming to the Armed Services Radio. The women of the church gave considerable financial support to the media ministry, and the division formed solid links with the mission work of the denomination.[2]

Even though television was just emerging on the American cultural horizon, Presbyterians during this decade were more than peripherally involved. A sampling of Presbyterian television programming includes a five-minute, 26-week series originating in Kentucky, a 13-week half-hour production carried on 33 television stations in the West, and a weekly program distributed to 60 hospitals.[3]

Early Assumptions

Both PCUSA and PCUS General Assembly Minutes reveal the Presbyterian bias toward ecumenical programming. As early as 1944, for instance, when both denominations were considering the use of radio, the PCUSA General Assembly stated:

> What goes over the air into every home should not be labelled with one part of the Christian Church, calling attention to Christian diversity. Rather, it should be our common, universal Gospel. Moreover, we do not want to start competition with other denominations.[4]

PCUS Presbyterians were perhaps more intentional than their PCUSA cousins in producing specifically Presbyterian programming—as early as 1945 they were beaming the "Presbyterian Hour" over twelve radio stations—but they were nonetheless consistently involved ecumenically.

In 1949, for instance, they report that "we cannot use time given us by the radio stations for denominational propaganda and promotion."[5]

The Protestant Radio Commission (P.R.C.), with a leadership board that drew heavily upon Presbyterians, was inaugurated in 1949 as a cooperative venture of sixteen denominations. It became the initial vehicle by which Presbyterians engaged in ecumenical programming. Convinced that radio and television should be used to "enlarge the faith and understanding of their constituency, to win converts, and to create goodwill among people of different beliefs," the P.R.C. set the policy for programming by mainline denominations:

> The Protestant Radio Commission will produce many programs on behalf of all and in the name of cooperating Protestantism. The P.R.C. will also help its constituent bodies in any distinctive aspect of their radio and television ministry that may be carried on by them. The P.R.C. will ask for network time only for the programs it produces, but will advise constituent denominations and interdenominational agencies how to ask for network time and will encourage these bodies to make their programs both distinctive and representative of Protestantism as a whole.[6]

Not incidentally, that statement from the Protestant Radio Commission also helped define mainline Protestantism's relationship to the commercial media industries. It committed the churches to the essentially passive policy of requesting free air time from the networks and their affiliates. Preachers and faith healers like Oral Roberts, who were not among the chosen sixteen denominations, were forced to pay for their air time. In the 1950s, when local television stations were hungry for programming and when Federal Communications Commission guidelines tied the broadcaster's license to serving community needs, mainline denominations were quite pleased with their free Sunday morning broadcasts.

Presbyterians, albeit wrapped in an ecumenical quilt so that their name was indistinguishable from other denominations, thrived in this broadcast environment. In cooperation with the Broadcasting and Film Commission of the National Council of Churches and television networks, Presbyterians helped produce several weekly television programs: "Lamp Unto My Feet," (CBS), "Look Up and Live" (CBS), "Frontiers of Faith" (NBC), "Morning Chapel" (Dumont network five mornings a week), and "I Believe . . . " (ABC).

The PCUSA in particular made every effort to benefit from a close relationship to those who ran commercial broadcast interest. In 1950, when the Department of Radio and Television made its report to the General Assembly, Dr. George D. Crothers, Director of Religious Broadcasts of CBS, addressed the Assembly. At that same Assembly, forty-four "consultants" to the department were named, all of whom were drawn from the industry.[7] And mindful of the fact that church programming was dependent upon the policy of asking for free air time, it is not unusual to find expressions of appreciation to the networks in the Assembly Minutes over a period of several decades.[8]

Alongside the commitment to produce programming ecumenically and the policy of asking for rather than buying broadcast time, both the PCUSA and the PCUS sought to train church leaders in the use of mass media. During the 1950s, there was widespread involvement in radio and television production at the level of synods, presbyteries, and seminaries, and church-related colleges. For instance, in the PCUSA the 1952 General Assembly recommended that synods and presbyteries form broadcasting committees, and by 1956, 36 synods and 242 presbyteries had done so. Moreover, in response to an earlier resolution from the Council on Theological Education, six out of ten Presbyterian seminaries could report that they offered a variety of courses in broadcast writing or broadcast production.[9]

There was also an early plan to have local "expediters" who would seek to relate the church to literally every radio and television station in the country. To assist in this task, the church media departments developed a massive card file to keep track of Presbyterians involved in any aspect of the broadcast industry—an idea that was resurrected again in each of the next three decades.

Perhaps one effect of such widespread interest in developing a media-wise membership base was that the church made extensive use of the electronic media in several subunits within the organization. In the PCUSA, the Board of Christian Education reported that its audiovisual department was preparing a number of radio and television productions. It also produced a twenty-minute motion picture designed for television use and installed a sound studio in its Philadelphia headquarters.[10]

As the 1950s drew to a close, church media experts wanted more money for more programming, but they seemed content, even confident, with the nest of relationships that had been established. The gospel message was being well served by Presbyterians who, in league with other denominations and the broadcast industry itself, anticipated a friendly future. Presbyterians and mass media ministries were as American as apple pie and Howdy Doody.

Middle-Age Ambivalence

As the church strode into the 1960s, there was an apparent eagerness among church media experts to press even more vigorously for the use of media in spreading the church's message. The PCUSA and the UPCNA had united to form the UPCUSA in 1958. The UPCUSA Presbyterians had a photogenic and media-astute Stated Clerk in Eugene Carson Blake. He came to that position with a background in parish work and religious broadcasting, and encouraged the Division of Mass Media in nurturing industry contacts. The PCUS was pleased with progress made in electronic media, but definitely wanted more. Mixing evangelistic zeal with industry statistics, the PCUS sounded an urgent note of appeal. With "half the world lying in unbelief," the PCUS insists, "our generation must not fail to master the art of mass communications" lest it stand accused of having "merely toyed with one of the

mightiest means of lifting men within sight of the Cross."
During the last decade, America had grown from a land of
four million television sets to a nation of fifty-two million
television homes. "Why," the report virtually thundered,
has "our Church not yet entered the door of TV?" Without
financial resources the report was left with prophecy: "The
Church which is satisfied with yesterday's methods of
communication for today's hungry world stands to lose
tomorrow's spiritual opportunity."[11]

The question of "why not television?" is difficult enough
to answer at the dawn of the 1960s. It becomes increasingly elusive as the decade unfolds. During this period of
church life, it is not easy to capture those underlying conflicts that ultimately led to the decline of church use of
mass media. Nor can one assume that both denominations
experienced identical struggles regarding the media.

In a general sense, it would appear that media experts in
both bodies experienced competition for resources within
their respective denominations, but from different directions. In the PCUS, television monies competed against
radio monies. In the PCUSA, electronic media monies
competed against print media monies. In both cases, television ultimately lost. To cite one example, one 30-minute
radio broadcast of "The Protestant Hour," released over
350 stations, cost as much as a single three-minute film
production for one station.[12] The church invariably chose
radio.

In any event, competition among media for financial
support was masked by the larger competition between
any media and virtually every other church program. Education, global mission, home mission, administration—all
these aspects of church life have their built-in financial
needs as well as a history of financial support. For either
radio or television to dislodge them in the course of one
decade would have been highly unlikely and, in fact, did
not occur.

Given the political and intellectual climate of the 1960s,
possibly a more interesting reason for the eventual demise
of television programming than the struggle for resources

was competition within the denominations regarding the composition of the message—what it should be and who should control its production. This is also a difficult factor to measure, but it is one that no doubt severely complicated the use of electronic media. During the 1960s, the PCUS dealt with such issues as alcoholism, abortion, the Black Manifesto, and the Vietnam War—the same issues that confronted their Presbyterian relatives north of the Mason-Dixon line.

In the UPCUSA, Long-Range Planning Committee reports supplement the Assembly Minutes in uncovering the denomination's involvement with media during the 1960s, a period that characterized the denomination's most energetic and most controversial engagement with television. Theological justification for using media was paramount. For instance, the 1960 report stated boldly:

> For the Church of the 20th century not to make extensive use of both television and radio would be as unthinkable as if St. Paul had refused to travel in ships or Luther and Calvin had regarded the printing press as unworthy of use.[13]

The 1960 report reiterated the denomination's commitment to produce programming cooperatively with the twenty-eight denominations of the National Council of Churches. The budget of the Division of Mass Media (formerly the Department of Radio and Television) had grown from $27,500 in 1949 ($6,000 of which was for programming with the Protestant Radio Commission) to $186,000 in 1960 ($107,450 of which was for programming with the Broadcasting and Film Commission of the National Council of Churches). In brief, monies spent for ecumenical programming increased from 22 to 58 percent of the division's total budget.[14]

Although the Long-Range Planning Committee report did express some general concern regarding television broadcast fare, it maintained the denomination's basic alignment with the broadcast industry. The church, stated the report, should be concerned over the presence of violence, sex, and the exaltation of materialism on television.

However, the report went on to insist that the fault lay with the "tastes of the audience" and not with the medium or the broadcasters: "Broadcasting is the eighth wonder of the world. . . . Our church takes the affirmative position of trying to help the broadcasters to provide the general public with a better balanced viewing and listening diet."[15]

The UPCUSA's Division of Mass Media pursued its commitment to media by taking its internally conflicted messages to the air in a strategy that might have won them the 1960s but lost them the 1970s and 1980s. In 1962, the Division of Mass Media approached Hollywood producer Stan Freberg on behalf of the Presbyterian Church and invited him to produce thirty- and sixty-second radio and television spots. Freberg's spots—which featured such items as a Christian hippie and a cowboy God figure—won the Presbyterian Church public attention.[16]

The Division of Mass Media found it difficult to measure, and hence to justify, the effectiveness of these creative spots. First of all, the spots were aimed at an audience identified only as the predominantly unchurched "grey American." Although this target audience is never defined, it seems to be that faceless individual who has, in his or her quest for security, seldom confronted existential questions and cried out for God.[17] But market surveys could not show that the spots prompted a spiritual awakening in this person. In test markets such as St. Louis, Freberg's own analysis showed that 79 percent of those polled who acknowledged being exposed to the spots (14 percent of 2,000) admitted that the spots "made them wonder about living with God." However, that same poll showed that 88 percent of those exposed to the spots already claimed to be church members. Presumably, they were wondering about God prior to viewing a thirty-second spot.

If the division could not show that its radio and television spots confronted the audience with a deeper understanding of the Divine, neither could it prove that the spots advanced the cause of church growth. For example, another study made several years later in Columbus, Ohio, showed that only 26 percent of the respondents had seen the "God Is Alive" spots, and less than 2 percent could recall seeing the closing tag.[18] But the closing tag was ecumenical in nature and not Presbyterian. Even had the "grey American" remembered the closing, this recall would not necessarily have prompted the unchurched "grey American" to become a Presbyterian.

Response to the Freberg spots helps uncover the conflict over the form and content of the message that UPCUSA Presbyterians faced at this point in the church's life. The spots were described as both "catchy"[19] and a "venture which applies to the Gospel jingles beneath the dignity of cigarettes, cereals and soap."[20] Some church members were offended by the spots, whereas others were fearful they would jeopardize the church's institutional integrity.[21] Charles Brackbill, associate director of the division, explained to the general presbyter of the Presbytery of New York City that the division had spent two years developing a strategy to reach the unchurched. A colleague of Brackbill's, who was on the Board of National Missions, criticized the spots for their "theological primitivism" and "naive supernaturalism." Church messages, this writer maintained, should instead be directed toward issues of civil rights, social values, and interpersonal communications. Unsolicited audience response ranged from "Shame on you for playing that commercial for 'buying God!'" to "Clever and subtly done . . . the message can be taken philosophically, especially if you're fed up with the orthodox messages that are usually handed out."[22]

Freberg himself—who by this time had become a close friend of Brackbill—was rather proud of his Presbyterian messages:

> I believe it is the first major step the Christian church has taken in broadcasting to attempt to reach the subconscious mind of the young American, who will do anything in his power to sluff off anything of an even remotely religious nature.[23]

The decade of the 1960s ended the most vigorous chapter in the UPCUSA's use of electronic media, if also its most hotly debated one. But it should also be noted that during this time, synod and presbytery involvement, measured by functioning broadcasting committees, decreased to virtual nonexistence.

Old-Age Dismantlement

During the 1970s, denominational support for using electronic media to distribute church messages to mass audiences dramatically changed. In the UPCUSA, the 1973 General Assembly effectively dismantled the Division of Mass Media by moving it to a subsidiary place in the church structure, cutting its production budget, and not offering to the division's executives equivalent job descriptions in the new structure.

Church executives who were involved in or affected by those decisions offer several reasons to explain the change in the church toward media, especially television. For example, Frank Heinze, former director of communications, said in a personal interview that for several reasons the Division of Mass Media was a "target" of the 1973 church restructure. Money was a major issue; the division's production budget was approximately a quarter of a million dollars.[24] In addition, William P. Thompson, the Stated Clerk of the General Assembly, was never a supporter of media. "At times he was almost paranoid about the media," Heinze said. Moreover, a decision had "evolved" that "might have been a grave mistake," namely, to emphasize internal communications. "It was felt that if the people in church, the folk in the pew, knew what we [the national church] are doing, they will like it and support it. Consequently the church lost out in their relationship with mass media."

Richard Gilbert was the director of the Division of Mass Media from 1964 to 1973, arriving at his post from a background in evangelism. Asked for his account of the demise of the division he directed, Gilbert said in a personal interview that this question could be accounted for at two levels. First, no segment of the church claimed the division as "theirs." Education, social action, and evangelism units were "glad to see us go, because of competition for a diminishing budget." Second, the overall church context had changed considerably. The Angela Davis affair had cost the church dearly, according to Gilbert, in terms of members and financial support; white backlash turned against the church for its litany of civil rights stands; the Sunday school curriculum was "dull as hell."[25] Gilbert's remarks regarding Stated Clerk Thompson and his attitude toward media were considerably less gracious even than Heinze's. Gilbert was also one of the executives not offered a position in the new structure; he began working instead for NBC.

From 1973 until the early 1980s, the national headquarters of the UPCUSA was not involved in television production.

In 1978, six presbyteries sent overtures to the General Assembly (UPCUSA) requesting the formation of a task force to reconsider the establishment of a mass media ministry. In 1980, the General Assembly established a Communications Unit, with minimal staff and virtually no budget for television production. The managing director for electronic program resources in this unit reported that in 1987 the only television program produced by that office was "Video One," a thirty-minute program sent via satellite once a month for interested cable franchises.

During the 1980s, what attention the Presbyterian Church gave to television production seemed to occur primarily at the regional levels. The Presbytery of San Francisco, the Presbytery of Cascades (Seattle), and the TriSynod Media Mission Board (Philadelphia) each produced several television spots. The Presbytery of San Francisco and the Presbytery of San Jose were briefly involved in a Bay Area ecumenical cable venture. The Presbyterian Media Mission (Pittsburgh) produced a biweekly cable program, and the Synod of Lakes and Prairies (Minnesota) produced educational videotapes to supplement Sunday school curriculum.

A 1988 survey of policy statements from the seventeen regional Presbyterian synods showed that "communications" was generally mentioned as a priority. But communications in this context was always understood to refer to print media and usually emphasized reaching current church members rather than a mass audience. Some synods also indicated that television should be a primary medium used by the church, but only one synod had made a significant investment in television production equipment. However, because the technology called television had changed significantly since the PCUSA's original Department of Radio and Television—with the rise of cable television, industrial television, and home video tape recorders—a reference to television is not necessarily a reference to broadcast television. It is often not clear from the context of synod statements on communications what type of television is referred to, but several synods have established offices of communications with task forces, committees, and staff whose portfolios include the goals of making the church and its messages more visible in the electronic media. When these groups and individuals refer to television, that term includes documentaries, thirty-second spots, cable television programming, and educational videotapes.

Observations

At the midcentury mark, American Presbyterians seemed well launched on an extensive mass media ministry. At every level of the organization, from theological seminaries to broadcast Sunday school programming, Presbyterians were carrying out their mandate of spreading the message of the gospel through the electronic media. As the century enters its last decade, however, this situation has clearly changed dramatically. Clergy are not leaving seminary well trained in either radio or television production. Only one synod has production facilities, the national offices have few people on staff with professional television production experience, and interest in using the mass media to reach the unchurched appears in only a few regional pockets.

A cluster of factors account for the change in denominational policies regarding media between the 1940s and the 1990s. Certainly, the cost of producing media materials (especially broadcast television programming) and the consequent competition for resources to cover those costs cannot be discounted as a major consideration. But costs cannot be divorced from such matters as agenda setting and theology. Presbyterians are in general not a poverty-stricken denomination. They have a demonstrated ability to raise major amounts of money for buildings, schools, and missions. Had a broadcast ministry to proclaim a church message to the unchurched been a major theological conviction, and thus a central denominational priority, one suspects that Presbyterians could have accomplished this goal. "Television" means, literally, "far vision." In the area of electronic broadcasting, Presbyterians have demonstrated a blurred vision.

As the preceding discussion also makes clear, however, this lack of a clear vision to reach the unchurched with a church message has to do, in part, with the fragmented and conflicted message within the organization itself. This has kept the church from having a consistent set of symbols that can be readily transmitted to an audience unfamiliar with those symbols. When someone sees a golden arch from the highway, for instance, they know that it stands for McDonald's and for a familiar menu of hamburgers and fries. But even though there has been a Presbyterian "franchise" in America for more than two hundred years, Presbyterians have no such identifiable golden arch or menu. Because both radio and television are highly selective media that clarify some elements of a message at the expense of others, and because Presbyterians have been unable to agree upon which gospel elements to clarify, conflicting groups within the organization have been unable or unwilling to assemble sufficient resources to produce any mass-mediated message.

If one grants that the original decisions in the 1940s and 1950s to enter the broadcast field with Presbyterian-produced messages was a correct one, then it is further possible to consider that the church's failure to sustain those decisions comes from a failure to understand the nature of the media themselves. Bluntly put, the early decisions to wrap Presbyterian messages in an ecumenical blanket failed to appreciate that a major value of television and radio advertising comes from brand recognition. It is true that Crest advertising sells the need to brush teeth, but the advertising is successful only if the consumer selects Crest instead of Colgate.

Presbyterians, especially those in the PCUSA and later the UPCUSA, seemed reluctant to frame a message that was distinctly and identifiably Presbyterian. This made for solid ecumenical relationships, especially during the tenure of Stated Clerk Eugene Carson Blake, with his major emphasis on church union. But it made for poor television marketing strategy. The reluctance to frame a uniquely Presbyterian message also made mobilizing support and resources for television increasingly difficult. And, as was seen with the Freberg spots, evaluating the effectiveness of ecumenical messages for Presbyterians was difficult, if not impossible.

Perhaps most critically, however, Presbyterians exhibited a certain naïveté regarding television. Television is itself a message-producing system that completely embraces the culture. Children are born into television; they watch thousands of hours of television before they learn to speak. Young adults have spent nearly two years of their life in front of a television set by the time they finish high school. Moreover, people watch television indiscriminately, not selectively. When Nielsen ratings show that in the average home the television set is on for six or seven hours a day, the real impact of this statistic is that people are exposed to the flow of television messages, not to intentional channel selection in order to find the "best" program available.[26]

Moreover, the values that comprise the flow of television programming are in large measure in opposition to the values Presbyterians—or most other mainline denominations—hold most dear. Women and minorities are severely underrepresented and greatly exploited in the television world. The world portrayed on prime-time television exalts violence, cultivates fear, esteems materialism, and denies the consequences of behavior. "Good" and "bad" are increasingly interchangeable, and with the proliferation of cable television, graphic sex and profane language are not uncommon.

Presbyterians have never seriously considered how thoroughly and fundamentally the messages television institutions produce challenge the confessions, doctrines, and beliefs of the church. Nor have they evaluated the extent to which people who grow up in a television culture and who are continually exposed to television's messages may have chosen television's values over church values. The inability of the church to hold even the children of its own members, much less attract new members, suggests there may be some correlation between television viewing habits and Christian beliefs.

As the twentieth century draws to a close, Presbyterians join other mainline denominations in considering, sometimes quite anxiously, the future. One certainty on that oftentimes uncertain horizon is the presence of television. The extent to which Presbyterians understand both the challenges and the opportunities which that medium presents may in large measure determine the church's ability to carry out its historic mandate of producing and distributing messages.

8

A Presbyterian Dilemma: Ecclesiastical and Social Racial Policy in the Twentieth-Century Presbyterian Communion

Joel L. Alvis, Jr.

The relationship between and among various races in the United States in the twentieth century has been tortured, confrontational, and divisive. Presbyterians of all races have participated in the conflagration. It would be worthwhile to examine the relationships of various racial groups within and without the Presbyterian Church. But the relationship of Black and white Presbyterians (and Americans) will be specifically examined here because: (a) it influenced (though was not exclusively responsible for) divisions within the Presbyterian Church prior to, during, and after the Civil War; (b) it was an important barometer of the development of ecclesiastical ties between the northern and southern Presbyterian churches throughout the twentieth century; and (c) it shows how Presbyterian denominations confronted issues of racism in their structure and moved toward a recognition of ethnic pluralism as an organizing principle.

The relationship of Black and white Presbyterians is similar to that of Black-white relationships in American society and within other Christian denominations. It reflects the American pattern of developing segregated bodies and organizations. Yet there were always groups that protested such policies and practices. Thus, like other Christian churches, Presbyterians struggled with the imperatives of the gospel while determining which policies and practices fostered conformity to God's love and hope for humankind.

What did it mean for Presbyterian denominations to be composed overwhelmingly of white men and women? What did the presence of Black Presbyterians mean to whites? Why were there Black Presbyterians, and what did their existence mean to others both in and out of the church? How did Black and white Presbyterians construct and respond to issues of racial identity as they were confronted with them in the church and the larger society? In order to answer these questions, this essay examines three periods: one from the end of the Civil War to the firm establishment of segregated practices; another from the establishment of segregation through World War II; and finally, the post–World War II period.

The Development of Segregated Practices

The Civil War created new and difficult circumstances in the southern region of the United States. An entire way of structuring life was eliminated with the abolition of slavery, and new structures needed to be developed. The churches of the nation and the South in particular had to respond to this situation. For Presbyterians, the situation was difficult. Almost all white southern Presbyterians had joined together in a church bounded by their ill-fated nation of 1861–1865. Many Blacks remained on the rolls of these churches but most of these quickly left for other opportunities.[1] A small Black remnant remained within the white-controlled Presbyterian Church in the U.S. (PCUS).

The Presbyterian Church in the U.S.A. Old School and New School General Assemblies sought to respond to the new situation. Both denominations established committees for this purpose. However, the Old School committee and its chair, S. C. Logan, were much more vigorous in their efforts, and he became chair of the Board of Missions for Freedmen that was based in Pittsburgh after 1870. At the same time, the PCUS concluded that a separate church for Blacks was the solution. They lacked the resolve, however, to carry the process through until they could be satisfied that Blacks could effectively operate as Presbyterians. Their paternalistic and racist concerns actually came to prohibit the realization of their goal.[2]

Northern and southern Presbyterians did have significant interchange concerning the evangelization of freedmen. A sharp exchange occurred in 1868–1869 between Logan and John Leighton Wilson, the executive secretary of the PCUS's Committee on Sustentation. Wilson asserted that it was the PCUS's exclusive right to deal with freedmen and organize them into a church. According to Wilson, the northern churches' role was to cooperate with the plans developed by southerners.[3]

No cooperative efforts in this field resulted from such interchange. This should not be surprising, for the atmosphere was so highly charged in the wake of sectional tensions that the exchange of fraternal delegates to the various General Assemblies did not occur until the 1880s. Even then there were grave suspicions and doubts about the others' integrity and patriotism.[4]

A second attempt to coordinate work among and for Black Presbyterians did not occur until the 1890s. In 1891, the PCUS General Assembly organized an Executive Committee on Colored Evangelization. A. L. Philips was its secretary, and his office was based in Birmingham. Under the impetus of this PCUS committee, plans were made to hold a conference for personnel of the Board of Missions for Freedmen and the Executive Committee on Colored Evangelization. The meeting was put off in 1893, but a gathering was held in January 1894 in Birmingham. A plan for joint work was proposed, but it satisfied no one.[5] Evidence of acrimony and competition reappeared in the work. Thereafter there was little possibility of cooperation, with the exception that both agencies supported the work of John Little in Louisville, Kentucky, in 1908–1909.[6]

This early period corresponded with the development

and application of a whole range of administrative practices for the Protestant churches. "Efficiency" became the
catchword of the day, though it remained undefined. The
result was to try to target specific groups and causes that
needed the churches' attention and to respond by making
them causes for the churches. These causes began to be
identified with "the" work of the church.[7] This can be seen
in the establishment of the Board of Missions for Freedmen in Pittsburgh and the later Executive Committee on
Colored Evangelization in Birmingham. When the Pittsburgh board's location was questioned and the suggestion
was made that New York might be a more suitable location, the board balked and claimed such a move "would
work great injury" to its efforts.[8]

Women became active in behalf of the Board of Missions for Freedmen during this time. The Women's Executive Committee for Home Missions, one of several
women's organizations at the time, organized a Department of Work for Freedmen in 1885. This followed two
years of interest and effort on behalf of women to participate in the work of the church through this board.[9] Women
in the PCUS were not organized and did not become involved in comparable work until the twentieth century.

Women participated in this work largely through raising
funds for the support of schools. To do this, each synodical
and presbyterial had a secretary for freedmen. She advocated the board's cause among the various organizations.
The relationship between the board and the women's organizations was primarily cordial. However, at times it became tense, for there was little control by women of the
distribution of funds raised by their organizations.[10]

Black Presbyterians also organized themselves during this
time. The Black church courts were, of course, interested in
the work of the Board of Missions for Freedmen, because
much of their synod, presbytery, and particular church support came from the board. But they were not limited to that
board's work. African missions, Sabbath schools, and temperance efforts were all causes that various predominantly
Black church courts advocated in the latter nineteenth cen-

tury. A periodical, *The Africo-American Presbyterian,* was started, and all Black Presbyterians were encouraged to subscribe. They even adopted and urged the use of the General Assembly's programs of systematic beneficence. These programs aimed at producing an efficient income for the denomination.[11]

The purpose of the Board of Missions for Freedmen and the predominantly Black church courts was to produce Presbyterians. But the test of success for the board and many other Presbyterians was how much like white Presbyterians the Black Presbyterians looked and sounded. This was particularly true in worship, because music that had once been tolerated within the confines of slavery was deemed inappropriate for "decent and orderly" worship. It should not surprise anyone that in recent years Black Presbyterians have responded forcefully to this tradition of repression.[12]

A massive missionary effort established the Black Presbyterian church courts and their constituent churches. They covered the states of North and South Carolina, Georgia, and Florida by 1871. This represented a significant investment of church resources and energy. Because of the economic uncertainty in much of the South, the costs of the work could not be supported by the newly emancipated people who were also the object of the work. But as the effort became better established, there was an increasing emphasis that the Black Presbyterian churches become self-sustaining. Consequently, the Board of Missions for Freedmen and later the Executive Committee on Colored Evangelization began to uphold self-support as the model for which Black churches should strive.[13]

There was an immediate and pressing need for educated ministers. Originally, the missionaries of the Old School and New School agencies were white, but they quickly recruited Black leadership. White males filled the positions of ministers, and white women and men served as teachers. Black men with promise for the ministry often served as catechists who assisted the minsters in visitation and helped teach in the Sabbath schools. In a number of places, this work was dangerous for whites and Blacks. Often, to ensure the safety of the catechists, the white minister supervisors had to travel with them.[14]

The Presbyterian Church in the U.S.A. (PCUSA) Assembly's philosophy of linking church schools and congregational organizational development grew into a system for meeting the needs of an educated clergy.[15] The system started with the establishment of both "parochial" (or day) schools and boarding schools. These provided a complete program of education that allowed individuals to acquire all of their formal education through the denominational schools. At one time, there were over 157 Presbyterian institutions for Black education sponsored by the PCUSA. Over time, the ability of the denomination to support all of these institutions was tested by changing social and economic conditions. The first to disappear were the primary schools, as more states implemented segregated primary schools and as the economic uncertainties of the 1930s strained denominational resources. Secondary boarding schools lasted for a longer period but were gradually phased out, so that by 1970 only four institutions, three colleges, and one secondary school remained. Another college, Johnson C. Smith, had attained independent status.[16]

The church agencies and General Assemblies looked to the institutions of higher learning to produce the Black ministers that were needed. The PCUSA Assembly's most significant effort was the establishment of Biddle Institute in Charlotte, North Carolina, in 1867. A theological department was added in the 1880s. But the administration of Biddle, which is now known as Johnson C. Smith University, had numerous difficulties with the Board of Missions for Freedmen over a variety of issues. In 1891, Daniel J. Sanders was selected to be the first Black president in spite of local opposition and the resignation of three of the white faculty members.[17]

The PCUS was not as systematic or sympathetic in its educational efforts, but it did sanction the establishment of the Tuscaloosa Institute for Training Colored Preachers in 1876. This institution developed out of the interest of

Charles Stillman, pastor of the Presbyterian Church in Tuscaloosa, Alabama. The support of the Institute by the denomination was minimal, though it was only through the education of Black ministers that the PCUS's plan to establish a separate Black church could be fulfilled. When Stillman resigned as superintendent of the Institute in 1893, there were twenty-four Black ministers in the PCUS. Nineteen of these had been educated in Tuscaloosa. After Stillman resigned, his name was attached to the Institute, and it eventually became Stillman College.[18]

At the turn of the century, industrial education as the means for Black development gained many adherents, as Booker T. Washington modeled his approach at the Tuskegee Institute in Alabama. Both the northern and southern churches incorporated such programs into their educational institutions, though not without some resistance. But throughout it all, there was still the rhetoric that these institutions would also provide an educated clergy.[19]

What was the Presbyterian communion trying to do and say as it provided educational and church opportunities for Blacks? The message is mixed and confused, reflecting the mixture and confusion of white Presbyterians during that time. David Reimers has identified the southern white churches' reaction to emancipation as one of providing segregated structures.[20] That is clearly what occurred in the Cumberland Presbyterian Church, and there was significant sentiment in that regard in the PCUS. Segregation occurred in the PCUS, but not as it did in other southern denominations; and in the PCUSA, Black courts were not given secondary status in church polity. However, the Cumberland experience did have a bearing on the PCUSA in the 1906 merger.

The Cumberland Presbyterian Church confronted the reality of Black Presbyterians in a manner similar to that of the larger Protestant denominations in the South during Reconstruction. A temporary plan of segregation was adopted in 1869 by the Cumberland General Assembly after feeble encouragements for missionary work among the freedmen.[21] This temporary arrangement was made permanent in 1874 by the white General Assembly. The separation was not accompanied with financial support for the "Colored Cumberland Presbyterian Church" (which later was known as the Second Cumberland Church), nor was it started with a well-organized system of church courts. Consequently, it lost many of its members, and a completely segregated denomination was established.[22]

This segregated pattern was important in the merger negotiations with the PCUSA in the early 1900s. The Cumberland Presbyterians wanted to have racial separation in the South, where they had significant numbers of members. The PCUSA members in the same region were from the Black presbyteries and synods that had developed since the Reconstruction period. Reimers suggests that creating segregated church courts was a small price to pay for the enlargement of the denominational standard. But at another level, this accommodation was part of a larger cultural pattern whereby white northerners in general were accepting segregated patterns of life and law that southerners had developed.[23]

There was opposition to the Plan of Union among Black Presbyterians because of the segregated church government provisions. Francis Grimké, a Black PCUSA pastor in Washington, D.C., opposed the proposal because he thought it allowed the PCUSA Presbyterians to capitulate to an increasing tide of racial hatred that was prevalent in the nation. He argued that the church had standards other than expediency.[24] Though racial separation did have a place in the arguments for this Plan of Union, doctrinal debate was a more significant barrier to overcome.[25]

As previously indicated, whites in the PCUS were uncertain as to how to respond to the reality of emancipation. Soon, however, they adopted the idea that eventually Black Presbyterians should be gathered into a separate and segregated church. To this end, they provided small sustentation to Black ministers and congregations and encouraged the support of the Institute at Tuscaloosa. Only grudgingly did the PCUS General Assembly permit Black elders to be elected and serve in these churches.[26] This policy was hardly one to foster the growth of congregations that would eventually develop into a separate and healthy denomination.

The policy continued to stay in place through the 1890s, when an executive committee was organized to form the Afro-American Presbyterian Church. The Reverend Oscar B. Wilson, an agent of the Executive Committee, attended the organizing meeting in January 1899 in Chester, South Carolina. Yet even at that time and place, confusion remained. "I took the most charitable view possible," Wilson recorded, "but failed to see [the new church's] *raison d'être*—as a separate body."[27] Some Black Presbyterians also objected. Many of the ministers educated at Stillman Institute objected to the Afro-American Church. Two presbyteries, Ethel and Central Alabama, were permitted to remain attached to the PCUS General Assembly. Thus, the viability of the new denomination was called into question from the very beginning.[28]

The Afro-American Presbyterian Church was judged a failure by 1915, when the General Assembly incorporated three segregated presbyteries into a segregated synod. The new synod was named for James G. Snedecor, executive secretary for colored evangelization from 1903 to 1910. This policy committed the PCUS to maintaining a Black constituency within the limits of Presbyterian polity. But at no point was a serious effort made to determine the opinion of Black Presbyterians in the various churches and presbyteries. This was no doubt a significant reason for the ecclesiastical failure.[29]

From Segregation to World War II

Segregation of the races within Presbyterian polity was finally and firmly established in both the PCUSA and PCUS Assemblies by 1915. But the Black churches, presbyteries, and synods continued to participate in the life of the Presbyterian communion. Their existence was a witness to the abuse and inequity of power present in the human condition. During this period, Black and white

Presbyterians struggled with the meaning of being Presbyterian in the midst of denominational turmoil engendered by cultural biases. At the same time, the ecumenical movement further complicated the situation, for its emphasis on brotherhood came to occupy an important place in Presbyterian Christian identity.

Black Presbyterians continued to participate in the programs of the church as they had in the post-Reconstruction period. The largest segregated Black synod in the PCUSA, the Catawba Synod, recorded its pleasure with prohibition, as did many other Presbyterians, but regretted the lack of uniform acceptance and compliance in society at large. Alcohol presented a special problem to the young, and the synod resolved that this threat should be attacked and not ignored or dismissed.[30]

Debate was also present in Black Presbyterian life as to the best means to carry out denominational policies. The *Africo-American Presbyterian* supported the use of quotas in developing stewardship and benevolence programs. The editor encouraged Black churches to subscribe their quotas so that denominational programs in the 1920s could be funded. This editorial wisdom was not universally accepted. A North Carolina reader argued that Black churches should keep the money they raised and use it to become self-supporting rather than have to depend on the church agencies to support their ministers.[31]

From the 1870s, the *Africo-American Presbyterian* helped Black Presbyterians stay abreast of ecclesiastical developments of consequence and helped provide a Black voice within the Presbyterian communion. It was endorsed by several of the Black courts in the PCUSA. Though it was not an official paper, it did offer a view of issues significant to numerous Black Presbyterians. Though Black Presbyterians had long supported the cause of missions in Africa, a Black missionary was not appointed until the 1920s. The editor took note of this discrepancy and urged that this injustice be corrected.[32]

The paper also carried numerous pieces about racial violence and injustice. One incident given extensive coverage in April 1925 was racial friction in Hampton, Virginia. Statistics compiled by Tuskegee Institute on lynchings were also carried, and the editorial page voiced strong condemnations of such violence. The PCUSA General Assembly did support some antilynching legislation in 1923. But white Presbyterian concern at the time was of much less intensity, because the threat of violence against them was much less of a reality than that against Blacks, Presbyterian or not.[33]

Voting rights were denied to the overwhelming majority of Black southerners prior to the landmark legislation of the 1960s. But the *Africo-American Presbyterian* supported the exercise of the franchise by Blacks wherever it could be obtained. "The man who cannot express his convictions at the ballot," wrote the editor, "is not a free man."[34] It may be concluded that this stance was not supported by either General Assembly because of their silence on the subject.

These issues put the Black constituency of the church at odds to greater or lesser degrees with the power structure of the denominations at the time. This was a period of tremendous theological ferment for Presbyterians, embroiled in the modernist-fundamentalist controversy of the 1920s.[35] Black Presbyterians, at least that portion represented in editorial opinions of the newspaper, tended to affirm a conservative theological stance. An *Africo-American Presbyterian* headline in May 1925 announced: "Colored Presbyterians Loyal to the Standards of the Church." This statement went on to affirm support of "the standard of the church," that is, "in the infallibility of the Bible, in the deity of Christ, and in the doctrine of salvation through faith."[36] This is a significant affirmation, when placed in the context of that issue of the paper where the news of the General Assembly debate on modernism and fundamentalism was given much coverage.

The theological stance of Black Presbyterians may also be gauged by the presence of material in newspapers. One series of articles was written by faculty members at the fundamentalist Moody Bible Institute in Chicago.[37] It is reasonable to assume that conservative theology did play a role in Black Presbyterian life in the 1920s.

Black Presbyterians in this period were very knowledgeable of the arguments of the Presbyterian tradition. The editor again displayed this when he wrote in favor of a Supreme Court decision that held an Oregon compulsory education law unconstitutional. This decision was "a great victory for Christian education and an inestimable blessing to the country."[38] Requiring public education would be one way to disallow private religious education. Because the work of the PCUSA placed great emphasis on the use of private schools, a compulsory public education law would have been a threat to this system. In addition, the racial climate of southern segregated society in this period did not favor providing adequate public instructional opportunities for Black children, regardless of religion.

The post–Civil War concern for an efficient working of church organizations escalated in the twentieth century. This resulted in elimination of special cause committees and the consolidation of church structures to execute the work of the church. The PCUS Assembly reorganized itself in 1910 and 1947 in the name of efficiency, thereby reducing the number of independent organizations attached to various church courts.[39] In both cases, denominational work with Black Presbyterians was affected by the elimination of autonomous entities with separate personnel and budgets.

The PCUSA Assembly's major reorganization of the period was finalized in 1923 after several years of planning. In this action, the work of the Pittsburgh-based Board of Missions for Freedmen was incorporated into the Board of National Missions. There was heavy opposition to this new arrangement from the Pittsburgh board. A debate centered on whether or not it was more efficient to have the work separated with a single object or to relate it to other projects with the same general goal and similar methods but without the specificity of a cause. Advocates of keeping the work separate in Pittsburgh noted that two-thirds of the funds for freedmen's work was raised in western Pennsylvania. Moreover, the board staff and members knew all the details of the work. This would be lost with a larger, noncause-specific board. In the end, these arguments did not carry the necessary weight, and the reorganizational plan adopted by the General Assembly made the work a unit of the larger board.[40]

Not all Black Presbyterians lived in the southern region of the country. Since the colonial period, there were some Black congregations in northern cities. After the Civil War, they remained free from the work of the Board of Missions for Freedmen because its work was confined to the newly emancipated. No organization existed for northern Black Presbyterians until the Afro-American Presbyterian Council was formed in 1894 at the First African Presbyterian Church of Philadelphia. It functioned as a fellowship group and later changed its name to the Council of the North and West. The council was very active in opposing the union of the northern and southern churches in the 1950s because the plan continued racially segregated presbyteries. At the same time, Black and white Presbyterians were heeding the call for "nonsegregation." This led to the integration of the council, with the hope that such a move would further integrate the church.[41]

Leaders of the Afro-American Council, as well as leaders in southern presbyteries and synods, were often educated in institutions founded and supported by the PCUSA. The northern church's success was in large measure due to its development and retention of leaders. In contrast, the ability to retain such leadership was a noticeable failure of the PCUS. Indeed, much Black leadership in the PCUS came from the educational institutions of the PCUSA. Catawba Synod isolated the distinction between these two denominations as being the willingness to invest resources in Blacks without the intent of separating them into their own denomination.[42]

White women's organizations gave substantial support to the educational effort in the twentieth century, as they had in the previous century. They continued their auxiliary organization to the Board of Missions for Freedmen and worked through the synodicals and presbyterials. But just as the support of the board was confined largely to Pittsburgh and the western Pennsylvania area, so too was women's support of the work. Their support at this time was not without its cultural biases. A discussion on the Black race was held and summarized in this cryptic but revealing way: "The idea was expressed by several ladies that it was very unfair to judge the whole race by the few that came north for excitement or other reasons."[43]

This racist mind-set alongside some support work for Blacks was not unique to northern women. White women in the PCUS became involved in supporting the limited programs for Blacks in the Presbyterian Church in the early years of the twentieth century. But PCUS women did not have a denominationwide organization until 1912, and the major support by southern presbyterials and synodicals for Black organizations came after this. The Woman's Auxiliary, as it was originally known, supported Stillman Institute monetarily, as did the women's organizations for the northern board. But the PCUS women's groups also organized a series of conferences for Black women at the synodical and Assembly level. Beyond this, the Auxiliary prodded the PCUS to an interracial awareness. Hallie Paxson Winnsborough, the main force behind the organization of the Auxiliary, was active in a number of organizations for interracial justice such as the Committee for Interracial Cooperation (CIC) and the Association of Southern Women for the Prevention of Lynching (ASWPL). Not all southern Presbyterian women approved of Winnsborough's role in such organizations or the advocacy of interracial programs for Presbyterians. Even those who disagreed thought there was some obligation of whites to help improve or better the lives of Blacks.[44] Thus, southern Presbyterian women struggled through their encounter with the racism of their own culture.

These activities came during the dawning of the modern ecumenical movement, when "brotherhood" was a concept gaining currency among many in the Protestant establishment. The churches seemed unable to move beyond

words and rather superficial expressions such as the establishment of Race Relations Sunday by the Federal Council
of Churches. This day was designed to promote interracial
worship and fellowship, but it rarely got beyond a handful
of pulpit exchanges in a very few northern towns. Nevertheless, enough of a consciousness had been developed by
the time of World War II that racial attitudes came in for a
complete reexamination by most Protestant churches.[45]

The Presbyterian communion certainly experienced this
phenomenon, for there were numerous statements made
concerning racial toleration and hatred in all of the Presbyterian denominations during and immediately after World
War II. In 1946, the Federal Council of Churches adopted
a statement calling for the denunciation of racial segregation in theory and practice by all its churches. This was an
impetus for the PCUSA to adopt a similar statement, and
it stirred debate in the PCUS.[46] Yet despite the call for
"nonsegregation" in the churches, dismantling the segregated church courts was not immediate.

Post–World War II

There were Black Presbyterians in both the PCUSA and
PCUS who were outside the pale of segregated church
courts. They were located for the most part in urban areas,
and their churches were members of the local presbytery.
These church members accounted for 12,000 of the 40,000
Black communicants of the Presbyterian Church in the
1950s. The remaining ones were stuck in the segregated
patterns associated with the South.[47] The geographic predominance of Black Presbyterians in the PCUSA and
PCUS meant that the segregated system had to be confronted not only by social pronouncement but with polity
adjustments as well. This geographic distribution continued throughout the postwar period as the Presbyterian
Panel found Black pastors concentrated in the synods of
the Piedmont and the South in 1973.[48]

Calls were issued in 1950 in both the PCUSA and PCUS
for the abolition of segregated church courts. Catawba

Synod issued a position paper in the PCUSA in which it charged that the thrust of the denominational program had been paternalistic. This pattern had begun immediately after the Civil War, when a separate agency was established for doing church work with Black Presbyterians. The continuance of this pattern said that Blacks were different from white Presbyterians, even when they were doing the same thing, such as applying for a grant to build a new church. To remove this paternalism, the synod called for the elimination of segregated synods and presbyteries.[49]

In the PCUS, the proposal to abolish segregated church courts was issued by Walter Lingle in the *Christian Observer*. His proposal was to eradicate the practice of segregation as official policy for organizing church courts. Segregationists opposed this move, but the more serious critiques came from whites concerned that if the system was totally eliminated at one time, the few Black Presbyterians that there were in the denomination would simply disappear.[50] Even when segregation was acknowledged as wrong, southern Presbyterians held on to past patterns, hoping that gradual means would rid the denomination of its paternalistic legacy.

The PCUSA started to dismantle segregated church courts by merging Black and white synods in 1957 and 1958. Presbyteries could still cover the same area, depending on racial factors. In 1964, the General Assembly acted to eliminate this discrepancy and placed a plan in motion for this purpose.[51] When the PCUS abolished its one segregated synod, the segregated presbyteries were attached to other synods with similar but not exact boundaries. This system stayed intact until 1964, when the General Assembly ordered that the segregated presbyteries be abolished and those churches assimilated into the presbyteries within which they were located. The plan was not without controversy, but the order was eventually completed in 1968.[52]

The PCUS had also integrated its presbyteries by developing Black churches in predominantly white presbyteries. This was done systematically beginning in 1946 with the Negro Work Program. At the time, there were approximately 3,000 Black Presbyterians in the PCUS, but by 1970 there were over 7,000 Black Presbyterians. Many of these were added through the organizational efforts that involved whites and Blacks in laying the groundwork and finding the resources for new church development. These churches were often located in new subdivisions and often near schools or colleges. Outside of the deep South, the churches became members of the local presbytery. This integration was not congregational, but it afforded an opportunity for some meaningful interracial interchange within the denomination.[53]

What became of desegregated structures and new Black churches? One critic has argued that Black Presbyterians were in worse condition in the early 1970s than they had been previously. In 1946, the PCUS had thirty-four Black clergy, but in 1971 there were only twenty-seven. In the UPCUSA, the number of Blacks fell drastically in the late 1960s and early 1970s. Gayraud Wilmore has provided a more extensive treatment of the recent predicament of Black Presbyterians in his book *Black and Presbyterian.* His work addresses the identity and meaningful role that Blacks can have in a predominantly white denomination.[54]

The civil rights movement served to remind Presbyterians and all Americans that religious and national ideals were not available equally to all people. A new era was at hand after the 1954 Supreme Court decision *Brown v. Topeka Board of Education,* which declared segregation unconstitutional. The number of church actions related to race did increase after that.[55] The theological assumptions, however, that undergirded the segregated order in church and society had been undermined prior to the 1954 Court case. Much attention was given to a PCUS "Statement to Southern Christians," which was issued less than a month after the *Brown* decision was rendered. The statement was not a spur-of-the-moment action, but one that had been refined over the course of several years and was predicated on a theological base.[56] When theological positions were placed in the context of the times, a volatile combination resulted. The Presbyterian denominations made state-

ments on events of the civil rights movement and worked
through a variety of agencies to address civil rights issues.

Making statements about various issues and events was
a long-standing Presbyterian means of stating and shaping
opinion. Presbyterian church courts began addressing issues of race in the 1920s in a paternalistic manner that was
consistent with their programs and polity. Like most other
Protestant churches, their statements through World War
II lagged behind the real concerns of Blacks as expressed
by Black organizations such as the National Association
for the Advancement of Colored People. After World War
II, there was some reduction in this gap, enough so that
Eugene Carson Blake, the Stated Clerk of the UPCUSA in
the 1960s, could say to Martin Luther King, Jr., at the
Washington March in 1963: "Rather we come late, late we
come." Blake then quoted Abraham Lincoln's dictum,
"Never say God is on our side; rather pray that we may be
found on God's side."[57]

The UPCUSA organized a special committee in 1958 to
find means of implementing the 1946 Federal Council of
Churches' plea to create a truly racially integrated church.
The Committee of Eighteen called for change in the church
first by having the General Assembly disband the segregated synods and presbyteries. Later it called upon the denomination to help prevent blockbusting of neighborhoods
and to affirm the availability of housing to all people regardless of race. "A Covenant on Open Occupancy for
Presbyterians" was implemented in several communities
and met with some success, and it was seen as a model by
various groups.[58]

During the late 1950s and early 1960s, the civil rights
movement emphasized protest against the denial of basic
guarantees of citizenship in the states. White Presbyterians
could often agree in condemning this "un-American" situation, and they found religious themes that resonated in
the language of nonviolence. But as the 1960s unfolded,
the language of Black Power overtook the rhetoric of nonviolence. The emphasis on integration that was appropriate
in the South did not have the same meaning in the North.[59]

Presbyterians continued to be concerned, but the controversy in society took its toll in the church as well. The sociologist Jeffrey Hadden argued that the events of the 1960s relating to civil rights and other issues highlighted a divergence of clergy and laity in Protestant churches. Evidence from the Presbyterian Panel in the late 1970s argued that, as the fervor of civil rights subsided in the 1970s, laity gave a lower priority to the necessity for continued work to establish racial justice.[60]

Black Power was felt in the Presbyterian communion in two specific events: the Black Manifesto and the response of the UPCUSA to Angela Davis. Both the UPCUSA and the PCUS were addressed in the Black Manifesto, which was issued in April 1969 by James Forman of the National Black Economic Development Conference, and both denominations responded in their 1970 General Assemblies. Forman's Black Manifesto was widely publicized in its call for "reparations" from white churches and synagogues because of the guilt of the religious community in supporting racism. Presbyterians rejected this call, but the UPCUSA approved a plan that would aid in the self-development of Blacks and other oppressed groups. Self-development sprang from the Black Manifesto, though the term was not used in the document.[61]

In response to Forman's challenge, the PCUS adopted a paper that rejected its "Marxist ideology," "black racism," and advocacy of "revolution." But at the same time, the General Assembly called Presbyterians not to reject the challenge completely, for "to do this would be to close our ears to an impassioned cry of the neighbor, to ignore the urgency of the present moment, and—quite possibly—to miss an opportunity to hear the word of God." The paper called on Presbyterians to acknowledge that racism was a serious problem in the United States and in the church from which whites had benefited and Blacks had suffered. One responsibility of predominantly white churches was to support financially projects that Blacks wanted, without the assurance that there would be benefits to whites. To this end, the Assembly supported a Black denominational caucus.[62]

The Angela Davis affair in the UPCUSA was prompted when the Council on Church and Race (COCAR) donated $10,000 to the legal defense of Davis at the request of a synod and particular church. Davis was accused of murder, kidnapping, and conspiracy in a 1970 confrontation in Marin County, California. The reaction to this grant was immediate and much of it was negative. The 1971 General Assembly questioned the propriety of the gift, but it was left standing. Yet several years later, to say "Angela Davis" in the Presbyterian Church is to stir up a whole range of emotions.[63]

Important in both of these developments was the organizing of Black Presbyterian leadership into its own caucus. This trend was common in most of the predominantly white Protestant churches in the late 1960s and early 1970s. The caucuses were formed as part of the Black Theology movement that called for greater degrees of Black control over the Black religious experience.[64]

Self-development continues to be the major programmatic response of the Presbyterian Church (U.S.A.). It reflects ideas of Black Power but is not overcome by them. It is far advanced over the early years of the civil rights movement and calls for integration. Physical presence of Blacks in white churches does not properly witness to the integrity of Black Presbyterians. Self-development also moves beyond the attempt of Black Presbyterians simply to get more pieces of the American pie. Self-development, as it was intended to be, transforms persons as they participate more fully in the life of the nation and the world. The challenge for this approach lies in the ability to develop and sustain projects that are able to accomplish this goal. The theme has continued to be incorporated into programs of the Presbyterian Church (U.S.A.) in the Self-Development of People program. But the program is difficult to implement, because it is driven by concerns and ideas that are generated by persons outside of the normal channels of denominational bureaucracy. Presbyterians have difficulty acknowledging that such irregular processes can produce viable results.[65]

Another approach that has not received the systematic adoption of self-development in the Presbyterian Church is that of indigenization. Taking his cue from missionary developments as well as Black Theology, Frank O. duCille, Sr., argues that the problems of Black Presbyterianism can be traced to a lack of African American identity among Black Presbyterians. This is both the result of Presbyterian programs that have founded and fostered Black churches, often in a paternalistic pattern, and of Black Presbyterians who often choose a perceived privilege of being Black and Presbyterian over being Black and Christian in some other tradition. A program of redevelopment is needed that will recognize the appropriateness of including Black traditions in Black Presbyterian churches. Although worshiping the same God and Lord, Black Presbyterians do not have to go about it in the same way as do white Presbyterians.[66] This approach seems to lack the same scope of self-development at the present time, but it is one that calls for more attention at the local level and is more congregationally oriented.

Conclusion

The Presbyterian dilemma was a dilemma of cultural and religious proportions. At the most basic level, it was and is a dilemma of power: Who has power? How does one group make decisions for others? For much of the period from the Civil War to the present, white men have controlled the structures of power in the Presbyterian denominations. Their decisions have been modified on racial policy as well as in other areas by the work of white women. Sometimes the change has been quite significant. Only in the last period have the voices of Black sisters and brothers come to be heard as worthy of inclusion in the meeting halls of decision making. And still the task is not complete.

Throughout the period examined, white Presbyterians never completely surrendered control over activities designed for, or even by, Blacks. The only real exception to

this is found in the Cumberland Presbyterian experience
when, for reasons of social expediency undergirded by racism, Blacks were excluded through the creation of a separate Black denomination. Southern Presbyterians were
trapped by the tensions of their racism. Blacks could not
be given complete control over their own churches, but
whites refused to participate in the creation of an effective
Black denomination. The tension persisted even into the
1950s, when the abolition of Black church judicatories was
questioned for fear that the few Black southern Presbyterians there were would completely disappear. The PCUSA
experience witnessed the establishment of Black churches
but also included segregation after 1906. Most often, Black
leadership was seen only within the work of the institutions and churches created for and by Blacks. The substantive contributions Blacks made to the Presbyterian
denominations have been often without appreciation or
even acknowledgment.

The Presbyterian dilemma with power amid Black and
white race relations always held in tension biblical messages as well as sociological ones. The historical effect was
to create a remnant people cut off from the decision-
making process of their denominations and often isolated
from the "Black Church" as well. Slowly, Black Presbyterians have established links to both of these groups. It is now
evident that the story of race relations between Black and
white Presbyterians in the twentieth century had two effects: (a) it created questions about the ability to make
Presbyterian Christianity and Blackness compatible; and
(b) it increasingly forced white Presbyterians to ask questions about the distribution of power within their denominations and whether they were acting in a manner
consistent with the gospel. What has happened in this
story is not a question limited to one racial ethnic group or
even to one denomination. It is something that should interest all people, for it is the occasion of rethinking the
human and religious experience in our own time, and of
recasting the vision of hope, given our present realities.

9

Identity and Integration: Black Presbyterians and Their Allies in the Twentieth Century

Gayraud S. Wilmore

There is a statement by Vincent Harding that accurately describes the condition in which we Blacks have found ourselves since our introduction to American Christianity in the seventeenth century:

> Indeed, one might say with confidence that whatever its other sources, the ideology of Blackness surely grows out of the deep ambivalence of American Negroes to the Christ we have encountered here. This ambivalence is not new. For we first met the American Christ on slave ships. We heard his name sung in hymns of praise while we died in our thousands, chained in stinking holds beneath the decks. . . . When our women were raped in the cabins they must have noticed the great and holy books on the shelves. Our introduction to this Christ was not propitious.[1]

I would submit that the "deep ambivalence" of which Harding speaks is not as much about Jesus Christ as it is about the white Christian church. My thesis for this essay rests upon this critical modification of Harding's observa-

This essay first appeared in the inaugural volume of The Presbyterian Presence series, *The Presbyterian Predicament* (© 1990 Westminster/John Knox Press).

tion. I have come to the tentative conclusion that since the 1890s, if not earlier, the prevailing attitude among Black members of the Presbyterian Church toward this predominantly white, middle-class denomination has been deep and persistent ambivalence. Throughout the twentieth century Black Presbyterians have oscillated back and forth between a desire for African American cultural identity and a desire for racial integration as an indispensable characteristic of any church that is truly Christian and visibly united.

Ambiguity denotes uncertainty, lacking clarity and definiteness. Ambivalence, on the other hand, denotes double-mindedness and conflict, but not necessarily confusion. Ambivalence frequently tolerates the coexistence of opposite points of view without befuddlement and mystification. Within Black Presbyterianism these two positions—racial and cultural identity and racial integration—while frequently conflictual and contradictory, have actually reinforced each other on the way to liberation and reconciliation within one inclusive and united church. In any case, it appears that a certain ambivalence has been necessary, if most Black members were to remain all these years within the folds of American Presbyterianism.

Of course, Blacks have not held ethnic self-consciousness and total assimilation in tension without the cooperation of sympathetic allies. Over the years, many white Presbyterians, known and unknown, have been associated with us in the struggle. It is necessary, however, to differentiate between friends or associates and allies. Not all white liberals who have been friends have also been allies. Perhaps the major qualification for being considered an ally of the Black movement is to have somehow understood, empathized with, and supported this ambivalence, even when convinced that Black consciousness sometimes impeded what white liberals believed to be best for the struggle against American racism and oppression.

Another conclusion of my study is that not only is it possible to hold identity and integration in a creative tension, but some subtle combination of the two positions is likely to be needed as this church moves into the twenty-first century. As

Presbyterians of the recently reunited church seek to explore the values and benefits of diversity-within-unity, perhaps the historic ambivalence of African Americans will prove to be one of the most important contributions to the denomination's ability to survive the twentieth century and demonstrate in the twenty-first what true pluralism looks like and is able to achieve in a truly united church.

Black Presbyterians Organize
for Racial Identity and Elevation

On September 27, 1894, a small group of Black Presbyterian clergy and laity gathered at the First African Presbyterian Church of Philadelphia to form the Afro-American Presbyterian Council (AAPC).[2] This was not the first time Black Presbyterians had caucused, for as early as 1857 their clergy had regular meetings with Black Congregational clergy to address matters of common concern.[3] Read in terms of the militant nationalism of Black Presbyterians United (BPU) in the 1960s, the statements of the Afro-American Presbyterian Council in 1894 sound strangely benign. In 1934, on the occasion of the fortieth anniversary of the Afro-American Presbyterian Council, John W. Lee, D.D., at that time pastor of the First African Presbyterian Church of Philadelphia, spelled out the reason for this second Black caucus.[4]

> The purpose for which the Council was organized was the mutual fellowship of the ministers and the churches of our group along religious, moral and social lines, who, by reason of our relation to white Presbyteries in the North, were deprived of those helpful privileges which our group enjoyed in the Southern section of the country through their own Presbyteries and Synods, where they constitute the entire body.[5]

A major concern of the council was the lack of influence in the judicatories of the North and West compared with the power Blacks exercised in the four segregated synods of the South. What the northerners yearned for was the power to participate in the church on an equal footing with whites. It does not appear, however, that political considerations predominated in the decision to form a Black caucus in 1894. In keeping with the mood of the era of Booker T. Washington, the primary purpose of the AAPC seems to have been the cultivation of Afro-American unity and racial advancement. It was assumed that both required a certain freedom from white control. The overarching concern of most Blacks in both major divisions of Presbyterianism was to elevate themselves through racial self-help, solidarity, and identity. This is not to suggest that all of the organizers of the council were followers of Booker T. Washington. Actually, the early AAPC was staunchly opposed to Washington's position of racial accommodation, but there was no impulse to become a political pressure group for racial integration either. Basically conservative in their theology and genteel in their methods of pursuing individual and collective goals, these elite Black Calvinists of the early twentieth century sought to prove their worth to both friends and detractors by their demonstrable intelligence, middle-class life-style, and moralistic values.

It is no accident that the idea for creating a national American Negro Academy (ANA), an organization for intellectual and cultural elevation, was conceived the year before the AAPC was founded. The principal architects of this famous academy were two distinguished clergymen, Francis J. Grimké, pastor of the Fifteenth Street Presbyterian Church in Washington, D.C., and Alexander Crummell, rector of St. Luke's Episcopal Church in Washington and perhaps the most celebrated Black churchman in the nation at the time.[6] The interests of the two movements— the ANA and the AAPC—parallel each other across the turn of the century and show many similarities. Much of the elitism of the ANA is reflected in some of the papers and addresses of the annual meetings of the AAPC, of which Grimké served as the second president.[7] It is significant that among the early members of the academy were no less than four highly esteemed and influential Black Presbyterian clergymen: John B. Reeves, pastor of the

Central Presbyterian Church of Philadelphia and former head of the theological department of Howard University; Daniel J. Sanders, the first Black president of Biddle Institute (later to become Johnson C. Smith University); Matthew Anderson, pastor of Berean Presbyterian Church in Philadelphia; and Francis J. Grimké, pastor of the Fifteenth Street Presbyterian Church in Washington, D.C.[8] More than any of the others, Grimké and Anderson, who were towering figures in both the ANA and the AAPC, illustrate the complex relationship among members of the AAPC between middle-class proprieties and Black religion, voluntary segregation and pressure politics, ethnic identity and the desire for integration.

Grimké was the most influential in the early days of the caucus. The son of a Black slave woman and a white planter of South Carolina, educated at Lincoln University, in Pennsylvania, and at Princeton Theological Seminary, a distinguished preacher and lecturer, he fought bitterly against the proposed union with the southern church in 1888 and against union with the Cumberland Presbyterian Church in 1905.[9] At the same time he expressed serious doubts about the commitment of white Presbyterians in the North to racial equality.[10] Although he was a member of the anti-Bookerite faction of the Black clergy, Grimké was by no means a radical Black nationalist. Indeed, according to the testimony of a contemporary who knew him well, he kept a certain distance and aloofness from the caucus he had helped to bring into existence.[11] Like W. E. B. Du Bois, with whom he worked to create the Niagara Movement—the predecessor of the NAACP—Grimké combined pride of race and a deep concern for Black history and culture with a fierce moral integrity and sense of fair play. Throughout his life he refused to compromise with segregation. But like Du Bois, and unlike his fellow Presbyterian Matthew Anderson, Grimké seems to have lacked the common touch that would enable him to associate with ordinary folk. Such identity with the Black lower class might mean, and often did mean, postponing justice due from whites for the sake of operational unity among Blacks.

Regional and Denominational Differences
Between Black Presbyterians

For most of the first half of the twentieth century, Black Presbyterians in the North and South were out of touch with each other. They had, to some extent, different perspectives on an appropriate posture for African Americans in the two major Presbyterian bodies. In North and South Carolina and Georgia men like Daniel J. Sanders; Albert M. McCoy, successor to John M. Gaston, secretary of the Unit of Work for Colored People of the Board of National Missions of the Presbyterian Church U.S.A. (PCUSA, referred to here as the northern church); William L. Metz, a highly respected pastor on Edisto Island; Henry L. Mc-Crorey, dean of Johnson C. Smith Seminary; A. H. Prince and Frank C. Shirley, field representatives for Atlantic and Catawba synods, were forced by the circumstances under which they labored to make necessary adjustments to the restrictive policies of the South.[12] Although they were ministers of the northern church, these men accepted the "separate but equal" dictum of *Plessy v. Ferguson* as applicable to the church as well as to the society.

Moreover, at the end of the nineteenth century, it was the intention of the Presbyterian Church U.S. (PCUS, referred to here as the southern church) to actually separate the races into two denominations. Between 1898 and 1916 an independent Afro-American Presbyterian Church was created by the southern church. It was only brought back into that denomination as the Snedecor Memorial Synod when it proved too weak to make it on its own.[13] Until the 1950s, the segregated PCUS Synod of Snedecor and the equally segregated PCUSA synods of Catawba, Atlantic, Canadian, and Blue Ridge represented Black Presbyterian power in the South, unrivaled by anything comparable in the northern-based Afro-American Presbyterian Council or its successor caucuses. It is true, nevertheless, that the ecclesiastical power that the Black judicatories enjoyed at the General Assembly level did not protect them or their congregations from the onerous paternalism that both

white Presbyterian churches carried over into the twentieth century from their missionary activity among the freed
people during the Reconstruction.

Bryant George, formerly of the mission strategy staff of
the UPCUSA Board of National Missions and an astute
observer of the power alignments of the church in the
Southeast, tells how Dr. John M. Gaston, who joined the
Board of Missions for Freedmen in 1910 and for nearly
three decades directed the northern church's work with
Blacks, maintained a private residence on the campus of
Johnson C. Smith University. Gaston kept a close eye and
tight rein on the Black churches by commuting back and
forth between Charlotte and Pittsburgh, where the purse
strings of the mission programs were held. Gaston was
from the old school and enjoyed all the deferences and
privileges of a plantation manager before the Unit for Colored Work was finally dissolved in 1938.[14] It is not difficult
to imagine why Black Presbyterians in the North wanted at
all costs to avoid the tender mercies of the freedmen's
board. Thomas J. B. Harris, for many years the executive
of the AAPC, has said that one of the primary reasons for
the foundation of the council was to prevent Black
churches in the North from being patronized by the national boards and agencies.[15] In an address before the
128th General Assembly, meeting in Atlantic City in 1916,
Matthew Anderson spoke for the entire AAPC when he
said:

> I express the unanimous sentiments of the ministry and the
> intelligent laity of the colored Presbyterians in the north
> when I say that we do not want any special ecclesiastical
> legislation for our churches, nor special Boards for their su-
> pervision and direction; we must stand precisely where the
> white churches stand, having the same rights and privileges,
> absolutely the same status, if we would be Presbyterians. For
> this reason, therefore, we are not willing to be placed arbi-
> trarily under the Freedmen's Board or any other Board got-
> ten up specially to manage colored work.[16]

Throughout this period the relationship was strained between Blacks in the North and those in the four segregated

synods of the South, not to mention between both of those groups and Blacks in the Presbyterian Church U.S. and the Second Cumberland Presbyterian Church. Class and perhaps even color differences were exacerbated by this lack of communication and by the disinclination of the northern clergy to be drawn into the orbit of the Board of Missions for Freedmen. It was not until after the consolidation of several agencies of the Presbyterian Church U.S.A. into the Board of National Missions in 1923, bringing work with Blacks in both regions into one Division of Missions for Colored People, that the feeling of estrangement began to dissipate.

During the next decade, the council, with its name changed to the Afro-American Presbyterian Council of the North and West, with four regional directors to "supervise, encourage, develop and extend the interest of the Churches in their areas," received fraternal delegates from the four Black synods at its annual meetings and attempted to present a united Afro-American front to the denomination.[17] Already by 1934 it was meeting regularly with national staff people to advise and coordinate the work with Black congregations. Thus, a subtle change in orientation occurred among Blacks in the northern church between the wars. As the Andersons, Reeveses, and Grimkés of the earlier period passed from the scene, Black Presbyterians began to shift from elitist racial identity emphases. They took a greater interest in church growth and institutional development, pressing the denomination for Black staff and committee appointments. They sought increased funds to help their churches become self-supporting, and they gave more attention to racial integration in all aspects of Presbyterian life and work. With the retirement of Gaston in 1938, the change of the title of the Unit of Work *for* Colored People, to the Unit of Work *with* Colored People, and the appointment of Albert B. McCoy, the first Black to serve as a board executive in the denomination, a new era began. Elitist solidarity and cultural identity concerns became increasingly subordinated to the widely accepted goal of racial integration.

By 1947 the council issued a public statement.

> The Afro-American Presbyterian Council is definitely a movement of interim strategy. The council has never entertained the idea of setting up a segregated group within the Presbyterian church. It has no brief to support a perpetuation of local Negro churches, nor does it desire or intend to become a pressure group within the church. Nevertheless, the council takes the strongest stand against segregation everywhere and in every form. . . . The sum total of the council's aims and objectives is to help the church to become a truly inclusive fellowship.[18]

If Anderson and Grimké typified Black Presbyterian leadership before World War I, Albert B. McCoy and George Lake Imes, the latter a field representative appointed by the Boards of National Missions and Christian Education in 1945 to serve as liaison between themselves and the Council of the North and West, typify the leadership in the interim between the Great Depression and the critical years of the 1950s and 1960s. The decades of the 1940s and 1950s called for the special talents of Black bureaucrats who could fill the vacuum left by the freedmen's board and the white-led Negro work of the newly consolidated Boards of National Missions and Christian Education. What was initially a white paternalism rapidly became a Black paternalism under white supervision. National Missions funds designated as salary supplements continued to be used to hold rebellious ministers and their churches in line with the conservative policies of New York and Philadelphia. This was particularly true in the case of the Synods of Catawba and Atlantic. Some of the younger clergy complained that Dr. McCoy and later Dr. Jesse B. Barber, who assumed the office upon McCoy's death in 1951, were veritable dictators who held the allocations of the mission program in trust for the "Great White Fathers and Brethren" of the northern church. This may be an unfair judgment upon several men and women who were appointed to staff positions between 1938 and 1958, but it is certain that the commission given to a few Blacks to lead others had implicit reservations built in and was never intended to supersede the prerogatives of middle judicatories and a General Assembly that repeatedly rejected the petitions of the AAPC and had neglected the nonwhite constituencies of the denomination during most of the century.

Black Presbyterians in the Era of Desegregation

The Presbyterian Historical Society in Philadelphia has preserved a memorandum sent by Rev. John Dillingham, pastor of the 13th Avenue Presbyterian Church in Newark, New Jersey, to Rev. L. Charles Gray of the Lafayette Church in Jersey City, dated November 19, 1953, that sets the stage for the dissolution of the Afro-American Council of the North and West in 1957. Dillingham spoke for some key Black Presbyterian clergy of the time when he wrote:

> From the time I first joined the Council in 1940 to the present, I have always looked upon it as an unfortunate, though NECESSARY organization. Being a southerner by birth, I have been rather sensitive about conditions that suggest segregation. I have cooperated with the Council, however, because I recognized that we faced certain facts and not just theories. Moreover, I interpreted our role as being that of "working ourselves out of a job." . . . New occasions, however, do teach new duties and time makes ancient good uncouth. The higher judicatories of our Church in the North and West are recognizing Negroes and electing them as Commissioners. In Synods like New Jersey, all ministers and elders in the Synod may attend its annual meeting. Furthermore, Negroes are being recognized in presbyteries not only as members of important Committees, but also as moderators (Detroit, Philadelphia, etc.). One Negro also has served as moderator of the Synod of California and Nevada.[19]

In this memo Dillingham alludes to an important action of the National Council of Churches in 1946, which was adopted and made its own by the General Assembly of the northern church—the famous call for "a non-segregated church in a non-segregated society." This action, more than any other prior to the civil rights movement of the 1960s, impelled the church toward the goal of desegregation.

Dillingham was impressed. "If General Assembly," he writes, "will go so far as to adopt a resolution calling for the dissolution of Negro Synods and Presbyteries as submitted by the Standing Committee on Social Education and Action at the 165th Assembly, then it is high time for us to rethink the place and function of the Council." Dillingham went on to recommend that the council should go further to renounce racial identity.

> To implement this ideal, it might be necessary to change our name again just as it was changed from "Afro-American Presbyterian Council" to "Presbyterian Council in the North and West." The new name should reflect not only a change in emphasis, but also the fact that we are talking about a United Church today.[20]

The Dillingham proposal was never implemented. But in 1957, in the glow of an unprecedented era of good feeling—largely generated by Clifford Earle, Margaret Kuhn, and other white allies in the national program of Social Education and Action of the Board of Christian Education—the council voluntarily voted itself out of existence. Almost everyone was satisfied with this surprising turn of affairs, but some clergy and laity felt that the action was premature and excessively optimistic about the demise of racism in the Presbyterian Church. Leroy Patrick, who at that time pastored Fifth Church in Chester, Pennsylvania, makes the following comment about those heady days:

> We—all of us—were in a state of euphoria, a shameful confession for those to make who had studied under Niebuhr. The Supreme Court had spoken. The Church's pronouncements were unequivocal. Freedom had finally arrived. Segregation's death knell had been sounded. Discrimination was over. Away with our little black organization. We would miss the fun, the fellowship, the camaraderie, but we had to give ourselves to the New Day.[21]

Two of the persons who readily conceded that a grave error had been made were Elo L. Henderson, the founder and pastor of the Grier Heights Church in Charlotte, elected in 1955 as the executive of the Synod of Catawba, and Edler G. Hawkins, a past president of the council and founder and pastor of St. Augustine Presbyterian Church in the Bronx. Henderson in the South and Hawkins in the North represented a new, militant posture for Black Presbyterians so recently beguiled and pacified by the attitudinal-change approach to race relations that came out of the Board of Christian Education prior to Clifford Earle, Margaret Kuhn, and H. Ben Sissel. A third Black leader came to the fore in the southern church, but with a somewhat different orientation. Lawrence W. Bottoms, perhaps the best known Black minister in the Presbyterian Church U.S., joined Alex R. Batchelor as assistant secretary of the Division of Negro Work in 1951. Although the social action wing of the southern Presbyterian church, comparable to Social Education and Action in the northern church, introduced the policy changes of the 1950s, Dr. Bottoms initiated an emphasis on Black new church development that brought the first leap in the membership of Black Presbyterians in the Presbyterian Church U.S. from approximately 3,000 in 1949 to almost 7,000 in 1958.[22] The increasing sensitivity of southern Presbyterians to the demands of the 1950s and 1960s was due in part to this infusion from the Black urban middle class as a result of Bottoms's style of leadership, which was based on his conviction that "brotherhood is deeper than a political issue, it is a moral issue."[23] His position rarely failed to get a respectable hearing in conservative Presbyterian U.S. circles, where the "spirituality of the church" was a major theological tenet. In the meantime, many white clergy and laity in both branches of Presbyterianism had changed during the decade of the 1950s. In the South, the change was massive. Ernest Trice Thompson analyzes what was happening among southern Presbyterians during this period.

> A number of factors led them to reassess their Christian obligation; among them a second world war in which Negroes fought for a country which denied them first-class citizenship, the mood of the returning soldiers, the Fair Employ-

ment Practice Commission (FEPC) of the war years, the drive for civil rights, the stepped-up activity of the NAACP, a series of court decisions admitting Negroes to institutions of higher learning and threatening segregating education in the public schools.[24]

But it was in 1954, just prior to the Supreme Court decision in the Brown case, that the Council of Christian Relations grasped the nettle. The church then affirmed that "enforced segregation of the races is discrimination which is out of harmony with Christian theology and ethics." At the forefront of this development were people like Malcolm Calhoun, John Marion, Aubrey Brown, Rachel Henderlite, and later, George Chauncey of the Division of Christian Relations. Joseph L. Roberts, a Black northern Presbyterian minister who joined the staff of the Board of National Ministries in 1970 to begin the new unit on Corporate and Social Missions, says that by that time "there were thirty to forty Southern Presbyterian allies in pastorates and on the national staffs who could be depended upon to put their bodies where their mouths were on the issue of racial justice."[25]

In 1947, William H. McConaghy, a white minister from Albany, New York, and Jesse B. Barber, from Lincoln University, were selected by the northern church to set up a new Institute on Racial and Cultural Relations, which became the rallying point for white allies.[26] During the 1950s, these friends and allies tended to coalesce around the Department of Social Education and Action of the Board of Christian Education and the program of urban and industrial work of the Board of National Missions. With the election of William A. Morrison and Kenneth G. Neigh as general secretaries of the Boards of Christian Education and National Missions respectively, a new day dawned for race relations in the United Presbyterian Church U.S.A. (UPCUSA). With the cooperation of John Coventry Smith, general secretary of the Commission on Ecumenical Mission and Relations, and Eugene Carson Blake, Stated Clerk of the General Assembly, who had been carefully educated to the realities of Black-white relations by Edler Hawkins and other members of the Black caucus, the three program boards launched the Commission on Religion and Race (CORAR) in 1963. Thus, the UPCUSA became the first national denomination to respond with a Black-led staff and a generous program budget to the civil rights movement of Dr. Martin Luther King, Jr., and must be given major credit for catalyzing the policy decisions and funds that produced the first Commission on Religion and Race in the National Council of Churches earlier that year.[27]

It is important to mention that during this period many Black Presbyterian women came to the forefront of the struggle for equality in the church. One thinks particularly of Emily Gibbes, Gladys Cole, Mildred Artis, Evelyn Gordon, Mildred Davis, Thelma Adair, and Mary Jane Patterson, to mention a few. Of course, from the early days of the Afro-American Presbyterian Council, women played a critical role as presenters of papers and leaders of discussion groups on education, the Black family, and youth activities. At the beginning of this century, most of the female leaders were the wives of ministers, many well-educated and talented in their own right. But by the 1940s and 1950s, other church women began to take their places at the annual meetings of the AAPC, the summer conferences at Lincoln University, near Oxford, Pennsylvania, and the popular "Workers Conferences" that convened each summer at Johnson C. Smith University in Charlotte, North Carolina. It would not be an exaggeration to say that without the leadership of extraordinarily gifted women, the National Black Presbyterian Caucus of today would not exist.

Black Presbyterian Militance
During the Civil Rights Period

The ferment that led to the creation of new caucuses within both Presbyterian churches began in the United Presbyterian Church U.S.A. with the organization of what was called Concerned Presbyterians by Bryant George and

Edler Hawkins in 1963. This new group was not patterned
after the old Council of the North and West. It was un-
abashedly political and played a key role in the campaign
Bryant George managed, which helped to elect Edler G.
Hawkins Moderator of the 176th General Assembly in
1964—the year after the caucus was founded, essentially
for that purpose. Having lost by two votes to Herman
Turner of Atlanta at the Des Moines Assembly in 1963,
Edler Hawkins, with strong interracial lobbying across the
church for a year, was finally elected the first Black Moderator at Oklahoma City the next year.

It is not possible to discuss here the role of the Commission on Religion and Race, which under a new mandate in
1968 became the Council on Church and Race (COCAR)
and the most impressive achievement of Black Presbyterians and their allies in the 1960s. Both Presbyterian
churches established Councils on Church and Race in the
1960s and 1970s; and these programs, staffed by Blacks
and strongly supported by Black and white caucuses outside the official structures, represent the apex of Presbyterian involvement in racial justice issues during the most
difficult years of the civil rights movement. In the northern
church, the ground was prepared for the Commission on
Religion and Race by the Committee of Eighteen of the
Board of Christian Education, which included the always
dignified but irrepressible Edler Hawkins, and the recon-
stitution of the old Council of the North and West as the
Concerned Presbyterians (note the absence of any racial
designation in the name) in 1963.[28]

In the southern church, the Council on Church and Race
was preceded by the strategic appointment to the national
staff in 1970 of Joseph L. Roberts, a Black UPCUSA pastor from New Jersey. It is significant, however, that Roberts's appointment was preceded by the creation of the
Black Presbyterian Leadership Caucus of the PCUS in
1969.[29] In both instances, it is doubtful that anything
would have happened without aggressive Black caucusing,
or without the support of white allies both within and outside the boards and agencies.[30]

The same year that Concerned Presbyterians recaptured the initiative of Blacks for increased visibility and power in the United Presbyterian Church U.S.A., a new interracial caucus was founded that was to become a major source of white support during the 1960s and 1970s. On May 16, 1963, a group of Black and white commissioners and visitors to the Des Moines Assembly came together to form a "mass membership organization" that called itself the Presbyterian Interracial Council (PIC). Its purpose was to recruit individuals for direct action work in the civil rights movement on behalf of the UPCUSA, to "identify with and work directly and openly with Negro and other minority groups in a persistent daring witness to minority communities," and to "give timely attention to immediate local and national issues whenever and wherever trouble breaks out."[31] Headquartered in Chicago under the leadership of Kenneth Waterman, its first executive secretary, PIC had more than a thousand members organized in twelve local chapters by the end of its first year.[32] It was undoubtedly one of the most successful programs in race relations ever launched by Presbyterians. PIC played a critical role in electing Hawkins to the office of Moderator at the 176th General Assembly. Its local chapters educated white Presbyterians on the etiquette of race relations at a time when few had any association with Blacks. Members of PIC chapters worked on fair housing programs, formed voting blocs that helped to get supportive policies adopted by presbyteries and synods, and recruited Presbyterian and other clergy for participation in the CORAR direct action project in Hattiesburg, Mississippi. PIC also cooperated with the Council on Church and Race in various relief efforts during the northern city rebellions between 1964 and 1968.[33]

The Dream of Integration Unfulfilled

A relevant question at this point in our discussion is: Why, at the highest point of United Presbyterian participation in the civil rights movement, which saw CORAR and PIC created in 1963 and Hawkins elected Moderator in 1964, was an unbreakable seal not cemented between Black and white Presbyterians, with the consequence of the truly integrated church that was the goal of the Council of the North and West and the reason for its admittedly premature dissolution in 1957?

The answer is complex. Obviously, the efforts made between 1963 and 1973 were not sufficient to make up for more than two hundred years of segregation and paternalism in both churches. Despite the historic contribution of the northern church to Black education in the South after the Civil War, its post–World War II sponsorship of aggressive community organization, urban ministries, and the civil rights movement, and its integration of several important staff and committee positions in the national church and lower judicatories, Presbyterians continue to be an overwhelmingly white denomination with Blacks greatly underrepresented in proportion to their numbers in American Protestantism. Black Presbyterian congregations are still small and are generally unable to remain integrated where they have evolved from previously white congregations in changing neighborhoods. Although some downtown and suburban churches have received Black members without difficulty, the price of amicable relations has usually required that African Americans divest themselves of any conspicuous cultural Blackness and become quietly assimilated to a white, middle-class milieu. Almost no healthy white congregations have called Black pastors, and the Black masses, on the whole, have not been attracted even to all-Black Presbyterian congregations in the numbers in which they have been drawn since the turn of the century to Baptist, Methodist, Pentecostal, or even Roman Catholic churches.

Another answer to the question about the failure of full-scale integration in the Presbyterian Church has to do with internal contradictions between racial integration and ethnic identity. If the ambivalence of Black Presbyterians toward the white church requires a strong interracial caucus as well as a strong Black caucus, it is certain that we have not yet learned how to manage both at the same time. A study of the activity of the Presbyterian Interracial Council will show that it began to decline as Black Presbyterians United (BPU), the new Black caucus established in the northern church in 1968, became more politically active on the presbytery level and more successful in forcing the church to recognize and appreciate the African American cultural heritage on the national level.[34]

It seems evident that there has been a reciprocal relationship between the failure of the church to become fully integrated and the swing of many Black Presbyterians, disillusioned by that failure, back to cultural identity and Black consciousness in recent years. Similarly on the national scene, the call for Black Power, the founding of the National Committee of Black Churchmen in Dallas in 1967, and a new emphasis on a more Afrocentric culture arose partly from the disappointment of the masses, particularly the youth, with the pace and quality of integration under Dr. King and the liberal coalition he had been able to put together with northern Democrats and the labor movement. But out of what was essentially a negative reaction in the ranks of mass-based organizations and community groups, a positive thrust toward Black pride and cultural nationalism developed in the late 1960s to give impetus to a movement for theological renewal in both Black Protestant circles and Black Roman Catholicism. The National Committee of Black Churchmen, the National Black Evangelical Association, the National Office of Black Catholics, the Society for the Study of Black Religion, and the Black Theology Project of Theology in the Americas were all institutional expressions of the remarkable flowering of African American theological reflection and praxis in the United States between 1964 and 1975.[35]

The Manifesto and Angela Davis Crises

The ability of Black Presbyterians in the northern church to stand together was subjected to its most stringent test less than three years after Black Presbyterians

United was created in the fall of 1968, immediately following the Second Annual Convocation of the militant interdenominational caucus, the National Committee of Black Churchmen, in St. Louis, Missouri. The first test came at the San Antonio General Assembly in 1969, when the caucus urged the church to respond favorably to the Black Manifesto of James Forman and the Black Economic Development Conference, which BPU and NCBC supported. The Manifesto was rejected, but the demands of the caucus for radical change did not go unheeded. The Program for the Self-Development of People was one of the consequences of the confrontation at San Antonio.

The second test involved one of the most controversial and least understood developments in the recent history of American Presbyterianism—the infamous Angela Davis affair.[36] The new alliance between Black Presbyterians and the bureaucracy of the boards and agencies of the national church was shaken to its core by the crisis over the young Communist woman from California, but the coalition held firm despite cries of outrage from the grass roots. With an unprecedented flood of letters and telegrams pouring into local church offices and to harried officials at 475 Riverside Drive in New York City, an incensed laity mounted a well-organized campaign to punish and possibly discharge the Council on Church and Race at the 183rd General Assembly, meeting in Rochester, New York, in May of 1971.

In a memorable address to the Assembly, Edler Hawkins reviewed the details of a grant of $10,000 from the Emergency Fund for Legal Aid that COCAR had made to ensure that Ms. Davis would receive a fair trial. As usual, Hawkins's approach was the soul of moderation, but no one at the Assembly could mistake his gentility for the lack of will to keep the Assembly supportive of the mandate it had given for its racial justice agency to represent the UPCUSA on the cutting edge of the civil rights movement.

> Our hope is that no one confuse the issue in a discussion of Miss Davis' political affiliation. This case was before our Council for help because of a legitimate appeal of a judicatory of the church, a Session of a local church situated in the area

in which Miss Davis is being held, and because our mandate is on the basis of the implications of race, we made the grant because we knew this Black lady needed help in securing an adequate defense *just* because she was Black, and a woman, and because she too, must be treated as "innocent" until proven guilty. . . . That grant for legal aid by which hundreds have been helped, is an investment in . . . the American system of justice, as an act of faith, that the rule of law, and the administration of justice in this land will be laid-on fairly and without discrimination to all Americans, be they Black, or White, Red, Yellow or Brown, or poor.[37]

The Standing Committee on Church and Race of the Rochester Assembly nervously considered the various proposals floating around the church to denounce the grant, discipline COCAR, and exonerate the denomination from the taint of communism. Many agreed with the conservative group, the Presbyterian Lay Committee, Inc., that the Legal Defense funds had been misused in the case of Angela Davis and that, in this and many other instances since its creation in 1963, the Council on Church and Race had far exceeded its mandate.[38] In its final report, the Standing Committee refused to repudiate unequivocally the COCAR action. It did, however, accept from the floor amendments to its cautious recommendation that the General Assembly continue the Emergency Fund for Legal Aid under the administration of COCAR. After one of the stormiest debates in the recent history of Presbyterian General Assemblies, the following motion was approved in connection with the report of the Standing Committee on Church and Race: " . . . that the 183rd General Assembly communicate to COCAR its serious question concerning the propriety of allocating $10,000 to the Marin County Black Defense Fund."

During the weeks following the Rochester Assembly, it became clear that Black Presbyterian leadership across the nation was unified behind Edler Hawkins, the chairman of COCAR, and resented the way the majority of white Presbyterians had cast aspersion upon what Blacks considered to be the good judgment, patriotism, and moral integrity of the COCAR staff. As in the past, a small minority of white Presbyterians at national and regional levels and in the Presbyterian Interracial Council held the line against an onslaught of several thousand communications from people in the local congregations bemoaning the "ill-advised action" of the Council on Church and Race in giving money to "that Black communist bitch," or words of similar effect.

In a much neglected but historic document entitled "Why Angela Davis?" (prepared by the National Race Staff, an interagency secretariat coordinated by COCAR staff), an ideologically and theologically cohesive response was made to its critics. In a section that refers to the support it was receiving from the powerful office of the Stated Clerk of the General Assembly, the statement of the national staff reads in part:

> The Council on Church and Race, by recommendation of the National Race Staff and under the criteria established for the Emergency Legal Aid Fund, made the grant to the defense fund for Angela Davis *because it believed in what the United Presbyterian Church has always professed about justice, liberation and reconciliation.* There is room for honest disagreement with this decision. But as the Stated Clerk of the General Assembly, Mr. William P. Thompson has said, "It's easy for us to provide help for people who conform to our standards. It is a real test of our commitment to the principles involved if we are prepared to help those who don't conform to our standards." The Stated Clerk expressed his willingness to defend the right of members of the church to disapprove of the Council's action, but he also expressed the hope that objectors would continue to support the church. If that counsel goes unheeded by the members of this predominantly white church not only will the United Presbyterian mission suffer untold injury, but perhaps even more important, a rupture will open up in our church between black and white that may be irremediable.[39]

The fear of an irreconcilable breakdown in relations between Black and white Presbyterians was real. During the summer and fall of 1971, chapters of Black Presbyterians

United fought off the criticism of friends and associates in the presbyteries by a critique of their own. BPU criticized what it regarded as the inconstancy of the church on the issue of political dissension exacerbated by the all too familiar prejudice against Black people. The question arose, shortly after the Rochester Assembly, whether BPU should take some dramatic action to communicate to the denomination-at-large its feeling of betrayal by what appeared to be a large-scale abandonment by white Presbyterians of their previously advanced position on racial justice. When the logistics of assembling the caucus in an emergency session seemed unmanageable, Bryant George, Edler Hawkins, and Robert P. Johnson, the executive of the Presbytery of New York City, conceived the idea of returning the $10,000 at a press conference as a way of saying to the church, and particularly to the Black community across the nation, that prominent Black members were willing to do for Angela Davis what a predominantly white General Assembly regarded as an "unfortunate impropriety."

On June 15, 1971, twenty Black Presbyterian clergy and laity, the top leadership of the denomination and of BPU, were called by telephone. Within twenty-four hours each sent a check for $500.00, out of personal funds, to make it possible for the defense fund grant to be repaid to the church, thus rendering the original grant not from a reluctant white church, but from a group of unabashedly supportive and indignant Black Presbyterians. Many felt that this action was the least that could be done to vindicate the honor, independence, and fearlessness of BPU, although some of the official explanations fell short of such implications. In handing over the twenty personal checks to Kenneth G. Neigh, general secretary of the Board of National Missions, Robert Pierre Johnson, spokesperson for the caucus, said:

> We as Black Presbyterians acknowledge publicly our distress at the outcry generated within our Church as a result of . . . the allocation of funds to guarantee a fair trial for Angela Davis. . . . We are presenting $10,000 to the Church as an affirmation of our personal commitment to justice in our

land . . . at considerable sacrifice to ourselves and our families.[40]

Johnson added that what was being done that day was "an indication to the Black community that there are Black Presbyterians who are more willing to affirm the rectitude of the Church's legal aid to Angela Davis than many white Presbyterians are willing to reject that rectitude." It was obvious that some Black Presbyterians felt let down by their white allies and were embarrassed by indications that Black Presbyterians were being laughed at by Black Americans in general for being unequally yoked with racists in an overwhelmingly white church.

The issue of Black consciousness and pride had figured largely in the decision in 1968 to scrap the nondescript designation of "Concerned Presbyterians," reduce dependency on the goodwill and reconciliation strategy of the Presbyterian Interracial Council, link the fortunes of Black Presbyterians with the new National Committee of Black Churchmen (later to become the National Conference of Black Christians), and create a Black caucus in the church that white power was bound to respect. Edler Hawkins and several other seasoned activists agreed in St. Louis to recede into the background and permit a younger, more militant leadership to come forward. E. Wellington Butts, the young pastor of Bethany Presbyterian Church in Englewood, New Jersey, was elected the first BPU president, but Edler Hawkins, the chairman of the dissolved Concerned Presbyterians and the Commission on Church and Race, could not avoid being regarded as the spiritual father and mentor of the new caucus. Since the Council of the North and West and PIC had both emphasized integration, a theological and psychological adjustment had to be made by many of the pastors and lay leaders who gravitated to BPU. But younger leaders like Butts, Eugene Turner, and J. Oscar McCloud had no recollection of the policies of men like Dillingham, Leroy Patrick, and L. Charles Gray. They were much more attuned to the Black Power movement tactics of the Student Nonviolent Coordinating

Committee and the National Committee of Black Churchmen, that is, to Black consciousness and Black Theology. A
new style of leadership—reminiscent of Francis J. Grimké,
but even more of Matthew Anderson, John B. Reeves, and
Reuben H. Armstrong—developed around Edler Hawkins
and the younger churchmen who revered him. Throughout
the years between 1963, when he came into national prom-
inence, and his death in 1977, Hawkins had skillfully held
in tension the twin goals of Black cultural identity and
interracial integration.

Radicalization and Reconciliation

The Angela Davis affair radicalized Hawkins and other
Black Presbyterians even more than the Black Manifesto
crisis of 1969, which left them disappointed by the evasive
response of the denomination to the demand for reparations. At no time, however, did they reject its compromise
of agreeing to release certain National Missions properties
for economic development in the South and creating the
Program for the Self-Development of People.[41] Actually,
Edler Hawkins kept a balanced perspective about the interracial character of the Presbyterian Church through the
years. The battles with conservative whites over the Black
Manifesto and the Emergency Legal Defense Fund never
blunted his sensitivity to the need for white allies in the
struggle for justice and reconciliation between the races in
both the church and the society.

In the fall of 1963, Hawkins received a letter from a
former seminary classmate asking whether or not there
was a place for white liberals in the movement. His response, warm and engaging as always, yet insistent on the
point that there was still a need for Blacks to keep the
pressure on through their own organizations, shows how
he walked the fine line between Black radicalism and reconciliation with whites. After presenting the position of
Black leadership dismayed by a report that six out of every
ten northern whites believed that Blacks were being
treated "about right," or "too well," Hawkins concluded

his letter by expressing disagreement with radical opinion on both sides. He then sought to reassure his white friend about the desirability of interracial coalitions.

> Let no doubts disturb you in the days ahead as to whether you are needed, for despite the oft repeated feeling on the part of the Negro personality that his freedom will never come apart from his own involvement and leadership, it can never really be assured until the true liberal helps to prepare white America in all ways that he can, for the urgent business of civil rights that is the business of all America.[42]

The Black leadership of the United Presbyterian Church U.S.A. adopted one of the most radical strategies among the ethnic caucuses that came out of the civil rights movement. It constantly pressed the white constituency to recognize the necessity of the Black consciousness movement. But Black Presbyterians never espoused a doctrine of separatism. Rather they understood Black pride, solidarity, and the sharing of power with whites as both desirable and indispensable for racial justice and reconciliation in the United States and in South Africa.

The role of Edler G. Hawkins in both Black Presbyterians United and in the Presbyterian Interracial Council is a classic example of the creative ambivalence Vincent Harding wrote about in his insightful essay on "Black Power and the American Christ." One hopes that the appropriation of this heritage will neither impede the movement toward the one holy catholic and apostolic church of the great creeds, nor the empirical church in which every group finds its history and culture acknowledged, appreciated, and used for the benefit of all.[43] It remains for the present generation of Black Presbyterians and their allies to help the reunited church discover a reconciling inclusiveness that makes use of the African American cultural inheritance, and other ethnic inheritances, without dividing us up into warring camps that will destroy everything for which the faithful men and women, of every race and nationality who preceded us, struggled and prayed.

10

Native American Presbyterians: Assimilation, Leadership, and Future Challenges

Henry Warner Bowden

Native American Presbyterians can be found in scattered locations across the North American continent. Their major locations form an enormous triangle that starts at the eastern tip of New York's Long Island with a Shinnecock congregation and stretches to Pima churches along Arizona's Gila River, thence to Eskimo parishes at Barrow and other places in northwestern Alaska. Considering overall tribal populations and current denominational strength at over three million, the proportion of Native American Presbyterians is not very large. But these Native Americans embody three centuries of the church's experience in the New World, and they constitute a vital part of its present strength, determined as they are to meet whatever challenges and opportunities the future holds.

Overviews of the Past and Present

Presbyterians are currently listed in at least twenty Native American tribes as well as among the Eskimos and Aleuts. Their numbers amount to approximately seven thousand members who worship in some 125 churches and chapels with an estimated native leadership of over thirty persons. Although situated in more than twenty presbyteries, under the jurisdiction of seven synods, two-thirds of these churches and more than two-thirds of their aggregate membership cluster in six areas.[1] This essay will focus, therefore, on people and problems in these concentrated areas: the Choctaws in Oklahoma, the Pimas and Navajos in Arizona, the Sioux in the Dakotas, the Nez Percés in Idaho, the Tlingit, Haidas, and Tsimshians of southeastern Alaska, and the Eskimos in northwestern Alaska.

The history of nineteenth-century mission efforts in each of these six areas is rich. Work among the Choctaws began in Mississippi and continued after the United States government removed tribes to Indian Territory in the 1830s.[2] Evangelical efforts in Arizona took an upward turn in 1870 with the arrival of Charles Cook, who labored there for thirty years.[3] Missions among the Dakotas began with the American Board of Commissioners for Foreign Missions and its Presbyterian representatives, Stephen Riggs and John Williamson.[4] The Nez Percés benefited from lengthy contact with Henry Spalding and the McBeth sisters.[5] Work in Alaska, including education and logistics as well as preaching, was the last field that attracted Sheldon Jackson.[6] These earlier missions bore fruit, and at least one aspect of their success lies in the fact that Native American Presbyterian constituencies have persevered in each of these areas throughout the twentieth century.

Over the past decades, people have pursued Native American missions under a number of auspices. The primary focus here will be on the Presbyterian Church in the United States of America (PCUSA), which was the largest segment of the denomination in this century until 1958. After that, most data will derive from that parent body as it then became the United Presbyterian Church in the United States of America (UPCUSA), and, following reunion with the Presbyterian Church in the United States (PCUS) in 1983, the Presbyterian Church (U.S.A.). The PCUS conducted missions during its existence between 1864 and 1983. This southern branch of the denomination concentrated its efforts in Oklahoma, as did the Cumberland Presbyterian Church, which still maintains separate ecclesiastical status.

Missionary work sponsored by southern churches did not compare in size and scope to that sponsored by the northern, more national, denomination. During most of the nineteenth century, the Board of National Missions in the PCUSA supervised Native American evangelism. In 1885, though, the General Assembly ordered a gradual transfer of responsibility to the Board of Home Missions, and the process was completed in 1893. So this century began with Native American missions viewed as part of the domestic field.

Two milestones worth mentioning were the deaths of Sheldon Jackson in 1909 and Charles Cook in 1917. Those endings closed off the nineteenth century, signaling a move from the old era to a different context. Before that time, Native American missions were perceived to be part of a general outreach to foreign peoples. Thereafter, Native Americans were viewed as a segment of the national population, just another ethnic group in this country that needed missionary attention. Whatever else the twentieth century held in store, it meant that evangelization among Native Americans would follow the same policies held by those engaged in other parts of the home mission campaign.

Until 1923, the Woman's Board of Home Missions had its own leadership and collected its own funds to support personnel in various fields of endeavor. In addition to funds, the Woman's Board also provided a means of circumventing the male-dominated committees that were too parsimonious and intransigent to support missions adequately. In 1923, the General Assembly ordered a merger of the women's independent group and the denomination's Board of Home Missions, forming the Board of National Missions (BNM).[7]

This new coordinating agency faced immediate difficulties. It operated at a financial deficit for nine years between 1923–24 and 1932–33. Although recovering slightly during the late 1930s and early 1940s, its revenues did not match those of the early 1920s. Of course, the Great Depression influenced financial matters in this period to a considerable extent, but it is also worth noting that Presbyterian women lost much of their previous enthusiasm for missions. Their contributions had been of tremendous importance, but after ecclesiastical bureaucrats co-opted their work in 1923, their efforts never again reached the level of earlier years.[8]

In 1924, the BNM came into existence, and it was the only agency to supervise Indian missions for the next fifty years. The BNM is naturally the best source for understanding the motives, policies, and ongoing issues related to Native Americans during that fifty-year period. It may be of passing interest to note that in that same year President Calvin Coolidge signed Congressional legislation making all Native Americans citizens of the country. In 1973, the Program Agency superseded the BNM, and it supervised church work among Native American peoples until 1983, when the Racial Ethnic Ministry Unit of the Presbyterian Church (U.S.A.) assumed responsibility for this and other racial ethnic ministries.[9]

Any serious attempt to make sense of statistical reports in the twentieth century teaches the observer to use them with caution. Because it is difficult to learn how various pollsters defined tribal membership, church membership, and ministerial status, the results of their canvasses cannot be used with much confidence. Because we do not know how carefully they collected data on tribes and various enterprises, we may not rely on their numbers as definitive. With these caveats in mind, it is possible to hazard some generalizations about Native American Presbyterians over the course of the twentieth century.

Church membership has remained fairly stable. Early decades reflect numbers ranging between 8,000 and 10,000. Since the 1920s, reports show the roll of church members to hover around 7,000. As far as the statistics can be trusted, membership has neither advanced nor decreased markedly. However, because tribal populations have generally increased during these years, there probably has been a relative decline of Presbyterianism among Native Americans. The number of churches has remained steady. Early reports mention an average of 160 churches, with the highest claiming 236 and none going below 134. By midcentury, however, the total began to dwindle, and recent estimates range between 110 and 130 Presbyterian churches comprised of Native Americans.[10]

Change appears more noticeable in the number of tribes that received some degree of missionary attention. In the first two decades of this century, reports listed work in over 50 tribes, with one report (in 1916) claiming work in as many as 71. After that, the total went sporadically downward. One can discern a process of attrition, for the affected tribes totaled 40 in 1940, 33 in 1950, and 22 in 1979. If the decrease in tribes indicates a negative trend, the number of Native American ministers underscores that decline more dramatically.

In 1911, the earliest survey made in this century reported 92 ministers, but we must remember that numbers do not disclose how ministerial status was defined, whether part-time or full-time workers were counted, or whether lay leaders were included as well as those ordained. The number increased appreciably until 1923, that great watershed year when one tabulation cited 239 Native American ministers. In the following decades, things deteriorated rapidly. The next reports that mentioned ministers, those in 1950, counted between 32 and 54. By 1979, the number had gravitated to around 30.[11] This decrease of approximately 90 percent is clearly one of the most serious challenges facing Native American Presbyterians today. Although grave, it is just one of the many issues Presbyterians have had to confront over the years.

Assimilation: An Issue Resolved, Theoretically

In 1802, Presbyterians created a Standing Committee on Missions. In 1902, President Theodore Roosevelt addressed the General Assembly, convened that year in New York City, on the centennial of the denomination's missionary program. He spoke glowingly of efforts to spread the gospel across the land, "to lay deep the moral foundation upon which true national greatness must rest." There was a mutual dependence between Christianity and civilization in his view, and doubtless in the minds of all those who packed Carnegie Hall that May evening.[12]

Drawing on convictions almost universally shared in a society dominated by Anglo-Americans, the speaker declared that "it is because of the spirit that underlies the missionary work, that the pioneers are prevented from sinking perilously near the level of the savagery against which they contend. Without it the conquest of this continent would have had little but an animal side."[13] In such convictions, there was little room for Native Americans to coexist with their own distinctive cultures. Popular conceptions painted Native American life as nothing more than "savagery," a dire threat against which white people had to contend. Native Americans were placed on the "animal side" of the natural environment, an obstacle to be subdued in the conquest of this continent.

Roosevelt's speech on that occasion was typical of a triumphalist frame of mind that had long characterized the colonial and nation-building epochs. This attitude viewed the American Republic as an admirable achievement of Protestant values and technological know-how. It was confident that the country could absorb different ethnic groups, if those people adapted to the standards set by the capitalist, literate, individualistic, English-speaking majority. This was the notion behind the "melting pot" theory, and Native Americans were accepted as Americans only if they abandoned their traditional identity and assimilated to mainstream culture.

Assimilationist assumptions have directed most of the evangelical work among Native Americans until quite recently. Advocates of home missions in this century's early decades often spoke optimistically of how "the moral standards of the Indians are duplicating the standards of Christian homes, and the Indian is becoming a real factor in Christian community life."[14] This meant that Native

Americans were increasingly turning their backs on the "vices and frailties" of traditional ways, such as reliance on "superstitious" beliefs, tribal dances, and curing ceremonies. Salvation came through the destruction of cultural integrity; Native Americans could be turned into something useful only if they espoused values and behavioral patterns in a life-style manufactured by white Christianity.

Presbyterians in the BNM and on mission stations echoed these sentiments for decades. One of the clearest statements of this sort appeared in the *Year Book of Prayer for Missions* in 1932. It said the aim of the current secretary regarding Native Americans was "to establish the present generation as self-respecting and respected citizens. . . . In short, the Indians are to be assimilated into the life of the nation, as have peoples of other countries and races."[15] Another spokesperson extolled the virtue of such an approach the following year: "The fundamental mistake of our early policy toward the Indians was that they were subjugated instead of being assimilated." Apparently the only necessary corrective was to demonstrate how manifestly superior white civilization was, and Native Americans would voluntarily accept both its tangible and spiritual benefits. Then, perhaps in an afterthought born of misgivings about whether acculturation would occur that easily, he added: "The moral ideals taught by Indian Field Service workers and missionaries alike need the support of law and law enforcement to build up in the Indian that sense of obligation which is an important element in true religion."[16]

Missionaries frequently combined their claims for the superiority of their faith with an assumed superiority of their culture, because for centuries European culture had been a primary carrier of Christianity. Most missionaries uncritically combined biblical truths with parts of their own cultural framework, dispensing a gospel of soap alongside a gospel of grace. They urged industry, punctuality, and private enterprise as much as love of neighbor. Even those kindly disposed to Native Americans conveyed an ultimatum: Accept the anonymous safety of belonging to the homogenized whole or face cultural atrophy as a result of either hostile or indifferent social dynamics.

Native Americans were expected to abandon habits rooted in traditions going back millennia in order to embrace foreign concepts of land ownership and work, authority structure and family relationships. For example, signs at Presbyterian missions like the one at Ganado, Arizona, proclaimed this attitude with such slogans as "Tradition Is the Enemy of Progress." Another was more specific, striking at the roots of traditional role models and the concept of communal sharing:

> Success will not come
> To those who shirk,
> To get up in the world,
> Get down to work.[17]

Such maxims did not take Native American ideas or values seriously, of course, because virtually everyone accepted the notion that white culture was superior in every way. Native Americans needed a thorough transformation, and the overwhelming majority of those engaged in such efforts were convinced that "the assimilating power of our American civilization is steadily modifying the habits of all the Indians and inevitably fitting them into the models of our Christian social standards." In the 1930s, most commentators on missions anticipated "a great awakening among the Indians, and an adaptation to present day conditions." They saw successful evangelical work as an indication of "notable and rapid changes in the direction of cultural assimilation in the course of the next few years."[18]

Those rapid changes did not occur, but assimilationist expectations remained strong for another two decades. At midcentury, delegates to the General Assembly were once again informed that a "thick, black wall of [traditional Native American] prejudice and indifference" still existed, "at which Presbyterians have been hammering for one hundred and fifty years." Confident in superior ends and means, the BNM proclaimed that the wall was "beginning to crack and buckle. We need to add more hammers and put more power into our prayers at this really promising moment."[19] Another Presbyterian commentator in 1952 acknowledged that the history of red-white relations had been largely a shameful one. But although the government had treated Native Americans in a dishonorable fashion, home missions afforded one bright feature in the otherwise gloomy story. This analyst reiterated the commonplace solution to things, noting that "a considerable number still live on reservations, but more and more the Indian is being integrated into the total population."[20] Without ever questioning whether Native Americans wanted white behavioral patterns or cultural standards, the widespread assumption was that they needed to assimilate or they would be entirely overwhelmed, lost in both this life and the next.

Massive changes began to occur in the second half of the twentieth century. There was no single cause behind this slow change, but attitudes about people and society began to alter. The outcry of oppressed minorities around the world, plus the civil rights movement at home, showed white Americans that their naive altruism had been blind to injustice, racism, and genocide in contemporary society. This sobering realization led many to reassess their ideas about ethnic differences and to accept differing life-styles as equally plausible.

Within that reappraisal of assumptions about white superiority, the assimilationist policy was finally recognized as destructive and arrogant. The "melting pot" theory of a homogenized American society gave way to the "salad bowl" theory that affirmed rather than scorned ethnic diversity. Because various groups had proved to be "unmeltable" anyway, it seemed the better part of wisdom to accept the reality of the situation instead of perpetuating cultural antagonisms by attempting the impossible.

Evidence of this major change in American attitudes began to emerge in the 1960s, and Presbyterians embodied this improvement as clearly as anyone else. One can hear the death knell of assimilationism in single voices and in collective denominational proclamations.

Specific data substantiating this new attitude appeared in a 1962 study of Sioux (or Dakota) Presbyterians. The author of this report found that, despite centuries of rhetoric about assimilation, "a complex of mechanisms and processes serve to perpetuate a distinct way of life for Dakota Indians." This did not mean survival of aboriginal culture; Dakotas had experienced many changes and continued to do so at a rapid pace. But it was clear that the direction of change would not "lead to the absorption of the Dakota as a homogenous part of the larger White society." Presbyterians should recognize, this report urged, that any policy affecting Dakotas "cannot be built on the assumption that they will eventually be assimilated. The evidence points to their remaining a distinct entity for generations to come." Going beyond that declaration of ethnic integrity, the author also suggested something about managerial options: "Outsiders, in this case the Board of Missions, do not have a choice of assimilating or preserving Indian culture. The choice will be decided by Indians."[21] So the important lesson beginning to be stated was that Native Americans should be partners in mission, not the subjects of an overbearing program.

Before 1950, missionaries assumed that their own culture was superior and that it would be only a matter of time before Native Americans embraced both Christianity and Western culture. Since then, fewer people have accepted the superiority of Euro-American culture, and Native Americans may accept Christianity without its usual supporting cultural nexus. As changing attitudes permeated society at countless points of individual input, the Presbyterian General Assembly manifested reform on the theological level as well. Without asking whether events affect ideas or thought leads to action, one can still say that the Confession of 1967 was a notable landmark in adjusting relationships among the denomination's various racial and ethnic components.

The new theological affirmation beheld the church as a coat of many colors, peopled by adherents with different cultural preferences. So in the last third of the twentieth century, Presbyterians rejected uniform cultural standards because

> God has created the peoples of the earth to be one universal family. In his reconciling love he overcomes the barriers between brothers and breaks down every form of discrimination based on racial or ethnic difference, real or imaginary. The church is called to bring all men to receive and uphold one another as persons in all relationships of life. . . . Therefore the church labors for the abolition of all racial discrimination and ministers to those injured by it. Congregations, individuals, or groups of Christians who exclude, dominate, or patronize their fellowmen, however subtly, resist the Spirit of God and bring contempt on the faith which they profess.[22]

Edward A. Dowey, Jr., chair of the committee that created the revised confession, commented that it was important to envision an inclusive church because "there are not several saviors, several salvations, or several churches offered to men according to their color, culture, or customs." It may be natural for like-minded people to assume that their standards are best, he observed, but "it is also demonic and a blasphemy when it controls the life of the church." Bearing down on this point, he asserted that this attitude "makes the reconciling community into its opposite, an exclusive club."[23]

This rejection of exclusivism was a step in the right direction. At least the conscious policy of cultural dominance can be avoided in the future, and now there is churchwide theological warrant for doing so. But ideas about racial and ethnic superiority have produced deep scars in Presbyterian minority groups, and the presuppositions that have wounded so many can persist in many subtle forms. It will be necessary for church members everywhere to be vigilant against resurgent narrow-mindedness.

Perhaps one could take the language of an earlier BNM report and use it against the old ideas: The thick, black wall of prejudice and indifference against Native American cultures is beginning to crack and buckle. We need to add more hammers and put more power into our prayers at this really promising moment to succeed in razing cultural exclusivism and arrogance to the ground. Although it may be true that the more overt kinds of assimilationist self-congratulation have begun to recede, it would be wise to heed Edward Dowey's comment regarding this portion of the Confession of 1967. Stating a sociological truth as well as theological wisdom, he observed that, as harmful presumptions fade, "the patronizing attitude will be the slowest to die, not least within the doer of good who is often more anxious to give suggestions than to receive the true needs of his neighbor."[24]

It seems that the issue of expecting Native Americans to assimilate to white culture is on the decline. But talking about a new attitude is one thing; acting on it is another. The inertia of several centuries will make a reversal of policy in this case all the more difficult to achieve. One Native American response said as much by noting that such lofty sentiments could be "ceremoniously accepted and unceremoniously filed with other recommendations that were never implemented."[25] It is important to monitor these good intentions closely in order to see if they really take place. One test of whether Presbyterians are serious about incorporating Native Americans as partners in mission will be if there is an increase in Native American leadership within the church. If Native Americans are to be respected as equals in an inclusive community, their experience should determine policies in their spheres of interest.

Leadership: An Issue Still Unresolved

In 1947, a study of Native American ministers reported that 66 percent of them "believed they were weaker [in numbers and impact] . . . than fifteen years earlier."[26] Statistics already mentioned substantiate this general sense of impending crisis that has accumulated since the 1930s. Some respondents thought Caucasians should supervise Native American churches, but more thought Native

Americans themselves were better suited as ministers. They could speak native languages, were sympathetic to local customs, and could understand the problems of their people. Because of their racial compatibility, Native American ministers would be better received by parishioners, and thus service would be more effective.[27]

Many thought that providing a trained native leadership was crucial to future growth. But the average salary paid in Native American churches at that time was hardly more than $82 per year. Even if a minister served two or three congregations, often a hundred miles apart, the accumulated stipend was not enough to support a family. Problems were made worse by the fact that the average educational experience of Native American ministers was 8.9 years of schooling; 6 percent of them had received no formal education at all. So the long-range need was abundantly clear: "In the opinion of the ministers themselves, trained leadership is the greatest single need for effective Indian work."[28] But where would it come from, what form would it take, and how would it be structured for healthy congregations?

Native American Presbyterian ministers have labored faithfully over the course of this century. But as their numbers diminish, who will succeed them, and how will they be nurtured and authorized? There have been so many notable Native American clergy that it is impossible to produce a comprehensive listing here. A few references lead us to wonder, however, if the next generation will produce similar giants.

In 1946, Esau Joseph was appointed supervisor of all the Native American churches on the Pima reservations. He was the first Native American minister to receive such responsibility, and by means of that office he formed an association of elders and deacons to coordinate their efforts. Cecil Corbett, one of his successors in the Sacaton parish, worked to further cooperation among the fourteen Pima-Papago churches, stressing especially their summer camp meetings as events of central religious importance.[29] Corbett has also served on the General Assembly's Mission Council and ministered in the Dakota Presbytery. For the past twenty years, he has been the director and, more recently, the chancellor of the Cook Christian Training School (now known as Charles Cook Theological School). This school, located in Tempe, Arizona, was founded in 1911 for Native American theological education.

Perhaps less publicly visible but nonetheless dedicated through the years were ministers like Bert Kelley, the first Navajo to be ordained. He began serving as lay pastor at Leupp in 1956 and worked thereafter for the Presbytery of Northern Arizona. Ordained in 1967, Kelley continued his efforts in the Presbytery of Grand Canyon until retirement in 1976.[30] In 1980, Roe B. Lewis retired after thirty-two years of service as a Presbyterian minister and associate executive for Indian missions in the Synod of the Southwest. He held pastorates at Vah-ki on the Gila River Reservation and at an intertribal urban ministry in Phoenix. Long associated with Cook Christian Training School, he organized its department of rural ministries and was the first Native American elected as president of its Board of Trustees.[31]

Roy Ahmaogak of Barrow, Alaska, was born to parents who remembered when the first Presbyterian missionaries reached that part of the world. In 1946, he sought ordination, having already succeeded his father as ruling elder. In that year, he also began translating parts of the New Testament into Arctic Eskimo dialect so his people could read scripture in their own language. While studying in the United States, Ahmaogak completed an Inupiat alphabet, produced an illustrated primer, and translated Mark, Romans, and part of John's Gospel. His ordination in 1947 by the Presbytery of Yukon was evidence that "the most continuous, understandable, and fruitful ministry of the church comes from the leadership of those who receive the Gospel and share it with their own people."[32] Another notable Alaskan Presbyterian is Walter A. Soboleff, a Tlingit who served for 31 years in Juneau and Tenakee Springs. For nine years he also worked as itinerant evangelist for the BNM on the motor vessel *Anna Jackman.* In 1985, he was honored along with Samuel Simmons, an Inuit from

Wainwright, and Arthur Johnson, a Tlingit from Sitka, as Native Americans who had devoted 25 years to the Presbyterian ministry.[33]

A Choctaw minister similarly recognized was John Bohanon of Eagletown, Oklahoma. Notable Sioux ministers include Sidney H. Byrd, who served in the Dakota Presbytery, the only all–Native American judicatory in the Presbyterian Church today. Its nongeographical responsibility covers the states of North and South Dakota, Minnesota, and Montana, supervising ten ordained ministers and three lay missionaries who work in 21 isolated churches. Byrd has expanded his contacts to five other states and has ministered among seven tribes other than his own. He was the only Native American to serve as a member of the General Assembly's Commission on Religion and Race, later called the Council on Church and Race. He is also a former chairperson of the Native American Consulting Committee, as have been Paul Firecloud and Ralph Scissons. Firecloud was also a veteran of the BNM and its efforts up until 1973. Scissons, an ordained elder, served as associate for Native American mission development for the Program Agency, worked on the National Committee on the Self-Development of People, and has been active on committees within the Synod of the Pacific.

Other prominent Native American Presbyterians are the men and women who have chaired or moderated consulting committees as they emerged within denominational structure. They include Eugene Wilson, Mary McQuillen, Leander Winnie, Jo Ann Smith, Henry Fawcett, Sandra Wakeman, Ray Goetting, Florence Davis, Clarence Acoya, Marjorie Wheelock, Eugene Begay, Claire Manning, and Cyrus Peck. These patient and judicious counselors are trying to formulate suggestions, guidelines, and policies that will provide for continuity and growth in Native American ministry. The challenge is formidable, and the difficulties seem immense. Still, prominent Native American spokespersons are convinced that "the complexity of our modern life can be accommodated with thought and hard work." In attempts to break artificial boundaries and seek commonality, it is important to "realize that there are no insoluble problems, only restricted vision and misspent energies."[34]

In 1968, the Advisory Committee on Ministries met on the Nez Percé reservation in Idaho and drafted several recommendations to the Council on Church Strategy and Development for presentation to the BNM and the General Assembly. Ideas stemming directly from Native Americans suggested that (a) a Native American staff person be named as associate for Indian ministries, (b) a screening committee evaluate Native American proposals for mission, (c) emphasis be placed on youth ministries, (d) non–Native American missionaries receive a thorough orientation before entering Native American fieldwork, (e) the Board of Christian Education be encouraged to participate more fully in Native American ministries, (f) a program for leadership and resource development be established, and (g) Cook Christian Training School be utilized as a base for training and strategy implementation.[35]

In 1969, the 181st General Assembly directed the BNM to establish a $100,000 seed fund to be used "for purposes deemed wise by the Indian groups themselves."[36] Pursuant to this action, a Consulting Panel of Indian Ministries was created, Paul Firecloud as chair. The panel was set up to screen proposals, articulate guidelines, and authorize an all-Indian Steering Committee to allocate funds. Response among Native American leaders was sanguine. "This new fund 'primed the pump of creativity,' " they said. "For the first time, funds were available to implement some of the ideas that had been collecting dust. Stifled initiative gave way to creative exploration of mission. . . . Urban groups, who had formerly shown little interest in the Church, were amazed that the historic, self-serving Church was now interested in issues of justice, community involvement, and self-determination."[37]

By 1970, a Presbyterian Indian Consulting Panel emerged to serve two purposes: (a) to spend funds wisely, taking into account what natives themselves expressed as their most pressing needs, and (b) to defend the integrity of

Native American perspectives within the denomination's intricate administrative structure. In 1974, this group became the Native American Consulting Committee, and within a year the NACC issued a position paper that reminded Presbyterians of their theological commitment. In light of confessional reforms and subsequent enabling grants, the NACC registered its dismay when those funds were terminated and developmental offices eliminated without consultation. Were Native Americans partners in, or still the object of, missions?[38]

Bureaucratic reversals threatened to blight nascent hopes before any tangible change could be realized. The NACC could not "understand how paternalism can thrive so luxuriously again after all of the agonizing lessons of the sixties that we are integrally bound together and there should not be the appearance of the subordinate-inferior relationship." Native leaders wanted to proceed on the higher plane of revised thinking, namely, "that we are all engaged in mission and that we have a variety of gifts growing out of our diversity and experiences." The issue was cooperation, not budget; Native Americans focused on sustaining a proper attitude, not maneuvering for a bigger subsidy. "It is not compensation that is sought," declared this combined voice that wanted release from past mistakes. "Rather it is to be joint heirs and members of the household of faith."[39]

Perhaps the instrumental explanation for this lack of communication is that, in a major denominational restructuring, the administrative responsibilities of the BNM were given to a new Program Agency in 1973, and there were administrative faults in the transition process. But the NACC thought such measures threatened recent reforms in missionary policy, and it invoked theological principle: "The future of missions is posited upon the assumption that it will lead to the establishment of indigenous churches." Obstacles still stood in the way of such a strategy, but unless the indigenizing concept remained in the forefront of evangelical activities, "it is highly likely that it will bog down in the morass of the older colonialism and Christian imperialism."[40] Enabling funds and the consulting process were important, but the issue of being sincere about self-determination among ethnic constituencies was more central. If administrative procedures did not become more responsive, barriers between brothers and sisters would not be overcome, and bureaucratic lethargy would continue to bring contempt on the faith that everyone professed.

In its most powerful utterance, the NACC held that "the desire of men of color to be freed from the shackles of white domination is a handwriting on the wall. And behind the handwriting is the very finger of God, for He never meant that mission churches should be satrapies and dependencies." The fundamental reason why Native Americans should be viewed as equal to others and their churches be on the same footing with more stable institutions was simple and yet profound: "Christians are all one in Christ and their differences are swept away when they kneel before the same cross and partake of the same supper."[41]

Recruiting and nurturing leaders in Native American churches is crucial to future Presbyterian effectiveness among these peoples. Customarily, those who present themselves for ordination are expected to have completed seven years of advanced education, four at college and three at seminary. As early as 1973, natives asked the Vocations Agency to construct more realistic standards for Native American ministers, because few of them could meet the normal requirements. In discussing authorization, this group stated that it did not advocate lowering standards, ignoring them, or wasting time having ministers acquire irrelevant credentials. Native American leaders valued practical competency, not conformity to rules set up by outsiders who did not understand local needs. "The question is not whether we should have standards," they insisted, "but how standards should be set and by whom."[42]

White regulations for ordination have not produced the desired result. The basic reason is that "in Indian communities, an enumeration of academic achievements and degrees does not elicit a positive response from the people. . . . [Q]uestions are seldom asked about where a man went to school, but rather, what he is able to do."[43] This might be true everywhere, but it is particularly relevant among Native Americans; there a person's status is based on relationships with local inhabitants, knowledge of their needs, and skill in meeting those physical and spiritual requirements. As one panel observed, "In the Indian community, the 'mantle of leadership' normally is accorded to a person who proves himself and serves the community rather than self. Respect is not granted, it is earned."[44] The prerequisite of proving oneself and earning leadership responsibility may account for the relatively older average age of Native Americans entering the ministry. For instance, the median age of people who live on reservations is 20.4; the average age of a Native American entering the ministry is 54.[45] So there are many problems connected with recruiting effective ministers and facilitating their work.

Native American and white Presbyterians need to arrive at realistic standards for ministry within tribal groups. Otherwise, "why would any Indian young person, in his right mind, . . . go into the ministry and be a servant of some paternalistic board and receive a salary so inadequate that his children would have to drop out of school in order to support the family?" This is the basic challenge, because "at a time when many Indian young people are struggling with the question of whether you can be both Indian and Christian, and when young people have had only one model of a church vocation to experience, it is unrealistic to expect youth will come forth and beg to be considered as a candidate for the ministry."[46]

For centuries, the Reformed tradition has emphasized the importance of education in a well-trained ministry. But Native Americans wonder if formal schooling is the best means of preparing for effective spiritual service. Most Native American pastors are bilingual, bicultural, and older than their non–Native American counterparts. They are selected by their own people who care about capabilities more than certificates. So Native American clergy are less motivated to obtain degrees, and it is a waste of time to dwell on uniform standards without noticing how native churches themselves define leadership competencies. Any program that hopes to nurture Native American pastors must recognize that competency has priority over curriculum. A study by the NACC notes that "in most Indian parishes leadership is a shared function among many people, rather than the office of an educated individual."[47] This means that training for leadership involves the mutual growth of the whole parish as well as that of prominent individuals who spend their lives there. Various presbyteries would do well to note these different standards when defining leadership in Native American settings.

Other Pending Issues

Even if the number of Native American clergy increases significantly, other serious problems threaten the spiritual welfare of Presbyterian Native Americans. Some of these problems stem from the stark realities of grinding poverty and inadequate medical care. A survey of Nez Percés in 1963, for example, reported that almost half of the 1,151 people living on the reservations were unemployed; those who could find work received an average income of $672 per year.[48] Another study found that Dakotas on the Pine Ridge reservation had a median income of $851 per year.[49] Contemporary Navajos fared better with an average of $2,335, but 94 percent of them lived below the national median. Of the approximately 85,000 people on Navajo reservation lands, 85 percent of them had no running water or electricity.[50] In 1920, the death rate among Native Americans was twice that of the nation as a whole; as late as 1959, the average age at death for Native Americans was 41, compared with a national average of 62 years.[51]

Other problems relate to local autonomy and top-heavy bureaucratic control. Among the Nez Percés, for instance, kinship patterns are the basis for social regulation. The people depend on a decentralized system of egalitarian values, and they distrust larger organizations, ecclesiastical or political.[52] Small wonder, then, that they are suspicious when church agencies dictate policies about property and funds, or force mergers on them without prior consultation.[53]

An additional irritant appears when outside administrators discount Native American ideas about what their churches need in order to flourish. For example, the Dakota Presbytery is threatened with extinction because managerial theory does not approve of the present arrangement. Without following the advice of experienced ministers who know their people, the proposed change follows a more efficient design. This proposed model ignores human relationships and uses an "essentially cartographic" classification system, "bearing only an occasional resemblance to the natural population and social groupings on the reservation."[54] Theological convictions also present a difficulty here. Although Presbyterians now affirm the right of every ethnic group to preserve its cultural identity, they also wish to integrate them as members of a single church, analogous to one body in Christ. At times, such ideals and practical problems do not mesh easily, and everyone concerned must deliberate carefully in formulating feasible compromises.

Some of these problems may be resolved in a new era of mutuality in mission, but native churches cannot become self-supporting in the foreseeable future. In light of the abysmal physical conditions mentioned above, the optimum solution in this situation is for supervisory agencies in the Presbyterian Church (U.S.A.) to respect the wishes of local peoples and to continue supporting them with supplemental funding at the same time.

Another issue of particular importance to the vitality of Native American cultures concerns land. Centuries ago, Native Americans held all of North America. By mid-nineteenth century they had ceded most of it to whites and lived on reservations. There were still 138 million acres of Indian land in 1887 but then the government began breaking up reservations and allotting parcels to individuals. By the time this program of forced acculturation ended in 1934, Native Americans had lost an additional 90 million acres of what little land remained in their hands.

The Presbyterian Church can use its denominational strength to support Native American attempts to redress this grievous loss in federal claims court. The church's agencies can also return its locally owned properties to the tribes who use them. It is no less than Christian duty for Presbyterians to concern themselves with federal legislation and treaty rights that try to safeguard the use of land, minerals, and water. These matters are crucial, not just to the esteem and self-determination of Native American people, but, as several Presbyterians have said, to the survival of humanity and to an effective witness of God's continuing grace.[55]

General Assemblies have debated many such issues in recent times, and partial improvements encourage hope for more to come. It remains to be seen whether Presbyterians will encourage people at all social and political levels to show greater respect for Native American ways of life. This can be done by helping defeat legislation that would terminate reservations without the consent of resident Native Americans. It can also be done by encouraging Native Americans to develop their own administrative policies and control their own affairs. Another way is to plan new educational programs for Native American children so that their learning experience is consistent with their cultural values. By supporting Native American family life and physical welfare, Presbyterians could provide an enabling arm instead of just a helping hand.

A final area of challenge and opportunity has to do with Native Americans who no longer live on reservations. If churches struggle for survival on native lands, they are virtually nonexistent among Native Americans who have moved to urban areas. Fully half of the Native American population has relocated, and as yet no effective means of providing spiritual care have been developed.

The lonely city does not nurture individuals as people did at "home" on the reservation. Conflicting values beset these bewildered, rootless people. As one analysis put it, "here is a kind of Indian with a profound need. The [traditional] culture is not really of much value to him, neither is the white. He is adrift and needs an interpretation of life that will be meaningful for his condition plus a fellowship of concern that he misses at this point of no return."[56] Urban ministries are beginning to meet this problem. In a few places, such as Los Angeles, Duluth, and the Lincoln-Omaha area, some counseling services are being offered. These agencies have great potential for facilitating ecumenical understanding and intertribal solidarity.

Looking back at the twentieth century from the perspective of its last decade, we can say that some beneficial changes have occurred but that many more are needed. The issues will not go away, nor will the people. A hundred years ago, it was popular to speak of Native Americans as "the vanishing American." It is now quite clear that Native Americans are not vanishing, nor are they abandoning their identity to blend more fully with the white majority. Native Americans are remaining Native Americans, to the enrichment of our country's pluralism. And Native American Presbyterians are remaining true to both their different cultural orientations and their shared faith. They have been loyal Presbyterians for centuries, and they will continue to be so, hoping that their church will finally live up to its commitment to diversity and inclusivity.

Perhaps the Native Americans' current attitude was best expressed by Rev. Holly Haile Smith, who in 1986 became the first Native American woman to receive Presbyterian ordination. After pointing out that her pragmatic ministry has to cope with depression and despair due to loss of language and land, she still ended on a hopeful note. Her words may be the best assessment of past wrongs that have been endured and of future improvements that can be anticipated:

> If I had only one thing to say to the Presbyterian Church it would be "han-yo," an Indian word by which my mother raised us children. It means you are not horrible, nor are you the greatest, but you are very good and you can do better.[57]

11

Hispanic Presbyterians:
Life in Two Cultures

*Francisco O. García-Treto and
R. Douglas Brackenridge*

The 198th General Assembly of the Presbyterian
Church (U.S.A.) designated 1987 as the Year of Hispanic
Ministry in recognition of El Centenario, the one hun-
dredth anniversary of the first indigenous Hispanic Presbyterian congregation in the United States.[1] That small
congregation of twenty-six members, established on November 2, 1887, in San Marcos, Texas, signaled the beginning of a variety of evangelistic, educational, and social
ministries designed to attract Spanish-speaking peoples
into the fold of mainline Presbyterianism. These efforts,
supervised by Anglo leaders who were influenced by the
prevailing imperial cultural attitudes toward ethnic minorities, were never given a high priority in national mission
strategies. As a result, relatively few Hispanics joined Presbyterian churches, and those who did found themselves
isolated from the denomination-at-large by segregated governing bodies and by cultural and linguistic differences.
This essay recounts briefly the historical development of
three major groups of Hispanic Presbyterians (Mexican
Americans, Cubans, and Puerto Ricans), assesses their
present denominational status, and raises some questions
about their future prospects as ethnic minorities within the
Presbyterian Church (U.S.A.).[2]

Hispanics presently constitute a minuscule portion of PC(USA) membership; the most recent denominational statistics place them at 22,746, or 0.84 percent of the 2,714,747 members reported in the study.[3] If one adjusts the figure so that members in the Synod of Puerto Rico are counted in a separate category, the percentage is even smaller.[4] Hispanic members of the PC(USA) who reside in the fifty states amount to only 13,698, or 0.50 percent of the total membership.[5] The vast majority of these members live in the synods of the Sun, the Northeast, Florida, the Southwest, and Southern California/Hawaii, with the largest concentrations in the presbyteries of New York City, Mission (South Central Texas), and Santa Fe (see Tables 11.1–11.3).

Another important adjustment in the figures should be made before using them as an accurate profile of Hispanic Presbyterians in the United States. The statistics represent the number of Hispanic members in *all* the churches of the presbytery reporting racial ethnic composition, and not just the number of members in the "Hispanic" churches within the presbytery. The latter number is in every case

The figures in Tables 11.1, 11.2, and 11.3 are derived from information found in the *Minutes of the General Assembly of the Presbyterian Church (U.S.A.),* 1989, Louisville, Kentucky.

TABLE 11.1

Presbyteries Reporting Over 1,000 Hispanic Members

Presbytery	Synod	Hispanic Members	White Members	Total
Mission	Sun	2,090	28,205	30,597
New York City	Northeast	1,729	9,061	19,757
The Northwest	Puerto Rico	5,123	1	5,138
San Juan	Puerto Rico	1,856	27	1,903
Santa Fe	Southwest	1,220	6,158	7,554
The Southwest	Puerto Rico	2,069	0	2,069

TABLE 11.2

Presbyteries Reporting 300–999 Hispanic Members

Presbytery	Synod	Hispanic Members	White Members	Total
Grace	Sun	546	51,702	53,417
Los Ranchos	So. Calif./ Hawaii	607	24,390	26,920
New Covenant	Sun	617	34,119	36,410
San Gabriel	So. Calif./ Hawaii	349	10,678	13,178
SW Florida	Florida/South	380	50,338	51,393
Tropical Florida	Florida/South	362	19,377	20,571

TABLE 11.3

Presbyteries Reporting 100–299 Hispanic Members

Presbytery	Synod	Hispanic Members	White Members	Total
Central Florida	Florida/South	221	22,426	23,551
Chicago	Lincoln Trails	232	31,766	36,462
De Cristo	Southwest	197	7,115	7,645
Denver	Rocky Mtns.	214	15,324	15,973
Elizabeth	Northeast	131	21,961	22,978
Grand Canyon	Southwest	188	15,828	17,339
Hudson River	Northeast	114	17,010	18,239
Newark	Northeast	261	8,373	10,770
The Pacific	So. Calif./Hawaii	285	10,857	14,707
Palisades	Northeast	220	9,606	10,802
Philadelphia	Trinity	130	47,562	50,600
Pueblo	Rocky Mtns.	105	9,422	9,661
Riverside	So. Calif./Hawaii	169	8,805	9,109
San Fernando	So. Calif./Hawaii	278	11,135	12,010
San Francisco	Pacific	221	15,618	18,374
San Joaquin	Pacific	111	8,417	8,789
San Jose	Pacific	148	11,111	12,058
Tres Rios	Sun	288	8,017	8,388
West Jersey	Northeast	163	16,611	17,172

Of 169 presbyteries reporting fewer than 100 Hispanic members, 52 reported five or less Hispanics.

significantly smaller. In the four presbyteries with the largest concentration of Hispanics, the total Hispanic population exceeded membership in "Hispanic" churches by 25, 40, 35, and 43 percent, respectively. Unquestionably, the portrait of Hispanic Presbyterians cannot be drawn by looking solely at the "Hispanic" churches, but must take into account the apparent assimilation of Hispanic Presbyterians into predominantly Anglo congregations.

It should also be noted that Hispanic Presbyterians are a heterogeneous group and that their representation within the PC(USA) reflects their diversity. Although speaking a common language, Hispanics in the United States are of widely different ethnic and national backgrounds, historical experiences, and socioeconomic classes. Mexican Americans, Cubans, and Puerto Ricans form the three major groups of Hispanic Presbyterians, but Dominicans and Central Americans are also increasingly present. Many of the Mexican Americans, Cubans, and Puerto Ricans, including those who are recent immigrants, are second- and third-generation Presbyterians. We will focus our attention on these three major groups and attempt to describe both their uniqueness and their commonality as Hispanics in the PC(USA) and its predecessors.

Hispanic Presbyterians in the Southwest

The oldest and largest group of Hispanic Presbyterians is located in the Southwest and has historically been referred to by a number of titles—Mexican, Latin American, Spanish, and Mexican American.[6] Nineteenth-century Presbyterian attitudes toward "Mexican" missions are succinctly summarized in a letter written in 1870 to home missionary Sheldon Jackson by Henry Kendall, secretary of the Board of Home Missions of the Presbyterian Church in the United States of America (PCUSA). "With our present resources of men and money," he wrote, "our leading idea must be to preach the Gospel in English and to an English-speaking people. We cannot pay for school teachers, for colportage, or for any other work among other nationalities till we have first cared for our own. . . . The Spanish population cannot compare in importance with the English-speaking people."[7] Nevertheless, by the end of the nineteenth century, Presbyterians had formed Hispanic congregations in Texas, New Mexico, Colorado, and California[8] and had established a network of day schools and clinics for Spanish-speaking children in New Mexico.[9]

As the twentieth century began, Presbyterian missionaries charged with responsibility for "Mexican" missions had little reason for optimism. Because of financial restrictions, they were forced to close many schools and medical missions and to dissolve a number of congregations. The Mexican Revolution (1909–10), however, spurred the first substantial and permanent migration of Mexican nationals to American soil, spotlighted the Hispanic Southwest, and riveted national attention on a wide spectrum of social, racial, and religious problems. With the push of the Mexican Revolution came also the increasing pull of American labor needs, especially in agriculture and industry. Such an influx of people could not be ignored, and Presbyterians responded with concerted efforts to reach Hispanics through a variety of missionary programs, including social ministries (Houses of Neighborly Service), educational ventures, and evangelistic campaigns.[10]

Although the success of these ministries varied from place to place, they had common features. Hispanics were isolated from the dominant Presbyterian Anglo membership. Undoubtedly, a key reason was the different languages. Even though some pastors encouraged bilingualism, English-speaking members were reluctant to learn Spanish, and Hispanics preferred to sing, pray, and preach in their native tongue. Transcending linguistic problems was the attitude held by many Anglo church people that Hispanics represented an inferior culture and alien race. A result was that the mission-oriented Anglos built new churches and then donated the old structures to the Spanish-speaking members, thus giving birth to the "Second" Presbyterian Church in many southwestern towns and villages.[11]

In 1908, the Presbyterian Church in the United States (PCUS) formalized this ecclesiastical segregation with the creation of the Texas-Mexican Presbytery, an organization that had the name and structure of a governing body but functioned essentially as a "mission" supervised by Anglo leaders. At one level, the so-called Tex-Mex Presbytery was simply a channel used by the Synod of Texas for distributing its home mission funds to the Mexican American churches. During the entire life of the Texas-Mexican Presbytery, practically all of its congregations depended on such funds for their survival. Churches were usually located in rural areas with poor and transient membership. Often congregations had fewer than a dozen charter members. Unlike Anglo presbyteries, Texas-Mexican Presbytery bypassed normal procedures for calling and installing pastors, and the Synod of Texas never questioned its actions. The presbytery referred to Hispanic ministers as "evangelists," and Anglo leaders moved them from place to place frequently, against the wishes of the congregations.[12] Texas-Mexican Presbytery might have continued had not the combined pressures of economics and integration influenced the denomination to dissolve its segregated governing bodies. After considering a series of studies and reports completed with little input from Hispanic leaders, the Synod of Texas (PCUS) approved a resolution that Texas-Mexican Presbytery and its constituent churches be merged with existing Anglo presbyteries.[13]

Just as Hispanic Presbyterians experienced isolation from the denomination, they also found themselves alienated from their Spanish-speaking Roman Catholic neighbors whose religion Presbyterian missionaries condemned as "besotted and Rome-ridden."[14] Converts to Presbyterianism heard lurid tales of moral laxity among priests and nuns, and bitter denunciations of hierarchical leaders who allegedly were out to take away their freedom under orders from "an old gentleman in Rome." Hispanic evangelists in turn made anti-Catholicism an essential ingredient of their itinerant preaching. Although governing bodies occasionally noted with disapproval that some Hispanic evangelists "attacked Romanism too much and preached necessity for new birth too little," the enthusiastic converts were simply reflecting what they had learned from their Anglo supervisors, many of whom were reacting to negative encounters with Catholicism on the foreign mission field.[15]

In addition to their strident anti-Catholicism, Hispanic Presbyterians also absorbed from early Anglo leaders firm adherence to a rigid, moralistic code of personal conduct. Refraining from drinking, smoking, dancing, and card playing were considered to be self-evident essentials of a Christian life. These attitudes heightened the isolation of Hispanic Presbyterians, not only within their own predominantly Roman Catholic communities, but also from Anglo church members whose social attitudes had been gradually liberalized in the twentieth century. One Hispanic pastor, for example, expressed fear that if his elders should mix with Anglo elders at an integrated presbytery meeting and see Anglo elders smoking, they would go back home convinced that all moral restraint had been removed.[16]

A final characteristic of Presbyterian missions to Mexican Americans was the emphasis placed on "Americanization" as a means of integrating Hispanics into mainstream culture. Both in annual reports and popular articles, missionaries featured success stories where converts reportedly had abandoned stereotypical "Mexican" behavioral patterns, adopted the Protestant work ethic, and become model citizens.[17] One executive of the PCUSA Board of Home Missions, speaking of Mexican immigrants shortly after the Mexican Revolution, observed that "mentally, socially, religiously, they [Mexicans] are in a state of transition. . . . The question which is to be decided within the next few years is whether they are to be won to anarchy or to Americanism; to Bolshevism or to Democracy; to Trotzky or to Christ."[18] The cultural imperialism implicit in this and other similar statements was not questioned by denominational leaders until the 1960s.

Hispanic Presbyterians from Cuba
and Puerto Rico

The history of Presbyterian involvement with Cuba and Puerto Rico is a long one. Its most active chapters began to be written with the loss of the two islands to the Spanish crown in 1898 and their fall into the United States' political and economic shadow.[19] Most U.S. Protestant denominations had actively supported the entry of the United States into the war with Spain, and, in a style perhaps inevitably suffused by the spirit of "manifest destiny," they sent missionaries to establish work in the islands as soon as the war was over.[20]

From the beginning, the agenda of the missions was something larger than a simple denominational expansion. On the one hand, realizing the immense difficulties of the task they had undertaken and their limited amount of material and personal resources, the denominations chose a cooperative and mutually nonconflictive style.[21] This eventually led to the predominance of the tag *"evangélico"* (always in the sense of "Protestant" or "non–Roman Catholic Christian") over denominational labels in identifying their converts. On the other hand, the common adversary was the Roman Catholic Church. Protestant publications highlighted what one writer has termed "the satanization of the Spanish colonial system, with the Catholic Church as the major culprit of the social and moral degeneracy" of island society.[22] Whereas Catholic Spain represented ignorance and repression, the Protestant United States stood as the model of enlightenment and freedom.

The Presbyterian Church instituted an enormously successful program of establishing schools that made available a first-rate, modern, and idealistic brand of education to all children without regard to their socioeconomic class. The jewel in the crown of the Presbyterian system of schools in Cuba was La Progresiva, founded by Robert L. Wharton in 1900 in the city of Cárdenas. This school came to be one of the most influential college preparatory institutions in the island.[23]

Ecclesiastically, the links between the Cuban and Puerto Rican churches and the PCUSA were very tight. A successful effort was instituted in the church's educational system to prepare a native leadership for the church and to grant authority to that leadership as soon as it was practicable. The churches in Puerto Rico and Cuba also began as "home" (later "national") mission fields and would eventually be integrated into U.S. presbyteries: Puerto Rico into the former Synod of New York, and Cuba into the former Synod of New Jersey.

These historical factors continue to influence the Hispanic churches of the mainland, most notably in the service of a significant number of Cuban ministers who were products of the Presbyterian schools and of the united seminary in Matanzas, and of the massive migration of Cubans to the United States in the 1960s. Marcos Ramos singles out the Cuban Presbyterian church as the one among the major denominations on the island at the time of the revolution that "suffered changes like no other." In large part, those changes stemmed from the significant losses of ministerial and lay leadership through emigration.[24]

Cuban ministers who immigrated to the United States found it relatively easy to become integrated into the structures of the church in *"el Norte"* primarily because their presbytery had always been part of a synod in the United States. Some of them, notably Alfonso Rodríguez and Cecilio Arrastía, have exercised leadership in the church in the United States far beyond the boundaries of its Hispanic constituency. Many others continue to serve Hispanic (not necessarily, nor even primarily Cuban American) congregations throughout the United States. It is evident, almost thirty years after the Cuban exodus, that the absorption of Cuban-trained leaders into the Presbyterian Hispanic milieu in the United States was a one-time phenomenon. It may have helped to alleviate the chronic shortage of Hispanic ministers in the United States, but it certainly did not represent a long-term solution to the problem of clerical leadership.

New Strategies Since the 1960s

By the 1960s, both the PCUS and the UPCUSA leadership had come to realize that their respective missionary programs for Hispanics had stagnated. Membership in Hispanic congregations was declining. Few young Hispanic men or women were entering seminary, and the social ministry of the Houses of Neighborly Service appeared increasingly anachronistic in an era of rapid social change. In response, the PCUS created a Latin American Advisory Committee. For the first time in history, the committee was not entirely Anglo in membership. Its assignment was to develop a "master strategy" for the Synod of Texas. The strategy included continuing education programs for Hispanic ministers and the production of Christian education materials in Spanish.[25] The UPCUSA created a Departamento Hispano Americano in 1962, which combined responsibility for Hispanic churches in the Caribbean and in the United States. Its initial report in 1964, entitled "God Does Not Speak Only English," emphasized the need for increasing the availability of Spanish literature and raised questions about the vastness of the problems and the inadequacy of the church's programs for their solution.[26] Other ventures indicated a growing sensitivity to the special problems and needs of the Presbyterian Hispanic community.[27] These included the Hispanic-American Institute in Austin, Texas (1966), a combined effort of the PCUS and UPCUSA to promote the recruitment and training of Hispanic leaders, and the West Side Ministry in San Antonio, Texas (1967), sponsored by Alamo Presbytery to develop creative ministries at the local level.

Despite such projects, Hispanic leaders in both Presbyterian denominations were dissatisfied with progress being made as the decade of the 1960s drew to a close. They contended that the church was responding too slowly and had failed to grasp the extent of frustration and alienation building up in Hispanic communities throughout the United States. Spurred on by the success of other minority groups, Hispanics finally captured the attention of both the

PCUS and UPCUSA General Assemblies in 1969. With cries of "*Ya Basta!*" ("Enough!"), "*La Raza,*" and "Brown Power," Hispanics brought their case to the 181st General Assembly (UPCUSA) in San Antonio, Texas. Expressing feelings of frustration, resentment, and neglect, they chastised the church for lack of sensitivity to its Hispanic constituency. They further claimed that the denomination's outmoded missionary structures had produced a small nucleus of Hispanic Presbyterians characterized by a futureless image and a mark of inadequacy. Out of this confrontation eventually emerged La Raza National Presbyterian Caucus (1972) as an advisory and advocacy group established to monitor denominational programs and policies relating to Hispanic constituents.[28]

Indirectly, the 1969 UPCUSA General Assembly in San Antonio had an impact on Hispanic ministries in the PCUS. Noting what national publicity and direct confrontation could achieve, a group of Hispanic pastors and lay people presented their denomination with a series of resolutions passed on October 31, 1969, called the "Corpus Christi Declaration." Condemning cultural imperialism, the document called for a permanent synodical committee, entirely made up of Hispanics, to be established in order to support Hispanic ministries. It expressed "genuine disappointment" that Hispanics played such a marginal role in the policy and decision-making processes of the denomination. As a result, the Synod of Texas created the Mexican American Task Force, which began immediately to develop leadership conferences and to function as a consultant to churches and governing bodies in social issues affecting Hispanics.[29]

Even though Chicano militancy stimulated interest in Hispanic Presbyterianism in the late 1960s and early 1970s, other issues such as women's liberation, denominational reorganization, and budgetary crises diverted attention from its agenda for action. Nevertheless, both the UPCUSA and PCUS continued to support various racial ethnic ministries, including Hispanic concerns. In creating regional synods in 1974, the UPCUSA approved an over-

ture that required each new synod "to provide an instru-
mentality for its ministry among the ethnic minorities . . .
within its bounds."[30] Out of this directive has evolved such
organizations as the Mexican American Coordinating
Council in Texas, the Hispanic Commission in southern
California, the Jicarita Cluster in northern New Mexico,
and the Liaison Committee for Hispanic Ministries of the
Synod of the Southwest. These groups initiate programs in
leadership training and development, publish educational
materials and newsletters, and organize events designed to
enrich congregational life in Hispanic churches.[31]

At the national level, the La Raza Caucus functions as
an advocacy and advisory group for Hispanics in the
United States and Puerto Rico. Reflecting differences in
strategy and organizational philosophy, however, southwestern Hispanics have formed new organizations to
represent their constituency, such as the Consulting
Committee on Hispanic Ministries in the Southwest in
1980 and the Hispanic Council of the West (Concilio
Presbiteriano Hispano del Oeste) in 1985. Behind the decision to create the Consulting Committee lay almost a decade of dissatisfaction on the part of southwestern leaders
with the performance of the La Raza Caucus as the "official" representative of all Hispanic Presbyterians. Many
Hispanics protested that they had no voice in the selection
of caucus membership and that the small group of individuals who formed the Executive Committee were not accountable to the majority for their decisions. Moreover,
the La Raza Caucus was said to concentrate on theological
and racial ethnic issues at the national level and neglect
sufficient direction and guidance for local church development and regional concerns.[32]

The reunion of the UPCUSA and PCUS denominations
in 1983 raised concerns among southwestern Hispanics
about their organizational relationship to General Assembly agencies in the new mission design. In August 1984,
thirty Hispanic pastors from the western United States attended a professional development seminar in Guadalajara, Mexico. They drafted and approved the "Declaration

of Guadalajara," which called for the creation of a new southwestern Hispanic caucus that would represent the views of its constituency and be accountable to denominational structures. Consequently, the General Assembly instructed the Program Agency to consult with Hispanic leaders in order to determine the form of the new organization and its relationship to Hispanic caucus activities. In 1985, representatives from synods, the Consulting Committee, and La Raza Caucus met in Tempe, Arizona, and agreed to form the Hispanic Council of the West. This became the official caucus for southwestern Hispanic Presbyterians.[33]

While dealing with the question of its relationship with La Raza Caucus, the Consulting Committee also labored to develop policies that would guide future Hispanic ministries in the Southwest. It created a Task Force on Hispanic Policy that drew up position papers on historical, cultural, and theological issues facing Hispanic Presbyterians. After review and study by a Convocation on Mission in 1983, the Consulting Committee submitted a paper, "Church Policy on Hispanic Ministries in the Southwest," to the 1984 General Assembly. This document was approved, with minor modifications, to serve as official policy directions for the 1980s.[34]

The report identified a number of issues affecting Hispanics that had not been realistically addressed by the Presbyterian Church, including (a) adequate funding for church development and scholarships for minority students, (b) accessibility of culturally and linguistically relevant Christian education materials, (c) recognition by responsible governing bodies of the cultural diversity of Hispanic people, (d) involvement of Hispanics in decision-making structures that affect Hispanics, (e) awareness of the importance of special ministries for youth, women, and the aged, and (f) the recognition and acceptance of the integrity of the Hispanic theological experience by the larger church. The report also urged that Hispanic Presbyterians deal more seriously with questions of identity and leadership.[35]

The call for new strategies for Hispanic ministries in the 1980s carried an implicit assumption regarding the ineffectiveness of previous efforts. Although most Hispanic leaders might agree with this, they would also acknowledge that in the 1970s and 1980s minorities had improved their denominational status and secured both staff support and funding for a number of beneficial projects. The Council on Church and Race (PCUS and UPCUSA) and the Vocation and Program Agencies sponsored theological colloquia, provided funds for scholarships to Hispanic college and seminary students, and initiated efforts to improve the quality and quantity of Christian education materials published in Spanish. Descriptions of these programs can be found in annual reports to the General Assembly during the 1970s and 1980s.[36]

In recent years, the development of border ministries and of assistance for Hispanic women indicate the significance of changing emphases in Hispanic ministries. The 1981 General Assemblies of the PCUS and the UPCUSA commended to the church for study a major report, "Strangers Become Neighbors: Presbyterian Response to Mexican Migration." The report urged the church to develop strategies for supporting and strengthening existing Hispanic congregations in ministry and outreach to new Mexican immigrants and to organize new congregations able to attract and assist Spanish-speaking persons. Significantly, the report also called for cooperation with the Roman Catholic Church on both sides of the border in projects of service to human need.[37]

The adoption of the report culminated in a sustained effort to focus attention on border problems and stimulated the formation of a number of new projects. Puentes de Cristo (Bridges of Christ) in the lower Rio Grande Valley has programs for orphans and street children; Project Amistad at Piedras Negras ministers to people in a largely industrial area; Project Frontera de Cristo, between Douglas, Arizona, and Agua Prieta, Mexico, has a special ministry to returning undocumented workers; and Project Pueblos Hermanos (Brother/Sister Cities) addresses urban problems such as unemployment, undocumented workers, and drugs and drug-related crimes. Migration issues also involve the treatment of refugees from Central America and the application of U.S. immigration laws. In November and December 1986, a group of Hispanic leaders sponsored by the Presbyterian Hispanic Council of the West traveled to Costa Rica, Nicaragua, and Guatemala, pursuing the Council's desire "to raise consciousness and to address issues of human need and social justice."[38]

Especially in the last decade, Hispanic women have become a recognizable "minority within a minority" in denominational circles. UPCUSA General Assemblies approved seventeen overtures that amended the Form of Government to guard against discrimination of women in all aspects of church life. The PCUS established the Committee on Racial Ethnic Women (CREW) in 1981 and, along with the Third World Women's Coordinating Committee of the UPCUSA, worked closely with other agencies and women's organizations to represent the interest of racial ethnic women.[39] At the same time, the denominations encouraged minority women to enter the professional ministry. The numbers are small, because such recruitment must confront a culture that has been reluctant to break long-standing traditions of the subordination of woman to her own "sphere." Rebecca Reyes became the first Hispanic Presbyterian woman to be ordained when she became pastor of the Memorial Presbyterian Church in San Marcos, Texas, on July 22, 1979.[40] A recent *Presbyterian Panel,* however, indicates that Hispanic women and other minority women would have difficulty being accepted in non-Hispanic congregations, particularly in the South.[41]

Beyond these developments at the national level and in the Southwest, there also has been activity in the Cuban and Puerto Rican Presbyterian constituencies. The concentration of Cuban Presbyterians in the Miami area provides a representative cross section of this Hispanic group.[42] A visit to Miami's First Spanish Presbyterian Church confirms the statistical information that it is one of the denomination's most successful Hispanic churches.

During a recent visit,[43] we found the new 900-seat sanctuary filled to capacity for the 11:00 A.M. Sunday service. Furthermore, some 200 attended the 9:00 A.M. service, and the evening service drew over 100. Ten new members, one of them a Nicaraguan, were received at the 11:00 A.M. service. A perusal of its reports and conversations with its leaders witness to a very vital, self-confident, and active Presbyterian congregation whose leadership is prominent in the life of the Miami Cuban community.

On the day of the visit, a congregational meeting was held to elect a pulpit committee to search for a co-pastor. Pastor Martín Añorga gave the congregation three reasons why it should approve the appointment. First, the church's rapid growth necessitates a heavy administrative burden on the pastor, thus limiting his time for educational and evangelistic responsibilities. Second, although the church has been able to use the services of many retired pastors, teachers, and other leaders, these persons are aging or leaving Miami and cannot contribute as much of their time and effort to the church as in the past. Third, he himself is looking forward to retirement in three or four years, and a co-pastor, who would remain in place at his retirement, would ensure a smooth transition to new leadership.

The Reverend Ernesto Sosa organized the First Spanish Presbyterian Church in 1958 with a small group of Cubans who met in the historic building of the First Presbyterian Church of Miami on Brickell Avenue. Añorga came in 1964, when the congregation was beginning to swell with exiles from the island, many of whom were former teachers in the Presbyterian schools of Cuba. A striking phenomenon in the Miami Cuban community is the re-creation of many of the familiar institutions, businesses, brand names, and other landmarks of the home culture remembered and cherished by the exiles. It is not surprising, therefore, that Cubans established La Progresiva in Miami. The school, referred to in the church's documents as a "parochial school," has been a clear asset to the growth of the church. La Progresiva has 520 students and is fully accredited as a private elementary school (1971) and as a high school (1981). The session of the church is also the school's Board of Trustees, and Añorga, who holds an M.Ed. in school administration, is the principal, even though a director oversees the real day-to-day running of the school. The students are mostly second-generation Cubans, with only some thirty to forty Anglos among them. Only three or four of the thirty-two faculty and staff are Anglo. Añorga emphasized that the success of the school is based on the desire of the Cuban community to retain its Cuban tradition and on its mistrust of public schools, which are "entirely secular" and increasingly unsafe. Although the school teaches the basic subjects in English, it follows a maintenance plan in which Spanish is the language of instruction for other subjects, for example, in the arts.[44] The school still counts on the support of an active national Cuban alumni association, even though its curriculum and constituency differ greatly from its Cuban roots.

A comparison of First Spanish Presbyterian Church with other Hispanic Presbyterian churches in Miami, including among them the congregation that now meets at the old Brickell Avenue church, demonstrates that the case of the First Spanish Presbyterian Church is unique and probably impossible to duplicate. These congregations are much more heterogeneous—Dominicans and Central Americans in particular are a significant part of their constituency—smaller, and poorer. Their situation is more typical of the struggling Hispanic churches of the East Coast, which serve primarily Hispanics of the urban working class.

In the Northeast, where Hispanic Presbyterians are primarily Puerto Rican, there are no counterparts to Miami's First Spanish Presbyterian Church. Daniel Damiani is a young Presbyterian minister of Dominican descent in New York City; he serves a congregation of sixty-five members in Brooklyn. Based on a thorough survey of fourteen area Hispanic congregations, Damiani concluded that "the actual situation can be described, without the least degree of exaggeration, as deplorable, obscure and uncertain. . . .

[O]ne can easily perceive a sense of frustration, survival mentality, and an evident impotence to deal with complex problems and situations."[45] He is optimistic, however, to the extent of saying that, despite the frustrating realities, "a new light of hope has begun to emerge" in the renewal of interest in the Hispanic ministries of the church that he detects among the national leadership of the PC(USA). Damiani pointed to the establishment of 1987 as the Year of Hispanic Ministry as "truly a cause for optimism and great expectation among the leaders of the Hispanic Church."[46]

In a personal interview in July 1988, however, Damiani gave expression to both his frustration and his sense of cautious hope. Leadership for the churches represents one of the chronic problems. At the time of the Damiani study, there were seven ordained ministers—four full-time and three part-time, with some of these retired or about to retire; one commissioned lay preacher; and three student pastors serving the fourteen congregations, of which six did not have the services of a pastor.[47] He also perceived lay leadership as a problem area, particularly because "a great number of lay leaders in the Hispanic congregations lack knowledge and understanding about the system of Presbyterian polity and its form of government."[48] Damiani also identified conflict within congregations, or between pastors and sessions, as frequent and debilitating. He singled out as problems the small size of the congregations—ten were of less than ninety members—and their lack of adequate financial resources, which encouraged what Damiani called a "survival mentality." Bilingual Christian education or evangelism materials were not readily available, and many of the building facilities were in serious disrepair.

Speaking roughly a year and a half after his original study, Damiani expressed some signs of hope. For example, the ministerial situation had been improved by the introduction of four pastors from Puerto Rico (one from the Dominican Republic) and by his own ordination. He mentioned one congregation in particular, Trinity United in Brooklyn, for developing a new program of community outreach that is anchored in the provision of social services that respond to the needs of the immediate neighborhood. According to reported statistics, Trinity United went from 118 members in 1986 to 158 members in 1987, unlike the others in the presbytery, whose gains were modest or who reported declines in membership. The frustrations, however, remain. It is evident that U.S. Hispanic churches are still dependent for pastors on sources outside the mainland.

Conclusions and Questions

Our description of the three major Hispanic Presbyterian groups and denominational efforts to support them as a distinct constituency leads us to frame some conclusions and to raise some questions about the future. Hispanic Presbyterians are a varied lot, and no conceivable strategy could be developed by the church to tailor programs and resources for every possible variation. Nevertheless, it is clear that there are at least three groupings that should be taken into account in the development of resources and strategies.

The first could be identified as Hispanics who choose to remain in the traditional Hispanic churches. The prevailing concerns for this group are those of bilingualism and biculturalism; of the development, retention, and support of leadership; and of the continuation of their churches. To illustrate, the language issue has been one of the most divisive and painful in the history of many Hispanic congregations. Whether the services and the educational ministry of the congregation are conducted primarily in English, in Spanish, or in a combination of both has been the issue over which many a congregation has split. A variety of accommodations exist, from Spanish-only, to alternate services in English or Spanish, to bilingual services, to English-only.

It is also apparent that the language issue in many cases is a symbol for a deeper problem, namely, the question of biculturalism. Although on the one hand Hispanic Presbyterians want to be integrated into denominational structures, on the other hand they wish to retain their recognizable identity, which leads directly to the issue of biculturalism. Even in congregations where English is the prevalent language, or even the only language, of worship and instruction, members want to maintain a distinctively Hispanic identity.

The denomination has in the past done very little to support bilingualism and biculturalism within its membership. For example, studies to determine what sorts of worship patterns have developed and how the Sunday school curriculum should support the concerns of bilingual/bicultural churches have not been done. Not surprisingly, such materials have been extremely scarce, and when they have been produced, they are usually mere translations from the English, an expedient that does not address the needs of biculturalism. Hispanic PC(USA) churches today operate without a Spanish hymnbook, or worship book, or Sunday school curriculum produced by their denomination. Minimal efforts are being made, however, in the distribution of translations of the *Presbyterian Newsletter, Justice Jottings,* or the annual One Great Hour of Sharing materials, but presently Presbyterian Hispanics' choices for sources of Spanish-language study and worship materials are to go to other denominational or commercial producers or to do without.

If the scarcity of Spanish-language program and worship materials is troublesome, the predicament posed by the need to prepare, support, and retain Hispanic pastors remains critical, even though limited successes point to hope. Two PC(USA) theological seminaries, Austin and McCormick, have developed special interest programs for recruitment and training of Hispanics for the Presbyterian ministry. In spite of their efforts and the occasional Hispanic who graduates elsewhere, the major sources of ministerial training for the Hispanic churches are still not the denominational seminaries. Production of Hispanic ministers, however, is not all of the problem. Retention of the ablest, and particularly the U.S.-educated, Hispanic clergy in the parish churches has proved difficult. Many recent seminary graduates go to administrative positions in the structures of the church or to educational institutions after brief parish experiences. Whether this is a passing phase that will stabilize after more graduates become available is uncertain, but at the moment many of the small vacant Hispanic churches have little hope of obtaining their own pastors.

Is there a future for these churches? If Hispanic migration to the United States were to follow the pattern of the nineteenth-century and early twentieth-century migrations from Europe, the answer would be no—at least as Spanish-language churches. That is, a one-generation wave of ethnic immigration would produce descendants who would assimilate more and more into the American pattern, progressively becoming English monolinguals not disposed to retaining "ethnic" features other than those fully compatible with American social patterns and values. There are undoubtedly many Hispanics who do follow this pattern. Nevertheless, Hispanics as a whole constitute a larger "minority" than any of the classic immigrant groups, and, in parts of the country like the Rio Grande Valley of Texas, are actually in the majority. Their language is the language of the founders of cities like San Antonio or Santa Fe or Los Angeles, and their culture is an essential element of the culture of the American Southwest.[49] Replenished by constant inmigration and frequent contact, the Spanish language and Hispanic culture, it can plausibly be argued, are permanent and increasing parts of the United States reality. It would be presumptuous to say that the PC(USA) Hispanic churches *do* have a future. Given the Hispanic presence and the future of Hispanics in the United States, however, it is clear that they *should* have a future, and that the denomination *should* provide them with the support they need to develop into a valuable resource.

Hispanics entering the United States as political refugees, and those either crossing the U.S. border in search of a livelihood or living on the boundary zone between the First and the Third World that is the U.S.-Mexico border, constitute a second category. The list of efforts in their behalf, from aid offered to Cuban refugees in the 1960s to current transborder ventures like Puentes de Cristo, is long and worthy. Attention must be focused on the plight of Nicaraguan, Salvadoran, and Guatemalan "sojourners" currently flocking to the promise of freedom in the United States. Although the PC(USA) historically has responded strongly to perceived need in situations of social emergency, what has also historically not been present has been the ability to accommodate itself to those it serves so that they feel truly at home. The assumption has been that the newly arrived Hispanics would find places in traditional Hispanic congregations, based on the dubious theory that language is a sufficient factor to define a group. If the PC(USA) is truly to incorporate this group—or, more properly, groups—it must be prepared to deal directly with the great cultural and socioeconomic differences that separate Mexican and Central American immigrants from U.S. Hispanics, not to say Anglos. Will it be prepared, for example, to experiment with ecclesiastical forms, such as the "base communities," which have proved their worth in Latin America? In spite of their foreignness to traditional Presbyterian polity, they may well be the key to otherwise unreachable Hispanics.[50]

Finally, the statistics that opened this essay showed that there are many Hispanics in the Anglo Presbyterian churches throughout the country. This should not be surprising after more than one hundred years of "Hispanic work." The church can count this fact as a success. The question to be raised, however, is that of the self-perception of the entire PC(USA) as regards its ethnic rootage. Is the PC(USA) always to remain a "Scottish" or a Scots-Irish/English church? Perhaps it is time to recognize, not by way of occasional ceremony, but rather of meaningful integration, the presence of Hispanics—and other groups, like Koreans—within the Presbyterian family. Robert Wuthnow, a sociologist of American religion, has identified the formation of "special purpose groups" as a characteristic feature of contemporary U.S. denominationalism.[51] Perhaps it is well to heed his warning of the negative side of

this development—specifically his analysis of the increase
in size and diversity of bureaucratization within the denominational structure that it entails, and the potential for frac-
tionalization that it can foment. Organized efforts to
recognize and deal with the Hispanic presence in the
Presbyterian Church have arguably already produced examples of both kinds of undesirable result. Nevertheless,
Wuthnow's thesis is that special-purpose groups have been
a revitalizing influence on American religion by stimulating
its potential adaptability, particularly in the context of the
social change that the United States has experienced since
World War II. In a society where Hispanics are rapidly becoming a significant minority, their organized presence
within the Presbyterian Church may indeed become a stimulus toward revitalizing change. The church would gain
greatly by celebrating the diversity that its now centenary
history of mission to Hispanics has brought it, and by reflecting that diversity in the many ways in which it wor-
ships, and sings, and tells its own history.[52]

12

Contexts for a History of Asian American Presbyterian Churches: A Case Study of the Early History of Japanese American Presbyterians

Michael J. Kimura Angevine and Ryô Yoshida

Developing a history of Asian American Presbyterian churches is a task that can only be anticipated and not accomplished at this point.[1] This essay will instead address the larger sociohistorical contexts and theoretical considerations necessary for such a venture. It will then focus on the formative period (the late nineteenth and early twentieth centuries) of Japanese American Presbyterian history as a case study. This approach is intended to suggest a methodology for the larger task of the study of other Asian American Presbyterian groups.

A new movement within Asian American Presbyterian churches emerged in the late 1960s and 1970s, and is symbolized in the formation of the Asian Presbyterian Caucus in 1972. On March 16–19, Presbyterians of Chinese, Filipino, Taiwanese, Japanese, Korean, and Southeast Asian ancestry from around the United States met for the first time at White Sulphur Springs in St. Helena, California.[2] These participants knew that this was a unique moment in the history of Asian American Presbyterian churches. Out of it came "A Statement of Concerns of Asian Presbyterians" written around the theme of self-development. After citing the Confession of 1967 and 1 John 3:15, these Presbyterians declared: "For the past 100 years, since the initial and successive migration of Asians to America, this group has been the most silent of minorities. Because of the peculiar history of racism and the popular notion of the 'melting pot,' Asians have been forced to deny their cultural and historical background to become a part of America and suffered a loss of self-hood." The Asian Presbyterian Caucus was to be the vehicle to assure the "full self-hood and cultural integrity" of Asian American Presbyterians. This particular moment was but one expression of a revitalizing movement of Third World people in the United States in the mid-1960s and early 1970s. This resurgence of people of color, with their unique historical perspective, was not received easily by some in the Presbyterian Church.

The participants at the St. Helena assembly thought they were breaking the silence of a century, but a close examination of the history of that century reveals voices that cry out with the eloquence of their own age. The Third World movement in the United States gave some Asian Americans the motivation and the sensitivity of historical consciousness to listen for the voices of the past as part of their own process of empowerment.

Wesley Woo describes three characteristics of the history of Presbyterian work with Asian Americans:

1. The work was largely under the control of white missionaries, pastors, Sabbath school teachers, or volunteers.
2. The mission world was captive to the prevailing American Protestant worldview that America was to be both the agent and exemplar of the coming kingdom of God and that Protestant Christianity, American culture, and civilization itself were virtually coterminous accomplishments. Therefore evangelism, Americanization, and the civilizing of pagans were seen as interchangeable processes toward the same end.
3. Protestant work with the Asian in America was generally seen as an extension of foreign missions and a way to evangelize Asia through the many Asians who were returning home.[3]

These three characteristics are important for understanding one of the several sociohistorical contexts discussed in this essay, namely, white Protestant denominations in the United States, and, in particular, the Presbyterian Church. The study of the rich and complex texture of Asian American Presbyterian church history must be grounded in the sociohistorical context of the United States that reveals the power of racism and how this context was fashioned and shaped by religious institutions in general and the Protestant and Presbyterian churches in particular.

A second context for this study is the sociohistorical context of Asian societies. This reveals the power of European and American imperialism, particularly how Christianity developed in Asia, after it entered Asian societies under the aegis and protection of European and American imperial might.

A third context for this study is the development of the international political economy and the way it influenced the domestic social context of Asian countries of origin as well as that of the United States, with its history of racism. This history of racism in the United States is itself linked with the development of the international political economy.

Specifically, this essay provides an account of the Presbyterian Church and Japanese in northern California between the late 1860s to the mid-1920s. The study is situated in the sociohistorical context of late nineteenth-century California and Meiji-Taishô Japan.[4] It provides an interpretation of the relevant features of American Protestant mission work and the development of Christianity in Japan during this period.

Late Nineteenth-Century Presbyterian Mission to Asians in the United States

The mission of the Presbyterian Church to Asians in the United States began in 1852, when First Presbyterian Church in San Francisco asked the Presbytery of California (Old School) to petition the Board of Foreign Missions of the Presbyterian Church in the U.S.A. for a mission among the Chinese in California. William Speer, a missionary to China with four years' experience in Canton, was commissioned by the board and sent to San Francisco in 1852. In addition to Speer, names such as Loomis, Cameron, and Sturge reflect the reality of a mission largely under the control of "white missionaries, pastors, Sabbath school teachers, or volunteers." These were dedicated and loving people who had a passion tempered with compassion for their charges, but they embodied within their work and commitments the ethos of a nineteenth-century worldview.

The American Protestant missions to Asians in late nineteenth-century America provided a church tradition that was formative for Asian American Christian churches. This mission had a closely linked domestic and international focus. The work among Chinese in America was started by former missionaries to China. Mission work to Japanese started in missions among Chinese, and at first, a Chinese translation of the Bible was used, which was more accessible than English translations to educated Japanese trained in the Chinese classics.

These missionaries had the explicit goal to Christianize, civilize, and Americanize Asians, who were perceived to be from inferior and degraded cultures. When the anti-Asian movement developed, the missionaries' response was ambiguous. On Christian principles, they defended Asians in the United States. But the Christian witness of the missionaries was tainted by the Anglo-Saxonism, racism, and nationalism that typified the consciousness and activity of late nineteenth-century America.[5] An example of this racism can be seen in the way missionaries couched their defense of Asians in terms of the benefits provided by the cheap labor of Asians who were willing to do tasks undesirable to whites.[6]

Josiah Strong, secretary of the American Home Missionary Society, typified this tradition in this illustration of racial pride: "The Anglo-Saxon as the great representative of these two great ideas [of Christianity and civil liberty], the depository of these two greatest blessings, . . . is divinely commissioned to be in a peculiar sense his brother's keeper."[7]

Closely related to this racism was paternalism. This concept, as developed by Eugene Genovese, an American historian, helps us understand the relationship between white Protestant missionaries and the Asian subjects of their work. Genovese writes: "Paternalism in any historical setting defines relations of superordination and subordination. Its strength as a prevailing ethos increases as the members of the community accept—or feel compelled to accept—these relations as legitimate. Brutality lies inherent in this acceptance of patronage and dependence, no matter how organic the paternalistic order."[8]

The Protestant mission to Asians in America and its workers reflected nineteenth-century paternalism. This paternalistic relationship was reinforced and intensified by the passionate defense of Asians by white Christian workers, a defense required in the face of a powerful anti-Asian racism. The intensity of their defense of Asians and their own self-understanding of the situation are expressions of this paternalism. Asians were children who needed to be protected and nurtured. This paternalism nurtured the consciousness and identity of Asian American Christians, and reinforced their ability to resist American racism; however, this paternalism also made it difficult for Asian American Christians to critique the paternalism.

Late Nineteenth-Century California

California was a rapidly changing society in the late nineteenth century. In 1848, after gold was discovered, California attracted people from around the world. The port of San Francisco was the terminus for this migration, the gateway to the gold fields of the Sierra Nevada foothills.

After 1852, when the easily mined gold of the placers was depleting, gold production slowed. Mining became more capital intensive, requiring more sophisticated methods of extraction. As agriculture oriented toward the Eastern and European market developed, land became a valuable commodity. In 1869, the transcontinental railroad was completed. The development of California's economic infrastructure required large amounts of cheap labor in a state already labor poor. Chinese labor became the preferred alternative. Many Chinese laborers were those who had come for gold but were displaced when anti-Chinese violence and legislation severely limited their mining.

During the period when Presbyterian missionary activities to Chinese and California began, the influx of Chinese coolies continued (from 1847 to 1882); about 500,000 Chinese were brought in during this period.[9] They worked primarily in mines and on railroads, and made significant contributions to the development of the economic infrastructure of the American West, including the transcontinental railroad.

The railroad was completed in 1869, the year that the numbers of Chinese entering the United States made a dramatic increase, almost doubling the previous year's figure. This increase was due to the signing of the Burlingame Treaty of 1868, which, with previous commercial treaties signed in 1844 and 1858, further opened China to the American markets by assuring the free flow of population. This continued until 1882 when, over the protests of a weak Chinese government, the U.S. government unilaterally broke provisions of this treaty with the passage of the Chinese exclusion act. This act represented the culmination of years of intensive anti-Chinese agitation by various groups, dominated by labor unions. With the exclusion of Chinese, a vacuum was left in the labor market that was filled by Japanese.

The legacy of the rancheros existing prior to the conquest of California by the United States affected the development of California agriculture. Because of the existence of large, privately owned tracts of land, kept largely intact because of an international treaty, free land was not available for homesteading, as was the case in the Midwest. After the Gold Rush, commodity agriculture oriented to an international market became a significant source of revenue for California. This development was facilitated by the building of the transcontinental railroad.[10] Japanese immigrants in California were engaged primarily in agricultural labor. In spite of the fact that Japanese immigrants later developed and dominated a less capital-intensive but more labor-intensive type of farming, the primary demand for Japanese labor in California in the late nineteenth century was in large-scale commodity agriculture, especially after the exclusion act of 1882 cut off the supply of Chinese labor, which was increasingly organized and resistant to exploitation.

Transformations in Meiji Period and Japanese Emigration

Meiji Japan (1868–1912) was exciting. Signs of change were everywhere: in the dress, the mannerisms, the goods, the new institutions. But these changes were not without their costs. Old Tokugawa institutions from the final period of traditional Japanese order under a central shogunate were dismantled, and new structures inspired by and chosen carefully from among the competing models offered by the nations of Europe and America were built. This fostered both a self-confidence and assurance that all things were possible in the new future, but also a self-doubt as the repudiated past came forward to question the meaningfulness of the present. One of the problems of Meiji society was to discover in that repudiated past a usable one—a conception of the past that could be meaningfully related to the present with all of its ambiguities and that could provide a vision of the future. The task of Meiji was to create a new Japan. But it was also to discover what it meant to be Japan in the face of the loss of a past that for some represented only humiliation or inferiority when confronted by the power, innovation, and possibilities of the West.

This milieu formed the character of Meiji period Christians and emigrants to the United States. It is an essential ingredient for understanding the nature of paternalism in the development of Japanese American Presbyterian churches and why Japanese so readily entered into the kind of relationships they did with missionaries, both in Japan and in the United States.

These tensions pervaded Japan through developments such as a national system of education.[11] The level of education of Japanese immigrants in the late nineteenth century and early twentieth century was higher on average than the native and immigrant white population in America and California. Meiji educational policy, similar to the formation of a national conscript military, was geared toward the building of a national consciousness rather than the older clan and domain loyalties. It also sought to strengthen the nation's resistance to and competition with the Western imperialist powers.

In the 1890s, the type of Japanese in the United States changed from diplomats, merchants, and students to laborers primarily.[12] From 1900 to 1907, the number of emigrants from Japan to Hawaii, Mexico, and elsewhere in the Western hemisphere increased. They were employed primarily in agriculture in California and in the western United States. They were engaged in such projects as land reclamation in the Sacramento River delta area, replacing Chinese laborers and providing agricultural labor for California's agribusiness. In the words of an 1891 report to the Foreign Ministry by Consul Chinda Sutemi of San Francisco: "They are not students any more, but are laborers. . . . They planned to come to America without any definite purpose except to make a fortune at a stroke."[13] This shift was a result of transformations occurring in Meiji Japan.

One significant change that affected the immigration of Japanese to America was shaped by early Meiji agricultural policies. These policies encouraged trends existing prior to the Meiji period, characterized primarily by the shift from village-based cooperative farming to one oriented to individual families in a market economy that depended more and more upon tenant farming and hired labor.[14] Traditional bonds of family and community and

the moral commitments they implied already were changing. An influential agent here was the tension arising from
a utilitarian individualism in which individual actions and
desires became the only point of certainty in a society
dominated by the power of instrumental rationality as expressed in the logic of the market and the ideology of the
individual.

The power of instrumental rationality intruded into Japanese society, where individual choices began to be
couched in the language of the market, and the traditional
bonds of family (*ie*[15]), village, domain, and nation
(*kokutai*) began to lose some of the deep moral meaning
they enjoyed in the neo-Confucian tradition of Tokugawa
Japan.[16] Individuals were increasingly faced with questions
that required a reconstruction of older ideas about individual success and dedication to the larger good of family and
nation.

It is not clear whether the development of a modern
liberal society, dominated by the logic of the market and of
the individual, was the same in Japan as it was in Europe
and America. However, it is clear that these developments
in Bakumatsu (pre-Meiji) and Meiji Japan were accompanied by a transformation of Japanese cultural values and
practices relevant to the nature of community and the
identity of Japanese in the United States in this formative
period.

The development of the internal Japanese market was
transformed after the coming of Commodore Perry and
the "black ships," of the Far Eastern Squadron to Edo Bay
in 1853. Japan was thrust into the world market and had
to compete directly with the larger industrialized econo-
mies of the imperialist powers. This forced inclusion into
the world market led to strengthening the central government, developing a modern industrial market economy
and a modern military in order to compete in a global
political economy, and a global economy dominated by
imperialist powers in Europe and the United States whose
interests were projected and protected militarily.

One of the more significant of these Meiji policies was

the Land Law of 1873.[17] This law instituted a land tax, important because it was the primary financial basis by which the Meiji government funded its industrial and military policies.[18] This Meiji land policy had enormous significance for the Issei, pre-war immigrants who came to the United States before the exclusion act in 1924.[19] Most of these immigrants came from rural and peasant backgrounds. Between 1889 and 1903, over two-thirds (67.4 percent) of Japanese immigrants to the United States came from the primarily agricultural prefectures in the south.[20]

Both Thomas Smith and E. H. Norman note the different character of Japanese farmers who, in Norman's words, were both more radical and more conservative than their English counterparts.[21] Similar to that of America, the family farm remained the ideal if not the dominant form of farming, preserving the pattern of small rural settlements and blocking the growth of large capitalist agribusiness.[22] In Japan, however, land ownership tended to concentrate in the hands of fewer and fewer people, although large landowners rented their land to families of tenants. This contributed to the "double nature," the "Janus head" of the Japanese peasant.[23] Yet even in the midst of the Meiji changes, the particular organization of rural Japan contributed to the preservation of the old values. These continued to be strong enough to serve the purposes of the Meiji state, which was balancing the radical and liberal ideas associated with the industrial economy and contact with the international political economy. This created tension between the old and the new.

Peasants forced from their families into the cities to help pay high rents and a cash tax provided the bulk of the new industrial work force and immigrants to the United States. The Japanese word *dekasegi* was used to describe this movement from the family farm and village to the city.[24] It literally means to work away from one's home or home province. During the development of Japanese capitalism in the early Meiji period, the combination of government rural policies and economic opportunities in the industrializing urban areas precipitated and encouraged the emigration of surplus agricultural labor out of the rural areas. This emigration was destined not only for Japanese urban areas with its demand for an industrial work force, but also to Hokkaidô, which the government wanted to be developed; overseas to such places as Hawaii, the United States, Peru, Mexico, Brazil; and, after the Russo-Japanese war, to Japan's overseas territories such as Korea, Manchuria, and Taiwan.

In his analysis of the development of disciplined industrial labor in early Meiji, Andrew Gordon comments on the tremendous difficulties facing early capitalists in developing the proper consciousness and character necessary for industrial labor. He describes these *dekasegi* peasants-turned-workers as being unreceptive to discipline, uncommitted, and lacking diligence.[25] The rural origin of this unruly working class is similar to that of the Issei. Instead of moving to the urban areas of Japan, the Issei went to the United States. The *dekasegi* ideal of many of these emigrants was to earn a sufficient amount of money in their places of sojourn to return home wealthy.[26]

The values and culture of the agrarian village, already changing with the intrusion of the market, confronted a new world in the industrializing city. The decline of the solidarities of the past led to the possibilities of new types of associations in the cities. Traditional Japanese types of solidarity such as the *ie* and values such as *risshi* continued to shape Japanese social patterns and development, but in new directions.[27]

This cultural transformation is crucial for understanding the character of the Issei pioneers and the Yobiyose, meaning "those who are called" to come to the United States to help relatives. The latter came to the United States during this period and were part of the generation that came of age in the period after the Sino-Japanese War.[28] These were the first to have been socialized and educated within the new Japan. Before 1905, the majority of immigrants were young. Approximately 78 percent of these were around thirty years of age or younger. These immigrants came of age in Meiji, and their character and consciousness were formed within the milieu of the tensions and excitement over change that characterized Meiji Japan.

Christianity in Meiji-Taishô Japan

This swirling milieu of Meiji provided the context for the first Presbyterian work in Japan. Christianity first came to Japan in the sixteenth century through the efforts of the great Jesuit missionary St. Francis Xavier. Christianity was banned and finally driven underground in the seventeenth century.[29] It was not until after Japan was forced to sign a series of unequal treaties in the face of American and European gunboats that Christian missionaries were allowed into Japan in the nineteenth century. Ostensibly they came to serve the needs of the growing European and American trade and diplomatic communities, but they came also to proselytize the Japanese. The first Protestant service of worship in Japan took place on Sunday, July 11, 1853, on the deck of Commodore Perry's flagship. Richard Drummond notes that this was owing more to Perry's sense of what he should do to represent the United States rather than out of any personal habit of piety.[30] This first Protestant worship in Japan is an image that reveals the relationship between imperialism and the Protestantism of nineteenth-century America.

During this period in Japan, American Protestant missionaries taught a Christianity integrated closely with Euro-American social, political, and scientific learning and practices. In their struggles to create a meaningful present and succeed in the new world of Meiji Japan, Japanese were encouraged by the missionaries to adapt to Western life-styles and values. Their efforts were made easier because of the link made between Christianity and modern technology and civilization. J. C. Hepburn, a Presbyterian medical missionary, was typical of those who advocated medical and educational work as a method to proselytize the Japanese.[31] It was common for American Protestant missionaries, such as Captain L. L. Janes, to establish or teach in schools.[32] A Presbyterian graduate of West Point,

Janes was invited to teach military sciences and other subjects at the school for Western learning for young samurai
of Kumamoto *han*.[33] As the Japanese government and people began to realize their global disadvantage vis-à-vis Europe and America, Christianity was accepted as the
driving ethos behind the technological and economic success of the West.

Japanese began to convert to Christianity, primarily
through close association with particular missionaries,
such as Janes. Most converts at this time were either from
the *samurai* or the wealthy peasant or merchant classes.
These Christians found in the Christianity of nineteenth-
century American Protestant missionaries a way of life and
a structure of meaning that helped them thrive in the
changing world of Meiji Japan. Irwin Scheiner notes in his
study of the Kumamoto band that they tended to see the
strict and austere discipline of this Christianity as a fulfillment rather than a repudiation of their Confucian training.[34] Their close association with particular missionaries
bound these converts to each other and to the missionary
as siblings and parent respectively.

Japanese Christians converted because of the character
of a specific missionary rather than attraction to a specific
theological perspective or ecclesiastical polity. Belonging
first to churches with the denominational affiliation of the
missionary, Japanese Christians asserted their autonomy
from American mission boards by establishing self-supporting churches under Japanese leadership, developing interdenominational organizations, and ultimately creating
their own denominations as soon as possible.

In this early period, these local congregations tended to
organize themselves along the lines of traditional Japanese
organization patterns. Typically, a few Christian leaders
and specific *ie* controlled the local church, forming a kind
of expanded *ie*. Churches were composed primarily of
family units rather than individuals. Not unexpectedly, the
relationship between leaders and members resembled that
between master and disciple or parent and child. This incorporation of traditional Japanese organizational pat-

terns by the local church ensured its survival, even as it tried to maintain its independence from foreign mission boards' domination in a society where Christianity did not have any significant cultural and institutional supports.

Finally, Japanese Christianity developed in a social situation preoccupied with first resisting then competing with Euro-American imperialism. Because Christianity was associated in their society with this imperialism, Japanese Christians were careful to show that Christianity was a spiritual resource that would strengthen Japan, even as it was being strengthened by Western technology. This was important because the Meiji government was promoting the notion of *wakon yôsai* (Japanese spirit, Western learning). Nationalism and patriotism were important elements of Japanese Christianity during the Meiji-Taishô period, just as they were in nineteenth-century American Protestantism.

Origins of Japanese Presbyterian Churches

The mission of the Japanese Presbyterian churches in the United States began in 1869 when a group of Japanese attended Sunday school and studied a Chinese translation of the Bible at Howard Presbyterian Church in San Francisco.[35] The pastor of Howard Presbyterian Church at this time was Henry Martyn Scudder, who served between 1865 and 1871. Scudder, a former missionary to India, was the father-in-law of Captain L. L. Janes. He served as a missionary to Japan between 1887 and 1889. A sermon he preached in 1866 epitomized what F. G. Notehelfer calls the "expansive, confident, and messianic mood of mid-nineteenth-century American Protestantism."

> With Christianity for our religion, Republicanism for our form of government, the highest social, civil, educational and spiritual welfare of the multitudinous millions under our benignant sway for our aim, and with the examples of lofty national virtue for the residue of mankind, shall we not do much to usher in the day of millennial glory?[36]

In this millennial vision for the world, Scudder expresses
the manner in which Protestant Christianity and American values, practices, and institutions were woven together. This vision is expressive of late nineteenth-century
Presbyterian missions' paternalism toward Asians in
America.

In 1877, a Japanese group composed mainly of Methodists and Congregationalists organized the *Fukuinkai* (Gospel Society) at the Chinese Mission of the Methodist
Episcopal Church in San Francisco.[37] This was the first
Japanese organization in America. The *Fukuinkai*'s purpose was to study the Bible, to "recognize the love of Jesus
Christ," to lead their Japanese compatriots to Jesus Christ,
and to "remove bad habits" that the members thought
were thriving among Japanese in San Francisco.[38] Among
other things, this meant educating and promoting temperance in the early Japanese community in San Francisco.
"Removing bad habits" was an expression of the notion of
risshi. Understanding the meaning of the tradition of *risshi*
in the Meiji period was an important element of redefining
the past in the face of Japan's new world as well as a com-
ponent of the intellectual ferment within Meiji society.
Cultivating the habits of good character was not just an
end in itself; it also meant setting a good example for the
world as proof that Japan was to be counted among the
"civilized" nations of the world. One of the leading forces
behind the development of the *Fukuinkai* was a patriotism
peculiar to Meiji Japan. If some Japanese in San Francisco
behaved in ways considered disgusting or immoral to the
"civilized" Americans, it would reflect not only upon other
Japanese in San Francisco, but would also insult "Japanese
honor and the relationship between Japan and the United
States."[39]

The *Fukuinkai* was a nondenominational, independent,
Japanese Christian organization aided originally by the
women's group of the First Congregational Church of San
Francisco. It served as a locus for study and religious in-
struction and as a center to assist Japanese newcomers to
San Francisco in such matters as finding jobs and housing.

In addition, it provided instruction in English and performed other charitable and moral reform work.

The *Fukuinkai* split in May 1881 over the issue of leadership. The increasing power within the *Fukuinkai* of Otis Gibson, from the California Conference of the Methodist Episcopal Church's mission to the Chinese in San Francisco, was particularly opposed by non-Methodist members of the *Fukuinkai.* The dissidents left the original *Fukuinkai* and formed the *Taira Fukuinkai* (Taylor Gospel Society) named for the street on which they met. The issue of the domination of Gibson and Methodist missionaries again split the *Fukuinkai* in 1883. A majority of its members left, having objected to the authority wielded by American missionaries in the organization. This group formed *Sutevenson Fukuinkai* (Stevenson Gospel Society), which met on Stevenson Street. A year and a half later, the Stevenson group merged with the first dissident group and assumed the name of the *Taira Fukuinkai.* Rev. Robert MacKenzie, pastor of Howard Presbyterian Church, Elder James Roberts from the same church, and Rev. John Carrington helped organize the meetings and the evening school of the *Fukuinkai.*[40] Members of the Taylor group later transferred to Howard Presbyterian Church.[41]

After the split, the emphasis on moral education did not change. On the first anniversary of the founding of an Oakland branch of the *Fukuinkai,* the group renewed their intention to work toward the education, enlightenment, and correction of those whose behavior insulted all Japanese and Japan in the eyes of Americans. Christianity in the early Japanese American community was similar to the Christianity of Meiji Japan.

The origins and early development of the *Fukuinkai* occurred at the same time as the anti-Chinese exclusion movement. The latter resulted in the exclusion of Chinese immigrants in 1882. The *Fukuinkai* was meeting in the Chinese Methodist Episcopal Mission during this time, and their association with the Chinese Mission and Gibson was the significant reason for the two splits that occurred in the *Fukuinkai.* Japanese did not want to be under the paternal authority of Gibson, with whom most had no real ties. And just as significantly, the Japanese Christians were a part of a Meiji culture, one embracing the West even as it was rejecting its Chinese past. China was seen as a culture that could not resist the Euro-American imperialism that Japan was resisting. The exclusion of Chinese in 1882 reinforced this image to members of the *Fukuinkai*. They made sure to distinguish themselves from a group that had been excluded by America. This split between Chinese and Japanese would become even stronger as Japan's military, built along Western lines, confronted and then defeated China in the Sino-Japanese war.

As the Taylor *Fukuinkai* came under the guidance of the Howard Presbyterian Church, some of its members affiliated with this congregation. Carrington, A. W. Loomis, and Roberts encouraged the Taylor *Fukuinkai* members to organize a Japanese Presbyterian church. Accordingly, the members of the Taylor *Fukuinkai* proposed the organization of such a church at the meeting of the San Francisco Presbytery on April 28, 1885.[42] The presbytery approved this proposal and appointed Loomis, Carrington, Mac-Kenzie, and Roberts as the organizing committee. The first organizational meeting was held on May 9, at which time seventeen members were received on letter of transfer from various churches in America and Japan. On May 16, 1885, they established the First Japanese Presbyterian Church of San Francisco with these seventeen transferred members and also sixteen baptized members.[43] The original members of the First Japanese Presbyterian Church were primarily male students, merchants, and businessmen—a microcosm of the Japanese population in San Francisco at the time. The original thirty-three also included one woman who was studying in preparation for medical school. Jusaburo Morita and Kokichi Mitani were elected elders, and Carrington was appointed moderator of the session until other pastoral help could be found for the new church. The presbytery placed this church under the supervision of the Board of Foreign Missions of the Presbyterian Church in the U.S.A. One of the first acts of the new First Japanese Presbyterian Church was the establishment of the *Seinenkai* (Japanese YMCA) on August 27, 1886. Its purpose was to develop a community based on Christian faith and to educate unaffiliated Japanese in the Bible and English.[44] Because many Japanese came to San Francisco to learn about Western civilization, the *Seinenkai* provided a school, boardinghouse, library, athletic facilities, and so forth. The *Seinenkai* was an educational ministry under the supervision of the Presbyterian Board of Foreign Missions.

The Board of Foreign Missions directed its early work to Japanese students and intellectuals who made up the bulk of the early Japanese population in San Francisco. The Presbyterian Church felt an obligation to do mission work among this group because a large number of Japanese who converted to Christianity under the influence of the Presbyterian mission in Japan were coming to California to continue their study of Western civilization begun in the mission schools and churches in Japan.[45] The church wanted to ensure that these students would continue to receive a Christian education during their sojourn in the United States that they might return to Japan as Christian missionaries.[46]

E. A. Sturge served as superintendent of the Japanese Presbyterian Mission on the Pacific Coast from 1886 to 1922. Sturge was born in 1856 in Cleveland, Ohio, and was educated at the University of Pennsylvania, where he received an M.D. and a Ph.D. He worked as a medical missionary in Thailand for the Presbyterian Board of Foreign Missions from 1880 to 1885.[47]

Returning to the United States to recover their health after he and his wife Annie contracted cholera, Sturge and his wife arrived in San Francisco in the summer of 1885. Sturge's letter to F. F. Ellinwood at the Board of Foreign Missions describes what he did after his arrival:

> We have now been here seven months. We came as you know for the sole purpose of working among the Chinese of this

city, but it seems as though God intended it otherwise for since the day of our arrival much of our time has been given to the Japanese work of which there seemed to be a greater need. Yesterday, four more of our Japanese scholars made a public profession of religion and were admitted to the membership of our little Japanese Church. Seven of our boys have been led to take this important step since we began our work among them and we believe that others are learning to love and trust in our Savior. Our home for Japanese young men which we call the Japanese Y.M.C.A. is quite full. The school and religious services are well attended.[48]

The 29-year-old Sturge planned to work as a medical missionary among the Chinese in San Francisco and was being supported in this work by his uncle in England.[49] Sturge had approached the Board of Foreign Missions for permission to do this work, and this permission was granted.[50] However, A. W. Loomis, who was in charge of the medical mission to the Chinese in San Francisco, opposed Sturge's involvement because of the financial strain of adding a fourth medical missionary and because Sturge could not speak Chinese. Loomis instead encouraged Sturge to work with the Japanese.[51] In July of 1886, the Presbyterian Board of Foreign Missions officially appointed Sturge to work at the school for Japanese in San Francisco.[52]

Upon his appointment to the Japanese school in San Francisco in July 1886, Sturge taught at the school of the *Seinenkai,* guided the members of the First Japanese Presbyterian Church, and helped establish several Pacific Coast Japanese Presbyterian churches. Sturge worked as a teacher, preacher, doctor, and superintendent of the Pacific Coast Japanese mission until 1922, except for a period between 1889 and 1891 when he went to Germany to pursue further medical studies. Although Sturge gave virtually his entire salary and property to the Japanese mission, he never informed the Japanese of this.[53]

Sturge criticized anti-Japanese sentiment, pointing out how irrational such notions were and reminding people that all human beings are brothers and sisters under God.[54] He used a language and reasoning typical of late nineteenth-century American Protestantism. Reminiscent of the language used by other Protestant missionaries to defend the rights of Asians in America, he wrote:

> Our cry should not be: "Exclude the Japanese," but rather Americanize and Christianize them and all foreigners who find their way to our shores, for in this way we may best help to save America and the world.[55]

Sturge was one of the leading figures to urge interdenominational cooperation for Japanese mission work in America. Sturge was a leading participant in an interdenominational conference on the "Oriental question" at Mt. Hermon in 1907. At that conference, a permanent council on the "Oriental question" was formed. The organizing principles again reveal the nineteenth-century perspective of Protestant leaders:

1. The Lordship of Jesus over the whole earth.
2. The promotion of Justice and mutual welfare of the nations bordering the Pacific Ocean.
3. The unquestioned supremacy of the Anglo-Saxon in America.[56]

Japanese respected Dr. Sturge and his wife and were deeply influenced by them. This followed a pattern of Japanese Christians in Japan, who also identified with the missionaries under whose influence they were converted. When Sturge resigned late in 1889 in order to study in Germany, the Japanese associated with the mission mourned the loss of "their lovely parents."[57] Upon his return in 1891, Sturge resumed the position of superintendent of the Japanese mission on the West Coast, to the delight of the Japanese Presbyterians.

Sturge was held in such esteem that a special celebration was held every five years to honor the anniversary of the beginning of his work. For the occasion of the fifteenth anniversary of Sturge's work, one thousand dollars was collected among the Japanese. In October of 1903 the Sturges were presented with round-trip tickets to Japan, and *The Spirit of Japan,* a volume of Sturge's poetry, was published.[58] For the occasion of his twenty-fifth anniversary in 1911, a special evangelistic campaign was mounted that featured Masahisa Uyemura, a prominent Presbyterian from Japan and pastor of Fujimichô Church in Tôkyô. In November of 1912, Japanese Presbyterians in the United States opened the Sturge Library. Japanese who were influenced by Sturge were so attached to him that even when they returned to Japan, they maintained their ties and loyalties. In 1933, a Sturge Society was established in Japan whose purpose was "to remind us of Dr. and Mrs. Sturge, to send our respect to them, and to comfort Dr. Sturge who is still making efforts to save the spirit of the Japanese in America in spite of his old age."[59]

The Japanese love for the Sturges was the love of those who had left Japan and could no longer be close to their parents. They experienced this parental love through the Sturges.[60] Because the Sturges had no children, the Japanese they served were viewed as children. This relationship is an example of paternalism. It was reinforced, on the one hand, by the triumphalist notions of late nineteenth-century American Protestantism reflected in Sturge, and, on the other, by the Japanese American Presbyterians who were a part of the changing milieu of Meiji-Taishô Japan, in which the vertical integrative patterns of the Japanese relationship based on loyalty and duty between parent and child, teacher and student were being redefined.

This powerful relationship with Sturge had a lasting and significant influence on the life of Japanese American Presbyterians. Sturge worked closely with the Presbyterian mission to the Japanese from 1885 until 1934 when he died. Even when he began his work at the age of twenty-nine, he was using the term "boys" in reference to Japanese. He continued to work with his "beloved children" past his retirement as the superintendent of the Japanese mission on the Pacific Coast. He worked closely with the Japanese mission in San Mateo until his death. This mission now bears his name as the Sturge Presbyterian Church.

Beginning in about 1894, new immigrants were increasingly agricultural laborers. They came to fulfill the labor demands of California agriculture. The Japanese community in San Francisco began reflecting this change, as did the First Japanese Presbyterian Church. Influenced by Sturge, many of his students entered the ministry and then left San Francisco to begin churches in more rural parts of California. Churches were established in Salinas, Monterey, Los Angeles and, early in the new century, in Watsonville by ministers associated with the Japanese Presbyterian Church in San Francisco.

The increased numbers of *dekasegi* workers in the California agricultural industry encouraged the Presbyterian Church to expand its ministry. Presbyterians started to work among laborers who lived in local areas such as Watsonville and Salinas in the early 1900s. The mission emphasized educational work for Japanese students.[61] After 1913, the mission focused on the Japanese family and children and the strengthening of the Sunday school.[62] Besides education, it encouraged temperance work in every Japanese local church.[63] In addition, the Occidental Board of the Women's Foreign Missionary Society sought to help Japanese women in need. For example, a rescue program for Japanese women and a women's home were established.[64] This rescue work was closely associated with the work of Donaldina Cameron in San Francisco's Chinatown.

Anti-Japanese feelings strengthened as natives and immigrants of European extraction began to feel that their economic and political privileges were threatened, and as the Japanese began to resist anti-Japanese economic exploitation in the fields. Japanese Presbyterians worked to resist this anti-Japanese movement. They formed the Japanese Presbyterian Conference (JPC) in June 1905 in order to cooperate for effective mission work to Japanese in America.[65] Sturge took part in this Conference as the superintendent of the Japanese Presbyterian Mission on the Pacific Coast. At the Conference, the participants resolved to publish *Dokuritsu* (Independence) as the Conference newspaper, establish new Japanese mission stations, develop a special program for Sturge's anniversary, and unite with other denominations.[66]

Japanese Presbyterians felt much closer to the Conference, which was more practically meaningful, than to the Presbyterian denomination. The Conference forged solidarity among Japanese Presbyterians, thereby intensifying their consciousness as a minority group within the Presbyterian Church. Although a part of local presbyteries, they were still under the authority of the Board of Foreign Missions and its representative, Sturge.

The Pacific Coast Japanese mission under the Board of Foreign Missions was transferred to the Home Mission Board in 1923.[67] After Sturge retired, Philip Payne, assistant director of the Department of City, Immigrants, and Industrial Work, assumed the position of superintendent of Japanese work in America and moderator of the Japanese Presbyterian Conference. The primary activities of the Conference centered upon finding churches for ministers, helping churches in need, and planning special evangelistic campaigns.[68]

There were difficulties in the growth of Japanese Presbyterian missions because of developments such as the beginning of the *Jôdo Shinshû* Buddhist mission from Japan in the late 1890s, anti-Japanese hostility, and the enactment of the legislation aimed at restricting Japanese from owning property, immigrating to America, or having naturalization rights. But Japanese Presbyterian churches expanded through California, into Washington and Utah.[69] Presbyterians organized the *Dendô-Dan,* the Japanese Interdenominational Board of Missions, which cooperated with Japanese churches of other denominations in campaigns to educate and fight against alcoholism as well as resist and delimit anti-Japanese sentiment.[70] Sturge consistently argued for denominational unity and the independence of the Japanese churches on the Pacific Coast, and he supported the *Dendô-Dan.*[71]

The JPC organized resistance to anti-Japanese legislation, such as the California alien land law of 1913, which prohibited "aliens ineligible for citizenship" from owning land, and the immigration law in 1924, which excluded Japanese immigration to the United States. JPC helped in the organization and support of new Japanese Presbyterian churches, such as in Lompoc, Monterey, and Lodi. It assisted the Presbyterian Church's missionary efforts in Japan by setting up special committees with this purpose and sending contributions to the Board of Foreign Missions for this purpose. It tried to improve the increasing uneasiness of the United States and the Presbyterian Church over Japanese imperialism in Korea.[72]

But even as the ties among Japanese Presbyterian churches were being strengthened, these same churches and leaders were at the forefront of interdenominational efforts of cooperation and even union. These efforts began to grow in significance in the face of the rising anti-Japanese movements. Presbyterians were at the forefront of the efforts. For example, as a direct response to the events leading up to the San Francisco School Incident in 1906, the *Zaibei Nihonjin Kirisutokyôto Dômei,* the Japanese Christian Federation in America, was established.[73] Racism was becoming more overt in America since the Japanese victory over the Russians in the Russo-Japanese war. This symbolized for many the first defeat of a white nation by a nonwhite nation and gave rise to new efforts to control and exclude Japanese in the United States. The concern for moral cultivation of character is also found in the goals of its constitution:

1. To spread Christianity.
2. To stimulate our people to a higher plane of living.
3. To reform customs.
4. To reclaim and to lead to usefulness those who are careless, indolent, and wandering from the path of rectitude.
5. To encourage people to be studious, industrious, and thrifty.
6. To render assistance to innocent people who have been wrongly accused of doing evil.
7. To encourage others to a noble life by making public real success already obtained by other people.[74]

These goals of the *Dômei* were typical of many such goals

extending back to the origins of the *Fukuinkai,* and they resonated with the concerns of Japanese intellectuals and leaders as they tried to come to grips with the tradition of *risshi* within the context of modern Japan. However, in America, the threat of the West was not only felt on the level of the international political economy and the struggle for power. It was also experienced in the day-to-day struggles of Japanese with white racism. Racism limited their economic ability to compete, made land tenure difficult if not impossible, and tried to exclude all Japanese immigrants and strip those who were here of the few political rights they had. The interdenominational movement was an important ingredient in the efforts to resist the racism of the United States.

Japanese American Christians were not isolated. They had the encouragement and support of Japanese in Japan. One such leader, Danjô Ebina, was pastor of the Hongô Church in Tôkyô. He came to visit the Japanese community in America on his way to an international conference of the Congregational Church held in the summer of 1908 in Scotland. Danjô Ebina exhorted Japanese in America to improve their character and morals as a way to confront the anti-Japanese movement. He said that Japanese should begin to think of America as their permanent residence and should make efforts to learn English. In doing so, they would be working to establish the presence of *Dai Nippon* (Great Japan) and develop *yamato damashii* (the Spirit of Japan) in America. They must also fulfill their responsibility to Imperial Japan through diligence, patience, and temperance; they must overcome the racism of Americans through the principle of "true brotherhood" based on the Christian notion of "philanthropy" and in the spirit of "*daijihi shujô saido*" (salvation of all living things through the mercy of the Buddha).[75]

Another such leader was Tsuneteru Miyagawa, pastor of the Osaka Congregational Church. He visited the Pacific Coast Japanese American communities in 1909. He denounced anti-Japanese racism as anti-Christian and urged the improvement and cultivation of Japanese character.

For him, the way to resist white racism and win equality was to become independent of white missionaries and denominations and to establish an independent Japanese Church in the United States. He said Japanese Christians in America should become familiar with and master the American political process rather than compete with each other based upon denominational differences.[76]

The presence of these strong leaders, emerging from the struggles for identity and independence in Meiji Christian churches, encouraged Japanese Christians in America. Japanese Christians continued their interdenominational efforts and began focusing their efforts beyond cooperation to church union.[77]

The establishment of the *Sôkô Nihonjin Kirisuto Kyôkai* (San Francisco Japanese Church of Christ) in 1914 marks an important moment. Japanese American Presbyterians were crucial in the development of this merger of the First Japanese Presbyterian Church into the San Francisco Japanese Church of Christ. The present Christ United Presbyterian Church in San Francisco evolved directly from this church. In studying the development of this federated church, one can see how Japanese were responding to a racist sociohistorical context and were in the process of developing an autonomous racial ethnic church. They were able to reinforce solidarity among Japanese Americans and to nurture Japanese American consciousness and identity in a people who today are still neither Japanese nor assimilated into white American culture.

The *Sôkô Nihonjin Kirisuto Kyôkai* was the first of what was hoped to become an independent Japanese American denomination, the *Beikoku Kirisuto Kyôkai* (Japanese Church of Christ in America). This church developed through the efforts and support of key Japanese lay persons who worked through their organization, the *Kirisutokyôto Dômei* (Japanese Lay Persons' Federation), with pastors and white Christian workers who had been engaged in interdenominational work. The church established a confession and a constitution that closely followed Presbyterian polity, despite the presence of other denominational representatives in the group. Much of the liturgy, especially for baptism, is similar to that of the Presbyterian *Book of Common Worship.* The similarities between this church and the *Kirisuto Kyôkai* in Japan needs to have careful study, especially beginning with the first Japanese Protestant church in Yokohama, the *Yokohama Nihon Kirisuto Kôkai.* Like the San Francisco *Kirisuto Kyôkai,* it was a result of cooperative work between the Presbyterian and Congregational denominations. This church too was modeled closely on Presbyterian Church polity. After the *Kirisuto Kyôkai* was established in San Francisco, missions were established in South Park (1914), San Raphael (1924), and San Mateo (1924).[78]

As noted earlier, E. A. Sturge was a supporter of interdenominational work, and he worked for and encouraged the development of the *Kirisuto Kyôkai.* He worked closely on this with the superintendent of the Congregational mission to the Japanese. His failure at getting the cooperation of the Methodist Superintendent Johnson to work for union kept the Japanese Methodists out of the efforts to establish the *Kirisuto Kyôkai.* Johnson saw the importance of cooperative work, but he thought that moving from cooperation to union was too much.[79]

Sturge was elected an elder on the session of the newly formed *Kirisuto Kyôkai.* The *Kirisuto Kyôkai* represented the federation of the Japanese Presbyterian and Congregational church in San Francisco. Sturge also was involved in church administration, although he was not a pastor. He was consistently elected to the session, and the church was under his influence even while it attempted to assert independence from the American denominations.

The paternal relationship between Sturge and the members of the church dominated their life together and the decision making of the session. An example of this influence can be seen in the action of a special session meeting that occurred on November 17, 1914. At that time, the relationship between the *Kirisuto Kyôkai* and the *Seinenkai* was discussed formally. This culminated a process of discussion that had been ongoing for some time. The session

The session finally voted resolving that "the Seinenkai which has been under the guidance of the *Kirisuto Kyôkai* be separated from the church from now on." Sturge was the only person voting against this action. After hearing his objections, the session reconsidered and passed another resolution that canceled the previous motion, leaving the *Seinenkai,* for which Sturge was responsible through the Board of Foreign Missions, as a part of the *Kirisuto Kyôkai.* The *Kirisuto Kyôkai,* like its predecessor First Japanese Presbyterian Church, honored Sturge frequently. In 1923, it voted to make Sturge a session member for life.[80]

There were similarities during this period between the development of interdenominational cooperative ministry in both Japan and in Japanese American communities. There were also obvious differences. Japanese Christians in Japan worked closely together, because Christianity did not have an institutional infrastructure of support in Japan, and Christians were a minority. Japanese American Christians worked cooperatively because of the small numbers of Japanese in the United States, but also as a means to resist white racism. Interdenominational work helped Japanese Christians respond effectively within the racist context of late nineteenth- and early twentieth-century America.

The approach of Japanese American Christians to the cultural context of nineteenth-century America was to focus on *risshi,* that is, the development of the character as a means to improve social conditions and personal moral behavior. This activity was directed at education, moral reform, and assimilation.[81] This strategy was influenced by the perception Japanese Christians had about Christian civilization. Japanese American Christians believed that in becoming Christians they had become civilized, assimilating the spirit of Western civilization. In doing so, they expected that the anti-Japanese racism would be reduced. This belief was based on the idea that America was a Christian nation and that as a Christian nation, it would be guided by Christian principles such as humanitarianism and the equality of all as children of God.[82]

One view of this notion of assimilation from that period

is found in an article in the *Shin Tenchi.* This article argued for the idea of *gaimenteki dôka* (external assimilation).[83] Because of the persisting racism of American society, Japanese should assimilate only the outward forms of American society, but they should concentrate on improving their own character and virtue according to the tenets of *bushidô,* or the complex pattern of life, thought, and practice known as "the way of the warrior." These tenets were unique to Japanese and could contribute to the development of American society. The Japanese American Christians expected that this type of response would lead to a reduction of anti-Japanese racism, just as Meiji Japan's acceptance of Western technology and culture was seen as a way to make Europe and America see Japan as an equal.

The optimism about the ability to change American racism was challenged by the passage of the 1913 land laws directed at Japanese ownership of land in California. Disillusionment would increase as racism began to become more and more a part of public policy and further restricted the rights of Japanese immigrants and their children. The 1924 exclusion act was a final triumph of the anti-Japanese movement. It remained unmatched by any other development until the relocation and incarceration of Japanese Americans in 1942. This white racism forced Japanese American Christians to see that, despite its biblical rhetoric, American civilization was not a Christian civilization as they had been led to believe.

Japanese American Christians began to demand coexistence with white Americans. They urged white Christians to work together with Japanese American Christians to accomplish their purpose of making America a Christian civilization. A conception of Japanese tradition appealing to such notions as *bushidô* and *chûkun aikoku,* or "loyalty to and love of country," was used to combat white American racism and truly achieve a universal notion of being children of God. Japanese American Christians also began to recognize that a uniquely Japanese American identity with its own virtue was developing out of the complex interactions between Christianity, the sociohistorical context of Meiji-Taishô Japan, and late nineteenth- and early twentieth-century America. This virtue could contribute to the development of a truly Christian civilization, not only in the United States but throughout the world. They did so by taking a concept given to them by white missionaries and using it to unmask the hypocrisy of American society.

This identity was not limited to consciousness. Institutional developments like the *Kirisuto Kyôkai* were established, providing the institutional support for this consciousness. The work of the Japanese Presbyterian churches and cooperative efforts with other Japanese American Christian groups nurtured a sense of autonomy and their consciousness as an oppressed racial ethnic group. It helped develop a political consciousness and a practice of resistance within a context of oppression.

With the exclusion act of 1924 and the growing number of Nisei who began to come of age in the 1920s and 1930s, the Japanese Presbyterian churches began to change.[84] The transfer of responsibility for Presbyterian work among Japanese in America from the Board of Foreign Missions to the Board of National Missions in 1922 parallels this shift in consciousness and practice occurring within the Japanese community in the United States. Slowly, the Japanese in America began thinking about America more as a home rather than a temporary place of sojourn before returning to Japan.

The exclusion law also forced the Issei to reevaluate their own position in the United States. They could no longer come and go freely as before. The power of the Japanese Association (*Zaibei Nihonjinkai*) began to decline, and as it began to lose influence, Nisei organizations were being formed.[85] Those nascent Nisei organizations that were to survive World War II provided leadership in the ensuing years for the church as well as the rest of the Japanese American community.[86]

These changes in community influence were not singular events that occurred immediately, but rather gradual trends that escaped notice initially until they had gathered sufficient strength to be noticed. However, a change in consciousness was occurring. No longer could the Issei hope for significant help from Japan in the face of the hardships of immigrant life compounded by the harsh racism of prewar America. The constant flow of new blood and ideas from Japan slowly changed as the distinction between those Japanese who could stay in the United States legally and those who came only temporarily for a specific purpose began to emerge in the consciousness of the Japanese American community.

Those Issei who had imagined themselves in the United States as temporary workers before returning to Japan now had to make that decision more carefully, because departure might mean never being able to return. Their tenuous hold on America became even more acute for those without children who were citizens. Children became very important, not only as a psychological anchor in America, but as the closest contact Issei could have with the legal rights enjoyed by American citizens. Issei who were not allowed by law to become citizens, whose legal status in the United States was tenuous because they were unable to own land or lease it for any length of time, depended upon the legal security of citizenship held by their children, the Nisei. The Nisei's citizenship gave them the ability to work within the American economic structure, in spite of its racism, and without the severe legal limitations imposed upon the Issei. The Nisei also benefited from their American education and their command of American language, customs, and mores.

But the foundations established by the Issei in the earlier decades of existence were important ones that would help the Japanese American Presbyterian churches play a vital role in the Japanese American community as it became less and less Japanese. Rather than becoming more and more American, however, a new historical phenomenon developed—a Japanese American identity.

This new Japanese American identity emerged within the Japanese American community in the context of nineteenth-century American Protestantism's paternalism.

Japanese Christians in America were able to develop the values and institutions that made up this emerging identity. At the same time, though, it was difficult for these early Japanese American Presbyterians to recognize the paternalism in missionaries like Sturge or to see how much their lives were affected by this type of relationship. The developing identity of Japanese American Presbyterians helped them resist the degrading aspect of the paternalism and articulate a vision in which they would be treated equal to their white brothers and sisters. However, the paternalism made it difficult for these Christians to envision a radically different order, let alone develop the political institutions necessary for making those social changes.

In this essay, we have focused on a very specific period in the history of Japanese American Presbyterian churches. In doing so, we have excluded the many changes that occurred in the prewar period. We have not discussed the incarceration and relocation experience, which is a formative and basic part of a Japanese American identity. We have not discussed the reestablishment of the Japanese Presbyterian churches in the postwar period, nor the effect of the 1960s and 1970s, nor the present situation and concerns of Japanese Presbyterian churches. All the more lacking is a similar type of analysis of Chinese Presbyterian churches, which have an even longer history, or the other churches that are a part of Asian American Presbyterian church history.

Our purpose has been to develop a historical methodology, emphasizing an analysis of specific sociohistorical contexts as a way to understand the history of Asian American churches. It is hoped that this essay will be but a beginning point for historical research and reflection. It is only by reconstructing and remembering our sacred memories that we will be able to fashion a life together as a people of God.

13

Korean American Presbyterians: A Need for Ethnic Particularity and the Challenge of Christian Pilgrimage

Sang Hyun Lee

Korean Protestant immigrant churches have suddenly become a noteworthy factor in the American religious scene. Their number has grown at an unprecedented pace—from about seventy-five churches in 1970 to about two thousand in 1988, an increase of about twenty-seven times in less than twenty years. More than half of Korean immigrant Protestants either identify themselves as Presbyterians or have a Presbyterian background.

Because the Korean immigrant church is a relatively new phenomenon in America, a study of it in any definitive sense is an elusive proposition. So the aim of this essay is necessarily a modest one. The focus will be on the ways in which Korean immigrant churches, particularly the Presbyterians, are dealing with the new reality they face in American society in general and in the Presbyterian Church in particular. As will be explained in this essay, Korean immigrants as a nonwhite people are running into limitations in the degree to which they are permitted to be socially and structurally assimilated into American society and are led to maintain a strong and seemingly permanent attachment to their ethnic communities. How and to what extent, we will ask, is this general reality reflected in the particular situation of the Korean immigrant churches' encounter with their Anglo counterparts? How does this "limited assimilation" of Korean immigrants affect the future of their churches and the relationship of their churches to American denominations? The Christian church, of course, cannot be allowed to be overrun by social forces. What, then, is the biblical and theological imperative for the direction of the Korean immigrant churches as well as for their relationship with the Anglo denominations?

Later in the essay, specific attention will be focused on the Korean Presbyterian churches' relationship with the Presbyterian Church (U.S.A.). Although the Presbyterian case would not completely apply to all other American denominations, it does have some significant parallels in the relationship of Korean immigrants within other Anglo denominations.

The Sociocultural Context of Korean Immigrants: Marginality and "Adhesive Assimilation"

The earliest Korean immigrants to the United States were more than seven thousand predominantly male laborers who came to work on sugar plantations in Hawaii between 1903 and 1905. After Korea was tragically annexed to Japan in 1910, about nine hundred intellectuals and students, as well as approximately one thousand so-called picture-brides, came to America. The end of the Japanese occupation in 1945 brought about a slightly larger number of immigrants. Approximately ten thousand students, war brides, war orphans, and others came between 1951 and 1964.[1]

It was the relaxation of the quota system under the new immigration of 1965 that brought about a dramatic increase in Korean immigration to the United States. Approximately 90 percent of Koreans residing in the United States today are the "new immigrants" who came after 1965 and their children. The 1970 Census found about 70,000 Koreans, but since then approximately 30,000

Koreans have been admitted annually. The estimate of the number of Koreans in 1988 ranges anywhere between 700,000 and one million. The Population Reference Bureau's projections indicate that the size of the Korean population in the United States will reach 1,320,759 in the year 2000. It is worth noting that in spite of the substantial increase of the living standards in Korea in the 1980s, the number of immigrants to the United States has not decreased at all. The majority of the Korean population are concentrated in America's major metropolitan areas (especially Los Angeles and New York), but Korean immigrants are geographically more widely dispersed than other Asian counterparts.[2]

American mass media has portrayed Asian immigrants as a successful "model minority." Many Korean immigrants have indeed experienced a financially more rewarding life than they had "back home" (of course, with much backbreaking work) and are enjoying many other new opportunities in their newly adopted country. A more careful look, however, will reveal that their existence in this country is not all that rosy, especially in the sociocultural sphere.

The Korean immigrants' predicament in America, in one word, is "marginality," a situation that results in what has been called "adhesive assimilation." Marginality, first of all, means that Korean immigrants experience a social and cultural displacement or uprootedness. They are no longer in Korea, nor are they really part of America. They are very much "in between," feeling a sense of ambivalence and the cultural conflicts that naturally result.

All persons who leave a familiar environment experience marginality in this first sense to some degree. But there is a second dimension of Korean immigrants' marginality that is peculiar to nonwhite persons and is a severely alienating and dehumanizing factor. Marginality, in this second sense, refers to the experience of being not only "in between" but also "outside" or "at the periphery." This is so because Korean immigrants are not fully accepted by the host society. A white European immigrant, such as a Swede, would be instantly accepted as "one of us" by the dominant group in the United States, even if he or she did not speak one word of English. But a Korean or Vietnamese, even if she or he is born in this country with names like Esther and David, remains perpetually a stranger. Such questions as "Where are you from?" or "How come you speak English so well?" never cease. One Korean American sociologist concludes:

> Non-white immigrants may attain a high degree of cultural assimilation (adoption of American life-style), but structural assimilation (equal life-chances) is virtually impossible unless the immutable independent variable, "race," becomes mutable through miscegenation or cognitive mutation of the WASP. Koreans are no exception to this Lebensschicksal.[3]

Sociologist Milton Gordon pointed out some time ago that cultural assimilation may take place without structural assimilation. The former is a necessary but not sufficient condition of the latter. With Korean immigrants, the racial factor sticks, and assimilation is limited ("acculturation only").[4] To use still another distinction, Korean immigrants can easily achieve secondary relationships (relationships at work, for example), but primary relationships (close social contacts and friendships) are another matter. One clear indicator of the racial barrier that Korean immigrants encounter is what Emory Bogardus describes as the "distance" that white Americans in general feel toward other ethnic groups. Over a period of several decades, in the Bogardus "racial distance scale" Koreans have consistently ranked as one of the most "distant" racial ethnic groups by the white dominant group, and on one occasion were perceived by whites as the most distant racially.[5]

The sociocultural marginality, or the imposed limitation in the assimilation of Korean immigrants, has resulted in what has been called "adhesive or additive assimilation" and strong and seemingly permanent ethnic attachment. Until the early 1960s, when theories on ethnic pluralism began to emerge, the general assumption about immigrants' assimilation process was that progressive acculturation and assimilation would bring about regressive ethnic attachment. Studies by Korean American sociologists have shown that this assumption is not true with Korean immigrants. Their acculturation or length of stay in this country does not weaken their attachment to the Korean cultural ethos and the Korean ethnic community. So Hurh and Kim have coined the term "adhesive or additive assimilation."[6] That is, Korean immigrants maintain their ethnic attachment regardless of the degree of their cultural assimilation. They simply "add on" to their ethnic attachment a degree of their American acculturation.

The reasons for this phenomenon are complex. The large number of the newly arrived Korean immigrants, the lack of English proficiency among many of them, and their general human reluctance to leave the comforts of their ethnic attachment have all contributed. One prominent factor that has led Korean immigrants to a strong ethnic attachment, however, is the white dominant group's maintenance of a social distance from them. "The immigrants' perception of such structural limitations and definition of their own limited adaptive capacities and resources," write Hurh and Kim, "would invoke in the immigrants a defense—their desire to maintain and even enhance their ethnic attachment and identity."[7] All human beings need intimate relationships (*gemeinschaft*) as well as a community where they can play out their social roles (*gesellschaft*). When they cannot have these needs met in the larger American society, they have no choice but to turn to their ethnic community. It is true that a strong ethnic attachment can have the undesirable consequence of isolation and ghettoization. But such ethnic attachment does provide Korean immigrants with a sense of belonging without which they cannot live.

The second-generation youth, by virtue of their particular situation, face a more difficult predicament than do their elders. For one thing, they are far more deeply involved in the white American world than is the first generation. This means that they are self-consciously aware of their marginalization much more acutely than are their parents. In face of marginality, where the Korean Americans of the first generation have their ethnic culture and community to turn to, those of the second generation cannot do so because their ethnic attachment is not strong enough. They never belonged deeply to the Korean culture or social world and, therefore, cannot return to it.[8] They are truly in a wilderness, in the world of in-betweenness and homelessness.

Korean Immigrants' Marginality and Their Religious Participation

Korean immigrants' predicament of marginality and the resulting phenomenon of strong ethnic attachment cannot but have some effect upon their religious life, although the motives for their church affiliations are complex and cannot be reduced to sociocultural factors. At least one of the central reasons for the extremely heavy church affiliation of Korean immigrants is their search for a sense of community that the larger American society does not offer them. This section will discuss the religious participation of Korean immigrants in general, and the following section will focus on the Presbyterian situation specifically.

Studies show that for Korean immigrants, church participation is so extensive that it can be said to be an important "way of life" for them in America. According to a Chicago sample, about half of Korean immigrants (54 percent) were already affiliated with Christian churches in Korea. When they come to the United States, the church affiliation significantly increases to 77 percent. The majority of the church affiliates (83.5 percent in the Los Angeles sample and 78.3 percent in the Chicago sample) attend church at least once a week. This means that about half of the non-Christian Korean immigrants join churches after their arrival in the United States. This is a very heavy church affiliation for Koreans, especially when compared with figures for church affiliation in Korea (about 25 percent).[9]

How is this extensive church involvement to be explained? From a social-scientific point of view, several factors have been proposed: (a) the legacy of the church's heavy sociocultural role as the community center since the days of the earliest Korean immigrants in Hawaii in 1903; (b) the high degree of preimmigration church affiliation; (c) the inclusive character of Korean churches in terms of the variety of people who are accepted into these churches and also the regularity and frequency of church gatherings; and (d) the religious pluralism inherent in American society—that is, the public acceptability of minority ethnic associations under religious (especially Protestant) pretext.[10]

More important than any of the above reasons for the heavy church affiliation among Korean immigrants, however, is the church's spiritual and sociocultural significance. A Chicago study shows that the vast majority of respondents (86 percent) gave a religious reason (e.g., worship of God, salvation, and so forth) as their primary motivation for church affiliation. Of equal significance, almost all of them (96 percent) identified their communal need (e.g., meeting people, friendship, and so forth) as their secondary reason for church attendance.[11]

Sociologists see these religious and sociocultural needs as being intensified in the immigrant situation. The uprooted predicament of the immigrant makes the human being's inherent search for meaning more urgent. This spiritual need, however, is usually intermingled with the sociocultural need, as indicated in such statements as, "I attend church and pray because I am lonely and seek peace of mind." Moreover, the sociocultural need is truly magnified in an immigrant person, especially in the case of a nonwhite, marginalized immigrant. Hurh and Kim write:

> The involuntary ethnic containment and voluntary ethnic attachment of the Korean immigrants' life in the United States explain why they are so extensively and intensively involved in their *ethnic* church which provides a focal point of social belonging, recognition, and emotional comfort, recreation, and of maintaining a vital linkage to their old country—ethnic fellowship and solidarity.[12]

The importance of the sociocultural role of the church for the immigrant communities of various ethnic groups in this country is well known. As Andrew Greeley puts it, "In the United States, the churches came to serve an ethnic role; they helped to sort out 'who one was' in a bewildering complex society."[13] In the case of Korean immigrants, there is an exceptionally heavy church affiliation. This is at least partly explained by the heightened importance of the church's communal role intertwined with its spiritual function that is in turn precipitated by the immigrants' social marginality in this country. The immigrants fill not only the Korean immigrants' need for intimate friendship, according to Hurh and Kim, but also their search for a society in which they can play out their social role. Hurh and Kim explain:

> The ethnic church usually provides not only a communal bond (the primary group) but also a *Gesellschaft* (the secondary group), which the immigrant also left behind. In other words, the immigrants are drawn together in the ethnic church not only to meet intimate friends but also to see "new faces" other than their family members, relatives, and close friends. In short, they miss both the informal and formal aspects of the Korean society back home, and the ethnic church seems to provide a microcosm of both.[14]

We may note in passing that it is precisely the Korean immigrants' deprivation of the fulfillment of their social roles in the larger American society that makes the holding of church offices (elders, deacons) so important to them. The same factor is behind so much of the intrachurch conflict that arises regarding the election of officers.

What is the outcome of our discussion in this section? One thing is clear: The "adhesive assimilation" and the resulting strong ethnic attachment of Korean immigrants are central among the factors that have led to an unusually heavy church affiliation of Korean immigrants. This also implies that when Korean immigrant churches become part of an American denomination, they will be coming into that relationship with all the social dynamics involved in their marginalization, adhesive assimilation, and ethnic attachment.

The Scattering of Korean American Presbyterians

It has been noted that Korean immigrants maintain strong and lasting attachment to their ethnic roots, and this attachment occurs predominantly through their affiliation with Korean ethnic churches. A central reason behind the Korean immigrants' strong ethnic attachment is the marginality or racial distance they experience in American society and their consequent return to their own countrymen and women for identity and community. In this overall context, some Korean ethnic churches have become part of American denominations, the membership of which are predominantly white. What happens, we may ask, when Korean ethnic churches, whose function is very much ethnic in nature, become part of a predominantly white denomination? We shall address this question at a later point.

Out of approximately two thousand Korean ethnic churches in the United States, the Southern Baptist Convention counts the largest number (470) of congregations, although the size of those congregations is often quite small. Probably the relatively flexible polity and the evangelistic ethos of the Baptist churches are the main reasons for the large number of Korean churches. The Presbyterian Church (U.S.A.) and the United Methodist Church claim an equal number of Korean congregations, approximately three hundred each. Many Korean churches have also been attracted to the Pentecostal ethos of the Assemblies of God, which claim about 160 Korean congregations. About forty Korean churches have joined the Presbyterian Church in America. Both the Reformed Church in America and the Christian Reformed Church claim about twenty-five Korean congregations each.

What about those Korean congregations that have not joined American denominations? A considerable number of Korean immigrant Presbyterians have organized themselves as a denomination of their own. The Korean Presbyterian Church in America, organized in 1976, has 170 congregations and four presbyteries (including one in Canada). This denomination is a member of the National Council of Churches and carries out all of the various ecclesial functions of a denominational body, including examination and ordination of ministers. There are obviously many other independent Korean ethnic churches that have not joined either an American or a Korean denomination.

Korean American Presbyterians are truly scattered across American denominations. About 70 percent of Korean Protestants in Korea are Presbyterians. In America, however, the percentage of Korean immigrant Protestants who are formally members of Presbyterian churches (whether of American denominations, the Korean denomination, or independent) seems to fall far short of the 70 percent. In fact, many Korean American Presbyterians attend churches of other denominations, although their exact number is unknown.

What also should not go unnoticed here is that the Presbyterian Church (U.S.A.), which historically played the central role in the American missionary work in Korea, claims barely three hundred Korean immigrant churches. This is the denomination of Samuel A. Moffett, who in 1901 helped organize the first presbytery in Korea and then the first Presbyterian theological seminary in that country. This is the church to which many Korean Presbyterian immigrants have a vague and yet real sense of closeness.[15]

But what are some of the reasons why more of the very fruits of their own missionary work have not become part of this denomination? One reason certainly is the rather strict polity in the American Presbyterian system. From the Korean point of view, the strictness in procedures insisted upon by presbytery committees and other governing bodies in their dealings with Korean immigrant clergy can be inflexible in the face of the concerns of persons of rather different background and ministerial context. What often are adhered to in the name of "high standards" are fit and appropriate for Anglo ministerial candidates and ministries. An elitist streak in American Presbyterianism may be causing the ironic situation where the church that sent the missionaries to Korea is structurally unable to welcome into its midst the fruits of its own labor who are at its doorstep seeking assistance.[16]

Another reason for the relatively low number of Korean churches in the Presbyterian Church may be the evangelistic and conservative character of the Korean Presbyterian churches. This, of course, is the reason why some Korean Presbyterian churches themselves do not want to join the Presbyterian Church. It would not be surprising, however, if the conservative ethos of Korean churches has not made some segments of the Presbyterian Church itself somewhat uneasy about the increasing number of Korean churches. It will be interesting to see whether or not any alignment between the conservative sector within the Presbyterian Church and Korean churches occurs in the future.

Korean American Presbyterians in an American Presbyterian Denomination

With the above general picture of the Korean Presbyterians in America, what can be said of the relationship between Korean Presbyterians and the Presbyterian Church (U.S.A.) in particular? First, we consider some of the positive things that the denomination has done in relation to the Korean American Presbyterians. In 1974, there were only twenty-two Korean congregations in the former United Presbyterian Church in the U.S.A. (UPCUSA). Stimulated partly by the issue of how the American denomination would relate to the newly emerging Korean presbyteries, in 1975 the UPCUSA appointed a Special Committee to Study the Needs of Korean American Ministries. The hoped-for union of the emerging Korean presbyteries with the UPCUSA did not work out. But the special committee's report to the 190th General Assembly

in 1978 did commit the denomination to a positive posture toward receiving some of the rapidly growing Korean
churches into the denomination.

In 1978, the Program Agency appointed the Consulting
Committee on Korean American Ministries with the mandate to encourage and support the growth and ministry of
Korean churches. By 1981, four regional consultants were
appointed to help meet the special needs of the growing
Korean congregations and to facilitate the Korean church's
participation in the life of the denomination itself. The
consultant for the southern region was appointed jointly
by the UPCUSA and the Presbyterian Church in the U.S.
(PCUS) to serve the southern synods of the former and to
act as the national Korean staff for the latter. Both the
northern and southern churches in 1982 organized the
Joint Korean Consultant Advisory Committee to help with
Korean church development in the southern United
States.

With the reunion of the two churches in the Presbyterian Church (U.S.A.) in 1983, some reorganization has occurred. The Joint Committee merged with the Consulting
Committee, which itself ended its work in 1988. A new
committee with the same name as before (the Consulting
Committee on Korean American Ministry), however, has
been organized under the Racial Ethnic Ministry Unit. A
new national staff position in the Racial Ethnic Ministry
Unit has been created to provide coordination to the denomination's work with the Korean congregations. At this
time, there are eight Korean American persons in the
church governing bodies at the national level and several
others serving on national level committees.

These staff appointments and establishment of committees have been much publicized and are indeed significant.
But how do the denomination and Korean American Presbyterians actually relate to each other? The basic mode of
that relationship is a combination of the denomination's
recognition and legitimation of the Korean churches'
strong maintenance of their ethnic attachment at the congregational level, and the expected integration and partici-

pation of these churches in the denomination's life and
work at presbytery and synod levels as well as in all other
aspects of the denomination. This duality in the relationship between the Korean churches and their American denomination is bound to cause difficulties. The likely
question is, How is the strong ethnic emphasis that is legit-
imately expressed on the congregational level going to
stand in harmony with the congregation's expected participation in the denominational life on various levels?

The simple fact is that there is no meaningful participation of Korean American clergy and laity in the life and
work of presbyteries and synods. There are exceptions to
this generalization, but they are few in number. Most Korean American clergy and lay leaders will confess that they
just do not feel comfortable at presbytery or synod meetings and have a hard time being motivated even to attend
the meetings. I submit that what is happening here is exactly what happens to Korean immigrants in the larger
American society. The social realities of marginalization,
racial distance, and strong ethnic attachment, with the
consequent segregation, prevail inside the American denomination.

What exacerbates this situation is the particular ethos of
Korean churches and their members that asserts itself
alongside the Korean churches' strong ethnic role. As mentioned earlier, Korean American Presbyterians are usually
more conservative than most Anglo American Presbyterians. Korean preaching is strongly Bible oriented. Most Korean churches hold early dawn prayer meetings a few times
a week and occasional all-night prayer meetings.

There are also some differences in church organization
and procedures. A well-known case in point is the Korean
church's understanding of both the qualifications for and
tenure of elders. Korean churches are also "conservative"
on the issue of women's ordination, either as ministers or
as elders. The Korean American ministry, at least for the
first generation, is a ministry in the Korean language.
These and other aspects of the particular ethos and practices of the Korean ethnic Presbyterian churches do not

make any easier the already difficult idea of their enthusiastic and dynamic participation in the denomination's life and work.

The Presbyterian Church has made efforts to recognize the high ethnicity of Korean congregations without giving up the ideal of their integration within the total life of the denomination. Some presbyteries are trying the idea of a Korean Presbyterian Ministries Committee (also called in some cases Korean Presbyterian Ministries Network). Their membership includes representative clergy persons from Korean congregations within the given presbytery or from several presbyteries. These committees or networks discuss the matters pertaining to Korean congregations that would normally have come up in one of the presbytery committees, and then offer recommendations to the presbytery committees.

Another way in which the Presbyterian Church and many other denominations have recognized the Korean churches' need to be ethnic communities is to organize ethnic caucuses. The National Korean Presbyterian Council sends delegates to the National Asian Presbyterian Council and meets once every year with clergy, laity, and youth delegates from all of the Korean congregations in the denomination. It is truly a moving experience for the Korean American Presbyterians scattered across the nation to come together for worship, fellowship, and mutual encouragement. Feeling no racial distance and a welcomed sense of oneness, one can say, "Ah! I belong to something!" This body discusses wide-ranging issues, passes resolutions to be sent to appropriate church governing bodies, and launches worthwhile projects. Korean churches also gather regionally for various activities, and there are Korean Presbyterian Women, Korean Presbyterian Men, and Korean Presbyterian Youth Councils. These Korean American gatherings, together with the dedicated work of the Korean national staff, regional consultants, and the Committee on Korean American Ministries, have certainly made indispensable contributions to the life of Korean Americans in the Presbyterian Church.

The above measures, however, do not really address the fundamental problem. Sitting in the National Korean Presbyterian Council and other similar ethnic gatherings, one feels encouraged and even exhilarated. But one also experiences a subtle sort of helplessness, and this feeling arises as one realizes that all these caucuses and other ethnic gatherings do not have any governing power, nor do they have any substantive budget to implement anything.

However, these measures are far from useless; they are indeed indispensable in the absence of anything better. But the fundamental problem facing the denomination as well as the Korean American Presbyterians themselves is not really dealt with by having caucuses and advisory committees. The fundamental issue is this: In the present situation, the Presbyterian Church and its Korean American members are caught in a dilemma. On the one hand, the Korean immigrant churches' predicament of having to be ethnically particular for their constituency's all-essential communal needs is fully legitimated and recognized by the denomination. Yet, on the other hand, the ethnically particular communal needs of the Korean American Presbyterians are not allowed to be fulfilled in other aspects of the denominational life. The heightened ethnic role of Korean American churches is affirmed on the local congregational level and then denied on other levels of the church's life and work. What is expected of the Korean American churches beyond the congregational level is what goes against the very essence of their social function. That, in a nutshell, is the problem. And this problem will undoubtedly demand a resolution of some sort.

There has been a widespread assumption, especially on the part of Anglo members of the Presbyterian Church, that as Korean immigrant Presbyterians become more acculturated in the American way of life, there will be an increasing tendency and ability among Korean immigrants to participate fully in the life of the denomination. But, as we have seen, studies show this to be untrue. The strong ethnic attachment is not in any way diminished by the length of residence or by the educational or economic accomplishments. The dilemma is not going to go away.

One possible solution that naturally presents itself is the Korean language presbytery. In 1983, the uniting General Assembly in Atlanta approved the establishment of such a presbytery, consisting only of Korean churches. Hanmi (translated literally, "Korean-American") Presbytery with fifteen Korean congregations was organized in January of 1984 within the bounds of the Synod of Southern California and Hawaii. The original understanding was that this presbytery would continue for ten years, with the possibility of an extension at the end of that period. Hanmi Presbytery now has grown to claim over thirty congregations and has exercised its governing body functions (e.g., the power to make overtures to the General Assembly) with a sense of exhilaration. The rationale behind the ten-year limitation for the existence of Hanmi Presbytery may very well have been the assumption that increased acculturation will bring about total assimilation. But as noted earlier, this simply does not happen. The felt need and justification for nongeographical presbyteries will continue to exist as long as the social realities remain what they are, both inside and outside the church.

This approach may have its own problems. For one thing, the language: presbyteries and synods will require many bilingual and bicultural Korean American leaders who can relate both to the very traditional first generation and to the church governing bodies. The training of such leadership would be essential. Further, ethnic language presbyteries by their very nature are in danger of some degree of isolation from the total structure and life of the denomination. Whether or not the denomination will accept such a strong ethnic assertion by Koreans is yet another question. This approach, however, is worth further study.

One wonders at this point about what the Korean churches' posture may become if the Presbyterian Church in the future fails to be more receptive to the ethnic self-affirmation of Korean churches in all aspects of the denominational life. Would some Korean Americans leave the denomination? Some might. However, it would be hard to imagine at this point the absence of a significant Korean American presence in the denomination. For one thing, Korean immigration is likely to continue, and the new arrivals always can use the assistance of an American denomination, especially that one with which Korean Presbyterians feel a historic connection. Furthermore, there is the all-important issue of the future of the second- and third-generation Korean American Presbyterians. We have already described their particularly difficult sociocultural predicament in this country. They are going to need a very strong affirmation of themselves in their bicultural *Korean American* identity and community. For this self-affirmation, they are going to need the support of the larger American society as well as their first-generation parents. And, assuming that the Presbyterian Church is sensitive to their special needs and is willing to translate that sensitivity into active programs, the first generation's continued relationship to the denomination can prepare, to some degree anyway, for an ecclesial framework within which their future generations can live as active Christians. In other words, Korean American Presbyterians separating themselves from the denomination will not solve all of their important problems.

So Korean American Presbyterians face a delicate task of maintaining ethnic identity and community without bringing about excessive isolation. Whether the American denominations will help them in this task, of course, is for those denominations to answer.

Pilgrimage Toward "A Better Country"

The delicate task we just mentioned is not going to be easy to carry out. Theologically speaking, human beings inevitably tend to avoid the narrow path; they are prone to avoid the problems through self-defeating and destructive means. The problem, therefore, goes deeper than sociology. What is needed is the widening of the imagination, an ongoing transformation of the persons, peoples, and churches. The church is going to have to be guided and empowered by the biblical vision of Christians as pilgrims—that is, as a people who are willing to leave the comfortable status quo always in search of "a better country," "the city whose builder and maker is God" (Hebrews 11). The American denomination needs to take leave of its captivity under the American culture and create in its midst the space in which people of all colors can dwell and make their home. Anglo Americans and their denominations need to be for the first time true pilgrims. This will involve a leave-taking or, as H. Richard Niebuhr once wrote about essentially the same immigrant church issues, "a resolute turning away from all those loyalties to the lesser values of the self, the denomination, and the nation, which deny the inclusiveness of divine love."[17]

The biblical symbol of pilgrimage demands a widening and deepening of the imagination for Korean American Presbyterians as well. Korean immigrant Presbyterians need to learn that their very human migration to this new land and the leave-taking involved in it can have a meaning, if appropriated with the biblical vision. Their departure from their homeland can have a purposefulness if it is taken as a God-given opportunity to embark upon a pilgrimage toward a new task, an unexpected vocation—namely, that of joining with all other "homeless" pilgrims in this land and working to build "a better country." Such an awakening to the possible meaningfulness of the immigrant existence is required if Korean Americans are going to have the will and tenacity to live their dual vocation of keeping ethnic particularity without excessive isolation. In other words, they need to know that neither ethnic particularity nor participation in the American world is an end in itself, an ultimate goal. They are rather the means toward a greater goal—the goal of participating in God's own work of establishing God's reign in the world. Only such a deeper vision will sustain Korean Americans as they carry out their delicate and difficult task.[18]

The deeper vision of that "better country" for which all Presbyterians have been called includes the construction of a church that is inclusive not only in word but also in deed. In moving toward such a vision, all concerned would have their particular responsibilities. The host or dominant church has the greater responsibility, in a sense, simply because of its position of power. Unless the host denomination becomes more just and more hospitable to the stranger, the powerless minority church can hardly be expected to be motivated to stay around. But by the same token, the minority church also has the responsibility to challenge the existing structure and work to reform the larger church as well as itself. Korean ethnic churches themselves must take leave of certain cultural traditions while reaffirming and cherishing many other aspects of them. The traditional Korean attitude toward the position of women, for example, is a cultural tradition from which Korean American Presbyterians as pilgrims should make a permanent departure. They have the responsibility to enter the wilderness of American society and the American church in order to try to make a contribution with their tradition of fervent evangelistic faith. Of course, all this needs to be done without losing or ignoring their own particular dignity and particular needs.

American denominations are themselves becoming in some ways "marginal" in the larger American society. This marginalization is not the all-encompassing sort that Asian Americans experience in this country. However, American denominations are becoming powerless in the fabric of American life. American denominations could react to this powerlessness with the strategies of retrenchment, something that would be in the long run detrimental both to the denominations and to the ethnic minorities. Or the churches can appropriate this powerlessness as part of their nature as "earthen vessels" and learn to let the transcendent power work through them. This could be turned into an opportunity for Anglo American churches to acknowledge their own nonultimacy and to embark upon a search for Home which, when found, could be the true Home for all people of all races. And that search surely is a vocation that should unite all of us.

Notes

Series Foreword

1. Arthur M. Schlesinger, Sr., "A Critical Period in American Religion, 1875–1900," first appeared in the *Massachusetts Historical Society Proceedings* 64 (1930–32) and is reprinted in John M. Mulder and John F. Wilson, eds., *Religion in American History: Interpretive Essays* (Englewood Cliffs, N.J.: Prentice-Hall, 1978), pp. 302–317.

2. Robert T. Handy, "The American Religious Depression, 1925–1935," *Church History* 29 (1960), 3–16, reprinted in Mulder and Wilson, *Religion in American History,* pp. 431–444; Handy, *A Christian America: Protestant Hopes and Historical Realities,* 2nd ed. (New York: Oxford University Press, 1984), pp. 159–184.

3. Sydney E. Ahlstrom, "The Radical Turn in Theology and Ethics: Why It Occurred in the 1960s," *Annals of the American Academy of Political and Social Science* 387 (1970), 1–13, reprinted in Mulder and Wilson, *Religion in American History,* pp. 445–446; Ahlstrom, "The Traumatic Years: American Religion and Culture in the 1960s and 1970s," *Theology Today* 26 (1980), 504–522; Ahlstrom, *A Religious History of the American People* (New Haven: Yale University Press, 1972), pp. 1079–1096.

4. Wade Clark Roof and William McKinney, *American Mainline Religion: Its Changing Shape and Future* (New Brunswick, N.J.: Rutgers University Press, 1987); Robert Wuthnow, *The Re-*

structuring of American Religion: Society and Faith Since World War II (Princeton, N.J.: Princeton University Press, 1988).

5. John V. Taylor, *The Primal Vision: Christian Presence Amid African Religion* (Philadelphia: Fortress Press, 1964), chapter 13, "The Practice of Presence," pp. 196–205.

Introduction

1. This image of the Cheshire cat is borrowed from Os Guinness, where it is quite skillfully used in his chapter on the "Cheshire Cat Factor," in *The Gravedigger File: Papers on the Subversion of the Modern Church* (Downers Grove, Ill.: InterVarsity Press, 1983), pp. 49–70.

2. See *The Confessional Mosaic: Presbyterians and Twentieth-Century Theology,* the second volume of the series The Presbyterian Presence: The Twentieth-Century Experience (Louisville, Ky.: Westminster/John Knox Press, 1990).

3. Meister's conclusions are confirmed by a recent study by Dennis N. Voskuil, "Reaching Out: Mainline Protestantism and the Media," in William R. Hutchison, ed., *Between the Times: Travail of the Protestant Establishment in America, 1900–1960* (New York: Cambridge University Press, 1989).

1: Presbyterian Evangelism: A Case of Parallel Allegiances Diverging

1. Robert S. Paul, "Presbyterians and Evangelism: Historical Background," *Austin Seminary Bulletin* 100 (April 1985), 15–23; Ephesians 4:11–13.

2. *Minutes of the General Assembly of the Presbyterian Church in the United States of America* [cited hereafter as GA, PCUSA], 1901, Part I, pp. 119, 170–171; *Minutes,* GA, PCUSA, 1902, Part I, p. 34; *Minutes,* GA, PCUSA, 1903, Part I, p. 38; Board of National Missions, "First Annual Report," in *Minutes,* GA, PCUSA, 1924, Part II, pp. 44–46; "Seventh Annual Report," in *Minutes,* GA, PCUSA, 1930, Part II, p. 168.

3. *Minutes of the General Assembly of the United Presbyterian Church of North America* [cited hereafter as GA, UPCNA], 1903, p. 849; *Minutes,* GA, UPCNA, 1956, p. 12. *Minutes of the General Assembly of the United Presbyterian Church in the United States of America* [cited hereafter as GA, UPCUSA], 1959, Part I, p. 262.

4. *Minutes,* GA, PCUSA, 1902, Part I, pp. 35, 37–39; *Minutes,* GA, PCUSA, 1905, Part I, pp. 29–30; and Board of National Missions, "First Annual Report," in *Minutes,* GA, PCUSA, 1924, Part II, p. 44.

5. *Minutes,* GA, PCUSA, 1904, Part I, pp. 30–31; *Minutes,* GA, PCUSA, 1905, Part I, pp. 30–31. The focus of the Simultaneous Movement on urban areas was in part a consequence of a territorial agreement between the Special Committee on Evangelistic Work and the Board of Home Missions in 1906. This compact assigned the special committee responsibility for larger towns and cities where evangelism would be conducted on an interdenominational basis, and the board would cover all evangelism within its territories. *Minutes,* GA, PCUSA, 1906, Part I, p. 24.

6. Richard William Reifsnyder, "The Reorganizational Impulse in American Protestantism: The Presbyterian Church (U.S.A.) as a Case Study, 1788–1983" (Ph.D. diss., Princeton Theological Seminary, 1984); Dale E. Soden, "Anatomy of a Presbyterian Urban Revival: J. W. Chapman in the Pacific Northwest," *American Presbyterians* 64 (1986), 51–56.

7. Quoted in Soden, "Anatomy of a Presbyterian Urban Revival," 54.

8. *Minutes,* GA, PCUSA, 1910, Part I, pp. 40–42; *Minutes,* GA, PCUSA, 1912, Part I, p. 37; *Minutes,* GA, UPCNA, 1909, p. 338; *Minutes,* GA, UPCNA, 1910, p. 667; Albert Dimmock, interview held at Montreat, N.C., June 6, 1988.

9. *Minutes of the General Assembly of the Presbyterian Church in the United States* [cited hereafter as GA, PCUS], 1908, pp. 34, 47; *Minutes,* GA, PCUS, 1910, p. 114. Thacker had participated with Chapman in one of the simultaneous campaigns in Boston during 1909 and had acquired quite a reputation for his evangelistic skills. J. E. Thacker, scrapbooks, MS, Presbyterian Study Center, Montreat, N.C.

10. *Minutes,* GA, PCUS, 1910, p. 107; Executive Committee of Home Missions, *Minutes,* February 21, 1911, and June 2, 1913, MS, Presbyterian Study Center, Montreat, N.C. Evangelists like Thacker were hired throughout the century by the PCUS. In fact, at certain points early in the century, the Board of Home Missions carried several assembly evangelists on its roster. But the PCUS did not adequately fuel its evangelism program with the necessary financial supplies for long-term planning until the mid-1940s.

11. Executive Committee of Home Missions, *Minutes,* June 2, 1913; September 8, 1914; and June 11, 1918, MS, Presbyterian Study Center, Montreat, N.C. *Minutes,* GA, PCUS, 1914, pp. 46–47, 57, 60.

12. *Minutes,* GA, PCUS, 1938, pp. 69, 143–144; *Minutes,* GA, PCUS, 1942, p. 141; *Minutes,* GA, PCUS, 1943, pp. 32, 151–153.

13. Chapman's evangelistic exploits had led him to conduct revivals in Great Britain and the lands "down under." The press of his fame, with its attendant opportunities, occasioned his resignation. *Minutes,* GA, PCUSA, 1909, Part I, pp. 31–32; *Minutes,* GA, PCUSA, 1912, Part I, p. 34; Board of National Missions, "Seventh Annual Report," in *Minutes,* GA, PCUSA, 1930, Part II, p. 169.

14. The official name for the new committee was the Permanent Committee on Evangelism. *Minutes,* GA, PCUSA, 1913, Part I, pp. 27, 33; Board of National Missions, "First Annual Report," in *Minutes,* GA, PCUSA, 1924, Part II, pp. 46–47; "Seventh Annual Report," in *Minutes,* GA, PCUSA, 1930, Part II, p. 169.

15. Board of Home Missions, "121st Annual Report," in *Minutes,* GA, PCUSA, 1923, Part II, p. 13; *Minutes,* GA, PCUSA, 1923, Part I, p. 28.

16. *Minutes,* GA, PCUSA, 1923, Part I, p. 120.

17. Ibid.

18. A final summary report on the previous work of the Board of Home Missions in 1923 specifically explained why that board had never included a separate division of evangelism. It indicates that all elements of its former structure kept evangelism as their primary function. Evangelism could not be delegated because it lay at the core of the board's purpose in all its manifestations. Board of Home Missions, "121st Annual Report," in *Minutes,* GA, PCUSA, 1923, Part II, pp. 15–16.

19. *Minutes,* GA, PCUSA, 1920, Part I, p. 394; *Minutes,* GA, PCUSA, 1921, Part I, pp. 350–351. *Pressing the Work of Evangelism Under Presbyterial and Pastoral Leadership: Observations on Presbyterial Responsibility, Together with an Outline of a Program for Presbyterial Evangelism* (Philadelphia: The General Assembly's Permanent Committee on Evangelism, n.d.).

20. Board of National Missions, "Seventh Annual Report," in *Minutes,* GA, PCUSA, 1930, Part II, p. 170; "Second Annual Report," in *Minutes,* GA, PCUSA, 1925, Part II, pp. 36–40.

21. In service to this goal, Mahy organized conferences of pastors to share the secrets of their evangelistic successes so that these could be compiled and distributed in a manual for churches. Board of National Missions, "Seventh Annual Report," in *Minutes,* GA, PCUSA, 1930, Part II, p. 170; and *A Manual of Evangelism for Ministers and Members: Prepared by Headquarters and Field Organization of the Board of National Missions Under the General Guidance of the Division of Evangelism* (New York: Division of Evangelism, Board of National Missions, n.d.).

22. Board of National Missions, "Sixth Annual Report," in *Minutes,* GA, PCUSA, 1929, Part II, p. 161. In 1932, the General Assembly tried to generate activity from the division by making an unsolicited request for the Division of Evangelism and the Spiritual Emphasis Committee of General Council to meet and develop a "consistent and continuing" program of evangelism throughout the church. *Minutes,* GA, PCUSA, 1932, Part I, p. 69.

23. Robert T. Handy, "The American Religious Depression, 1925–1935," *Church History* 29 (1960), 3–16; Charles G. Dennison, *Orthodox Presbyterian Church, 1936–1986* (Philadelphia: Committee for the History of the Orthodox Presbyterian Church, 1986). One later commentator on Klein's work made the claim that the slow rate of growth that the church experienced during the 1930s, despite the religious depression and the fundamentalist controversies, was a small triumph rather than the failure often assumed from a cursory look at the statistics. Richard R. Gilbert, "Evangelism from the Top: A 60-Year Study of the History, Growth, Aim and Relationships of National Evangelism," December 4, 1962, TS, PC(USA), Dept. of History, Philadelphia, p. 8.

24. *Minutes,* GA, PCUSA, 1940, Part I, pp. 33–35; *Minutes,* GA, PCUSA, 1941, Part I, pp. 183–186.

25. *Minutes,* GA, PCUSA, 1942, Part I, pp. 214–215.

26. *Minutes,* GA, PCUSA, 1945, Part I, p. 143.

27. The official dates for the New Life Movement were January 1, 1947, to January 1, 1950. *Minutes,* GA, PCUSA, 1946, Part I, pp. 123–130; *Minutes,* GA, PCUSA, 1947, Part I, pp. 162–165; Board of National Missions, "24th Annual Report," in *Minutes,* GA, PCUSA, 1947, Part II, pp. 9–15.

28. *Minutes,* GA, PCUSA, 1946, Part I, pp. 125–127.

29. Ibid., p. 124.

30. Ibid., p. 127; *Minutes,* GA, PCUSA, 1950, Part I, pp. 201–202.

31. In 1940, 1945, 1948, 1952, and 1955, the UPCNA announced new multi-year programs of evangelism, each with statistical goals to be achieved by the denomination and, in some cases, by congregations. *Minutes,* GA, UPCNA, 1940, p. 129; *Minutes,* GA, UPCNA, 1945, p. 399; *Minutes,* GA, UPCNA, 1948, p. 46; *Minutes,* GA, UPCNA, 1952, p. 34; *Minutes,* GA, UPCNA, 1955, p. 1310.

32. *Minutes,* GA, PCUS, 1944, pp. 47, 166; *Minutes,* GA, PCUS, 1946, p. 141.

33. These goals and the structure of the program indicated an interest in approaching the problem of assimilation of current church members and inactives first, and then reaching beyond to those who had not been a part of any denomination. The Committee on Evangelism suggested goals that emphasized bringing inactives back to the church in the early part of the program and later expected more new members from those who had never been members. In 1947–48, the denomination was to add 30,000 by profession of faith and 70,000 by letter or restatement of faith; in 1948–49, 35,000 by profession and 65,000 by letter or restatement; in 1949–50, 40,000 by profession and 60,000 by letter or restatement; in 1950–51, 45,000 by profession of faith and 55,000 by letter or restatement; and in 1951–52, 50,000 by profession and 50,000 by letter or restatement. *Minutes,* GA, PCUS, 1947, pp. 74–75, 151–152; *Minutes,* GA, PCUS, 1948, p. 138.

34. *Minutes,* GA, PCUS, 1947, pp. 74–75.

35. Ernest Trice Thompson, "The Board of National Ministries," in *Minutes,* GA, PCUS, 1973, Part III, p. 108.

36. *Minutes,* GA, PCUSA, 1951, Part I, pp. 206, 209. The UPCNA made a similar move with its United Evangelistic Crusade by planning a 2½-year extension of the program under the name the "United Evangelistic Advance." *Minutes,* GA, UPCNA, 1952. p. 34.

37. As the division described its situation, "No church ever drifts toward evangelism but always away from it. The natural inclination is for a church to concentrate on its present membership. The tendency is to let evangelism wait until the pastor and members catch up with their duties—which never happens. Without constant reminders, evangelism is left out. The Division of Evangelism keeps bringing these reminders to the churches." *Minutes,* GA, PCUSA, 1953, Part I, p. 92.

38. Millard Research Associates found that 3 out of 5 new members, or 58%, were only peripherally involved in church activities if at all; 4 out of 10 new members were no longer attending with any degree of frequency; and 4–6 out of every 10 new members were not closely related to their church by either attendance or activities after only 3–4 years. Millard Research Associates, Ltd., "A Research Study of Expectation Regarding the Church and Reasons for Membership. Prepared for the Division of Evangelism, United Presbyterian Church in the USA," 1963, TS, Presbyterian Historical Society, Philadelphia, pp. 63, 64, 151; *Minutes,* GA, UPCUSA, 1960, Part I, pp. 195, 218. The immediate response of the denomination was to foster "koinonia" groups where new members could be incorporated more readily by small-group gatherings within a congregation. *Minutes,* GA, UPCUSA, 1960, Part I, p. 194; Board of National Missions, "158th Annual Report," in *Minutes,* GA, UPCUSA, 1960, Part II, pp. 15–16; *Minutes,* GA, UPCUSA, 1961, Part I, pp. 253–256; Board of National Missions, "159th Annual Report," in *Minutes,* GA, UPCUSA, 1961, Part II, p. 91; *Minutes,* GA, UPCUSA, 1962, Part I, p. 214; and *Minutes,* GA, UPCUSA, 1963, Part I, pp. 250–251.

39. Gilbert, "Evangelism from the Top," p. 4.

40. Ibid., p. 23; *Minutes,* GA, UPCUSA, 1963, Part I, p. 244; and *Minutes,* GA, UPCUSA, 1964, Part I, p. 210.

41. *Minutes,* GA, UPCUSA, 1958, Part I, p. 461; Board of National Missions, "157th Annual Report," in *Minutes,* GA, UPCUSA, 1959, Part II, pp. 12–13; Division of Evangelism, Board of National Missions, United Presbyterian Church in the U.S.A., "A Prospectus on the Division's Structure and Services," 1967, TS, PC(USA), Dept. of History, Philadelphia, pp. 4–5; *Minutes,* GA, UPCUSA, 1963, Part I, p. 245.

42. Board of Church Extension, Presbyterian Church in the United States, *Minutes,* July 1958–February 1962, MS, Presbyterian Study Center, Montreat, N.C., p. 15; Board of Church Extension of the Presbyterian Church in the United States, *Eleventh Annual Report* (Atlanta: Board of Church Extension, 1960), pp. 35–36. The division envisioned a "Presbyterian Mission to the Nation" that would include the UPCUSA and the PCUS. The UPCUSA cooperated with the PCUS in preaching cavalcades in four border synods. Albert E. Dimmock, "Report to the Moderator of the General Assembly, Dr. Marion A. Boggs, on the Presbyterian Mission to the Nation," January 15, 1961, TS, in the author's possession (photocopy of typescript), p. 65.

43. Dimmock, "Report to the Moderator," pp. 33–38; Board of Church Extension, *Eleventh Annual Report,* pp. 35–36; and Board of Church Extension of the Presbyterian Church in the United States, *Twelfth Annual Report* (Atlanta: Board of Church Extension, 1961), pp. 5–8.

44. Dimmock, "Report to the Moderator," pp. 74–80; and Board of Church Extension, *Twelfth Annual Report,* pp. 5–80.

45. Patricia H. Sprinkle, "A History of Evangelism in the Presbyterian Church, U.S., 1959–1971," TS, Presbyterian Study Center, Montreat, N.C., p. 9; and Gilbert, "Evangelism from the Top."

46. Robert McAfee Brown, "The New Shape of the Gospel," in *Addresses on Evangelism to the Pre-Assembly Conference on Evangelism and to the 179th General Assembly of the United Presbyterian Church in the U.S.A., Portland, Oregon, May 16, 17, and 23, 1967* (New York: Division of Evangelism, Department of Mission Strategy and Evangelism, United Presbyterian Church in the U.S.A., [1967]), p. 26; *Minutes,* GA, UPCUSA, 1966, Part I, pp. 332–334; George Thomas Peters, *Evangelism Re-examined* (New York: United Presbyterian Church in the U.S.A., 1967), p. 11; "God, Church and World: A Position Paper," in Board of National Ministries, Presbyterian Church U.S., *Minutes,* April 27–29, 1971, TS, Presbyterian Study Center, Montreat, N.C. It is likely that pastoral counseling theory may have contributed as much as the civil rights movement to this period's emphasis on listening. Indeed, in the evangelism literature of this era, there is much concern that individuals listen to those whom they seek to evangelize, much as the church must listen to the world outside its doors.

47. *Minutes,* GA, UPCUSA, 1964, Part I, p. 220.

48. General Assembly Commission on Evangelism, United Presbyterian Church in the U.S.A., "Resolution of the Commission on Evangelism," 1964, TS, PC(USA), Dept. of History, Philadelphia.

49. *Minutes,* GA, UPCUSA, 1966, Part I, p. 333.

50. *Minutes,* GA, UPCUSA, 1967, Part I, p. 221.

51. Board of Home Missions, "121st Annual Report," in *Minutes,* GA, PCUSA, 1923, Part II, pp. 15–16; Board of National Missions, "First Annual Report," in *Minutes,* GA, PCUSA, 1924, Part II, p. 43; *Minutes,* GA, PCUSA, 1941, Part I, p. 151; Board of National Missions, "155th Annual Report," in *Minutes,* GA, PCUSA, 1957, Part II, p. 59; *Minutes,* GA, UPCUSA, 1958,

Part I, p. 328; and Board of National Missions, "157th Annual Report," in *Minutes,* GA, UPCUSA, 1959, Part II, p. 15.

52. Division of Evangelism, Department of Mission and Evangelism, Board of National Missions, "Evangelism Clichés," n.d., TS, Presbyterian Historical Society, Philadelphia, pp. 2–3; *Minutes,* GA, UPCUSA, 1967, Part I, pp. 221–223; Board of National Missions, "44th Annual Report," in *Minutes,* GA, UPCUSA, 1967, Part II, pp. 59–127; Brown, "The New Shape of the Gospel," pp. 30–31; Board of National Ministries, PCUS, *Mission in Motion: An Annual Report for 1967* (Doraville, Ga.: Foote and Davies, 1967), p. 15; Edward M. Huenemann, "Called to Be Advocate: An Exegetical and Theological Note," in *Occasional Papers,* no. 6 (N.p.: Division of Evangelism, Board of National Missions, UPCUSA, 1969); *Minutes,* GA, UPCUSA, 1970, Part I, p. 555; Donald G. Lester, *Congregation in Pilgrimage* (New York: UPCUSA, 1971), p. 6; and Board of National Missions, "47th Annual Report," in *Minutes,* GA, UPCUSA, 1970, Part II, pp. 1–2, 28.

53. Matthew 16:25; Mark 8:35; Luke 9:24; and John 12:25.

54. The General Assembly received 20 overtures in 1968 concerning the membership loss and/or evangelism; 7 overtures in 1970; 6 overtures in 1971; and 1 overture in 1972. *Minutes,* GA, UPCUSA, 1968, Part I, pp. 40, 57, 291–292; *Minutes,* GA, UPCUSA, 1970, Part I, pp. 40, 42–43, 53–56, 74, 84–85; *Minutes,* GA, UPCUSA, 1971, Part I, pp. 29–30, 39, 42, 52–53, 56, 74; *Minutes,* GA, UPCUSA, 1972, Part I, p. 67.

55. *Minutes,* GA, UPCUSA, 1968, Part I, pp. 293, 294.

56. *Minutes,* GA, UPCUSA, 1969, Part I, pp. 648–660.

57. "A Call to Repentance and Expectancy: A Message to the Church Adopted by the General Assembly of the Presbyterian Church in the United States at Montreat, North Carolina, April 1965," TS, Presbyterian Study Center, Montreat, N.C.; and *Guide to Be Used with "A Call to Repentance and Expectancy"* (N.p.: PCUS, 1965); Board of Church Extension of the Presbyterian Church in the United States, *Seventeenth Annual Report* (Atlanta: Board of Church Extension, 1966), p. 22.

58. "Evangelism Task Force: 1965–67," TS, Presbyterian Study Center, Montreat, N.C.; and Board of Church Extension, *Seventeenth Annual Report,* p. 16.

59. "A Look at the Implications," in a packet entitled *A Theological Basis for Evangelism,* TS, Presbyterian Study Center, Montreat, N.C.; Sherrard Rice, "An Introduction," in ibid. Al-

bert Curry Winn, interview held at White Library, Louisville Presbyterian Seminary, Louisville, Ky., September 20, 1988.

60. *Minutes,* GA, UPCUSA, 1964, Part I, pp. 214–216; *Minutes,* GA, UPCUSA, 1966, Part I, pp. 336–338; and Board of Church Extension of the PCUS, *Mission in Motion: An Annual Report for 1966* (Doraville, Ga.: Foote and Davies, 1967), pp. 22–23.

61. Board of National Ministries of the PCUS, *Report of the Board of National Ministries: Journey Outward—Conversion from Introversion* (N.p.: n. pub., 1970), pp. 17–28.

62. *Minutes,* GA, UPCUSA, 1976, Part I, pp. 336–397.

63. Ibid., pp. 382–383.

64. *Minutes,* GA, UPCUSA, 1977, Part I, pp. 543–553.

65. The first name given to this program was "New Age Dawning," but it was changed to "New Day Dawning" in 1989. The earlier title had fostered unintended and unwanted associations with the New Age religious movement popular in the culture. *Minutes of the General Assembly of Presbyterian Church (U.S.A.)* [cited hereafter as GA, PC(USA)] 1984, Part I, pp. 122–142.

66. *Minutes,* GA, PC(USA), 1984, Part I, pp. 93, 361, 364.

67. For UPCUSA Presbyterians supporting social action evangelism, an injunction in their Confession of 1967 regarding national security was applied equally to the church. The 1967 Confession maintained that the search for reconciliation and peace required that "the nations pursue fresh and responsible relations across every line of conflict, *even at the risk of national security,* to reduce areas of strife and to broaden international understanding" (emphasis added). *The Constitution of the United Presbyterian Church in the United States of America, Part I: Book of Confessions,* 2nd ed. (New York: Office of the General Assembly, UPCUSA, 1970), 9.45.

2: Twentieth-Century Presbyterian New Church Development: A Critical Period, 1940–1980

1. *Minutes of the General Assembly of the Presbyterian Church (U.S.A.),* 1988, Part II, p. 506. Other studies in the Lilly project will deal with racial ethnic ministries.

2. Everett L. Perry and Margaret T. Perry, "New Church Development Policies: An Historical Overview," *Journal of Presbyterian History,* 57 (Fall 1979), 245. The Perrys' article

summarizes new church development policies from the seventeenth-century beginnings of American Presbyterianism through 1978 and provided the basic outline for the narrative sections dealing with the PCUSA, UPCUSA, and UPCNA. Their citations in the principal period under consideration (1940–1980) have been checked against the original sources. This study is an extremely significant and helpful guide to all major developments.

3. Ibid., 247.

4. Ibid., 266.

5. Ibid., 247–251.

6. *Minutes of the Board of National Missions of the Presbyterian Church in the United States of America* [cited hereafter as BNM, PCUSA], vol. 21, pp. 141, 184, 222. Original volumes are in the archives of the PC(USA), Dept. of History, Philadelphia.

7. *Minutes of the General Assembly of the Presbyterian Church in the United States of America* [cited hereafter as GA, PCUSA], 1944, pp. 68–71, 178–184.

8. *Minutes,* BNM, PCUSA, vol. 22, pp. 194–198.

9. Perrys, "New Church Development Policies," p. 252.

10. *Minutes,* GA, PCUSA, 1945, pp. 176f., 182; *Minutes,* BNM, PCUSA, vol. 23, p. 71. Approval was given for "$400,000 to $500,000 a year until other provision can be made" and for consideration of using unrestricted board funds. *Minutes,* GA, PCUSA, 1946, pp. 164–169.

11. *Minutes,* GA, PCUSA, 1948, p. 155; *Minutes,* GA, PCUSA, 1947, p. 157; *Minutes,* BNM, PCUSA, vol. 28, pp. 246–247.

12. *Minutes,* BNM, PCUSA, vol. 26, p. 79.

13. *Minutes,* GA, PCUSA, 1951, p. 173; *Minutes,* GA, PCUSA, 1953, pp. 153–154.

14. *Minutes,* GA, PCUSA, 1955, pp. 126, 275; *Minutes,* BNM, PCUSA, vol. 33, pp. 175–176, 200ff.; vol. 34, pp. 109–110.

15. *Minutes,* BNM, PCUSA, vol. 35, pp. 242ff.; *Minutes,* GA, PCUSA, 1958, pp. 581ff.

16. *Minutes,* GA, PCUSA, 1959, pp. 251–252.

17. *Minutes of the Board of National Missions of the United Presbyterian Church in the United States of America* [cited hereafter as BNM, UPCUSA], vol. 3, pp. 207–208. Original volumes are in the archives of the PC(USA) Dept. of History, Philadelphia.

18. *Minutes of the General Assembly of the United Presbyterian*

Church in the United States of America [cited hereafter as GA, UPCUSA], 1960, pp. 186–187.

19. *Minutes,* BNM, UPCUSA, vol. 4, pp. 253, 273; *Minutes,* GA, UPCUSA, 1962, pp. 197–198, 435–436; *Minutes,* BNM, UPCUSA, vol. 8, pp. 7–8, 261–262; *Minutes,* GA, UPCUSA, 1966, pp. 289–291.

20. *Minutes,* GA, UPCUSA, 1966, p. 290.

21. Perrys, "New Church Development Policies," p. 258; *Minutes,* GA, UPCUSA, 1967, p. 263.

22. Perrys, "New Church Development Policies," p. 258.

23. Ibid., *Minutes,* GA, UPCUSA, 1971, pp. 379–382.

24. *Minutes,* BNM, UPCUSA, vol. 16, pp. 32–36.

25. Ibid., p. 36.

26. Ibid., p. 180; *Minutes,* GA, UPCUSA, 1972, p. 622.

27. Perrys, "New Church Development Policies," p. 259.

28. UPCUSA, Program Agency, October 19, 1973, p. 275; June 26–28, 1975, pp. 161ff.; October 21–23, 1976, p. 318. Microfilm copy of these minutes is on file in the archives of the PC(USA) Dept. of History, Philadelphia. Perrys, "New Church Development Policies," pp. 259–260.

29. *Minutes,* GA, UPCUSA, 1976, pp. 336–337, 396–397.

30. Ibid., p. 388.

31. Ibid., pp. 388–390.

32. *Minutes,* GA, UPCUSA, 1977, pp. 99f., 119, 547.

33. *Minutes,* GA, UPCUSA, 1978, pp. 51, 343.

34. Ibid., p. 343.

35. *Minutes,* GA, UPCUSA, 1981, pp. 209–210.

36. Compiled from the UPCUSA statistical tables in the annual General Assembly *Minutes,* Part II.

37. Wallace N. Jamison, *The United Presbyterian Story: A Centennial Study, 1858–1958* (Pittsburgh: Geneva Press, 1958), Preface, pp. 1, 222.

38. Ibid., pp. 70–75.

39. Ibid., pp. 172–177.

40. Ibid., p. 174.

41. *Minutes of the Board of American Missions of the United Presbyterian Church of North America* [cited hereafter as BAM, UPCNA] vol. 1, pp. 41ff., 149. Original volumes are in the archives of the Presbyterian Historical Society, Philadelphia.

42. *Minutes of the General Assembly of the United Presbyterian Church of North America* [cited hereafter as GA, UPCNA], 1931, pp. 336, 944.

43. Compiled from the UPCNA statistical tables in the Appendix of the annual General Assembly *Minutes* (includes American presbyteries only). Where discrepancies existed between total listed per year and sum of new churches organized by synod, we used the latter.

44. *Minutes,* BAM, UPCNA, vol. 2, p. 787.

45. *Minutes,* GA, UPCNA, 1944, p. 93.

46. *Minutes,* BAM, UPCNA, vol. 4, p. 1002.

47. Ibid., pp. 1087, 1097; *Minutes,* BAM, UPCNA, vol. 5, p. 1219.

48. *Minutes,* BAM, UPCNA, vol. 5, pp. 1120, 1140; *Minutes,* GA, UPCNA, 1950, p. 876; *Minutes,* GA, UPCNA, 1951, p. 1234.

49. *Minutes,* BAM, UPCNA, vol. 5, pp. 1233, 1254; *Minutes,* GA, UPCNA, 1952, p. 98.

50. *Minutes,* GA, UPCNA, 1965, p. 141.

51. *Minutes,* BAM, UPCNA, vol. 6, p. 144.

52. Ernest T. Thompson, "Annual Report of the Board of National Ministries," *Minutes of the General Assembly of the Presbyterian Church in the United States* [cited hereafter as GA, PCUS, AR], 1973, Part II, p. 90.

53. Ibid., pp. 90–94.

54. Ibid., pp. 93–94.

55. Ibid., pp. 94, 105.

56. Compiled from the PCUS statistical tables in the Appendix or Part II of the annual General Assembly *Minutes.*

57. *Minutes of the General Assembly of the Presbyterian Church in the United States* [cited hereafter as GA, PCUS], 1938, p. 69; Appendix, pp. 143–145; ibid., pp. 141–145.

58. See, for example, *Minutes,* GA, PCUS, AR, 1940, pp. 9–10.

59. See, for example, *Minutes,* GA, PCUS, AR, 1942, pp. 11–14.

60. *Minutes,* GA, PCUS, 1942, p. 79.

61. Presbyterian Church in the United States, Executive Committee of Home Missions, *Minutes,* July 17, 1947, p. 17. For a complete report on the Home Mission Emergency Fund, see Presbyterian Church in the United States, Assembly's Home Mission Council, *Minutes,* February 10–11, 1948, Appendix I. Copies of the minutes of the Executive Committee and its successor agencies (up to the 1973 PCUS reorganization) and of the Assembly's Home Mission Council are in the archives of the Presbyterian Study Center, Montreat, N.C.

62. *Minutes,* GA, PCUS, AR, 1948, p. 9.

63. *Minutes,* GA, PCUS, 1946, pp. 64, 85–86; AR, p. 45; *Minutes,* GA, PCUS, 1947, p. 76; *Minutes,* GA, PCUS, AR, 1953, pp. 3, 8.

64. Thompson, "The Board of National Ministries," p. 108.

65. *Minutes,* GA, PCUS, 1954, 93–95. Actual figures for 1955–57 were: 188 churches, or 1.2 per week (although 1955 [70] and 1957 [68] had the two highest number of churches organized between 1940 and 1980); net membership increase was 67,882 (26,771 from 1954 to 1955; 22,051 from 1955 to 1956; and 19,060 from 1956 to 1957). In 1956, losses were 63,198, and in 1957 they were 68,954! Data were compiled from the PCUS statistical tables. See note 56 above.

66. *Minutes,* GA, PCUS, 1961, pp. 55–56.

67. *Minutes,* GA, PCUS, 1953, pp. 82–85; *Minutes,* GA, PCUS, 1956, p. 70; *Minutes,* GA, PCUS, 1965, p. 59.

68. *Minutes,* GA, PCUS, 1955, p. 74; *Minutes,* GA, PCUS, 1959, p. 83; *Minutes,* GA, PCUS, AR, 1959, pp. 43–45.

69. *Minutes,* GA, PCUS, AR, 1961, p. vi.

70. Ibid., pp. vi–vii; Thompson, "The Board of National Ministries," p. 115.

71. *Minutes,* GA, PCUS, AR, 1961, p. 14.

72. *Minutes of the Board of Church Extension of the Presbyterian Church in the United States* [cited hereafter as BCE, PCUS], February 1961, pp. 152–153. See note 61 above.

73. Ibid., p. 153.

74. Data were compiled from the PCUS statistical tables. See note 56 above.

75. *Minutes,* GA, PCUS, AR, 1961, pp. 15–16.

76. *Minutes,* BCE, PCUS, October 1961, p. 172.

77. *Minutes,* GA, PCUS, 1962, p. 39; *Minutes,* GA, PCUS, AR, 1962, p. 7.

78. *Minutes,* GA, PCUS, 1964, p. 91; *Minutes,* GA, PCUS, AR, 1964, p. 10.

79. *Minutes,* GA, PCUS, 1965, pp. 48–51.

80. *Minutes,* GA, PCUS, AR, 1967, p. 24. Data were compiled from the PCUS statistical tables. See note 56 above.

81. *Minutes,* GA, PCUS, 1962, p. 57.

82. *Minutes,* GA, PCUS, AR, 1963, pp. 5, 21–22.

83. *Minutes,* BCE, PCUS, November 1963, 81ff.; *Minutes,* GA, PCUS, 1964, p. 92; *Minutes,* GA, PCUS, 1965, p. 69; *Minutes,* GA, PCUS, 1966, p. 71.

84. *Minutes,* GA, PCUS, AR, 1966, p. 7.

85. *Minutes,* GA, PCUS, 1967, p. 76.

86. $1,639,389 (*Minutes,* GA, PCUS, 1971, Part II, p. 144).

87. See, for example, PCUS, Board of National Ministries, November 7–9, 1969, pp. 9–10; February 24–26, 1970, p. 13; June 30–July 2, 1970, pp. 2, 9, 17, 21; November 10–11, 1970, p. 6; July 11–13, 1972, p. 3.

88. *Minutes,* GA, PCUS, 1968, p. 74.

89. *Minutes,* GA, PCUS, AR, 1968, pp. 17–24.

90. *Minutes,* GA, PCUS, 1976, p. 144; *Minutes,* GA, PCUS, 1974, Appendix, p. 254; *Minutes,* GA, PCUS, 1983, p. 597.

91. *Minutes,* GA, PCUS, AR, 1972, p. 47; *Minutes,* GA, PCUS, 1974, p. 190; *Minutes,* GA, PCUS, AR, 1974, p. 41.

92. See, for example, *Minutes,* GA, PCUS, AR, 1973, p. 48; *Minutes,* BNM, PCUS, March 8–10, 1972, pp. 12ff.

93. *Minutes,* GA, PCUS, 1979, Appendix, p. 317.

94. Data for this table and Tables 2–6 were compiled from the statistical reports contained in the annual General Assembly minutes of the denominations, except as otherwise noted.

95. *Minutes,* GA, PCUS, 1979, Appendix, p. 317.

96. Sources: U.S. Bureau of the Census, *Historical Statistics of the United States, Colonial Times to 1970,* Bicentennial Edition, Part 1 (Washington, D.C.: U.S. Government Printing Office, 1975), 211 [Series E 135–166]; and U.S. Bureau of the Census, *Statistical Abstract of the United States: 1988* (108th ed.) (Washington, D.C.: U.S. Government Printing Office, 1988), 450 [Table No. 738].

97. These figures are based on the author's own experience as the organizing pastor of the First Presbyterian Church of Allen, Texas, located 25 miles north of downtown Dallas, in the years 1983–1988. In our situation, land cost alone was $220,000, and the first unit estimate was close to $600,000, including architect's fees. These figures are typical for the Dallas area. The church has received funding from the Highland Park Presbyterian Church, Dallas, Texas, Grace Presbytery, the Synod of the Sun, and the General Assembly, as well as generous contributions of cash and goods from other individuals and congregations.

3: The Rise and Fall of Presbyterian Official Journals, 1925–1985

1. Martin E. Marty, "The Protestant Press: Limitations and Possibilities," in *The Religious Press in America* (New York: Holt, Rinehart & Winston, 1963), pp. 22, 62.

2. Robert Wuthnow, *The Restructuring of American Religion: Society and Faith Since World War II* (Princeton, N.J.: Princeton University Press, 1988).

3. The newspaper the *Presbyterian* was not included in this study because it was not under the control and direction of the church. As an independent newspaper, however, it considered itself representative of the views of the PCUSA, and when *Presbyterian Life* began full-scale publication in 1948, the editors of the *Presbyterian* decided to disband the newspaper in favor of the new magazine.

4. "On Running a Church Paper," *Presbyterian Magazine* 32 (October 1926), 461; "A Magazine Creed," *Presbyterian Magazine* 32 (February 1926), 59.

5. Ibid.

6. *Minutes of the General Assembly of the Presbyterian Church in the United States of America* [cited hereafter as GA, PCUSA], 1931, Part I, pp. 223–224.

7. Ibid., p. 224.

8. Ibid.

9. *Presbyterian Magazine* 36 (January 1930) and *Presbyterian Magazine* 37 (February 1931).

10. The typewritten manuscript of the report is in the PC(USA), Dept. of History, Philadelphia.

11. General Council Committee on a Church Paper, *Minutes,* 1941, in the PC(USA), Dept. of History, Philadelphia.

12. *Minutes,* GA, PCUSA, 1947, Part I, pp. 91–92.

13. *Presbyterian Life* 1 (January 17, 1948), 2; *Presbyterian Life* 1 (February 14, 1948), 2; *Presbyterian Life* 2 (February 5, 1949), 12–13.

14. Board of Directors of *Presbyterian Life, Minutes,* July 2, 1947, in the PC(USA), Dept. of History, Philadelphia.

15. Articles of Incorporation of *Presbyterian Life,* in the PC(USA), Dept. of History, Philadelphia.

16. Board of Directors of *Presbyterian Life, Minutes,* July 2, 1947, in the PC(USA), Dept. of History, Philadelphia.

17. Robert Cadigan, "Facing the Facts of Presbyterian Life," *Presbyterian Life* 2 (February 5, 1949), 12–13.

18. *Minutes,* GA, PCUSA, 1949, Part I, p. 85.

19. Ibid., p. 86.

20. *Presbyterian Life* 4 (June 23, 1951), 17.

21. See the financial statements for *Presbyterian Life* published

in the supplement to the General Assembly *Minutes* for these years.

22. *United Presbyterian* 99 (May 1, 1941).

23. In 1956, the *United Presbyterian* was under the financial control of the Board of Christian Education.

24. *United Presbyterian* 114 (October 7, 1956), 19.

25. Raymond L. Edie, "The Church Paper," *United Presbyterian* 115 (January 27, 1957), 11.

26. J. Oscar Lee, "Race Relations and the American Churches," *United Presbyterian* 115 (February 10, 1957), 4–6.

27. Theophilus M. Taylor, "Women and the Christian Ministry," *United Presbyterian* 114 (October 14, 1956), 22.

28. "Correspondence," *United Presbyterian* 115 (February 10, 1957), 22–23.

29. See the following issues of *Presbyterian Life:* October 14, 1950; June 11, 1953; and June 26, 1954.

30. *Presbyterian Life* printed a General Assembly report on "Relations Between Church and State" in the September 1, 1962, issue. Reaction to *Presbyterian Life*'s manner of reporting the news was printed in the issue for March 15, 1963, pp. 27–28. See also the letters published in the July 1, 1964, issue, p. 4. A considerable number of letters to the editor that were never printed in the magazine can be found in the PC(USA), Dept. of History, Philadelphia.

31. *Minutes of the General Assembly of the United Presbyterian Church in the United States of America* [cited hereafter as GA, UPCUSA], 1968, Part I, p. 141.

32. A copy of the brochure *A Magazine for a Church with a Conscience* can be found in the PC(USA), Dept. of History, Philadelphia. The full title is *A Magazine for a Church with a Conscience 1968—Presbyterian Life.* It is a report to the General Assembly in the twenty-first year of the magazine and was written by Daniel B. Carsat, president of the Board of Directors of *Presbyterian Life.*

33. Wittreich Associates Incorporated, a public opinion management service, authored the report.

34. Warren J. Wittreich, "Report on Readers' Attitudes Toward *Presbyterian Life,*" unpublished report prepared by Wittreich Associates, Inc., November 1971, p. 10. The report can be found in the PC(USA), Dept. of History, Philadelphia.

35. Ibid., p. 19.

36. Ibid., p. 23.

37. "Report of the First Board of Directors of *Presbyterian Life,"* in *Minutes,* GA, UPCUSA, 1973, Part I, pp. 891–895.

38. Ibid.

39. "Ruling Elder Robert J. Cadigan, Editor for a Quarter Century, Retires" *A.D.* 2 (February 1973), 2–3.

40. The abbreviation A.D. stands for *anno domini,* a time reference meaning "in the year of the Lord."

41. File of correspondence of editor Robert Heinze for 1976 in the PC(USA), Dept. of History, Philadelphia.

42. J. Martin Bailey, Report to the Board of Directors of *A.D.,* September 22, 1975, in the PC(USA), Dept. of History, Philadelphia.

43. "Presbyterian Church Periodicals and Editorial Comment," an unpublished report prepared by the Simmons Market Research Bureau, Inc., 1984, p. 32.

44. Ibid., p. 52.

45. *64th Annual Report of the Executive Committee of Publication and Sabbath School Work to the General Assembly of the PCUS,* 1925, p. 18, and *74th Annual Report of the Executive Committee of Religious Education and Publication,* 1940, p. 54.

46. "The Presbyterian Survey and Its Circulation," *Presbyterian Survey* 22 (March 1932), 131.

47. "If There Were No Church Paper," *Presbyterian Survey* 23 (September 1933), 519.

48. See especially "The Story of the American Negro," *Presbyterian Survey* 39 (February 1949), 68–73; and "States Rights and Human Rights," *Presbyterian Survey* 39 (October 1949), 454–456, 480.

49. *Minutes of the General Assembly of the Presbyterian Church in the United States* [cited hereafter as GA, PCUS], 1952, pp. 93, 94.

50. Ibid., p. 94.

51. *Minutes,* GA, PCUS, 1953, pp. 79–80.

52. John Mackay reported in October 1953 that there was a new idolatry afoot in the country; he labeled this idolatary "fanatical anticommunism." John A. Mackay, "The New Idolatry," *Presbyterian Survey* 43 (October 1953), 47–48.

53. "Our Church Is Showing Steady Increase in Selfishness," *Presbyterian Survey* 45 (October 1955), 8–10.

54. "Women—What Role Shall They Play in the Church?" *Presbyterian Survey* 46 (June 1956), 24–25, 62.

55. "In Review—94th General Assembly," *Presbyterian Survey* 44 (August 1954), 3.

56. *Presbyterian Survey* 45 (November 1955), 3; "Survey Campaign Picks Up Speed," *Presbyterian Survey* 48 (November 1958), 48.

57. *Minutes,* GA, PCUS, 1956, p. 123.

58. Compare the staff as listed in the February and March issues in the index volumes. *Minutes,* GA, PCUS, 1958, pp. 135–136.

59. *Minutes,* GA, PCUS, 1959, p. 120.

60. *Presbyterian Survey* 49 (December 1959), p. 17.

61. "Letters" and "Prefers Bombs," *Presbyterian Survey* 50 (July 1960), 5–6.

62. Ben Hartley, "Editor's Comments," *Presbyterian Survey* 51 (January 1961), 2.

63. Report of the Board of Directors of *Presbyterian Survey, Minutes,* GA, PCUS, 1964, p. 207.

64. Tape recording, Atlanta radio station WGST interview with Ben Hartley, January 3, 1966.

65. See letters in the February 1968 issue of the *Presbyterian Survey.* See also the Vietnam opinion poll in *Presbyterian Survey* 58 (February 1968), 24.

66. Elizabeth Lollar, "But We Didn't Give Ourselves," *Presbyterian Survey* 54 (January 1964), 29–32.

67. "Letters, Wrong Mag or Wrong Church?" *Presbyterian Survey* 54 (May 1964), 6–7.

68. "Letters, Criticism of NCC Is Just," *Presbyterian Survey* 54 (June 1964), 7.

69. *Presbyterian Survey* 58 (June 1968), 2–3.

70. "Letters," *Presbyterian Survey* 58 (August 1968), 4–6.

71. Report of the Board of Directors of *Presbyterian Survey, Minutes,* GA, PCUS, 1966, p. 126.

72. Report of the Board of Directors of *Presbyterian Survey, Minutes,* GA, PCUS, 1971, p. 265.

73. John Templeton, "Forum," *Presbyterian Survey* 61 (December 6, 1971), 14.

74. *Minutes,* GA, PCUS, 1971, pp. 119–121.

75. "Editor's Mail," *Presbyterian Survey* 62 (May 1972), 43.

76. Ibid., 44; (July 1972), 41.

77. "Editor's Mail," *Presbyterian Survey* 62 (August 1972), 42–43.

78. Robert J. Hastings, "Keep the Church Press Open," *Presbyterian Survey* 63 (March 1973), 26–27.

79. Bill Lampkin, "Please Don't Murder the Messenger," *Presbyterian Survey* 68 (August 1978), 2.

80. "Letters," *Presbyterian Survey* 70 (June/July 1980), 6.

81. *Minutes,* GA, PCUS, 1980, pp. 150–151.

82. *Minutes,* GA, PCUS, Part I, 1982, p. 312.

83. "Presbyterian Church Periodicals and Editorial Comment," an unpublished report prepared by the Simmons Market Research Bureau, Inc., 1984, p. xii.

84. Cary Patrick, "Paging Through History," *Presbyterian Survey* 74 (June 1984), 47–48.

85. Vic Jameson, "New Year's Ideas from a New Editor," *Presbyterian Survey* 74 (January 1984), 4.

86. Wuthnow, *The Restructuring of American Religion,* pp. 71–100.

4: A Poultice for the Bite of the Cobra: The Hocking Report and Presbyterian Missions in the Middle Decades of the Twentieth Century

1. Laymen's Foreign Missions Inquiry, The Commission of Appraisal, William Ernest Hocking, Chairman, *Re-Thinking Missions: A Laymen's Inquiry After One Hundred Years* (New York: Harper & Brothers, 1932), p. ix. For a secondary treatment of the Hocking Report and the controversy it generated within American Presbyterianism, see William R. Hutchison, *Errand to the World: American Protestant Thought and Foreign Missions* (Chicago: University of Chicago Press, 1987), pp. 158–175; Gerald H. Anderson, "American Protestants in Pursuit of Mission: 1886–1986," *International Bulletin of Missionary Research* 12/3 (July 1988), 106–108.

2. Hocking, *Re-Thinking Missions,* p. 18. Some of the thinking on Protestant missions that anticipated—and perhaps prompted—the conclusions of the Hocking Commission were James L. Barton, "The Modern Missionary," *Harvard Theological Review* 8 (January 1915), 1–17; J. P. Jones, "The Protestant Missionary Propaganda in India," *Harvard Theological Review* 8 (January 1915), 18–44; Daniel Johnson Fleming, *Attitudes Toward Other Faiths* (New York: Association Press, 1928); idem, *Ways of Sharing with Other Faiths* (New York: Association Press, 1929).

3. Hocking, *Re-Thinking Missions,* pp. 18, 19, 45.

4. Ibid., pp. 48, 326–327, 19.

5. Ibid., pp. 19–22, 292, 327.

6. Ibid., pp. 22–23.

7. Ibid., p. 326.

8. Ibid.

9. Pearl S. Buck, "The Laymen's Mission Report," *Christian Century* 49 (November 23, 1932), 1434.

10. Ibid., 1434, 1435.

11. Pearl S. Buck, "Is There a Case for Foreign Missions?" *Harper's Monthly Magazine* 166 (January 1933), 147.

12. Ibid., 149, 151.

13. Robert E. Speer, *"Re-Thinking Missions" Examined* (New York: Fleming H. Revell Co., 1933). Speer's review was never formally adopted as an official statement of the board; nonetheless, many Presbyterians accepted the treatise as an authoritative statement by the church's chief missionary theorist. Although Speer judged many findings of the report to be correct and worthy of implementation, he did not hesitate to voice his concerns about the faults of the report. Speer objected to the fact that the report, despite its claim to be the result of a "laymen's" inquiry, was not written by lay people. The select group of philosophers who had written the report, he argued, had little experience in the study of world missions and had wrongly assumed that the earliest leaders of the missions movement were evangelists who cared little for the social needs of nationals on the field. Although the report claimed to be unbiased and benevolent in its intent, Speer found it to be a partisan document that found little in the missions movement worthy of continuing support. And he accused the Commission of erring in their call that their report be accepted or rejected entire. The report, Speer claimed, had to be judiciously assessed; some of its recommendations were useful, others were not. Speer devoted the largest portion of his review to two major objections to the report. The first objection was theological. The report had construed "life in humanistic this-world terms" and had argued "that the spirit of Christ is not the Holy Spirit of the New Testament, who is nowhere mentioned." The report's "theological basis is the basis of the old Protestant liberalism . . . which passes over the ideas which give power both to evangelicalism and to the Roman Catholic faith. Nowhere is there any mention of prayer or of the supernatural forces of the Gospel" (p. 29). Speer believed that the report rejected the traditional claims of Christ's deity, the incarnation, and the resurrec-

tion. In short, Speer reckoned that the report had abandoned traditional Christian faith and sought to replace it with a lifeless humanism. Speer's second objection was largely pragmatic and centered on the report's proposal that Protestant missions should be carried out by a centralized, autonomous administrative body. His critique of this "Impracticable Plan" (p. 36) can be summarized in the charge that the report urged the churches to replace vibrant evangelism with mere secular philanthropy. These two objections would be echoed in subsequent statements of the board.

14. Hutchison, *Errand to the World,* p. 172. Buck herself faced stiff criticism in Presbyterian circles for her liberal views, and her standing eroded further when she "resigned" from the mission field and divorced her husband several years later. Ibid., p. 169. Buck herself was not technically a Presbyterian missionary. Even though she often referred to herself as a missionary, at other times she would insist that it was her husband who was the missionary.

15. This essay is based, in part, on information contained in the annual reports of the foreign missions boards of two branches of the American Presbyterian tradition. The bibliographic data for the various collections of reports read as follows: *Minutes of the General Assembly of the Presbyterian Church in the United States of America* (Philadelphia: Office of the General Assembly, 1930–1957) [cited hereafter as GA, PCUSA]; *Minutes of the General Assembly of the United Presbyterian Church in the United States of America* (New York: Office of the General Assembly, 1958–1972) [cited hereafter as GA, UPCUSA]; *Minutes of the Presbyterian Church in the United States* (Richmond: Presbyterian Commission of Publications, 1930–1951; Atlanta: Office of the General Assembly in Atlanta, 1952–1972) [cited hereafter as GA, PCUS].

16. *Minutes,* GA, PCUSA, 1933, pp. 157–159.

17. Ibid., pp. 159, 160.

18. *Minutes,* GA, PCUSA, 1934, p. 242.

19. *Minutes,* GA, PCUSA, 1935, p. 120.

20. Ibid.

21. *Minutes,* GA, PCUS, 1935, p. 39.

22. *Minutes,* GA, PCUSA, 1930, pp. 149, 150; *Minutes,* GA, PCUSA, 1931, p. 236.

23. *Minutes,* GA, PCUS, 1935, p. 39.

24. *Minutes,* GA, PCUS, 1934, pp. 56–57; *Minutes,* GA, PCUSA, 1932, p. 331.

25. *Minutes,* GA, PCUS, 1930, p. 74.

26. *Minutes,* GA, PCUSA, 1931, p. 237.

27. See, for instance, ibid., p. 234.

28. *Minutes,* GA, PCUSA, 1935, p. 120.

29. *Minutes,* GA, PCUSA, 1934, p. 241; *Minutes,* GA, PCUSA, 1935, p. 125.

30. *Minutes,* GA, PCUSA, 1956, pp. 170–171 (ellipsis in original).

31. *Minutes,* GA, PCUS, 1954, pp. 98, 147–165 passim.

32. *Minutes,* GA, PCUSA, 1933, p. 158.

33. *Minutes,* GA, PCUSA, 1943, p. 354.

34. *Minutes,* GA, UPCUSA, 1961, p. 309.

35. *Minutes,* GA, UPCUSA, 1963, pp. 289, 290.

36. *Minutes,* GA, PCUSA, 1937, pp. 199–200.

37. *Minutes,* GA, PCUSA, 1941, p. 245.

38. *Minutes,* GA, PCUSA, 1949, pp. 172, 169–170.

39. The uniting General Assembly of 1958 established the Commission on Ecumenical Mission and Relations, widely known by the acronym COEMAR, to formulate missions policy for the newly formed United Presbyterian Church in the U.S.A. Throughout its fourteen-year history, COEMAR in effect codified the ecumenical, inclusive impulses that had been gaining momentum since the publication of the Hocking Report. For an inside, albeit self-congratulatory account of COEMAR, see Donald Black, *Merging Mission and Unity* (Philadelphia: Geneva Press, 1986).

40. *Minutes,* GA, PCUSA, 1935, p. 120.

41. *Minutes,* GA, UPCUSA, 1971, p. 389.

42. *Minutes,* GA, UPCUSA, 1959, p. 273. Although missions efforts of the 1960s and 1970s were erected on a far more liberal theological platform than in the past, verbal proclamation and direct efforts aimed at individual conversions—the shibboleth and *raison d'être* of the traditional missions effort—did not disappear from the missions agenda. However, it is extremely difficult to determine the extent to which the verbal proclamation of the gospel message was actually de-emphasized under the reign of the new missions ideology. The rhetoric of the Assembly Minutes indicates that the church was reassessing, a half-century later and half a world away, the claims of the social gospel, in which the witness of word and deed were seen as inextricably bound to-

gether. Although this appears to argue for the triumph of the Hocking Report in the church, it remains a commonplace among historians that Presbyterian missionaries of the middle decades of the twentieth century were both committed to and adept at "personal evangelism" designed to win converts to the faith.

43. *Minutes,* GA, UPCUSA, 1963, p. 280.

44. *Minutes,* GA, UPCUSA, 1966, p. 295.

45. *Minutes,* GA, UPCUSA, 1967, p. 286.

46. *Minutes,* GA, UPCUSA, 1968, p. 403.

47. *Minutes,* GA, PCUSA, 1931, p. 234.

48. *Minutes,* GA, PCUSA, 1936, pp. 155, 156, 161, 166.

49. *Minutes,* GA, PCUSA, 1937, p. 199.

50. *Minutes,* GA, PCUSA, 1939, pp. 204, 211.

51. *Minutes,* GA, PCUSA, 1942, p. 222.

52. *Minutes,* GA, PCUSA, 1943, p. 349.

53. Ibid., p. 351.

54. *Minutes,* GA, PCUS, 1943, p. 69.

55. *Minutes,* GA, PCUSA, 1946, pp. 242–243.

56. *Minutes,* GA, PCUSA, 1944, p. 355.

57. *Minutes,* GA, PCUS, 1945, p. 80; see also *Minutes,* GA, PCUSA, 1947, p. 174.

58. *Minutes,* GA, PCUS, 1948, p. 74.

59. *Minutes,* GA, PCUSA, 1952, p. 177.

60. Ibid., p. 178; *Minutes,* GA, PCUS, 1952, p. 85.

61. *Minutes,* GA, UPCUSA, 1960, p. 205.

62. *Minutes,* GA, PCUSA, 1953, p. 172.

63. *Minutes,* GA, PCUSA, 1955, pp. 158–159.

64. *Minutes,* GA, UPCUSA, 1958, p. 346; *Minutes,* GA, UPCUSA, 1959, p. 273.

65. *Minutes,* GA, UPCUSA, 1961, pp. 304, 309.

66. *Minutes,* GA, UPCUSA, 1964, pp. 259–260.

67. See Hutchison, *Errand to the World.*

68. *Minutes,* GA, UPCUSA, 1973, pp. 382, 383.

69. Perhaps nothing illustrates this new attitude better than a statement by the UPCUSA in 1970: "The social, cultural, and historical forces which have forged the Vietnamese people into an independent nation are not familiar to us either as Americans or more specifically as Christians. Any future relationship with Vietnamese people must take seriously the need to engage in significant dialogue and cooperation with all those who share a common humanitarian concern including members of the Buddhist

and other religious communities." *Minutes,* GA, UPCUSA, 1970, pp. 529–530.

5: American Presbyterians in the Global Ecumenical Movement

1. W. Stanley Rycroft, *The Ecumenical Witness of the United Presbyterian Church in the U.S.A.* (Philadelphia: UPCUSA Board of Christian Education, 1968), p. 19.

2. Donald Black, *Merging Mission and Unity* (Philadelphia: Geneva Press, 1986), pp. 7–10.

3. Simeon Stylites [pseudonym of Halford E. Luccock], "Looking for a Word," *Christian Century* 75 (August 20, 1958), 959.

4. The background to and history of those ecumenical bodies most closely related to the World Council of Churches are surveyed in articles contained in *A History of the Ecumenical Movement, 1517–1948,* ed. Ruth Rouse and Stephen C. Neill, 2nd ed. (Philadelphia: Westminster Press, 1967), and *A History of the Ecumenical Movement,* vol. 2: 1948–1968, ed. Harold E. Fey (Philadelphia: Westminster Press, 1970). A third volume in this series is currently in progress, under the editorship of Paul Crow. Continuing discussion and debate within ecumenism is recorded in two journals published under the aegis of the World Council of Churches, *Ecumenical Review* and *International Review of Mission.* Ans J. van der Bent, librarian emeritus of the World Council of Churches (WCC), has provided a range of ecumenical bibliographies; see especially *Major Studies and Themes in the Ecumenical Movement* (Geneva: WCC, 1981) and *A Guide to Essential Ecumenical Reading* (Geneva: WCC, 1984). For background on the Lausanne Movement for World Evangelization, see C. Rene Padilla, ed., *The New Face of Evangelicalism* (Downers Grove, Ill.: InterVarsity Press, 1976), and Vinay Samuel and Chris Sugden, eds., *The Church in Response to Human Need* (Grand Rapids: Wm. B. Eerdmans, 1987). A statistical overview of global Christianity, recorded with a concern for world evangelization, is found in *World Christian Encyclopedia,* ed. David B. Barrett (New York: Oxford University Press, 1982).

5. Lefferts A. Loetscher, *A Brief History of the Presbyterians,* 4th ed. (Philadelphia: Westminster Press, 1983), pp. 95–96: "For some years before 1837 there had been those ominous rumblings of controversy between 'Old School' and 'New School' parties

within the church. . . . The Old School . . . felt that the Presbyterian Church should have its own denominational church boards, responsible to the General Assembly, rather than work in such nondenominational agencies as the American Education Society and the American Home Missionary Society." A continuing commitment to nondenominational, evangelical mission persisted in Presbyterian membership in the American Bible Society; see Rycroft, *Ecumenical Witness,* pp. 87–88.

6. Acts 8:36; 10:47f.; 11:22; 15:1–31. See also Edward W. Farley, "The Presbyterian Heritage as Modernism: Reaffirming a Forgotten Past in Hard Times," in Milton J Coalter, John M. Mulder, and Louis B. Weeks, eds., *The Presbyterian Predicament: Six Perspectives* (Louisville, Ky.: Westminster/John Knox Press, 1990), pp. 59–61; for commentary on New Testament accounts of the early Gentile mission, see George B. Caird, *The Apostolic Age* (London: Gerald Duckworth and Co., 1955), pp. 83–105. Receding farther in time, one could contrast the passion for religious and national purity in Esther and Ezra-Nehemiah with the cross-cultural motifs of Ruth, Jonah, and Isaiah 40–66.

7. "Address by the General Assembly: All the Churches of Jesus Christ Throughout the Earth," *Minutes of the Presbyterian Church in the Confederate States of America,* 1861, vol. I, pp. 51–59. The address, composed by James Henley Thornwell, takes a leaf from the U.S. Declaration of Independence, setting out the just causes for bringing to birth a new creature on the North American continent.

8. T. Erskine Clarke, "The History of Ecumenical Relations in the Southern Presbyterian Church," *Minutes of the General Assembly of the Presbyterian Church in the United States* [cited hereafter as GA, PCUS], 1976, Part I, pp. 466–477. Clarke notes that the stated theological reasons for separation were handsomely supplemented by unstated geographical and cultural reasons.

9. Ibid., p. 470. Clarke notes a statement by a contemporary PCUS Assembly that "the union of the Old and New Schools 'involved a total surrender of all the great testimonies of the Church for the fundamental doctrines of grace.' "

10. Rycroft, *Ecumenical Witness,* p. 90.

11. Ernest Trice Thompson, *Presbyterians in the South* (Richmond: John Knox Press, 1973), vol. 2, pp. 237–238.

12. Ben M. Barrus, Milton L. Baughn, and Thomas H. Campbell, *A People Called Cumberland Presbyterians* (Memphis,

Tenn.: Frontier Press, 1972), pp. 270–277. This conflict persisted despite attempts by the PCUS to enter into union discussion with Cumberland Presbyterians in the South.

13. Samuel McCrea Cavert, *The American Churches in the Ecumenical Movement, 1900–1968* (New York: Association Press, 1968), pp. 79–80.

14. Kenneth Scott Latourette, *A History of the Expansion of Christianity,* vol. 7: *Advance Through Storm* (New York: Harper & Brothers, 1945), p. 27, cites many forerunners of Edinburgh, among them the World Evangelical Alliance, the World's Student Christian Federation, the YMCA and YWCA, and the World's Christian Endeavor Union.

15. The Union Missionary Conference of 1854 was held in the Presbyterian Church at Nineteenth Street and Fifth Avenue in New York.

16. Kenneth Scott Latourette, "Ecumenical Bearings of the Missionary Movement and the International Missionary Council," in Rouse and Neill, eds., *A History of the Ecumenical Movement, 1517–1948,* p. 362, describes the hesitant and careful debate of 1910, followed by conference chair John R. Mott's visionary closing address, which began: "The end of the Conference is the beginning of the conquest. The end of the planning is the beginning of the doing."

17. Latourette, "Ecumenical Bearings," p. 357.

18. Cavert, *American Churches in the Ecumenical Movement, 1900–1968,* p. 82.

19. Robert Wuthnow, *The Struggle for America's Soul: Evangelicals, Liberals, and Secularism* (Grand Rapids: Wm. B. Eerdmans, 1989), p. 70.

20. John Coventry Smith, *From Colonialism to World Community: The Church's Pilgrimage* (Philadelphia: Geneva Press, 1982), pp. 155, 167.

21. G. Thompson Brown, *Presbyterians in World Mission* (Decatur, Ga.: Columbia Theological Seminary, 1988), pp. 49–56, provides a schematic representation of the development of American Presbyterian mission in the nineteenth and twentieth centuries.

22. Lesslie Newbigin, "Mission to Six Continents," in Fey, ed., *A History of the Ecumenical Movement, 1948–1968,* pp. 174–179.

23. Black, *Merging Mission and Unity,* pp. 74–75. Black observes that the ramifications of mutuality had not fully sunk in:

COEMAR unilaterally appointed committee members from other countries, rather than requesting partner churches to select their own representatives; the UPCUSA's relationship with the Presbyterian Church of Brazil, already perilous, never fully recovered from this and other miscommunications.

In addition to the text of the *Advisory Study* published by COEMAR, there was a fifteen-page confidential addendum (headed "Supplemental Paper No. 5") on "The Ecumenical Movement as a Factor Conditioning the United Presbyterian Church's Fulfillment of Mission Overseas." It discussed the impact of ecumenical involvement on COEMAR's relations with "daughter churches," the ancient Eastern churches, the Roman church, and "evangelical fundamentalists."

24. Smith, *From Colonialism to World Community,* p. 209. Smith adds that he showed the report "to another General Secretary of a Presbyterian agency" and was told "these things might be significant overseas but were of little or no value in the United States!"

25. Thompson, *Presbyterians in the South,* vol. 3, pp. 432–443. The Montreat consultation heralded a series of mutual mission pacts and led to Montreat II's ecumenical affirmation "The Nature of the Unity We Seek"; see G. Thompson Brown, "Overseas Mission Programs and Policies of the Presbyterian Church in the U.S.," *American Presbyterians: Journal of Presbyterian History* 65 (1987), 166–170; and "The Nature of the Unity We Seek," *Minutes,* GA, PCUS, 1978, Part I, pp. 165–180.

26. Johannes Verkuyl, *Contemporary Missiology,* ed. and trans. Dale Cooper (Grand Rapids: Wm. B. Eerdmans, 1978), pp. 197–204.

27. Arthur Judson Brown, *Memoirs of a Centenarian,* ed. William Wysham (New York: World Horizons, 1957), p. 37.

28. Rycroft, *Ecumenical Witness,* pp. 142–144.

29. Wuthnow, *Struggle for America's Soul,* p. 75, reports that a 1932 poll recorded by the Federal Council of Churches showed that northern Presbyterians supported the concept of church union by four to one, whereas "Southern Presbyterians . . . leaned moderately toward continuing the current divisions." See also H. Paul Douglass, *Church Unity Movements in the United States* (New York: Institute for Social and Religious Research, 1934), pp. 116, 444.

30. Tissington Tatlow, "The World Conference on Faith and

Order," in Rouse and Neill, eds., *A History of the Ecumenical Movement, 1517–1948,* pp. 406–417.

31. W. A. Visser 't Hooft, *The Genesis and Formation of the World Council of Churches* (Geneva: WCC, 1982), pp. 94–97.

32. Douglass, *Church Unity Movements in the United States,* p. 70.

33. Nicolas Zernov, "The Eastern Churches and the Ecumenical Movement in the Twentieth Century," in Rouse and Neill, eds., *A History of the Ecumenical Movement, 1517–1948,* p. 667.

34. Leon Howell, *Acting in Faith: The World Council of Churches Since 1975* (Geneva: WCC, 1982), p. 61.

35. See "The Nature of the Unity We Seek," *Minutes,* GA, PCUS, 1978, Part I, p. 171.

36. The response may be found in the *Minutes of the General Assembly of the Presbyterian Church (U.S.A.)* [cited hereafter as GA, PC(USA)], 1986, Part I, pp. 548–555, or in *Churches Respond to BEM* (Geneva: WCC, 1987), vol. 3, pp. 189–205.

37. Practicing as they preached, the writing team of the Presbyterian Church (U.S.A.)'s response was made up of six women and three men. See *Minutes,* GA, PC(USA), 1986, Part I, p. 555.

38. Bennett's remark is quoted by C. L. Patijn, "The Strategy of the Church," in *The Church and the Disorder of Society* (London: SCM Press, 1948), p. 159 n. 1.

39. Peter H. Hobbie, "Bringing Oxford Home," *American Presbyterians: Journal of Presbyterian History* 66 (1988), 27.

40. Barrus, Baughn, and Campbell, *A People Called Cumberland Presbyterians,* pp. 457–459, 481.

41. Hans Jochen Margull, "The Ecumenical Movement in the Churches and at the Parish Level," in Fey, ed., *A History of the Ecumenical Movement, 1948–1968,* pp. 365–368.

42. T. Watson Street, *The Church and the Churches* (Richmond: Covenant Life Curriculum, 1965).

43. Paul Abrecht, "The Evolution of Ecumenical Social Thought," in Pauline Webb, ed., *Faith and Faithfulness* (Geneva: WCC, 1984), p. 109.

44. On the UPCUSA and Vietnam, see Smith, *From Colonialism to World Community,* pp. 280–284. Shaull is quoted in *World Conference on Church and Society: Christians in the Technical and Social Revolutions of Our Time,* ed. M. M. Thomas and Paul Abrecht (Geneva: WCC, 1967), p. 25.

45. Paul Ramsey, *Who Speaks for the Church? A Critique of the*

1966 Geneva Conference on Church and Society (Nashville: Abingdon Press, 1967).

46. Donald W. Shriver, "One Voice in a Chorus," *Presbyterian Outlook* 149 (December 4, 1967), 6–7. On the same two pages, the *Outlook* published three other reviewers' comments on Ramsey's book: John C. Bennett, "Risks Are Involved"; Raymond J. Pontier, "Who Speaks for Humanity?"; and Richard Shaull, "Something New Is Needed." Mention of *Who Speaks for the Church?* is conspicuously absent from *Presbyterian Life, Monday Morning,* and *Presbyterian Survey,* magazines published by the UPCUSA and PCUS. *Outlook* is independently published.

47. Eugene Carson Blake, book review, *Theology Today* 25 (April 1968), 134–136. Defenders of the Geneva conference did not see it as a "social action *curia*" (Ramsey, *Who Speaks for the Church?* p. 13), but as a forum exercising no more than informal authority. Nor did Ramsey's respondents tend to address the methodological issues he raised as a Christian ethicist. It would be more than two decades before Richard John Neuhaus published this tribute in "How My Mind Has Changed," *Christian Century* 107 (July 11–18, 1990), 670: "During those years my chief intellectual antagonist was the late Paul Ramsey of Princeton. He did not so much defend the justice of the war as he challenged the reasoning of those who were so sure of its injustice. The extent to which my opposition to the war was honest was due in very large part to Paul Ramsey."

48. An overview of critiques is provided in Ans J. van der Bent, "Diversity, Conflict, and Unity in Ecumenical Theology," *Ecumenical Review* 41 (1989), 201–212. Paul Abrecht deals specifically with social ethics in "From Oxford to Vancouver," *Ecumenical Review* 40 (1988), 147–168. From a Presbyterian Church (U.S.A.) perspective, one critique of liberation thought is presented by Daniel L. Migliore, "Jesus Christ, the Reconciling Liberator: The Confession of 1967 and Theologies of Liberation," *Journal of Presbyterian History* 41 (1983), 33–42. Migliore investigates the commonalities and contradictions of Reformed and liberation thought, and shows how each can usefully critique the assumptions of the other. See also Harvey T. Hoekstra, *The World Council of Churches and the Demise of Evangelism* (Wheaton, Ill.: Tyndale House, 1979), and the review of Hoekstra's book by Robbins Strong in the WCC's *International Review of Mission* 70 (1981), 79–81.

49. Patricia M. Roach, "From San Antonio to Manila," *Mon-*

day Morning 55 (January 22, 1990), 4. For an evangelical critique of WCC missiology, see Hoekstra, *World Council of Churches.* An academic treatment of comparative contemporary missiology and extensive bibliographical references are found in Rodger C. Bassham, *Mission Theology: 1948–1975. Years of Worldwide Creative Tension, Ecumenical, Evangelical, and Roman Catholic* (Pasadena, Calif.: William Carey Library, 1979).

50. C. Rene Padilla, "Mission in the 1990s," *International Bulletin for Missionary Research (IBMR)* 13 (October 1989), 150, 152. Padilla's longtime leadership of a socially concerned stream within the Lausanne movement and his commitment to holistic evangelism, which he calls "integrity in mission," are noted by Robert T. Coote, "Lausanne II and World Evangelization," *IBMR* 14 (January 1990), 10–17. See also Samuel and Sugden, *The Church in Response to Human Need,* p. x.

51. John Wicklein, " '60 Minutes' Sounds the Alarm," *Christianity and Crisis* (February 21, 1983), 41–44, showed that CBS did little checking of facts for its broadcast of January 23, 1983, but based its argument primarily on Jean Isaac Rael's article in the January 1983 *Reader's Digest.*

52. "Special Committee to Study the National Council of Churches and the World Council of Churches," *Minutes,* GA, PC(USA), 1986, Part I, pp. 209–258.

53. Ibid., pp. 236–239.

54. *Presbyterian Panel* (June 1984), 1, 8.

55. Lewis Wilkins, "The Present Profile of Ecumenical Relations in the Presbyterian Church U.S.," *Minutes,* GA, PCUS, 1976, Part I, p. 478.

56. Madeleine Barot, "What *Do* These Women Want?" in Webb, *Faith and Faithfulness,* pp. 76–83.

57. Virginia Lieson Brereton, "United and Slighted: Women as Subordinated Insiders," in William Hutchison, ed., *Between the Times: The Travail of the Protestant Establishment in America, 1900–1960* (New York: Cambridge University Press, 1989), pp. 143–167. Brereton deals primarily with the Federal Council/National Council of the Churches of Christ in the U.S.A., concluding on p. 164 that women leaders of the 1940s and 1950s "basically agreed with their male counterparts about the social and religious agenda of the Protestant churches. When a conflict arose between male and female church groups, it was over the distribution of power and authority, not over vastly different worldviews."

58. "Special Committee to Study the NCC and WCC," *Minutes,* GA, PC(USA), 1986, Part I, p. 211.

6: Presbyterian Ecumenical Activity
in the United States

1. Robert McAfee Brown, "I Am Presbyterian—Therefore I Am Ecumenical," *Presbyterian Survey* (September 1987), 12–15.

2. The number of books and articles on the ecumenical movement is massive. Helpful bibliographies include Paul A. Crow, Jr., *The Ecumenical Movement in Bibliographical Outline* (New York: NCCC, 1965); Erminie H. Lantero, "Comprehensive Bibliography of Church Cooperation and Unity in America," in Samuel McCrea Cavert, ed., *Church Cooperation and Unity in America, A Historical Review: 1900–1970* (New York: Association Press, 1970), pp. 354–396; and more specifically on Presbyterianism, the bibliography in W. Stanley Rycroft, *The Ecumenical Witness of the United Presbyterian Church in the U.S.A.* (Philadelphia: UPCUSA Board of Christian Education, 1968), pp. 297–306. For official actions by Presbyterian General Assemblies, see *A Digest of the Acts and Proceedings of the General Assembly of the Presbyterian Church in the United States, 1861–1965* (Atlanta: Office of the General Assembly, 1966); *Digest of the Acts and Deliverances of the General Assembly of the Presbyterian Church in the United States of America* (Philadelphia: The Office of the General Assembly, 1938); *The Digest of the Principal Deliverances of the General Assembly of the United Presbyterian Church of North America* (Pittsburgh: United Presbyterian Board of Publication, 1942); *The Cumberland Presbyterian Digest* (Memphis, Tenn.: Board of Publication and Christian Education of the Cumberland Presbyterian Church, 1957); and *Digest of the Minutes of the General Assembly of the Presbyterian Church in America* (N.p.: The Stated Clerk of the General Assembly of the Presbyterian Church in America, n.d.).

3. See George M. Marsden, *The Evangelical Mind and the New School Presbyterian Experience* (New Haven: Yale University Press, 1970).

4. The term "interlocking directorates," although not technically accurate, points to the homogeneity of the leadership of the benevolent societies and the frequent appearance of the same names on the boards of different societies.

5. Of the seventy-five American participants in the first meeting of the Evangelical Alliance, forty-five were from Calvinist denominations—Congregational, Presbyterian, or Reformed. See *Evangelical Alliance: Report of the Proceedings of the Conference* (London: Partridge and Oakey, 1847), xcviii.

6. Various Covenanters and Seceders groups came together in 1858 and formed the United Presbyterian Church of North America. See Wallace N. Jamison, *The United Presbyterian Story: A Centennial Study, 1858–1958* (Pittsburgh: Geneva Press, 1958). The Associate Reformed Presbyterian Church, primarily in the South, did not participate and remains in the 1990s a separate denomination.

7. Major studies that cover Presbyterian history in the nineteenth century include Marsden, *The Evangelical Mind;* Ernest Trice Thompson, *Presbyterians in the South* (Richmond: John Knox Press, 1973), 3 vols.; and Lefferts A. Loetscher, *The Broadening Church: A Study of Theological Issues in the Presbyterian Church Since 1869* (Philadelphia: University of Pennsylvania Press, 1954).

8. See Sydney Ahlstrom, *A Religious History of the American People* (New Haven: Yale University Press, 1972), pp. 802–804; and Samuel McCrea Cavert, *The American Churches in the Ecumenical Movement, 1900–1968* (New York: Association Press, 1968), pp. 38–51.

9. Significant excerpts from the report can be conveniently found in H. Shelton Smith, Robert T. Handy, and Lefferts A. Loetscher, *American Christianity: An Historical Interpretation with Representative Documents* (New York: Charles Scribner's Sons, 1963), vol. 2, pp. 394–397. In spite of all of their intimate ties to American culture, the social concerns of the FCC were not simply an American phenomenon but part of a growing international movement of Social Christianity. The international dimension of Presbyterianism and the ecumenical movement is considered in the essay in this series entitled "American Presbyterians in the Global Ecumenical Movement."

10. Ahlstrom, *Religious History,* pp. 802–803.

11. Cavert, *American Churches,* p. 54. Cavert, although emphasizing the social agenda as the primary concern of the Federal Council, also calls attention to other activities of the Council, especially the Council's concern for evangelism. A Commission on Evangelism was created by the Council in 1912, and it sponsored a variety of evangelistic efforts such as preaching missions.

Even in these, however, the social agenda was never absent, for the "missions represented an effective fusing of evangelistic and missionary spirit with social and educational concern." Ibid., p. 142.

12. A classic treatment of reformers that emphasizes their need to maintain their own status is Richard Hofstadter, *The Age of Reform: From Bryan to F.D.R.* (New York: Random House, 1955).

13. Robert H. Wiebe, *The Search for Order* (New York: Hill & Wang, 1967), emphasizes the changing social status of the reformers and their quest for stability and order. Cf. Robert Lee, *The Social Sources of Church Unity: An Interpretation of the Unitive Movements in American Protestantism* (New York and Nashville: Abingdon Press, 1960).

14. *A Digest of the Acts and Proceedings of the General Assembly of the Presbyterian Church in the United States, 1861-1965,* pp. 455-456; Thompson, *Presbyterians in the South,* vol. 2, pp. 266-273.

15. *Minutes of the General Assembly of the Presbyterian Church in the Confederate States of America,* vol. I, 1861, pp. 52-53.

16. Reports of contributions to the NCC are printed each year in the *Presbyterian Layman,* along with percentages of totals and amounts per member. See, for example, May 1972; May 1974; September-October 1977; March-April 1982. In 1971, for example, the UPCUSA was the second largest contributor to the NCC. On a per capita basis, however, the UPCUSA was the largest contributor at $.65 per capita—nearly three times the amount of United Methodists at $.23. The PCUS—one-tenth the size of the largest contributor, the United Methodist—was the fourth largest contributor in total contributions, but contributed at more than twice the rate per capita ($.58) as the United Methodists.

17. "The Presbyterian Planning Calendar, 1988-89," p. 46.

18. Cavert, *American Churches,* p. 254. See Eugene C. Blake, *A Proposal Toward the Reunion of Christ's Church* (Philadelphia: General Assembly Office of the UPCUSA, 1961), and Robert McAfee Brown and David H. Scott, eds., *The Challenge to Reunion* (New York: McGraw-Hill Book Co., 1963).

19. Ahlstrom, *Religious History,* p. 1079.

20. Autobiographies provide important personal perspectives of these leaders. See *Charles Lemuel Thompson: An Autobiography,* ed. Elizabeth Osborn Thompson (New York: Fleming H. Revell Co., 1924); Charles Stelzle, *A Son of the Bowery: The Life*

Story of an East-Side American (New York: George H. Doran Co., 1926); William Adams Brown, *A Teacher and His Times* (New York: Charles Scribner's Sons, 1940). Cavert's fifty years of personal involvement in the ecumenical movement provided much of the insight for his *American Churches.* See also W. Reginald Wheeler, *A Man Sent from God: A Biography of Robert E. Speer* (Westwood, N.J.: Fleming H. Revell Co., 1956).

21. T. Erskine Clarke, "The History of Ecumenical Relations in the Southern Presbyterian Church," *Minutes of the General Assembly of the Presbyterian Church in the United States,* 1976, pp. 466–477.

22. See R. Douglas Brackenridge, *Eugene Carson Blake: Prophet with Portfolio* (New York: Seabury Press, 1978).

23. See, for example, John Leith, *Introduction to the Reformed Tradition* (Atlanta: John Knox Press, 1977), pp. 53–55; and Lefferts A. Loetscher, *A Brief History of the Presbyterians,* 4th ed. (Philadelphia: Westminster Press, 1983), pp. 182–184, 186. Lewis Lancaster, director of the Office of Ecumenical Relations for the Presbyterian Church (U.S.A.), has noted that one reason for the level of Presbyterian leadership involvement in ecumenical agencies is that Presbyterians tend to commit their top leaders to ecumenical work. Telephone interview with Lewis Lancaster, March 1989.

24. Leith, *Introduction,* p. 54.

25. Clarke, "History of Ecumenical Relations," p. 474.

26. A good example of the rise of the Sun Belt in an area strongly marked by southern traditions is Charleston Presbytery in South Carolina. By the time of the vote on church union, the largest congregation in the presbytery was the First Presbyterian Church of Hilton Head, whose membership was composed primarily of people who had moved there from outside the South. Charleston Presbytery voted for union by a majority of one. Union presbyteries had helped to prepare the way for the vote in many areas of the PCUS.

27. See George Marsden, *Reforming Fundamentalism: Fuller Seminary and the New Evangelicalism* (Grand Rapids: Wm. B. Eerdmans, 1987), pp. 107–110.

28. Ibid., pp. 264 and passim.

29. Telephone interview with Professor Paul Hiebert, Fuller Theological Seminary, March 1989. Leighton Ford serves as chair of the Lausanne Committee for World Evangelism.

30. See Paul Y. Glock and Rodney Stark, *American Piety: The*

Nature of Religious Commitment (Berkeley: University of California Press, 1968), p. 10.

31. David Bos, "Community Ministries: The Establishment of Ecumenical Local Ministries in North American Church Life," *Journal of Ecumenical Studies* (Winter 1985), 121ff.

32. Telephone interview with David Bos, March 1989. Bos is the chair of the National Steering Committee for Community Ministries.

33. Telephone interview with M. Anderson Sale, executive presbyter, Missouri Union Presbytery, March 1989. Ironically, this ecumenical pattern may be reversing with population shifts away from such areas and the struggle to preserve a particular denominational tradition.

34. Telephone interview with Barry Van Deventer, executive presbyter, Charleston-Atlantic Presbytery, March 1989.

35. "The Interchurch Conference," *Southwestern Presbyterian* (October 18, 1905), p. 2.

36. *Southern Presbyterian Journal* 13 (July 7, 1954), (July 16, 1954), (May 19, 1954), (September 1, 1954).

37. Perhaps the best known was J. Howard Pew.

38. The objectives of the Presbyterian Lay Committee were "to encourage ministers and laymen alike to take their place as individuals in society and, as led by the Holy Spirit, to become involved in such social, economic and political problems in which they have some competence, and to assert their position publicly as Christian citizens on all such matters"; and "to discourage public pronouncements by Church leaders speaking for the Church as a corporate body . . . on political, social and economic questions unless there are spiritual or moral issues which can be supported by clear-cut Biblical authority." The *Layman* may regard its clear if often indirect support of particular economic and social agendas as appropriate because the *Layman* is not speaking "for the Church as a corporate body." Or it may regard its position as being "supported by clear-cut Biblical authority." (Cf., for example, its call for withdrawal from the NCC and WCC, May–June 1984, where its ideological position is clear, or a typical headline: "4th World Council of Churches: Social Gospel, Revolution, Violence, Humanism, Share the Wealth Promoted.") The *Layman*'s use of the doctrine of the "Spirituality of the Church" to defend capitalism and U.S. interests is remarkably similar to the use of the doctrine by southern Presbyterians to defend slavery and southern independence. Cf. Erskine Clarke,

"Southern Nationalism and Columbia Theological Seminary," *Journal of Presbyterian History* 66 (Summer 1988), 123–133.

39. See, for example, "COCU Vote Demonstrates Mistrust Between Members and Leaders," *Presbyterian Layman,* October 1972.

40. Ibid., May 1968.

41. "Resolution of the Board of Directors of the Presbyterian Lay Committee on 'Consultation on Church Union,' " ibid., November 1970.

42. August J. Kling, "Changes in Structure and Authority That Will Affect United Presbyterians if the COCU Plan for a 25,000,000 Member Super-Church Becomes a Reality," ibid., January 1971.

43. William P. Thompson, in his "stinging rebuke" of the Assembly for withdrawing, declared that the action was "a retreat by the United Presbyterian Church into narrow Presbyterian parochialism." "Stated Clerk Rebukes COCU Withdrawal Action," ibid., August 1972.

44. "The Voice of the Assembly," ibid., June–July 1972; "COCU Vote Demonstrates Mistrust Between Members and Leader," ibid., October 1972.

45. The *Layman* continued to oppose COCU, but not with the same intensity or the same sense of COCU as a serious threat. Cf. "COCU Super Church Alarms Many," ibid., May–June 1986.

46. "General Board of NCC Calls for Many Changes in U.S. Foreign Policy," ibid., April 1968.

47. Cf. "World Council of Churches 6th Assembly: Soft on Soviet Aggression but Strong in Attacking U.S. Policy," ibid., September–October 1983; "World Council of Churches Ignores Sandinista Abuses" and "NCC Defends Aid to Sandinistas," ibid., September–October 1984.

48. The *Layman* complained in April 1972: "Isn't there anything in this country that deserves the support of our churches? Is our self-guilt so great that nothing in the life of this country is worthy of *any*thing but attack?" in "An Ecumenical Witness," ibid., April 1972.

49. See Christopher Lasch, *The Culture of Narcissism: American Life in an Age of Diminishing Expectations* (New York: W. W. Norton & Co., 1978), and Robert N. Bellah et al., *Habits of the Heart: Individualism and Commitment in American Life* (Berkeley: University of California Press, 1985).

50. No one has stated these concerns more forcefully than

Jacques Ellul in *The Technological Society* (New York: Alfred A. Knopf, 1963).

51. It is perhaps ironic that much of the opposition to ecumenical "bureaucracies" and to a "superchurch" came from prominent business leaders during a period when U.S. businesses exemplified the values of efficiency, centralization, and standardization.

52. Cf. Wade Clark Roof and William McKinney, *American Mainline Religion: Its Changing Shape and Future* (New Brunswick, N.J.: Rutgers University Press, 1987), pp. 19–20. Roof and McKinney propose a new "mapping" of religion in contemporary America in order to highlight the formation of what they regard as new clusters. These new clusters, they contend, have surpassed the denomination as the fundamental divisions in American religious life.

7: Presbyterians and Mass Media: A Case of Blurred Vision and Missed Mission

1. *Minutes of the General Assembly of the Presbyterian Church in the United States of America* [cited hereafter as GA, PCUSA], 1950, Part I, pp. 79–95.

2. *Minutes of the General Assembly of the Presbyterian Church in the United States* [cited hereafter as GA, PCUS], 1954, Part I, p. 87.

3. *Minutes,* GA, PCUSA, 1956, Part I, pp. 280, 284.

4. Quoted in the report of the Department of Radio and Television to the Long-Range Planning Committee, 1960, vol. 1. Presbyterian Historical Society, Philadelphia.

5. *Minutes,* GA, PCUS, 1949, Part I, p. 201.

6. *Minutes,* GA, PCUSA, 1950, Part I, p. 82.

7. Ibid., pp. 78, 80.

8. *Minutes,* GA, PCUSA, 1956, Part I, p. 279; *Minutes of the General Assembly of the United Presbyterian Church in the United States of America* [cited hereafter as GA, UPCUSA], 1961, Part I, p. 106; *Minutes,* GA, UPCUSA, 1966, Part I, p. 98 (26 out of 36 members of the Division of Mass Media are chairmen, presidents, or vice-presidents of commercial media organizations); *Minutes,* GA, PCUSA, 1971, Part I, pp. 292, 1047 (where at least 14 out of 24 members on the Council on Mass Media can be identified with commercial media organizations).

9. *Minutes,* GA, PCUSA, 1956, Part I, pp. 285ff.

10. *Minutes,* GA, PCUSA, 1950, Part I, p. 89.

11. *Minutes,* GA, PCUS, 1960, Part I, p. 177.

12. Ibid., Appendix, p. 177.

13. Report of the Department of Radio and Television to the Long-Range Planning Committee, 1960, vol. 1, p. 5. Presbyterian Historical Society, Philadelphia.

14. Ibid., pp. 33–34 (a summary of Department of Radio and Television budgets).

15. Ibid., pp. 5, 37.

16. "Bolstered by Test Run, Presbyterian Church Eyes Nation-wide Radio Drive," *Advertising Age* (April 27, 1964); *Time,* Religion Section (July 12, 1963).

17. *Minutes,* GA, UPCUSA, 1966, Part I, p. 374.

18. Columbus Study of "God Is Alive" radio spots, October 3, 1966. Conducted by the Market Opinion Research Company, Detroit, Mich. Presbyterian Historical Society, Philadelphia.

19. Jack Gould, "The Presbyterian Spots," *New York Times,* July 19, 1964.

20. *Christian Century* (August 7, 1963), 973.

21. Robert Lewis Shayon, "Transistorized Mission," *Saturday Review* (August 24, 1963).

22. Unpublished letter, Charles Brackbill, Jr., of the Division of Mass Media, to Rev. G. E. McClellen, general presbyter, Presbytery of New York City, August 27, 1963, Presbyterian Historical Society, Philadelphia; unpublished letter, George D. Colman, associate field administrator, Board of National Missions, to Rev. Edward Willingham, Detroit Council of Churches, January 2, 1964; unpublished report, Listener comments about Freberg spots to WRVR, New York, 1963.

23. Dave Meade, *Chicago Daily News* (June 6, 1964).

24. Frank Heinze, interview held at the Presbytery of Philadelphia office, Philadelphia, July 20, 1987.

25. Richard Gilbert, interview held at the Nassau Tavern, Princeton, N.J., August 5, 1987.

26. George Comstock, "The Evidence So Far," *Journal of Communication* 25 (1975), 25–33; George Gerbner, Larry Gross, Michael Morgan, and Nancy Signorielli, "Living with Television: The Dynamics of the Cultivation Process," in Jennings Bryant and Dolf Zillman, eds., *Perspective on Media Effects* (Hillsdale, N.J.: Lawrence Erlbaum Associates, 1986); George Gerbner, "TV's Changing Our Lives," *Presbyterian Review* (January

1982), 11–13; George Gerbner and Larry Gross, "Living with Television: The Violence Profile," *Journal of Communication* 26/2 (Spring 1976), 173–194; George Gerbner, Larry Gross, Michael Morgan, and Nancy Signorielli, "Charting the Mainstream: Television's Contribution to Political Orientations," *Journal of Communication* 32/2 (Spring 1982), 100–127.

8: A Presbyterian Dilemma: Ecclesiastical and Social Racial Policy in the Twentieth-Century Presbyterian Communion

1. Kenneth K. Bailey, "The Post–Civil War Racial Separations in Southern Protestantism: Another Look," *Church History* 46 (December 1977), 453–473.

2. *Minutes of the General Assembly of the Presbyterian Church in the United States of America* [cited hereafter as GA, PCUSA], 1869, pp. 992–993; *Minutes,* GA, PCUSA, Board of Missions to Freedmen [cited hereafter as BMF], October 14, 1869, Presbyterian Historical Society, Philadelphia; Andrew Murray, *Presbyterians and the Negro: A History* (Philadelphia: Presbyterian Historical Society (PHS), 1966), pp. 162–163; Ernest Trice Thompson, *Presbyterians in the South,* 3 vols. (Richmond: John Knox Press, 1973), vol. 2, pp. 203–222, 313–320.

3. *Report,* GA, PCUSA, Committee on Freedmen, 1869, pp. 28–42.

4. Thompson, *Presbyterians in the South,* vol. 2, pp. 242–256.

5. *Minutes of the Executive Committee on Colored Evangelization to the Presbyterian Church in the United States* [cited hereafter as ECCE], Historical note, n.d.; October 11, 1892; April 11, 1893; July 11, 1893; November 12, 1893; August 13, 1895; and miscellaneous clippings, Presbyterian Study Center, Montreat, N.C.; *Minutes,* GA, PCUSA, BMF, January 8, 1894, PHS.

6. *Minutes,* PCUS, ECCE, vol. 1, p. 117; vol. 2 passim.

7. Richard William Reifsnyder, "The Reorganizational Impulse in American Protestantism: The Presbyterian Church (U.S.A.) as a Case Study, 1788–1983" (Ph.D. diss., Princeton Theological Seminary, 1984), pp. 6, 239, 246, 269.

8. *Report,* GA, PCUSA, Committee on Freedmen, 1870, p. 23; *Minutes,* GA, PCUSA, BMF, May 12, 1884.

9. Lois A. Boyd and R. Douglas Brackenridge, *Presbyterian Women in America* (a publication of the Presbyterian Historical

Society and Contributions to the Study of Religion, No. 9) (West-port, Conn.: Greenwood Press, 1983), pp. 38–41; *Minutes,* GA, PCUSA, BMF, July 23, 1883; May 12, 1884; August 29, 1894.

10. Inez Parker Moore, *The Rise and Decline of the Program of Education for Black Presbyterians in the United Presbyterian Church U.S.A., 1865–1970* (San Antonio: Trinity University Press, 1977), pp. 20–23; *Minutes,* GA, PCUSA, BMF, May 19, 1890; May 1, 1893; June 25, 1895.

11. Atlantic Synod, *Minutes,* 1876, p. 9; 1879, pp. 5–11; 1879, pp. 10–11; 1883, p. 7; 1887, p. 16; 1893, p. 15; Catawba Synod, *Minutes,* 1888, pp. 5–7; 1897, pp. 14, 29–32; Catawba Presby-tery, *Proceedings,* 1873, pp. 13–21.

12. Murray, *Presbyterians and the Negro,* pp. 145, 191; Frank O. duCille, Sr., *Indigenization: How to Grow Black Churches in White Denominations* (Pineville, N.C.: Frank O. duCille and Co., 1983), pp. 55, 58.

13. Jesse Belmont Barber, *Climbing Jacob's Ladder: Story of the Work of the Presbyterian Church U.S.A. Among the Negroes* (New York: Board of National Missions, PCUSA, 1952), pp. 36–39; *Minutes,* GA, PCUSA, 1868, p. 603; *Minutes,* GA, PCUSA, BMF, November 19, 1888; Yadkin Presbytery, Data File, PHS; *Minutes,* GA, PCUSA, BMF, March 2, 1876; October 30, 1876.

14. *Report,* GA, PCUSA, Committee on Freedmen, October 1868, pp. 14–15; *Minutes,* GA, PCUSA, 1869, pp. 990–992; Moore, *Rise and Decline,* p. 19.

15. Atlantic Synod, *Minutes,* 1893, p. 11.

16. Moore, *Rise and Decline,* pp. 27-30, 57; Barber, *Climbing Jacob's Ladder,* pp. 62–65.

17. *Minutes,* GA, PCUSA, BMF, August 5, 1867; April 7, 1884; Murray, *Presbyterians and the Negro,* pp. 174–175, 193–194.

18. *Minutes,* PCUS, ECCE, June 6, 1891; July 7, 1891; Thompson, *Presbyterians in the South,* vol. 2, pp. 310–311.

19. Murray, *Presbyterians and the Negro,* pp. 175–177; Moore, *Rise and Decline,* p. 46; *Minutes,* PCUS, ECCE, June 17, 1902; July 14, 1902; December 10, 1907.

20. David Reimers, *White Protestantism and the Negro* (New York: Oxford University Press, 1965), pp. 25–50.

21. *Minutes of the General Assembly of the Cumberland Presby-terian Church,* 1866, pp. 80–81; 1867, pp. 10, 101–102; 1869, p. 23.

22. Murray, *Presbyterians and the Negro,* pp. 152–156; Ben M.

Barrus, Milton L. Baughn, and Thomas H. Campbell, *A People Called Cumberland Presbyterians* (Memphis, Tenn.: Frontier Press, 1972), pp. 167–169, 570.

23. Reimers, *White Protestantism,* p. 52.

24. Cape Fear Presbytery, *Minutes,* April 16, 1904, PHS; Murray, *Presbyterians and the Negro,* pp. 199–201.

25. John Ames, "Cumberland Liberals and the Union of 1906," *Journal of Presbyterian History* 52 (1974), 3–18.

26. Thompson, *Presbyterians in the South,* vol. 2, pp. 221–222.

27. Oscar B. Wilson, *Diary, 1896–1900,* January 20, 1899, Montreat, N.C.

28. *Report,* PCUS, ECCE, 1900, p. 12.

29. Joel L. Alvis, Jr., " 'The Bounds of Their Habitations': The Southern Presbyterian Church, Racial Ideology, and the Civil Rights Movement" (Ph.D. diss., Auburn University, 1985), pp. 23–24; duCille, *Indigenization,* p. 61.

30. Catawba Synod, *Minutes,* 1923, pp. 16–17.

31. *Africo-American Presbyterian,* August 13, 1925, p. 2; February 4, 1926, p. 2; March 11, 1926, p. 2; May 6, 1926, p. 2; November 15, 1926, p. 2.

32. Ibid., July 2, 1925, p. 2.

33. Ibid., January 1, 1925, p. 2; March 25, 1925, pp. 1, 2; April 2, 1925, p. 2; April 9, 1925, p. 1; Murray, *Presbyterians and the Negro,* p. 235.

34. *Africo-American Presbyterian,* June 24, 1926, p. 2.

35. George Marsden, *Fundamentalism in American Culture* (New York: Oxford University Press, 1980), pp. 141–195.

36. *Africo-American Presbyterian,* May 14, 1925, p. 2.

37. Ibid., January 8, 1925, p. 4; January 15, 1925, p. 4; January 22, 1925, p. 4; January 29, 1925, p. 4; February 5, 1925, p. 4.

38. Ibid., July 9, 1925, p. 2.

39. Thompson, *Presbyterians in the South,* vol. 3, pp. 365–383.

40. *Minutes,* GA, PCUSA, Special Committee on Reorganization and Consolidation of the Boards and Agencies, 2 vols., October 24–26, 1922, PHS; Reifsnyder, "The Reorganizational Impulse," pp. 334, 338.

41. Murray, *Presbyterians and the Negro,* pp. 210–212.

42. Atlantic Synod, *Minutes,* 1916, p. 25; Catawba Synod, "Catawba Synod's Position on the Question of Total Integration of Negroes Into the Total Life and Work of the Presbyterian Church in the U.S.A." (adopted at Synod, October 19, 1950), PHS.

43. *Minutes,* GA, PCUSA, BMF, Women's Executive Commit-

tee, *1902 or 1903–1915* By-laws, pp. 3–5, PHS; May 1902; December 1904.

44. Reimers, *White Protestantism,* pp. 90–92; Alvis, "Bounds" pp. 27–32.

45. Reimers, *White Protestantism,* pp. 110–111; Edward R. Orser, "Racial Attitudes in Wartime," *Church History* 41 (September 1972), 337–353.

46. Alvis, "Bounds," pp. 40–41; Murray, *Presbyterians and the Negro,* pp. 236–237.

47. Barber, *Climbing Jacob's Ladder,* pp. 86–87.

48. *Presbyterian Panel* 1 (June 1973), 4.

49. Catawba Synod, Paper n.d., n.p.

50. Alvis, "Bounds," pp. 58–60.

51. Murray, *Presbyterians and the Negro,* pp. 231–233.

52. Alvis, "Bounds," pp. 159–161.

53. Ibid., pp. 50–97; Ernest Trice Thompson, *The Spirituality of the Church* (Richmond: John Knox Press, 1961), pp. 35–36.

54. duCille, *Indigenization,* p. 7; Gayraud S. Wilmore, *Black and Presbyterian* (Philadelphia: Geneva Press, 1983).

55. Murray, *Presbyterians and the Negro,* p. 232; Barrus, Baughn, and Campbell, *A People Called Cumberland Presbyterians,* pp. 510–511.

56. James Smylie, "The Bible, Race, and the Changing South," *Journal of Presbyterian History* 59 (Summer 1981), 197–217; Alvis, "Bounds," pp. 108–110.

57. Frank S. Loescher, *The Protestant Church and the Negro* (New York: Association Press, 1948), pp. 28–50; *New York Times,* August 29, 1963, p. 21, quoted in Murray, *Presbyterians and the Negro,* pp. 229–230.

58. Office of Church and Society, UPCUSA, "The United Presbyterian Church and Race Relations, 1936–1963," mimeographed, pp. 5–13.

59. Gayraud S. Wilmore, "From Protest to Self-Development," *Church and Society* 61 (January–February 1971), 6–7; Lucius Walker, "Opportunities for Minority Development," ibid., 22–26; Paul E. Kraemer, *Awakening from the American Dream: The Human Rights Movement in the United States Assessed During a Crucial Decade* (Chicago: Center for the Scientific Study of Religion, 1973), pp. 69–81.

60. Jeffrey K. Hadden, "Clergy Involvement in Civil Rights," *Annals of the American Academy of Social Science* 387 (January

1970), 118–127; *Presbyterian Panel* 4 (November 1977), 1, 31, Appendix D.

61. Wilmore, "From Protest to Self-Development," p. 9.

62. "Race, Racism, and Repression: Statement of PCUS General Assembly 1970 in Response to 3 Overtures to Reject the Black Manifesto," *Church and Society* 61 (September–October 1970), 12–17.

63. "Angela Davis and the Presbyterians," *Christian Century* 88 (July 7, 1971), 823; Aurelia T. Fule, "Still Debating Angela Davis?" *Monday Morning* 52 (November 23, 1987), 10–11. An additional $10,000 was donated by Black clergy and lay leaders to offset the allocation of funds.

64. J. DeOtis Roberts, "The Black Caucus and the Failure of Christian Theology," *Journal of Religious Thought* 26 (Summer Supplement 1969), 19–25.

65. Wilmore, "From Protest to Self-Development," pp. 10–13; *Minutes of the General Assembly of the Presbyterian Church (U.S.A.),* 1986, Part I, p. 655; *Presbyterian Layman* 20 (November–December 1987), 8–9.

66. duCille, *Indigenization,* pp. 8–15, 30–47.

9: Identity and Integration: Black Presbyterians and Their Allies in the Twentieth Century

1. Vincent Harding, "Black Power and the American Christ," in Floyd B. Barbour, ed., *The Black Power Revolt* (Boston: Porter E. Sargent, 1968), p. 86.

2. John W. Lee, "Forty Years of Council Activity," *Africo-American Presbyterian,* November 22, 1934, p. 1.

3. Black Presbyterian and Congregational clergy met at Central Presbyterian Church in Philadelphia on October 28, 1857. It was evidently their second meeting. Elymas P. Rogers, moderator of the previous meeting, presumably in 1856, preached the sermon. Present at this meeting were eight Presbyterian clergy and five laymen, and three Congregational clergy—one from Massachusetts and two from Connecticut. *Minutes and Sermons of the Second Presbyterian and Congregational Convention* (New York: Daly, 1858).

4. Lee became pastor of First African on January 20, 1901, when the membership was only 48. By 1907 he had increased the membership to 225 and had made a substantial contribution to what was called that year the Presbyterian Council of Ministers

and Laymen. (Brochure of the *14th Annual Meeting of Presbyterian Council of Ministers and Laymen, October 24–28, 1907*; PC(USA), Dept. of History, Philadelphia).

5. Lee, "Forty Years of Council Activity."

6. Alfred A. Moss, Jr., *The American Negro Academy* (Baton Rouge, La.: Louisiana State University Press, 1981), p. 19.

7. See, for example, such titles as "Is Presbyterianism Adapted to the Masses?" by Dr. W. A. Alexander, and "Social Purity—Some Helps—Some Hindrances," by Mrs. Caroline V. Anderson, at the meeting in 1900; or "The Supreme Purpose of the Church as Expressed in the Gospels," by Rev. L. Z. Johnson, D.D., and "The German Gymnasia Versus the Laxity in Training of Colored Youth," by Rev. Matthew Anderson, D.D., at the Council meeting in 1916.

8. Moss, *American Negro Academy,* pp. 16–31.

9. Henry J. Ferry, "Racism and Reunion: A Black Protest by Francis James Grimké," *Journal of Presbyterian History* 50/2 (1972), 77.

10. Carter G. Woodson, ed., *The Works of Francis J. Grimké* (Washington, D.C.: Associated Publishers, 1942), vol. 1: *Addresses,* pp. 239–240, 268–269, 506; Grimké to the Presbytery of Washington City, October 4, 1908, ibid., vol. 4: *Letters.*

11. Interview with Rev. Thomas J. B. Harris, December 21, 1988.

12. Andrew E. Murray, *Presbyterians and the Negro: A History* (Philadelphia: Presbyterian Historical Society, 1966), p. 230.

13. Ernest Trice Thompson, *Presbyterians in the South,* vol. 3 (Richmond: John Knox Press, 1973), pp. 84, 89; and "Continuity and Change," an unpublished, undated manuscript in the Woodruff Library Archives, Atlanta University Center.

14. Personal correspondence, Bryant George to Gayraud Wilmore, August 4, 1988.

15. Interview with Thomas J. B. Harris, December 21, 1988.

16. Cited in C. James Trotman, "Matthew Anderson: Black Pastor, Churchman and Social Reformer," *American Presbyterian* 66/1 (Spring 1988), 19.

17. *Minutes of the 57th Annual Session of the Presbyterian Council of the North and West, October 4–8, 1950.*

18. *Monday Morning,* January 20, 1947.

19. Memorandum, John Dillingham to L. Charles Gray, November 19, 1953.

20. Ibid.

21. Personal correspondence, L. Patrick to Gayraud Wilmore, February 8, 1989.

22. R. Douglas Brackenridge, "Lawrence W. Bottoms: The Church, Black Presbyterians and Personhood," *Journal of Presbyterian History* 56/1 (Spring 1978). See also Thompson, *Presbyterians in the South,* vol. 3, p. 423.

23. Lawrence W. Bottoms, unpublished address to a conference with PCUS ministers, February 19–21, 1958, in the Woodruff Library Archives, Atlanta University Center.

24. Thompson, "Continuity and Change," p. 13.

25. Interview with Joseph L. Roberts, February 24, 1984.

26. Jesse B. Barber, *Climbing Jacob's Ladder* (New York: Board of National Missions, PCUSA, 1952), p. 92. A major feature of this program was the annual Lincoln University Summer Conference, which brought together Black and white clergy and laity for race relations training.

27. Interview, Jovelino Ramos with Kenneth G. Neigh, October 25, 1983, in *COCAR & CORAR Legacy, 1963–1987* (New York: New York Based Council on Church and Race, 1987), pp. 537–559 (limited edition in the archives of Johnson C. Smith Seminary, Atlanta).

28. *Minutes of the General Assembly of the United Presbyterian Church in the United States of America* [cited hereafter as GA, UPCUSA], 1963, Part I, p. 141.

29. The Black Presbyterian Leadership Conference of the PCUS was established at the 1969 General Assembly as an agency of the Assembly by recommendation of the General Council. Its purpose was to "recapture the historical Black experience so that the Black Church may work more concretely for the liberation of all Black people, move toward Black ecumenicity and work for world-wide Black unity so that Black people may be in a stronger position to challenge the white church with the truth of the gospel, and thereby usher in more quickly the day of authentic reconciliation among all the peoples of the world." *Annual Reports of Assembly Agencies* (PCUS, 1970), pp. 17–18.

30. Joseph L. Roberts credits John Anderson, executive of the Board of National Missions of the PCUS, for opening the way for the BPLC and the Commission on Church and Race. The 110th General Assembly received a recommendation to recognize an independent Black caucus called for in a BPLC paper, "Black Expectations," adopted by the caucus in Atlanta on September 28, 1969 (see *Minutes of the General Assembly* [PCUS, 1970], p.

151). This action was understood to supersede the previous recommendation from General Council. The caucus headquarters
was established in Tuskegee, Alabama. Lawrence F. Haygood,
Calvin Houston, Zeke Bell, Michael Elligan, and W. D. Tolbert
were key leaders in the founding of the Leadership Caucus. In the
UPCUSA the white allies at the national level were William Mor-
rison, Kenneth Neigh, Eugene Carson Blake, Marshall Scott, and
Clifford Earle. Among those most active in the founding of Black
Presbyterians United (BPU) one year before the BPLC was cre-
ated were Edler Hawkins, Bryant George, J. Metz Rollins, Robert
P. Johnson, E. Wellington Butts, and J. Oscar McCloud. See J.
Metz Rollins, "The Spirit of Black Presbyterianism: Part II,"
Periscope 2 (New York: Program Agency, UPCUSA, 1982), pp.
25–29.

31. "Profile of the Presbyterian Interracial Council," membership application brochure, 1964, in the Woodruff Library Archives of Atlanta University Center.

32. *NOW,* Newsletter of PIC, April 1964, p. 2.

33. See reports of COCAR in *Minutes,* GA, UPCUSA, 1964,
Part I, pp. 325–329; and 1965, Part I, pp. 394–402.

34. PIC was organized at the Des Moines Assembly for the
purpose of mobilizing white support for the Concerned Presbyterians' proposal for a national race relations agency related to the
General Assembly. Kenneth Waterman, its first executive, wrote
in *NOW* (April 1964): "Commissions will work conservatively
and quietly *within* the power structures of the establishment of
the church. PIC will organize large numbers of frustrated individuals (most of them laymen) into a movement to work *upon* the
establishment, as well as to militantly witness to and help the
Negro community gain justice in all areas of civic life." But by
1967 the coalition was in decline. James A. McDaniel, associate
for Poverty and Community Organization of the Board of National Missions, wrote in *NOW* (Summer 1967): "Presently many
PIC Chapters are 'paper' organizations, poorly financed and peopled by half committed members. Some chapters, when they hold
meetings, are not large enough to require a room larger than a
phone booth. Unable to harness the potential resources of their
constituencies, PIC cannot at present produce much worth co-
alescing with."

35. For a study of the origin of these groups, their documents
and contributions to theological renewal in the Black church, see
Gayraud Wilmore and James H. Cone, eds., *Black Theology: A*

Documentary History, 1966–1979 (Maryknoll, N.Y.: Orbis Books, 1979).

36. Angela Davis was a 27-year-old Black militant and former philosophy instructor at UCLA. A member of the Communist party in the United States, she was charged with murder, kidnapping, and criminal conspiracy resulting from a shoot-out in a San Rafael, California, courtroom in August 1970 that resulted in the deaths of Superior Court Judge Harold Haley, Jonathan Jackson, William Christmas, and James McClain. Davis was charged with supplying the guns used by the three prisoners. A codefendant, Ruchell Magee, was charged with firing the shotgun that killed Judge Haley. She was captured in a New York City motel and extradited to California, where she spent almost a year in prison and was finally exonerated after a sensational trial that galvanized the support of many Blacks and liberal whites who admired her courageous witness in behalf of civil rights and prison reform, but doubted that she could get a fair trial without the vigilant intervention of progressive forces across the nation.

37. Text of remarks by Rev. Edler G. Hawkins to the 183rd General Assembly of the United Presbyterian Church U.S.A., Rochester, N.Y., May 24, 1971, in *COCAR & CORAR Legacy, 1963–1987: The Angela Davis Papers* (New York: New York Based Council on Church and Race, 1987), p. 2 (limited edition in the archives of Johnson C. Smith Seminary, Atlanta).

38. James J. Cochran, executive vice-president of the Presbyterian Lay Committee, Inc., to J. Henry Neale, co-chair of the Council on Church and Race, November 27, 1972 (The Angela Davis Papers).

39. "Why Angela Davis?" (draft of the National Race Staff of the UPCUSA response to the protest, pp. 12–13; The Angela Davis Papers).

40. News release of the Presbyterian Office of Information, New York, June 15, 1971.

41. The Black Manifesto of the Black Economic Development Conference (BEDC) was presented on May 15, 1969, to the 181st General Assembly in San Antonio, Texas, by James Forman. It called for reparations of over $500,000,000 to be paid to Blacks for centuries of enslavement and exploitation from which the churches and synagogues of the nation derived enormous benefits. Although the Assembly did not respond directly to Forman's demands, it did vote certain extraordinary measures by recommendation of COCAR. The Standing Committee on Church and

Race said of the Manifesto: "We accept this new way of speaking to us, to affirm that it may be a necessary mode of God's coming to judge and to help to free us from racial attitudes that demean us." Each of the program boards, in specific terms, was called upon to make new funds and properties of the church available "in response to the critical needs that our brothers [of BEDC and La Raza, the Hispanic caucus] have focused for us." The report was adopted by the General Assembly. One of the consequences was the creation, by the 182nd General Assembly (1970) in Chicago, of a National Committee on the Self-Development of People to design criteria and allocate thousands of dollars to "local communities of need" through judicatory self-development committees. See Arnold Schuchter, *Reparations: The Black Manifesto and Its Challenge to White America* (Philadelphia: J. B. Lippincott Co., 1970); Robert S. Lecky and H. Elliott Wright, eds., *The Black Manifesto* (New York: Sheed & Ward, 1969); Gayraud Wilmore, *Black Religion and Black Radicalism* (Garden City, N.Y.: Doubleday & Co., 1973), pp. 202–210; *Minutes,* GA, UPCUSA, 1969, Part I, pp. 660–681; 1970, Part I, pp. 667–676.

42. Edler G. Hawkins Papers, Woodruff Library Archives, Atlanta University Center.

43. For analyses that African American theologians make of contemporary ecclesiology of the ecumenical movement, see David T. Shannon and Gayraud Wilmore, eds., *Black Witness to the Apostolic Faith* (Grand Rapids: Wm. B. Eerdmans, 1988).

10: Native American Presbyterians: Assimilation, Leadership, and Future Challenges

1. Statistics are notoriously difficult to ascertain, verify, and correlate in this area of endeavor. Some of the more reliable figures can be found in Clifford M. Drury, *Presbyterian Panorama: One Hundred and Fifty Years of National Missions History* (Philadelphia: Board of Christian Education, 1952), pp. 234–235, 251, 291–292; and R. Pierce Beaver, ed., *The Native American Christian Community: A Directory of Indian, Aleut, and Eskimo Churches* (Monrovia, Calif.: Missions Advanced Research and Communication Center, 1979), pp. 257–266. The pragmatic decision to focus on major population centers does not imply that work among the unmentioned tribes is insignificant or that their faithful witness is irrelevant. Space requirements simply demand

treating them with generalizations that do not recognize uniquenesses pertinent to every setting.

2. One of the more accessible sources for this early mission is W. David Baird, "Cyrus Byington and the Presbyterian Choctaw Mission," in Clyde A. Milner II and Floyd A. O'Neil, eds., *Churchmen and the Western Indians, 1820–1920* (Norman: University of Oklahoma Press, 1985), pp. 5–40.

3. For an introduction to this topic, see Minnie A. Cook, *Apostle to the Pima Indians: The Story of Charles H. Cook, the First Missionary to the Pimas* (Tiburon, Calif.: Omega Books, 1976); and Mark T. Banker, "They Made Haste Slowly: Presbyterian Mission Schools and Southwestern Pluralism, 1870–1920" (Ph.D. diss., University of New Mexico, 1987).

4. See Moses N. Adams, John P. Williamson, and John B. Renville, *The History of the Dakota Presbytery of the Presbyterian Church in the United States of America, from Its Organization to April 1890* (Good Will, S. Dak., 1892; reprint, Freeman, S. Dak.: Pine Hill Press, 1984).

5. See Mary M. Crawford, *The Nez Percés Since Spalding* (Berkeley, Calif.: Professional Press, 1936).

6. See J. Arthur Lazell, *Alaskan Apostle: The Life Story of Sheldon Jackson* (New York: Harper & Brothers, 1960); see also Theodore C. Hinckley, "The Alaskan Labors of Sheldon Jackson, 1877–1890" (Ph.D. diss., Indiana University, 1961).

7. The best place to learn about this sweeping change is Lois A. Boyd and R. Douglas Brackenridge, *Presbyterian Women in America: Two Centuries of a Quest for Status* (Westport, Conn.: Greenwood Press, 1983), pp. 61–66.

8. Banker, "They Made Haste Slowly," p. 394.

9. *Minutes of the General Assembly of the United Presbyterian Church in the United States of America* [cited hereafter as GA, UPCUSA], 1972, series 7, vol. 7, pp. 620–621.

10. For a collection of earlier statistical reports, see Beaver, *Native American Christian Community,* pp. 22–26.

11. Ibid., pp. 22–26, 257–266.

12. As cited in Hermann N. Morse, *From Frontier to Frontier: An Interpretation of 150 Years of Presbyterian National Missions* (Philadelphia: Board of Christian Education, PCUSA, 1952), pp. 18–19.

13. Ibid.

14. Gustavus E. E. Lindquist, *The Red Man in the United States: An Intimate Study of the Social, Economic and Religious*

Life of the American Indian (New York: George H. Doran Co., 1923), pp. 62, 67–68.

15. *Year Book of Prayer for Missions* (Philadelphia: PCUSA, 1932), p. 24.

16. George W. Hinman, *The American Indian and Christian Missions* (New York: Fleming H. Revell Co., 1933), pp. 164, 169.

17. Cited in George A. Lee, "Sourcebook on the Navajo: A Challenge for the Church in Arizona and Utah," typed manuscript produced for the Board of National Missions, September 1960, p. 12.

18. Hinman, *American Indian and Christian Missions,* pp. 160–161.

19. *Minutes of the General Assembly of the Presbyterian Church in the United States of America,* 1950, series 4, vol. 12, Part II, p. 107.

20. Morse, *From Frontier to Frontier,* p. 61.

21. Ernest Schusky, *Dakota Indians in Today's World: A Study of Dakota Indians' Needs in Relation to United Presbyterian Church U.S.A. Work* (New York: Board of National Missions, 1962), pp. 51, 62–63.

22. Confession of 1967, para. 44. See Edward A. Dowey, Jr., *A Commentary on the Confession of 1967 and an Introduction to "The Book of Confessions"* (Philadelphia: Westminster Press, 1968), p. 21.

23. Ibid., pp. 128–129.

24. Ibid., p. 131.

25. Excerpt from "We May Be Brothers, After All," as cited in *Indian Quest,* typed working paper of the Native American Consulting Committee, 1974, p. 9.

26. B. Frank Belvin, *The Status of the American Indian Ministry* (Shawnee: Oklahoma Baptist University Press, 1948), p. 68.

27. Ibid., pp. 48–49.

28. Ibid., pp. 116–117.

29. "Pima-Maricopa Indian Camp Meeting, 1981," in Pamphlet Folder Box 9211, PC(USA), Dept. of History, Philadelphia.

30. *Indian Quest* (October 1980), 2; ibid. (May 1984), 2.

31. *Indian Quest* (May 1984), 3.

32. Remarks made upon presentation of an honorary degree by Whitworth College in June 1965, transcribed for Luther M. Dimmitt for his planned history of Presbyterian missions in Alaska. See also *Presbyterian Life* (December 9, 1950).

33. *Indian Quest* (May 1984), 2; ibid. (June 1985), 3.

34. Ralph E. Scissons, "Dedication to Eugene Crawford," *Church and Society* 74/1 (1988), 4.

35. Excerpt from "We May Be Brothers, After All," pp. 4–6.

36. *Minutes,* GA, UPCUSA, 1969 vol. 4, Part II, p. 129.

37. Excerpt from "We May Be Brothers, After All," pp. 7–8.

38. "The Tribe Sends a Voice as They Come," a position paper of the Native American Consulting Committee, February 1975, p. 20.

39. Ibid., p. 21.

40. Ibid., p. 40.

41. Ibid., p. 24; see also pp. 26–27.

42. "The Hoop Is Broken," a position paper of the Presbyterian Indian Consulting Panel, October 1, 1973, p. 3.

43. Ibid.

44. "The Tribe Sends a Voice as They Come," p. 25.

45. *Minutes,* GA, UPCUSA, 1972, vol. 6, Part I, pp. 632–633.

46. "The Hoop Is Broken," p. 11.

47. Cecil Corbett and Gary Kush, "Mending the Hoop: Comprehensive Report of the Indian Church Career Research and Planning Project," a position paper of the Native American Consulting Committee, 1974, pp. 51, 89–90.

48. Grace Ann Goodman, "Nez Percé Presbyterians," Institute of Strategic Studies, Board of National Missions, UPCUSA, October 1966, p. 2.

49. Schusky, *Dakota Indians,* p. 30.

50. Lee, "Sourcebook on the Navajo," pp. 15, 20, 24.

51. Harold E. Fey and D'Arcy McNickle, *Indians and Other Americans* (New York: Harper & Brothers, 1959), p. 93; William A. Brophy and Sophie D. Aberle, eds., "The Indian: America's Unfinished Business," in *Report of the Commission on the Rights, Liberties, and Responsibilities of the American Indian* (Norman: University of Oklahoma Press, 1966), p. 163; U.S. Department of Health, Education, and Welfare, Public Health Service, *Illness Among Indians* (Washington, D.C.: 1961).

52. Deward E. Walker, Jr., "A Survey of Nez Percé Religion," A Report to the Research and Survey Staff, Institute of Strategic Studies and the Office of Indian Work, UPCUSA, January 1964, pp. 64–65.

53. Goodman, "Nez Percé Presbyterians," pp. 4, 9, 11.

54. Cited in Walker, "Nez Percé Religion," p. 34.

55. *The Presbyterian Church and Indian Lands: A Handbook on Native American Property,* prepared by the Institute for Devel-

opment of Indian Law and the Native American Consulting Committee of the Presbyterian Church (U.S.A.), 1979–1989, pp. 35, 37–38; see also "How Do You Spell Chancellor?" inaugural address by Cecil Corbett, Charles Cook Theological School, January 14, 1990.

56. Lee, "Sourcebook on the Navajo," p. 37.

57. *Horizons* (May/June 1989), 7.

11: Hispanic Presbyterians: Life in Two Cultures

1. *Minutes of the General Assembly of the Presbyterian Church (U.S.A.)* [cited hereafter as GA, PC(USA)], 1986, Part I, pp. 44, 826. In this essay we refer to the Presbyterian Church in the United States of America (PCUSA), which became the United Presbyterian Church in the United States of America (UPCUSA) in 1958; the Presbyterian Church in the United States (PCUS); and the Presbyterian Church (U.S.A.), or PC(USA), the reunion of the UPCUSA and the PCUS in 1983.

2. For a survey of the history of the Presbyterian Church (U.S.A.), see Lefferts A. Loetscher, *A Brief History of the Presbyterians,* 4th ed. (Philadelphia: Westminster Press, 1983).

3. *Minutes,* GA, PC(USA), 1989, Part II, pp. 506–508.

4. The three presbyteries of the Synod of Puerto Rico reported their membership—almost totally Hispanic—as follows for 1989: Presbytery of the Northwest, 5,123; Presbytery of San Juan, 1,856; and Presbytery of the Southwest, 2,069.

5. For comparison, note that the same report lists Asians as comprising 1.4 percent, Blacks as 2.51 percent, and Native Americans as 0.24 percent of the denomination, leaving 95.01 percent who report their racial ethnic classification as white.

6. For a detailed historical narrative of Mexican American Presbyterianism, see R. Douglas Brackenridge and Francisco O. García-Treto, *Iglesia Presbiteriana: A History of Presbyterians and Mexican Americans in the Southwest,* 2nd ed. (San Antonio: Trinity University Press, 1987).

7. Henry Kendall to Sheldon Jackson, July 18, 1870, in Jackson Correspondence, vol. 3, pp. 893–894, PC(USA), Dept. of History, Philadelphia.

8. Brief histories of the Hispanic churches in southern California have appeared in a recent collection edited by Jane Atkins-Vásquez, *Hispanic Presbyterians in Southern California: One*

Hundred Years of Ministry (Los Angeles: Synod of Southern California and Hawaii, 1988).

9. Brackenridge and García-Treto, *Iglesia Presbiteriana,* pp. 34–62.

10. Brackenridge and García-Treto, *Iglesia Presbiteriana,* pp. 127–128, 141–146.

11. One Presbyterian missionary gave this description of her pupils in New Mexico: "I have learned much about the habits and customs of Mexicans. They do not get a decent living in their homes. Decency and true refinement are not found among the Mexican people." *The Church at Home and Abroad* (September 1889), 21. For other similar examples, see Brackenridge and García-Treto, *Iglesia Presbiteriana,* pp. 49–53.

12. Brackenridge and García-Treto, *Iglesia Presbiteriana,* pp. 87–125.

13. *Minutes of the Synod of Texas (PCUS),* September 15, 1953, p. 164. See also *Latin-American Presbyterian Churches in Texas: A Study Prepared for the Ad Interim Committee on Latin-American Work, Synod of Texas (PCUS)* (Austin, Tex., 1952). Cited hereafter as *LAPCT.* The amalgamation was completed on January 1, 1955. A number of Mexican American pastors protested the action because they considered Texas-Mexican Presbytery to be an important factor in maintaining their self-identity.

14. *Minutes of the General Assembly of the Presbyterian Church in the United States of America* [cited hereafter as GA, PCUSA], 1881, pp. 532–533.

15. Brackenridge and García-Treto, *Iglesia Presbiteriana,* pp. 60–62.

16. *LAPCT,* p. 8.

17. *Christian Observer* (December 11, 1901), 6.

18. *Minutes,* GA, PCUSA, 1913, p. 208. See also Brackenridge and García-Treto, *Iglesia Presbiteriana,* pp. 127–155.

19. For a basic source on the story of Presbyterian missions to the two islands, written by an important participant, see Edward A. Odell, *It Came to Pass* (New York: Board of National Missions of the PCUSA, 1952). For the history of the Protestant churches in Cuba, with a solid presentation of the Presbyterian story, see the definitive work by Marcos Antonio Ramos, *Panorama del Protestantismo en Cuba: La presencia de los protestantes o evangélicos en la historia de Cuba desde la colonización española hasta la revolución* (San José, Costa Rica: Editorial Caribe, 1986). Not a history, but a critical analysis of U.S. Protes-

tant missions in Puerto Rico as bearers of U.S. colonialism, is Daniel R. Rodríguez, *La Primera Evangelización Norteamericana en Puerto Rico, 1898–1930* (Mexico, D.F., and Rochester, N.Y.: Ediciones Borinquen, 1986).

20. See Ramos, *Panorama del Protestantismo,* pp. 159ff. Among the denominations that were to establish significant work in the islands, the notable exception to supporting the war was the Society of Friends.

21. Signs of that choice can be seen as early as 1898, when the northern and southern Methodist Churches, the northern Baptists, the northern Presbyterian Church, the Society of Friends, and the Congregational Church entered into a Comity Agreement concerning Cuba, Puerto Rico, the Philippines, and the islands of Micronesia (see Rodríguez, *La Primera Evangelización,* p. 185); or in the history of the Presbyterian Church in Cuba, which is the result of the consolidation of the Congregational Church missions (1909) and the PCUS and Disciples of Christ missions (1918) into the PCUSA work. It is also notable that the two seminaries that to this day continue to serve the churches in Puerto Rico and Cuba—the Seminario Evangélico de Puerto Rico in Río Piedras (1919) and the Seminario Evangélico de Teología in Matanzas (1946)—were the results of interdenominational cooperation (see Ramos, *Panorama del Protestantismo,* pp. 298–305, 475–478).

22. Rodríguez, *La Primera Evangelización,* p. 239.

23. Like all other private schools, La Progresiva was nationalized by the Castro government in 1961. Ironically, it recently received praise from Fidel Castro in his long conversations with the Brazilian Frei Betto, published as *Fidel and Religion.* Castro singles it out as a "prestigious" school and notes that many of its alumni are "with the Revolution," and that, unlike the Jesuit Colegio de Belen he himself attended, La Progresiva served the humbler sector of society. See *Fidel y la Religión* (La Habana: Oficina de Publicaciones del Consejo de Estado, 1985), p. 210.

24. Ramos, *Panorama del Protestantismo,* p. 540, says: "Beginning with the end of 1960, a large part of the membership of the [Presbyterian] congregations began to leave the country. The take-over of the numerous and influential Presbyterian schools, the closing of the church's social programs, and the departure from the country of the majority of the church's clergy, as well as of its lay leadership, determined a drastic drop in membership" (translation by Francisco García-Treto).

25. *Minutes of the Synod of Texas (PCUS),* 1964, p. 652; and 1965, p. 172.

26. *Annual Report of the Board of National Missions of the United Presbyterian Church in the United States of America* (Philadelphia, 1964), pp. 32–47.

27. Brackenridge and García-Treto, *Iglesia Presbiteriana,* pp. 202–204.

28. Ibid., pp. 213–217.

29. *Minutes of the Synod of Texas (PCUS),* 1972, pp. 400–410.

30. *Minutes of the General Assembly of the United Presbyterian Church in the United States of America,* 1972, Part I, p. 110.

31. Brackenridge and García-Treto, *Iglesia Presbiteriana,* pp. 228–229.

32. Ibid., pp. 229–230. In a recent editorial in the newsletter of La Raza Caucus, Idalisa Fernández says: "We can see with joy that changes have come about . . . as a result of our conversations with the Hispanic Council of the West, through which we have realized that we need the united voice of the Hispanic Presbyterian people . . . that both la Raza and the Council have common goals towards which we can strive together for the honor and glory of God. We are in agreement that we must have a single organization representing our people and our culture, as the other ethnic/racial groups have, at the General Assembly level." *La Voz Presbiteriana del Caucus Hispano Presbiteriano "La Raza"* 1/2 (June 1988), 2. The same issue reports a meeting in March 1988 in Los Angeles, where a joint committee of La Raza/National Hispanic Caucus and the Hispanic Council of the West discussed coordination of efforts in matters of common concern.

33. *Minutes,* GA, PC(USA), 1986, Part I, p. 539; and Brackenridge and García-Treto, *Iglesia Presbiteriana,* pp. 230–231.

34. *Minutes,* GA, PC(USA), 1984, Part I, pp. 303–304.

35. Ibid.

36. For a summary of some of these activities, see *Minutes,* GA, PC(USA), 1985, Part I, p. 447. The reports of the Program and the Vocation agencies are particularly useful for these purposes.

37. *Minutes,* GA, PC(USA), 1981, Part I, pp. 257–293.

38. Marj Carpenter, "Help at the Border," *Presbyterian Survey* (May 1986), 32–33.

39. *Minutes,* GA, PCUSA, 1975, Part I, p. 361, and 1980, Part I, p. 244; *Minutes of the General Assembly of the Presbyterian*

Church in the United States, 1982, Part I, p. 263; and *Minutes, GA, PC(USA)*, 1983, Part I, p. 406. See also Brackenridge and García-Treto, *Iglesia Presbiteriana*, pp. 235-236.

40. *Minutes, GA, PC(USA)*, 1980, Part I, p. 296.

41. *Presbyterian Panel* (New York: The Vocation Agency, 1986), p. 8. See also Eva Stimson, "The Road Is Uphill," *Presbyterian Survey* (May 1988), 15–16.

42. There were 640 active members and $376,900 in receipts in 1987, according to *Minutes, GA, PC(USA)*, Part II, p. 438. In a personal interview during the summer of 1988, however, Martín Añorga placed current membership at 914.

43. July 10, 1988.

44. Interview with Rev. Martín Añorga, July 10, 1988.

45. Daniel A. Damiani, *Study of the Hispanic Presbyterian Congregations in the Presbytery of New York City*, a study submitted to the Hispanic Presbyterian Pastors' Association of the Synod of the Northeast, October 1986, p. 2.

46. Ibid., p. 3.

47. Ibid., p. 13.

48. Ibid., pp. 15f.

49. See, for example, Jesse Miranda, "Realizing the Hispanic Dream," *Christianity Today* (March 3, 1989), 37–40. Hispanic population in the United States increased 34 percent between 1980 and 1988. There are presently 19.4 million Hispanics, representing 8.1 percent of the total population.

50. On an experimental basis, First Presbyterian Church in San Antonio sponsors a worker who is living in the west side of the city and promoting the formation of an ecclesiastical base community. Time will tell whether the project will succeed.

51. Robert Wuthnow, *The Restructuring of American Religion: Society and Faith Since World War II* (Princeton: Princeton University Press, 1988). See especially chapter 6, "The Growth of Special Purpose Groups."

52. *The Presbyterian Hymnal: Hymns, Psalms, and Spiritual Songs* (Louisville, Ky.: Westminster/John Knox Press, 1990) includes over a dozen Hispanic hymns, with both Spanish and English text. La Raza Caucus has identified publication of a Spanish hymnbook "inclusive of the new hymnology that is now emerging in our communities" as one of its priority projects. *La Voz Presbiteriana del Caucus Hispano Presbiteriano "La Raza"* 1/2 (June 1988), 1–2.

12: Contexts for a History of Asian American Presbyterian Churches: A Case Study of the Early History of Japanese American Presbyterians

1. Portions of this essay are developed more fully in the authors' previous work, most specifically: Michael J. Kimura Angevine, "A Sociohistorical Context of Theological Education in the United States," *Pacific Theological Review* 21/1 (Fall 1987), 28–37; Christ United Presbyterian Church, *The Church's One Hundred Years in the Japanese American Community* (San Francisco: CUPC, 1988); Ryô Yoshida, "A Socio-Historical Study of Racial/ Ethnic Identity in the Inculturated Religious Expression of Japanese Christianity in San Francisco, 1877–1924" (Ph.D. diss., Graduate Theological Union, Berkeley, 1989); Ryô Yoshida, "A Study of the Early Japanese Churches in California, 1869–1906," in Dôshisha Daigaku Jinbun Kagaku Kenkyûjo, ed., *Kaigai Nihonjin Imin to Kirisutokyô* [Japanese Christian Church Overseas] (Tôkyô: PMC Shuppan, 1990).

An essay on the history of Asian American Presbyterian churches is a difficult task. The term "Asian American" masks a complex phenomenon. Asians include people more numerous and more diverse than those of Europe, and historical generalizations about Asians in America run a greater risk of error than do similar generalizations about Americans of European ancestry. "Asian American" includes such diverse people as Burmese, Cambodian, Chinese, Filipino, Hmong, Indonesian, Japanese, Korean, Laotian, Malaysian, Mien, Thai, Vietnamese, to mention but a few. Even groups described by terms like "Indian," "Filipino," and "Indonesian" derive from the historical experience of European imperialism, which forced a unity by subjugation of many different ethnic groups with differing languages, cultures, and histories. China itself encompasses a larger and more complex diversity of people than does Europe. The diversity of China is further compounded by the presence of large Chinese communities throughout Asia itself.

2. One of the reforms precipitated by the civil rights movement was the change in federal immigration policy, which for the first time attempted to eliminate the racist restrictions within the immigration quotas. This opened the doors for a large influx of Asian immigrants for the first time since restrictive legislation was passed in the late nineteenth and early twentieth century. This influx would change the complexion of Asian American

communities and lead to the tremendous growth of Asian American churches. Prior to 1965, the situation was a bit less complex, with fewer than fifty Asian American Presbyterian churches. Today there are over three hundred Korean churches and new church developments alone in the Presbyterian Church (U.S.A.), with over sixty of other Asian groups.

3. Wesley Woo, "Asians in America: Challenges for the Presbyterian Church (U.S.A.)," (New York: Program Agency, Presbyterian Church (U.S.A.), 1987), p. 20.

4. The Meiji period began with the overthrow of the Tokugawa government in 1868 and ended with the death of the Meiji Emperor in 1912. The Taishô period began with the death of the Meiji Emperor and ended with the death of the Taishô Emperor in 1923.

5. Wesley Woo, "Protestant Work Among the Chinese in the San Francisco Bay Area, 1850–1920" (Ph.D. diss., Graduate Theological Union, Berkeley, 1983), pp. 91, 132–136.

6. Rev. Otis Gibson, superintendent of the Methodist Episcopal Mission to the Chinese in San Francisco, is a typical example. He wrote the following in defense of Chinese in the face of the anti-Chinese movement in the early 1870s: "At rates of labor which exist in the early days of California, or at rates of labor which would instantly prevail were the Chinese removed from our midst, not one of the few manufacturing interests which have sprung up on these shores, could be maintained a single day." Otis Gibson, *Chinaman or White Man or Which?* (San Francisco, 1873), p. 10. Cited in Ronald Takaki, *Iron Cages* (New York: Alfred A. Knopf, 1979), p. 232.

7. Josiah Strong, *Our Country: Its Possible Future and Its Present Crisis* (New York: Baker and Taylor Co., 1885), p. 86.

8. Eugene Genovese, *Roll, Jordan, Roll* (New York: Vintage Books, 1974), p. 6.

9. See Mary Roberts Coolidge, *Chinese Immigration* (New York: Henry Holt & Co., 1909).

10. Edna Bonacich, "Some Basic Facts: Patterns of Asian Immigration and Exclusion," in Lucie Cheng and Edna Bonacich, eds., *Labor Immigration Under Capitalism* (Berkeley: University of California Press, 1982), pp. 60–78.

11. The profound conflicts, contradictions, and debates occurring in Japanese society during the Tokugawa and Meiji eras were mirrored in the educational system. From a system composed of private, religious, or clan-sponsored schools in late Tokugawa Ja-

pan, the educational system became at first a system of universal education dominated by a type of Western liberalism. After the imperial rescript on education of 1890, the educational system tried to embody the decision of a faction of the Meiji government to combine Western science and technical training with those elements of Japanese morality that were important to the policy-makers of that time. These government officials feared that the liberalism of Western ideas would be corrosive to Meiji Japan.

12. According to labor statistics of Japanese immigrants between 1886 and 1908, 21.5% of Japanese in the United States were merchants; 21.4% were students, 21.1% were laborers, 14.1% were farmers and fishermen, and 3.8% were artisans. See Yamato Ichihashi, *Japanese in the United States* (1932; repr. New York: Arno Press, 1969), p. 67.

13. Matsuzô Nagai, *Nichi-bei Bunka Kôshôshi, 5. Ijû-hen* [A History of Japanese American Cultural Relations, v. 5: Emigration] (Tôkyô: Yoyosha, 1955), p. 44.

14. Thomas Smith, *Agrarian Origins of Modern Japan* (Stanford: Stanford University Press, 1973), pp. 201–213. See also Yamamura Kôzô, "Returns of Unification: Economic Growth in Japan, 1550–1650," in John Whitney Hall, Nagahara Keiji, and Yamamura Kôzô, eds., *Japan Before Tokugawa* (Princeton: Princeton University Press, 1981) for a more detailed description of these policies instituted primarily between 1550 and 1650. Like the Meiji policies, they radically transformed Japanese agriculture from a primarily locally oriented market to a nationally oriented one. The transformations of the Meiji can thus be interpreted as the transformation from an internal orientation to an orientation to the international political economy.

15. "*Ie*" is sometimes translated "house" or "home" in the sense of a building where one lives. It also means family or household. It has a meaning similar to the English word *house* in the sense of "the Plantagenet House." It refers to a whole complex of meaning and relationships, each with certain obligations and responsibilities to past (deceased), present, and future members of the *ie*. Although the concept has undergone numerous transformations in Japanese history, many of the formal characteristics were influenced by Confucian and later neo-Confucian ideas and practices.

16. Robert N. Bellah, "Baigan and Sorai: Continuities and Discontinuities in Eighteenth Century Japanese Thought"; Tetsuo

Najita, "Method and Analysis in the Conceptual Portrayal of Tokugawa Intellectual History"; H. D. Harootunian, "The Consciousness of Archaic Form in the New Realism of Kokugaku"; in Tetsuo Najita and Irwin Scheiner, eds., *Japanese Thought in the Tokugawa Period* (Chicago: University of Chicago Press, 1978), pp. 3–38, 63–104; and Maruyama Masao, *Studies in the Intellectual History of Tokugawa Japan,* trans. Mikiso Hane (Princeton: Princeton University Press, 1974).

17. The new Meiji government instituted policies, in addition to those directed at agriculture and education that included policies for the abolishment of *han* (domains) and the rigid class structure of Tokugawa society. It also established a national conscript army, replaced the *han* with prefectures, and set up new status classifications of *Kazoku, Shizoku,* and *Heimin. Kazoku* was the title given primarily to the old court nobility (*kuge*) and the former heads of clans (*daimyo*). *Shizoku* was the designation of the former samurai class, and *Heimin* was the designation given to the remainder of the common people.

18. Thomas Smith estimates that this tax accounted for 78% of government revenues until 1881; by 1890 it decreased to 50%. Smith, *Agrarian Origins of Modern Japan,* p. 211. The framers of Meiji land policy took a crucial step in its formation with the passage of a law removing the Tokugawa ban on the selling of land. This was a necessary step in the institution of a land tax because of the importance of having a recognized landowner who was legally responsible for that tax. In 1873, a land tax was passed that consisted of three elements that were significantly different from previous tax policy. The tax was based on the value of the land and not the value of the harvest. The tax was not adjusted for the quality of the yield, and the tax was paid in cash, not in kind. This meant that the landowner rather than the direct producer of the crops was liable for a unified tax, set initially at 3% of the value of the land, to be paid to the central government. E. H. Norman, *Japan's Emergence as a Modern State: Political and Economic Problems of the Meiji Period* (New York: Institute of Pacific Relations, 1940), p. 143.

19. The Meiji land policies contributed to the tremendous social transformations occurring in Japan at this time. That portion of the rural population who could not find work or who were from families who could not support them were forced into the cities in search of work in the burgeoning industries. As the modern industrial economy developed, this trend was accelerated as

more and more of the rural domestic industry collapsed in the face of urban competition. This trend, coupled with the increasing pressure of overpopulation in the rural areas, forced younger members of the family into the urban areas in the hopes of supplementing the meager income of the family left on the farm. It was this group who formed the bulk of the emigrants.

20. Ichihashi, *Japanese in the United States,* pp. 78–81. Twenty-six percent came from Hiroshima prefecture, and 13% from neighboring Yamaguchi. Emigrants from the Kyûshû prefectures of Kumamoto and Fukuoka constituted 15% and 9% respectively, and 4.4% came from the old Tokugawa domain of Kii, the present Wakayama prefecture. The preponderance of emigrants came from the four southwestern prefectures of Yamaguchi, Hiroshima, Kumamoto, and Fukuoka, a pattern similar to immigration to Hawaii and Peru, although Okinawa was much more significant in the Hawaiian and Peruvian pattern. The reasons for the significant contribution of these four prefectures is not entirely clear. However, part of the explanation lies in the nature of agricultural production and land tenure, differing implementation of Meiji agricultural policies among the prefectural governments, and the recruiting practices of emigration companies. Alan Moriyama, *Imingaisha: Japanese Emigration Companies and Hawaii, 1894–1908* (Honolulu: University of Hawaii Press, 1985), pp. 158–159. Hishiki suggests that climatological similarities made a difference within Peru, which was dominated by Okinawan emigrants. An interesting anomaly to the pattern, showing the effect of recruitment patterns, is seen in the fact that the majority (47%) of the first labor group of 790 to Peru were from Niigata. In 1974, the Peruvian Japanese Community was approximately 60% Okinawan in origin. Patricia Chieko Hishiki, "Acculturation and Cultural Transmission in the Japanese Colony of Lima, Peru" (Ph.D. diss., Stanford University, 1986). Emigration companies, however, played a less significant role in immigration to the west coast of the United States than to such places as Hawaii, Peru, Brazil, and Mexico.

21. Smith, *Agrarian Origins of Modern Japan,* pp. 11ff., 24ff., 110ff., 155ff., 180ff.; Norman, *Japan's Emergence as a Modern State,* pp. 155ff.

22. This was so except in California, which from the beginning was dominated by large-scale farming oriented to the world market.

23. Norman, *Japan's Emergence as a Modern State,* p. 156.

The other side of the Janus head in Norman's conception can be seen in the rise of the new religious movement in Bakumatsu and early Meiji, as well as in the peasant rebellions and movements of this time—movements such as *yonaoshi, ee ja nai ka,* and *uchi kowashi.* However, many of these peasant movements can be seen as a form of nostalgia for a past, before the intrusion of the market changed the basic relationships of the village such as that of the *ie.*

The *honke-bunke* relationship came to have more of an economic rather than a moral significance, as Hashimoto Mitsuru has pointed out. Hashimoto Mitsuru, "The Social Background of Peasant Uprisings in Tokugawa Japan," in Tetsuo Najita and J. Victor Koschmann, eds., *Conflict in Modern Japanese History* (Princeton: Princeton University Press, 1982), pp. 145ff. The *honke* is the head, or primary, family, and the *bunke* are the branch, or collateral, families. This is an example of the significance of vertical relationships in Japanese traditional patterns of organization. Robert N. Bellah has an important discussion of this vertical integration, which is a characteristic of Japanese society, in his *Tokugawa Religion* (New York: Free Press, 1985), pp. 11–57, 178–197.

Rather than labeling these movements as either radical or conservative, however, one can make finer distinctions. Some were movements that used the past and its traditions for a vocabulary that was then used to describe a new vision, as Irwin Scheiner's study of *yonaoshi* (literally "world renewal") movements has shown. These were not simply a longing for the old. Irwin Scheiner, "Benevolent Lords and Honorable Peasants," in Najita and Scheiner, eds., *Japanese Thought in the Tokugawa Period,* pp. 39–62.

24. *Dekasegi* from the Japanese compound *kanji,* formed with the character for *(de)ru,* meaning "to leave or go out," and the nominal form of *(kase)gu,* meaning "work or labor."

25. Andrew Gordon, *The Evolution of Labor Relations in Japan: Heavy Industry, 1853–1955* (Cambridge, Mass.: Harvard University Press, 1985), p. 15.

26. Yuji Ichioka, *The Issei* (New York: Free Press, 1988), p. 3.

27. One of the best-sellers on Meiji Japan was Samuel Smiles's book *Self Help.* The Japanese translation of the book had the title *Saikoku Risshi hen.* Cited in Earl Kinmonth, *The Self-Made Man in Meiji Japanese Thought* (Berkeley: University of California Press, 1981), pp. 1ff. Both Kinmonth and Masao Maruyama,

"Patterns of Individuation and the Case of Japan: A Conceptual Scheme," in Marius B. Jansen, ed., *Changing Japanese Attitudes Towards Modernization* (Princeton: Princeton University Press, 1965), pp. 489–531, point out that the word *risshi* in early Meiji referred to the idea of the independence of individuals. This was grafted to the Confucian ideal of improving the family's reputation through education and was linked to the early Meiji ideal of strengthening the country. By the end of Meiji, the word lost its larger referent. Despite Kinmonth's assessment, it would be difficult to equate this with the extreme forms of individualism found in the West, although Maruyama's argument is more convincing. However, by the end of Meiji, it is clear that contemporary Japanese, commenting upon the new Japanese character, perceived it to be comparable, if not worse. Cited by Maruyama, Kazutami Ukita describes this Japanese character at the end of the Meiji period in *Shin-kokumin no Shûyô*: "Now in the Business World of Japan, individualism is going to be put into practice much more violently than in England, America, Germany, and France. Apart from times of national crisis, there are no people on the earth who are more individualistic than the Japanese."

This is an expression of the decline of the traditional symbols and ideals of solidarity in the face of the new relationships encouraged by the instrumental rationality of the market. Maruyama Masao tries to reserve the notion of individualism to something less privatistic and similar to the older Confucian notion of *risshi* by saying that this phenomenon "was in fact nothing but a naked egoism into which the *risshi* of the former days was transformed by privatization." Masao, "Patterns of Individuation," p. 508.

28. See Maruyama, "Patterns of Individuation," pp. 43–98. See also Kenneth Pyle, *The New Generation in Meiji Japan* (Stanford: Stanford University Press, 1969).

29. During this period, the impact of Christianity, first under the Jesuits and then the Franciscans and Dominicans, was significant. Cathedrals, schools, hospitals, and other institutions multiplied. Many powerful families converted and forced the conversion of their domains. The history of this period is complicated, but by the mid-seventeenth century, Christianity was actively and forcefully suppressed, after the Tokugawa family consolidated its control over Japan. One of the primary reasons for this was the connection between the Roman Catholic Church and European powers. Spain, in particular, had established the

Philippines as the bulwark of its Pacific Empire. These measures to control and eradicate Christianity continued on the books, as well as in practice, into the Meiji period. One such law instituted to control Christianity, for example, was the requirement that each person be registered at a local Buddhist temple.

30. Richard Drummond, *A History of Christianity in Japan* (Grand Rapids: Wm. B. Eerdmans, 1971), p. 143.

31. Hepburn's letters: March 11, 1861; March 17, 1861; December 9, 1862; April 24, 1868. In Tetsuya Ohama, *Meiji Kirisuto Kyôkaishi no Kenkyû* [Study of the Christian Church in Meiji Japan] (Tôkyô: Yoshikawa Kobunkan, 1979), p. 23.

32. Janes was to go to Kumamoto in 1871, before missionaries were allowed into the interior of the country. Janes had met Japanese Sunday school students in Howard Presbyterian Church, San Francisco, where his father-in-law was Pastor. The Kumamoto band was converted through the ministry of Captain Janes. See Irwin Scheiner, *Christian Converts and Social Protest in Meiji Japan* (Berkeley: University of California Press, 1970); F. G. Notehelfer, *American Samurai: Captain L. L. Janes and Japan* (Princeton: Princeton University Press, 1985); Pyle, *The New Generation.*

33. This refers to both a geographical domain and a clan-type network that ruled the domain in what some scholars called the "*baku-han*" (***bakufu-han***) system of the Tokugawa period.

34. Scheiner, *Christian Converts,* pp. 44ff.

35. "Report of Superintendent" (February 17, 1869) in *Annual School Report of Howard Presbyterian Church* (1860–1869, San Francisco Theological Seminary). Notehelfer, *American Samurai,* p. 97, also mentions this group.

36. Henry Martyn Scudder, *A Discourse Delivered in the Howard Presbyterian Church, San Francisco, Thanksgiving Day, November 29, 1866* (San Francisco: Edward Bosqui, 1866), p. 36, cited in Notehelfer, *American Samurai,* p. 82.

37. It is not clear what relationship existed between the group of Japanese students who gathered at Howard Street Presbyterian Church in the late 1860s and early 1870s and the founding of the *Fukuinkai.*

38. *Fukuinkai Enkaku Shiryô* [Historical Records of the Gospel Society] (1881–1897, Japanese American History Room in San Francisco and the Japanese American Research Project Collection at UCLA).

39. "The Gospel Society Established in San Francisco in the U.S.," *Shichi-ichi Zappô* (January 30, 1880), 5–6.

40. John Carrington's letter to F. F. Ellinwood, July 27, 1885; J. Roberts's letter to F. F. Ellinwood, October 27, 1884. PC(USA), Dept. of History, Philadelphia.

41. According to the session *Minutes* of Howard Presbyterian Church, Akamine and Shirafuji became members of the Howard Church on February 4, 1883. On February 18, the following became members: Mr. and Mrs. Yanagisawa, Yuna Yanagisawa, Sôbei Kishimoto, S. Kaneko, Nakamura, Hamada.

42. San Francisco Presbytery, *Minutes,* April 28, 1885.

43. San Francisco Presbytery, *Minutes,* September 8, 1885. As for the history of the Japanese Presbyterian Church of San Francisco, see Christ United Presbyterian Church, *The Church's One Hundred Years.*

44. "Japanese Young Men's Christian Association," *Occident* (September 21, 1887).

45. Presbyterian Board of Foreign Missions, *Annual Report,* 1886, p. 152.

46. "It is the duty of the Church, therefore, to look after these men on this side of the ocean as well as on the other, and especially to so develop their faith and Christian grace that they may become laborers in the great vineyard of their native land." Presbyterian Board of Foreign Missions, *Annual Report,* 1886, p. 152. See also the reports for 1901 and 1902, and "Report of Japanese Work in San Francisco," *Occident* (July 24, 1889).

47. "Personal Record of E. A. Sturge, M.D.," April 25, 1902, PC(USA), Dept. of History, Philadelphia. See also Kohachiro Miyazaki, *Sutoji Den* or *A Life of E. A. Sturge M.D., Ph.D.* (Tô-kyô: Sturge Zenshû. Kankokai. 1935).

48. E. A. Sturge, letter to F. F. Ellinwood, January 3, 1886. PC(USA), Dept. of History, Philadelphia.

49. Ibid.

50. E. A. Sturge, letter to F. F. Ellinwood, February 4, 1886; and F. F. Ellinwood, letter to E. A. Sturge, February 17, 1886. PC(USA), Dept. of History, Philadelphia.

51. A. W. Loomis, letter to F. F. Ellinwood, May 3, 1886. PC(USA), Dept. of History, Philadelphia.

52. F. F. Ellinwood, letter to E. A. Sturge, July 6, 1886. PC(USA), Dept. of History, Philadelphia.

53. Shokichi Hata and S. Satow's letter to Halsey, June 15, 1920. PC(USA), Dept. of History, Philadelphia.

54. E. A. Sturge, "Should We Exclude the Japanese?" (June 1907), in Kohachiro, *Sutoji Den,* pp. 150–164.

55. Presbyterian Board of Foreign Missions, *Annual Report,* 1920, pp. 186–187.

56. "The Oriental Problem," *Pacific* (July 4, 1907), 14.

57. "Report from San Francisco," *Kirisutokyô Shimbun* [Christian News] (February 14, 1890).

58. "Insecure Behavior," *Nichibei* [Japanese American News] (October 25, 1903). See also Kohachiro, *Sutoji Den,* pp. 91–106.

59. "Pamphlet for the *Sôkô Heito Kai*" (November 15, 1933). In the Oka Shigeki Collection, Japanese American Research Project Archives, UCLA.

60. *Shin Sekai* [New World] (June 6, 1911), 3.

61. Missions emphasizing education were started in Alameda (evening mission school); Hanford (school, kindergarten, Japanese Women's Society); Los Angeles (educational classes); Monterey (library); Sacramento (YMCA); Salinas (evening school, library, kindergarten); San Francisco (day and night school, library, Prospect Place school); Stockton (YMCA); Visalia (school); Watsonville (educational classes, YMCA, kindergarten); Wintersburg (educational classes, kindergarten). Presbyterian Board of Foreign Missions, *Annual Report,* 1902, pp. 311–312; 1905, pp. 414–416; 1906, pp. 451–454.

62. Presbyterian Board of Foreign Missions, *Annual Report,* 1914, pp. 195–196. According to this *Annual Report,* a large number of Japanese women came to America after the enactment of the Gentlemen's Agreement. The result of this influx was an increased number of Japanese American children. There were now approximately seven or eight thousand Japanese American children in California, and one thousand children were born every year. Although 80% of these Japanese American children attended American public schools, they did not attend Sunday school.

63. Presbyterian Board of Foreign Missions, *Annual Report,* 1895, pp. 77–78; 1896, pp. 254–255.

64. Presbyterian Board of Foreign Missions, *Annual Report,* 1891, pp. 63–64; 1892, pp. 90–91; 1900, pp. 334–335; 1902, pp. 311–315.

65. Nenkai Junbi Iin, ed., *Zaibei Nihonjin Chôrôkyôkai Rekishi* [The History of the Japanese Presbyterian Church in the Pacific Coast] (Dendô 25 Shunen Shukkai Iin. 1911), pp. 40–46.

66. Ibid., pp. 40–44.

67. Presbyterian Board of Foreign Missions, *Annual Report,* 1923.

68. Sumio Koga, "History of Japanese Presbyterian Conference" (unpublished manuscript, 1980). PC(USA), Dept. of History, Philadelphia.

69. Presbyterian Board of Foreign Missions, *Annual Report,* 1912, pp. 26–27; 1913, pp. 441–443; E. A. Sturge's "Report of Work for the Japanese on the Pacific Coast," 1917. PC(USA), Dept. of History, Philadelphia. The Japanese churches in Hollywood and Long Beach had difficulty in obtaining a church building because of the anti-Japanese opposition. Pacific Japanese Mission, Methodist Episcopal Church, *Official Journal* (1923), 26–27.

70. Sumio Koga, comp., *"A Centennial Legacy": History of the Japanese Christian Missions in North America, 1877–1977,* vol. 1 (Chicago: Nobart, 1977), pp. 112–115.

71. Nenkai Junbi Iin, ed., *Zaibei Nihonjin Chôrôkyôkai Rekishi,* pp. 85–88; "New Phenomena in the Mission Field," *Shin Tenchi* [New Heaven and New Earth] (December 1912), 3. Sturge also played a significant role in establishing in 1914 the *Sôkô Nihonjin Kirisuto Kyôkai* (Japanese Church of Christ of San Francisco), made by the federation of the San Francisco Japanese Presbyterian and Congregational churches. "Full History of the Establishment of the San Francisco Japanese Church of Christ," *Dendôsha* [The Evangelists] (October 1914), 2.

72. "Annual Meeting of the Japanese Presbyterian Conference in the U.S.," *Fukuin Shimpo* [The Gospel Newspaper] (June 17, 1920).

73. This development represented a final indication of the inability of the Japanese government to protect the interests of the Japanese in the United States, as it had done so successfully in the San Francisco school incident of 1906, when President Theodore Roosevelt intervened after the San Francisco school board had segregated Japanese students into separate schools. Although the Gentlemen's Agreement, which was a result of the school crisis, represented a defeat for the free immigration of Japanese to the United States, it was also seen as a sign of the effectiveness of the Japanese government in asserting its interest in the arena of world politics and within the United States. By voluntarily limiting emigrants to close relatives of those already in the United States, the Japanese government was able to delay the efforts of the anti-Japanese movement to exclude Japanese immigration. This role as

a global power, however, was a two-edged sword. As Japanese diplomatic efforts devoted more and more attention to the promotion of Japan's China policies and the expansion of its influence in Manchuria, Japan was unable to be as insistent on the protection of Japanese living within the United States.

Because of the Gentlemen's Agreement, a large number of Issei women were allowed to enter the country as wives of Japanese already in the United States, transforming the Japanese community from one dominated by bachelors to one dominated by families. This was a very different situation from that of the early Chinese immigrants, who were excluded in 1872 before any significant number of women were allowed to immigrate. Likewise, the Gentlemen's Agreement allowed a group of younger Issei, who were the children of Issei already working in America, to come to the United States. These younger Issei, sometimes called Yobiyose, formed an important core of leadership in the prewar community. This emigration from Japan was abruptly cut off with the passage of the exclusion law of 1924, which, except for temporary educational, diplomatic, and commercial purposes, totally excluded Japanese from immigrating to the United States.

This exclusion had immediate international repercussions and contributed significantly to the steadily increasing tensions between the United States and Japan. After passage of the act, anti-American demonstrations erupted in Tokyo.

74. Pacific Japanese Mission, Methodist Episcopal Church, *Official Journal* (1905), 8.

75. Danjô Ebina believed that the notion of Christian brotherhood advocated by white Christians was distorted by the racism of whites toward people of color. The word "true" here distinguishes his notion from the racist notion of European and American Christians. *Shin Sekai* (June 7–9, 14–16; November 14, 30, 1908).

76. Ibid. (July 1, 27; August 11–19, 1909).

77. For more of this interdenominational movement and its significance, see Yoshida, ch. 6 in "A Socio-Historical Study of Racial/Ethnic Identity."

78. Christ United Presbyterian Church, San Francisco. San Francisco Japanese Church of Christ, *Yakuinkai Kiroku* [Minutes of the Session], 1914–1925, at the Christ United Presbyterian Church, 1700 Sutter St., San Francisco, Calif.

79. Pacific Japanese Mission, Methodist Episcopal Church, *Official Journal* (1913).

80. Christ United Presbyterian Church, San Francisco, San Francisco Japanese Church of Christ, *Yakuinkai Kiroku* [Minutes of the Session], 1914–1925.

81. This is a very different understanding of assimilation than that which dominates the work of many scholars of Japanese American history and experience. In fact, the notion of assimilation discussed by Japanese Americans during this time was directed more at developing a Japanese American identity than at assimilating into the white dominant groups.

82. Yoshida, ch. 6 in "A Socio-Historical Study of Racial/Ethnic Identity."

83. "Discussing Assimilation," *Shin Tenchi* (August 1913; September 1913).

84. Issei marriages took place primarily between 1905 and 1924. Most of the Nisei were born in the three decades between 1905 and 1935. During this period, framed by the Gentlemen's Agreement of 1907 and the rising tensions between the United States and Japan over hegemony in China, a large group of children were born to Japanese in the United States. These children were the result of the large influx of Issei women and the establishment of families that took place during this time. In the early years of marriage, the birth of children interfered with the work responsibilities of the Issei women, so a significant number of children were sent back to Japan for child care and education.

85. The Japanese Association's control over movement to and from Japan was preempted by the ban on all immigration. No longer could it control the entrance of wives and children or intervene as effectively on behalf of the community.

86. The emergence of the Japanese American Citizens League as an important organization in the Japanese American community in the postwar period is a notable example of this change.

13: Korean American Presbyterians: A Need for Ethnic Particularity and the Challenge of Christian Pilgrimage

1. Joseph Ryu, "Jae-Mi-Han-In-Kyo-Doe (Korean Churches in America)," in Sang Hyun Lee, ed., *Korean American Ministry: A Resourcebook* (The Consulting Committee on Korean American Ministry, Program Agency, Presbyterian Church (U.S.A.), 1987), pp. 49–50; see also Won Moo Hurh and Kwang Chung Kim, *Korean Immigrants in America: A Structural Analysis of Ethnic*

Confinement and Adhesive Adaptation (Rutherford, N.J.: Fairleigh Dickinson University Press, 1984), pp. 46–49; Hyung Chan Kim, ed., *The Korean Diaspora* (Santa Barbara, Calif.: ABC-Clio Press, 1977); Bong Youn Choy, *Koreans in America* (Chicago: Nelson Hall, 1979), pp. 253–260.

2. Won Moo Hurh, "The Korean Community in America: Future Prospects and Issues." Paper presented at the annual meeting of the Korean American University Professors Association, Atlanta, Ga., October 2–4, 1987, p. 3.

3. Won Moo Hurh, "Comparative Study of Korean Immigrants in the U.S.: A Typological Study," in Byong-suh Kim et al., *Koreans in America* (Montclair, N.J.: The Association of Korean Christian Scholars, 1977), p. 95. See also Everett V. Stonequist, *The Marginal Man: A Study in Personality and Culture Conflict* (New York: Russell & Russell, 1973). Other important studies of Korean immigrants include Eui-Young Yu, "Koreans in America: An Emerging Ethnic Minority," *Amerasia Journal* 4 (1977), 117–131; and Ilsoo Kim, *New Urban Immigrants: The Korean Community in New York* (Princeton: Princeton University Press, 1981). For studies of Korean immigrant women in America, see, for example, Inn Sook Lee, ed., *Korean-American Women: Toward Self-Realization,* (Mansfield, Ohio: Association of Korean Christian Scholars, 1985); and H. H. Sunoo and D. C. Kim, eds., *Korean Women,* (Memphis, Tenn.: Association of Korean Christian Scholars, 1978).

4. Milton M. Gordon, *Assimilation in American Life* (New York: Oxford University Press, 1964), p. 77.

5. Emory S. Bogardus, "Comparing Racial Distance in Ethiopia, South Africa, and the United States," *Sociology and Social Research* 52 (January 1968), 152; Hurh, "Comparative Study," p. 66.

6. Hurh and Kim, *Korean Immigrants in America,* pp. 73–86.

7. Ibid., p. 86.

8. Ibid., pp. 148–149.

9. Won Moo Hurh and Kwang Chung Kim, "Religious Participation of Korean Immigrants in the United States." Paper presented at the annual meeting of the Association of Asian Studies, Washington, D.C., March 17–19, 1989, p. 7.

10. Ibid., pp. 12–19; Hurh and Kim, *Korean Immigrants in America,* pp. 133–137. The last point about American pluralism was recently elaborated and supported by the American sociologist R. Stephen Warner, "Change and Continuity in the U.S. Re-

ligious System: Perspectives from Sociology." Lecture delivered at Princeton Theological Seminary, February 6, 1989, pp. 16–17.

11. Ibid., pp. 131–132.

12. Hurh and Kim, "Religious Participation," p. 18.

13. Andrew M. Greeley, *The Denominational Society: A Sociological Approach to Religion in America* (Glenview, Ill.: Scott, Foresman, 1972), p. 125, quoted in Hurh and Kim, *Korean Immigrants in America,* p. 133.

14. Hurh and Kim, *Korean Immigrants in America,* p. 135.

15. For a brief survey of Korean church history, see Kyung Bae Min, "The Presbyterian Church in Korean History," in Lee, ed., *Korean American Ministry: A Resourcebook,* pp. 15–27; and Samuel Hugh Moffett, "Missions to Korea: A Brief Summary," ibid., pp. 38–47.

16. R. Stephen Warner, an American sociologist, takes a somewhat optimistic view on the possibility that a mainline denomination like the Presbyterian Church will respond positively to the ethnic church's demands. See Warner, "Changes and Continuity," p. 22.

17. H. Richard Niebuhr, *The Social Sources of Denominationalism* (New York: Henry Holt & Co., 1929), p. 284.

18. The ideas suggested here were elaborated upon in the author's essay "Called to Be Pilgrims: Toward an Asian American Theology from the Korean Immigrant Perspective," in Lee, ed., *Korean American Ministry: A Resourcebook,* pp. 90–120.

Index